Paul Cooke (Ed.)

The Lives of Others and Contemporary German Fil...

Companions to Contemporary German Culture

Edited by
Michael Eskin · Karen Leeder · Christopher Young

Volume 3

Paul Cooke (Ed.)

The Lives of Others and Contemporary German Film

A Companion

DE GRUYTER

ISBN 978-3-11-026810-2
e-ISBN 978-3-11-026847-8
ISSN 2193-9659

Library of Congress Cataloging-in-Publication Data
A CIP catalog record for this book has been applied for at the Library of Congress.

Bibliographic information published by the Deutsche Nationalbibliothek
The Deutsche Nationalbibliothek lists this publication in the Deutsche Nationalbibliografie;
detailed bibliographic data are available on the internet at http://dnb.dnb.de

© 2013 Walter de Gruyter GmbH, Berlin/Boston
Cover image: *The Lives of Others* – Ulrich Mühe © Sony Pics/Everett/Rex Features
Printing: Hubert & Co. GmbH & Co. KG, Göttingen
∞ Printed on acid-free paper
Printed in Germany

www.degruyter.com

MIX
Papier aus verantwor-
tungsvollen Quellen
FSC
www.fsc.org
FSC® C016439

Table of Contents

Acknowledgements

This volume is the product of a two-year project, supported by the British Academy, The World Wide Universities Network and the Faculty of Arts at the University of Leeds. It was initially developed during a roundtable session at the German Studies Association meeting in Louisville, Kentucky in 2011. This was followed by a two-day workshop at the University of Leeds. In addition to the individual contributors to the volume, I would like to thank all my colleagues in German and World Cinemas at the University of Leeds for their support of the project and active participation at the Leeds workshop. Thanks also to Bernadette and David Cooke for their help preparing the manuscript. I am very grateful to the series editors for their invitation to produce this collection, and to Christopher Young, in particular, for his work involving Florian Henckel von Donnersmarck in the project. Finally, I would like to thank the director himself for his engagement with the volume and for his permission to reproduce his University of Cambridge 'X-Changing Lecture on German culture'.

Paul Cooke

Introduction
The Lives of Others and Contemporary German Film

Florian Henckel von Donnersmarck's *The Lives of Others* belongs to a small but growing number of recent German-language films that have caught the imagination of audiences around the world, bringing the nation's film industry a level of international attention it has not enjoyed since the early 1980s with the success of the New German Cinema. Set in 1984, and described in its critical reception, *inter alia*, as a melodrama, a heritage film and a spy thriller, the film offers the spectator a suitably Orwellian image of pre-unification life under East Germany's totalitarian regime. An internationally renowned GDR writer Georg Dreyman is placed under surveillance by the state's infamous security service, the Ministerium für Staatssicherheit (Ministry for State Security, commonly referred to as the MfS or Stasi), on the advice of a corrupt party official, Minister Bruno Hempf, who claims to suspect him of dissidence. This is an accusation which, at the start of the narrative at least, is entirely false, and we quickly realize that Hempf's real motivation is his lust for the writer's partner, the beautiful and talented actress Christa-Maria Sieland. During the surveillance operation, the controlling Stasi officer, Captain Gerd Wiesler, a man initially convinced of the GDR's status as the better of the two post-war German states and the need of his organization to protect it against Western counter-revolutionary forces, begins to lose faith in the ruling communist party's draconian understanding of its 'socialist' project. He is drawn, instead, to the humanistic artistic world that he discovers through eavesdropping on the couple from his surveillance suite above their apartment. As a result, rather than relaying to his superiors Dreyman's gradual turn to dissidence, he protects him, producing innocuous reports and even removing an incriminating typewriter from the man's flat which would have provided his Stasi colleagues with evidence that Dreyman was the author of an inflammatory essay published in the West. At the same time, we witness the psychological destruction and suicide of Sieland. Initially forced into an affair with the Minister to protect her career, she ultimately cooperates with the Stasi's investigation of her partner, working as one of the thousands of *Inoffizielle Mitarbeiter* (unofficial collaborators, commonly referred to as IM) employed by the organization, the guilt for which she cannot endure. For his part, Dreyman is entirely ignorant of the surveillance operation against him and the reasons for Sieland's death until after unification, at which point he requests access to his Stasi file. Reading the reports prepared by

Wiesler, he discovers the protection he received from the officer, subsequently uncovering the man's identity, whom he finds working now as a lowly distributor of advertising flyers. Dreyman chooses, however, not to make contact with him. Instead he simply dedicates his first post-GDR novel – and the first work he has written since Sieland's death – to HGW XX/7, Wiesler's Stasi code name, an action that signals to the former officer the writer's gratitude. Moreover, it is a gesture that signals to the spectator how both men can now draw a line under their respective pasts. In the immediate aftermath of unification, Dreyman, still suffering the trauma of his GDR experience, seemed to lose the ability to write. Publication of the novel two years later points to the rediscovery of his voice and with it his ability to imagine a future for himself in the unified country. Equally significant, Wiesler now knows that his good deed has been recognized, his contentment captured in the film's closing shot: a medium close-up of the man, his trouble-worn face breaking into a quiet smile as he buys a copy of the book.

The aim of the following collection of essays is twofold. First, it hopes to offer new insights into the film, examining some of the reasons behind its success, placing *The Lives of Others* within its wider historical, political, aesthetic and industrial context. However, as I shall discuss in this introductory chapter, the reception of the film generated a debate that went well beyond the merits, or otherwise, of this box-office hit, ranging from the political potential of the history film and the status of the GDR in the pre-history of the Berlin Republic in the first decade of the new millennium to the nature of film funding in Germany and the cultural value of popular cinema. Consequently, the volume also uses the film as a case study to take stock of the state of both German film and German film studies, highlighting some of the key fault lines at work in contemporary critical discourses. In so doing, it provides the various authors collected together here – many of whom have shaped academic and professional discussion of German cinema in recent years – with the opportunity to reflect on and further develop the debates to which the film spoke.

The Director, His Project and the Road to International Acclaim

Born in 1973 to an aristocratic family of Silesian expellees, Florian Henckel von Donnersmarck spent his childhood living in New York, Berlin, Frankfurt/Main and Brussels, his family moving with his father's postings as a senior manager for Lufthansa and giving him a native command of both English and German. After school he initially moved to St Petersburg to study Russian before taking up a place at Oxford, where he studied politics, philosophy and economics and where, most importantly for his future career, he won an internship to work for Richard Attenborough on *In Love and War* (1996). From there he went to film school, studying at the Munich Academy for Television and Film, whose alumni include Wim Wenders, Bernd Eichinger and Roland Emmerich. At this point he had the initial idea for *The Lives of Others*. This came from an account he had read of a conversation between Maxim Gorky and Lenin, during which the Russian leader pointed to what he viewed to be the dangerously humanizing power of art. In the director's retelling of the conversation, Lenin suggested that he could not listen to Beethoven's *Appassionata* – his favourite piece of music – too often, as he feared it would prevent him from taking the necessary action to complete the revolution, making him want to whisper 'sweet, silly things' into the ears of those he should be prepared to destroy without compassion.[1] This became the story of a hard-line Stasi operative who mutates into a sensitive guardian angel through his exposure to poetry and music.

Although he had the idea for the film as a student, *The Lives of Others* had a long genesis, taking eight years to come to the screen, the director initially finding it difficult to secure the necessary financing. Nonetheless, after a slow start the project began to gain momentum and by the time it was scheduled for theatrical release in Germany on 23 March 2006 it seemed destined for success. By this point it had already received four Bavarian film awards. These were quickly followed by seven German Film Awards, three European Film Awards and dozens of other nominations and prizes, culminating in February 2007 in the award of an Oscar for Best Foreign Language Film. It also did well commercially, grossing over $77 million worldwide, a figure that places it in the same commercial league as other recent German hits such as Wolfgang Becker's *Good Bye, Lenin!* (2003, $79 million) and Oliver Hirschbiegel's *Der Untergang* (Downfall, 2003, $92 million).[2] However, the success of *The Lives of Others* is, to some extent, more impressive than either of these films or, indeed, other recent German-language Oscar winners, Caroline Link's *Nirgendwo in Afrika* (Nowhere in Africa, 2001) and Stefan

---

1 Florian Henckel von Donnersmarck, '*Appassionata:* Die Filmidee', in *Das Leben der anderen. Filmbuch* (Frankfurt am Main: Suhrkamp, 2006), pp. 169–70 (p. 169). This is retold in more detail in von Donnersmarck's contribution to this volume, from where this translation is also taken. For a detailed discussion of the way von Donnersmarck uses this story in the film itself and how this compares to Lenin's original motivations see Jennifer Creech, 'A Few Good Men: Gender, Ideology, and Narrative Politics in *The Lives of Others* and *Good Bye, Lenin!*', *Women in German Yearbook. Feminist Studies in German Literature & Culture*, 25 (2009), 100–26 (p. 109–10), as well as Silberman's contribution to this volume.
2 All figures taken from *Box Office Mojo* (http://boxofficemojo.com/).

Ruzowitzky's German-Austrian co-production *Die Fälscher* (The Counterfeiters, 2007). This was von Donnersmarck's debut feature, produced for a meagre $2 million. Compare this to the $8 million budget of *Nirgendwo in Afrika* or the $15 million at Hirschbiegel's disposal. These are still modest sums by Hollywood's standards, but nonetheless of a different order to that available to von Donnersmarck. Moreover, one would not expect a low-budget project to attract a cast of such well known film and television actors, including Ulrich Mühe (*Der letzte Zeuge* [The Last Witness, Bernhard Stephan, 1998–2007]), Sebastian Koch (*Die Manns – Ein Jahrhundertroman* [The Manns – Novel of a Century, Heinrich Breloer, 2001]) and Martina Gedeck (*Bella Martha*, Sandra Nettelbeck, 2001), all of whom agreed to waive a large proportion of their fee to take part. Equally remarkable, the director managed to engage the composer Gabriel Yared – best known for his Oscar-winning work on Anthony Minghella's *The English Patient* (1996) – to write the soundtrack. He also clinched important deals with major distribution companies, including Walt Disney's Buena Vista International in Germany and Sony Pictures Classics in the US, as well as a prestigious contract with the publisher Suhrkamp for a book to accompany the film. Although well connected through his background and education, von Donnersmarck is himself a very resourceful man who, even at this early point in his career, was happy to approach established members of the industry, confident that he would be able to convince them of the value of his project.

His confidence, as well as his tenacity and energy, also stood him in good stead during the Oscar campaign, which played a hugely significant role in the commercial success of the film and in the subsequent development of the filmmaker's career. There are numerous reasons why *The Lives of Others* did well at the Academy Awards. Like both other post-unification German-language winners and the vast majority of nominations, this is a film that engages with the nation's problematic past, while conforming to mainstream genre conventions. As Georg Seeßlen notes, in order to be successful in this category, a 'film has to be "foreign enough," but must also not flout the aesthetic codes of the dream factory too flagrantly'.[3] However, also important was Sony's carefully orchestrated promotion campaign. The film opened in Los Angeles for one week in December 2006 in order to qualify for the 'Critics' Awards', an important event that often indicates subsequent Oscar success. This was then followed by special screenings for critics and other key opinion-makers to create a word-of-mouth 'buzz' around the film. It did not go on general release in the US until February 2007, in the immediate run up to the ceremony, at which point von Donnersmarck was in the US,

---

3 Georg Seeßlen, 'So gewinnt man einen Auslands-Oscar', *Die Zeit*, 22 February 2007.

travelling the length and breadth of the country, giving up to twenty interviews a day, his fluency in English making him an easy guest for US talk-show hosts.[4] This is a director who understands the modern film industry well and is very comfortable with the glitz of Hollywood.

Mapping the Contours of Success: the 'Authenticity Debate' and Beyond

Although the global success of *The Lives of Others* can be compared favourably with that of *Good Bye, Lenin!* or *Der Untergang*, unlike these other films, its success was largely international. It grossed over $11 million in the US on its theatrical release, amounting to 14% of its total gross. This compares with $4 million for *Goodbye, Lenin!* (5.1%) and $5.5 million for *Der Untergang* (6%). In Germany, on the other hand, Becker and Hirschbiegel's films earned $41 million (9%) and $39 million (16.5%) respectively, *The Lives of Others* only $19 million (5%). By any usual measure of success for a German film, *The Lives of Others* did well domestically in terms of ticket sales. It achieved an audience of over 2 million during its theatrical release, a German film generally being deemed a hit if it sells more than a million tickets. Yet this is a long way short of *Good Bye, Lenin!'s* audience of 6.5 million. It is also far removed from the domestic success of Til Schweiger's *Keinohrhasen* (Rabbit Without Ears, 2007, 6 million) or the monster hits of Michael 'Bully' Herbig, *Der Schuh des Manitu* (The Shoe of Manitu, 2001, 10.5 million) and *(T)Raumschiff Surprise – Periode 1* (Dreamship Surprise – Periode 1, 2004, 9 million).[5]

If one looked closely, this divergence in international and domestic reception could also be sensed in the prizes the film received. Von Donnersmarck received nominations and prizes at festivals around the world, but while the film did well at the German film awards, it was snubbed by Berlinale director Dieter Kosslick, who did not invite it to compete at the 2006 festival. Similarly, in its international press reception it was almost uniformly praised for its gripping, beautifully shot narrative, which ostensibly gave its audience an authentic and detailed presentation of the oppressive reality of life in the GDR. 'It's hard to believe that this is von

---

4 For a discussion of von Donnersmarck's campaign to win the Oscar see Seeßlen, 'So gewinnt man einen Auslands-Oscar', Susan Vahabzadeh and Fritz Göttler, 'Dabei sein ist längst nicht alles', *Süddeutsche Zeitung*, 23 February 2007.
5 All ticket sales figures are taken from the Filmförderungsanstalt Filmhitlisten (http://www.ffa.de/).

Donnersmarck's first feature', David Ansen declares. 'His storytelling gifts have the novelistic richness of a seasoned master'.[6] Peter Bradshaw was similarly effusive in his praise, describing it as an 'intensively crafted liberal tragedy' that provides an effective 'antidote to *Ostalgie*', the much discussed 'nostalgia for the days of the Berlin Wall', that had, Bradshaw suggests, so gripped the nation of late and was to be found most obviously in the success of Becker's *Good Bye, Lenin!*, a film that 'frankly, came close to indulging the shabby communist regime'. At last, it appeared, a German filmmaker was revealing the true face of the GDR and uncovering the inner workings of its most despised state organ.[7] In Germany, however, its reception was far more mixed, sparking a major, and at times hugely vitriolic, debate. On the one hand, there were those who also saw the film as a corrective to *Ostalgie*, or to the 'Sun-Alley-ization of GDR memory', as Sebastian Handke puts it, here referring to that other key *Ostalgie* film, Leander Haußmann's coming-of-age teen comedy *Sonnenallee* (Sun Alley, 1999).[8] Indeed, no less an authority on Stasi oppression than Wolf Biermann praised the film for its authentic image of the GDR, a remarkable achievement for a 'debut director who grew up in the West'.[9] The film's ostensible quest for authenticity and painstaking attention to detail was repeatedly cited by those who praised it. It seemed that every aspect of the set was an accurate reconstruction of the period, down to the bugging devices installed in the writer's flat, as von Donnersmarck was at pains to point out in interviews he gave during the film's theatrical release.[10] And, as he was also keen to mention in these same interviews, although he grew up in the West, he did have some first-hand experience of life in the GDR gained on family trips there as a child, underlining his 'right' to tell this kind of story.[11] The film's apparent authenticity, moreover, was a major reason behind the level of

---

6 David Ansen, 'A Waking Nightmare. Sex, spies und audiotape in corrupt East Germany', *Newsweek*, 12 February 2007. For an overview of the film's critical reception see Lu Seegers, '*Das Leben der Anderen* oder der "richtige" Erinnerung an die DDR', in *Film und kulturelle Erinnerung. Plurimediale Konstellationen*, ed. by Astrid Erll and Stephanie Wodianka (Berlin: Walter de Gruyter, 2008), pp. 21–52; Nick Hodgin, 'Screening the Stasi: The Politics of Representation in Postunification Film', in *The GDR Remembered. Representations of the East German State since 1989*, ed. by Nick Hodgin and Caroline Pearce (Rochester: Camden House, 2011), pp. 69–91 (pp. 78–84).

7 Peter Bradshaw, 'The Lives of Others', *The Guardian*, 13 April 2007.

8 Sebastian Handke, 'Die Wanzen sind echt: Kinodebatte über *Das Leben der Anderen*', *Tagesspiegel*, 8 April 2007.

9 Christina Tilmann, 'Wer ist Florian Henckel von Donnersmarck?', *Tagesspiegel*, 25 February, 2007.

10 Handke, 'Die Wanzen sind echt'; Dieter Radow, 'Die innere Wiedervereinigung', *Frankfurter Allgemeine Zeitung*, 12 April 2007.

11 Lars-Olav Beier, 'Endstation Hollywood', *Der Spiegel*, 12 February 2007.

official endorsement the film received.[12] Along with Biermann, the former and, then, current Federal Commissioner for the Stasi archives, Joachim Gauck and Marianne Birthler, were also effusive in their support. 'Yes, that's how it was!', declared Gauck emphatically in *Stern* magazine, praising the film for its presentation of 'authentic images, figures and events'.[13] For the Federal Agency for Political Education, the film's attention to detail also made it an ideal text for teaching school children about the oppressive reality of life in the East,[14] and the positive reviews of the various film screenings specifically for children seemed to support its view, the organizers of such events precisely seeing the film as a way for the younger generation to gain a non-*Ostalgie*-tainted picture of the GDR.[15]

On the other hand, there were those who condemned the film precisely for its *lack* of authenticity. As Anna Funder notes in one of the few critical foreign reviews the film received, the Stasi would never have let a lone individual run an operation like this. Consequently, a single officer betraying the Stasi could never have had such a large impact on an operation, and this is not to mention the fact that there is little or no evidence that such conversions amongst members of the organization ever took place.[16] Similarly Stefan Wolle, along with numerous other commentators in Germany, found various inaccuracies in its representation of the inner workings of the MfS, from the film's incorrect use of titles in the way the characters address each other to the unlikelihood that a member of a party elite known for its prudish nature would, or could, order an expensive surveillance operation in order to have an affair.[17]

---

12 Peter Zander, 'Im Ausland wird man immer zuerst auf Nazis angesprochen. Das nervt', *Die Welt*, 21 March 2006.

13 Joachim Gauck, '*Das Leben der Anderen*: "Ja, so war es!"', *Stern*, 25 March 2006.

14 Marianne Falck, *Filmheft. Das Leben der Anderen* (Bundeszentrale für Politische Bildung: Bonn, 2006).

15 Torsten Harmsen,'Irgendwie geht's um Stasi: 700 Schüler sehen auf Einladung Klaus Bögers *Das Leben der Anderen*', *Berliner Zeitung*, 4 April 2006; Ingo Rössling, 'Film und Diskussion: Enkel von Stasi-Opfer zeigt Flagge', *Die Welt*, 29 March 2006.

16 Anna Funder, 'Eyes without a Face', *Sight and Sound*, 5/17 (2007), 16–20 (p. 18). It is interesting to note that, while the initial international press reception was very positive, there were some significant commentators, like Funder, with a particular interest in the former Eastern Bloc who were similarly critical in terms of the film's historical accuracy, including Timothy Garton Ash, who was nonetheless very positive in terms of the film's overall value (Timothy Garton Ash 'The Stasi on Our Minds', *New York Review of Books*, 31 May 2007) and Slavoj Žižek, who saw little very little of merit in the film. Slavoj Žižek, 'The Dreams of Others', *In these Times*, 18 May 2007 (http://www.inthesetimes.com/article/3183/).

17 Stefan Wolle, 'Stasi mit menschlichem Antlitz', *Deutschland Archiv*, 3 (2006), 497–99.

Others went far beyond pointing out specific historical inaccuracies to challenge the film's underlying ideological position. One of the most scathing appraisals in this regard came from Rüdiger Suchsland, who condemned the film as 'Disney's GDR-Melo[drama]', a reference to its distribution in Germany by Buena Vista. Suchsland is particularly contemptuous of both the film's official endorsement and its potential educational value:

> This is one of those films that culture ministers like. A palatable melodrama, from the brown, dusty days of the GDR, seasoned with some sex and art, lots of horrible repression, some dead people, still more heartache, a few cold, evil perpetrators, lots and lots of German victims and a Saul who becomes a Paul. [... von Donnersmarck] presents the GDR so simplistically, clearly and unambiguously that one doesn't have to think about it much. One knows where one stands. He divides the past up into small, bite-sized, consumable pieces, into teaching units. School classes will be shown it until they can't stand it anymore.[18]

Of course the authorities liked the film, Suchsland suggests. Its straightforward melodramatic narrative allows a clear-cut reading of the past that requires no reflection. In similar vein, Gerhard Ehrlicher argues that the film 'trivializes the misdeeds of the State Security Service'.[19] While Günter Jenschonnek goes further, suggesting provocatively that its ultimate aim is to turn Wiesler into 'a State Security Schindler', making a straight-edged perpetrator into a sensitive good person, then into a hero and finally into a pitiable victim.[20] Both its detractors and supporters make the point that *The Lives of Others* is a feature film and not a historical treatise. Indeed, this is a point von Donnersmarck himself increasingly made in response to some of the comments the film received about specific historical inaccuracies, while still insisting upon the overall authenticity of the film's depiction of the period.[21] However, for its detractors this fundamental claim to authenticity meant that the film must, in fact, be judged not only aesthetically but also as history. In this regard, while the 'bugs' used in the film might well be 'real', its presentation of the workings of the Stasi are not and so cannot stand as a useful depiction of the period. Instead, Thomas Lindenberger, for example, argues that the Stasi is used as the backdrop for a classic 'exploitation film', designed primarily to attract international audiences.[22]

---

18 Rüdiger Suchsland, 'Mundgerecht konsumierbare Vergangenheit', *Teleopolis*, 23 March 2006.
19 Gerhard Ehrlicher, 'Die Realität war eine andere', *Frankfurter Allgemeine Zeitung*, 21 June 2006.
20 Jenschonnek, 'Sehnsucht nach unpolitischen Märchen'.
21 Hodgin, 'Screening the Stasi', p. 79.
22 Thomas Lindenberger, 'Stasiploitation – Why Not? The Scriptwriter's Historical Creativity', *German Studies Review*, 31.3 (2008), pp. 557–66.

Others also argue that this was not the first film to address seriously the legacy of the Stasi, as some critics claimed, pointing to numerous documentaries and dramas that have presented the machinations of this organization since unification, including Volker Schlöndorff's *Die Stille nach dem Schuß* (The Legend of Rita, 2000), Connie Walter's *Wie Feuer und Flamme* (Never Mind the Wall, 2001) and Christian Klemke and Jan Lorenzen's *Das Ministerium für Staatssicherheit: Alltag einer Behörde* (The Ministry of State Security: The Daily Routine of an Agency, 2003).[23] Indeed, rather than marking a new stage in the historical representation of the GDR, both the film itself and elements of its reception could be seen as a throwback to the early 1990s when the role of the Stasi was central to discussions of the East German State, and German public life was regularly punctuated with scandals about the collaboration of public figures with the MfS, scandals that came to light as the miles of Stasi files accumulated in its forty years of existence were gradually worked through. In the wake of the *Wende* (the German term used to describe the collapse of the GDR), numerous figures were outed as IMs, from Lothar de Maizière, the GDR's only democratically elected President, to some of the country's most prominent cultural figures such as Christa Wolf and Heiner Müller, fuelling the impression that life in the GDR was like living in an Orwellian Big Brother state where, as Jürgen Habermas famously described it, a giant octopus-like organization stretched its tentacles through the whole of society, leaving no aspect of life free from its influence.[24] In recent years such scandals have become less frequent, although the film itself generated another one when Mühe made the claim that his former wife, the actress Jenny Gröllmann, had spied on him for the Stasi. This seemed further to point to the authenticity of the film, Gröllmann playing a version of 'Sieland' to Mühe's real-life 'Dreyman'.[25] However, any connection between the actual experience of the actors and the film's representation of history ultimately appeared to reside instead in the unreliability of the Stasi archive as an accurate record of the past, Gröllmann herself claiming that her

---

23 See, for example, Seegers, '*Das Leben der Anderen* oder der "richtige" Erinnerung an die DDR', p. 35.

24 For further discussion see David Bathrick, *The Powers of Speech. The Politics of Culture in the GDR* (Lincoln: University of Nebraska, 1995), p. 221.

25 Seegers also notes that this was not the only way in which the film seemed to play to external Stasi debates, pointing to a demonstration just before its German premiere when 200 former Stasi officers protested against the manner in which the MfS was being characterized in the Stasi Prison Museum at Hohenschönhausen. Seegers, '*Das Leben der Anderen* oder der "richtige" Erinnerung an die DDR', p. 34. The impact of these events on Mühe is further discussed in von Donnersmarck's contribution to this volume.

file was a fabrication by an ambitious Stasi officer.[26] Moreover, in relation to the way the film played into broader debates on the history of the GDR and its representation in contemporary German society, its supporters' claim that *The Lives of Others* was a corrective to *Ostalgie* ignored the fact that such nostalgia was at least partially a response to the very post-unification perception of the GDR as an Orwellian Stasi state we find in the film, where all activity was monitored and manipulated by the MfS, and where anything resembling a 'normal' life, as one might understand it in the West, was impossible. *Ostalgie*, with its fetishization of aspects of everyday life in the GDR was, for better or worse, in part a declaration of such normalcy.[27]

Despite its subject matter and the claim that it was intent upon challenging the apparent revisionism of *Ostalgie*, for its detractors, the film trivialized the Stasi's crimes in its focus on a 'good' officer and so ultimately offered an equally revisionist image of the past. In this regard, *The Lives of Others* was also repeatedly condemned as a 'consensus film', a pejorative term used to describe much recent mainstream German cinema.[28] Coined by Eric Rentschler to define a wave of romantic comedies that enjoyed a good degree of domestic success during the 1990s, it suggested an approach to filmmaking far removed from the aesthetically challenging and politically abrasive work of the New German Cinema. These mainstream comedies instead appeared to present a self-congratulatory image of life in the recently united Germany.[29] Although hardly a romantic comedy, the term is used here to describe a film that was accused of wilfully misrepresenting the reality of the Stasi's activities, turning the past into an easily digestible melodrama, its straightforward narrative and comfortable mainstream aesthetic undermining any potential it might have as a useful intervention in debates on the legacy of the GDR. Returning for the moment to Suchsland's attack, it is revealing that he twice cites Fassbinder as a counterpoint to von Donnersmarck. For Suchsland, Fassbinder embodies a far more aesthetically and politi-

---

26 Jennifer Creech points to the research carried out by Petra Weisenburger for her 2008 documentary on Gröllmann's life, *Ich will da sein* (I Want to Be There), where she came to this conclusion, also noting that there was no document containing Gröllmann's signature to prove that she had been an IM. Creech, 'A Few Good Men', p. 121.

27 For further discussion see Paul Cooke, *Representing East Germany. From Colonization to Nostalgia* (Oxford: Berg, 2005).

28 von Beier, 'Endstation Hollywood'; Katja Körte Bauer, 'Die feine Grenzlinie auf dem Weg zum Verra', *Stuttgarter Zeitung*, 27 February 2007.

29 Eric Rentschler, 'From New German Cinema to the Post-Wall Cinema of Consensus', in *Cinema and Nation*, ed. by Mette Hjort and Scott Mckenzie (London and New York: Routledge, 2000), pp. 260–77.

cally interesting German film tradition, one that understands the self-reflexive, critical potential of melodrama, served up here as unreconstructed kitsch.[30]

In response to the views of critics such as Suchsland, Günter Rohrbach, President of the German Film Academy, produced a similarly vitriolic attack in *Der Spiegel*, condemning these German feuilletonists as 'autistic', their invariable condemnation of mainstream German films revealing them to be out of touch with the cinema-going public. He questions what he views to be the patronizing implications of the term 'consensus film' as it is used by numerous critics in the German press. Instead, he celebrates the term and the role such films have played in the rediscovery of mainstream domestic cinema by German audiences; he goes on to question the purpose of those critics who seem to approach popular film with a preconceived resentment, unable to see any potential artistic merit in such work, however this might be defined.[31] Von Donnersmarck, for his part, supported Rohrbach, taking on those who condemned his film as 'consensual', redefining the term positively:

> If 'consensus film' is supposed to mean the same as 'trivial' or even 'bad film', then I want to make a lot more bad and trivial films in my career. What would those critics say of films like *Casablanca* or *Godfather Part II*? They must be the worst films of all time, for absolutely everyone thinks that they are good, and not – as in my case – almost everyone. I wish that *The Lives of Others* was much more of a consensus film![32]

For von Donnersmarck, it is possible to be 'consensual', in the sense of being popular with audiences and aesthetically mainstream, but to still have artistic credibility.

The Lives of Others and Contemporary German Film

What began as a discussion of an individual film became a debate on the ethics of representing Germany's problematic history as well as the type of film industry the country should support. In the rest of this volume these discussions are revisited, re-evaluated and extended, building on the growing body of scholarship that has emerged since the film's initial reception while also taking into account later developments in von Donnersmarck's own career as well as in the broader

---

30 Suchsland, 'Mundgerecht konsumierbare Vergangenheit'.
31 Günter Rohrbach, 'Das Schmollen der Autisten', *Der Spiegel*, 22 January 2007.
32 Quoted in Annette Maria Rupprecht, 'Florian Henckel von Donnersmarck: XXL', *German Film Quarterly*, 3 (2006), 16–17 (p. 17).

landscape of German film. Part I of the volume (Making the Film) focuses on the immediate production context, beginning with two contributions from people directly involved in the project. Chapter One is a lecture given by von Donnersmarck at the University of Cambridge, introduced by Christopher Young who organized the event. The director talks very personally about his approach to filmmaking and in particular his conceptualization of colour and music. Some of this account appears in the various interviews he gave during the film's initial release. However, the lecture format gives him the space to provide a far greater level of detail than is found elsewhere. Throughout, a sense of von Donnersmarck's tenacity dominates, born of the conviction he had of the value of his project and which helped him bring together a cast and crew of a calibre one would not expect for a debut director. At the same time, he addresses some of the key issues raised in the wider debate the film sparked, issues that will be explored throughout this volume. Not least, he revisits the question of historical authenticity and his right, as a Westerner, to tell this story, reflecting on the pressure he felt from the media to find a link in his own biography to the GDR. In Chapter Two Manfred Wilke addresses the issue of authenticity further, giving an account of his experience working as von Donnersmarck's historical consultant on the film. Wilke has spent his career analysing the workings of the SED dictatorship and was involved, during the 1990s, in the Federal Enquete Commissions on the official historical appraisal of the GDR period. He discusses the specific historical sources which fed into the narrative – including the historical evidence for the type of conversion we see in Wiesler – as well as the wider political and social realities of life in the GDR, particularly towards the end of the state's existence. Chapters Three and Four complement the accounts of these two direct participants. Randall Halle (Chapter Three) looks at the broader production context within which von Donnersmarck was operating as a debut feature-film director, examining the fault lines between, and asymmetries in, the experience of filmmakers from the former GDR and the Federal Republic, along with the specific cultural habitus of von Donnersmarck's training in Munich. Halle examines the unique place the director occupies within what he terms the postwall 'matrix of production', as well as the broader implications of von Donnersmarck's success for the rest of the industry and the challenge it presents more established filmmakers to achieve more with ever smaller budgets. Jaimey Fisher (Chapter Four) discusses the pivotal role played by Ulrich Mühe (Wiesler) in the success of the film, the importance of his contribution having already been highlighted in von Donnersmarck's lecture. Fisher looks at Mühe's participation in the film from the perspective of 'star studies', exploring the place of the actor's biography in the critical discourse that initially surrounded the film, offering a different perspective on the question of historical authenticity to that found in Wilke's chapter.

This he contextualizes within Mühe's entire oeuvre, and the way his star persona has a particular memorializing dimension either not found, or ignored, in discussions of stardom in Anglo-American star studies.

Fisher begins to move the discussion of the film beyond its initial production context, opening it up to reinterpretation from a range of theoretical and cultural perspectives. In Part II (Re-positioning the Film) this is developed further, the film being read in ways that re-evaluate and re-configure the initial debates it generated. Chapters Five and Six focus on issues of genre. On the one hand, Andrea Rinke continues the discussion of the specific contribution made by von Donnersmarck's cast, looking now at the way in which Martina Gedeck helped shape the character of Christa-Maria Sieland. Rinke brings out ambiguities in the character of Sieland ignored in much of the film's initial critical reception, exploring her complex place within the melodramatic economy of gender relations in the film and, in turn, the film's appeal to pathos. This, she argues, challenges any straightforwardly Manichean conceptualization of melodrama in the film, offering instead a more nuanced understanding of its presentation of power-relations than has often been acknowledged. David Bathrick, on the other hand, examines the film as the first post-89 Cold War spy film, a generic approach that he uses to re-evaluate the film's engagement with history in its form as well as narrative content. Bathrick continues the discussion begun by Wilke, returning to the historical record in his account of the way the Stasi carried out its surveillance operations. However, he quickly moves from the historical to the aesthetic, placing the film within a trajectory of film production that moves from James Bond to John Le Carré before landing on Roland Gräf's little discussed East German drama *Der Tangospieler* (The Tango Player, 1991), produced by DEFA, the state's centralized film production company. In the process, Bathrick also develops aspects of Halle's chapter, contrasting approaches to coming to terms with the GDR past in contemporary (unified) German cinema against the approach that was beginning to emerge in GDR state-sponsored films produced just before DEFA was wound up in 1992.

In his lecture, von Donnersmarck is keen to highlight the literary nature of his screenplay and the efforts he went to in order to have it published by Suhrkamp. In Chapter Seven, Marc Silberman reflects further on the literary dimensions of von Donnersmarck's project, extending the volume's discussion of the film's initial production context to the publication context of the screenplay. At the same time, he explores the literary forms and allusions that permeate the film itself, from Lessing to Brecht, examining the ways in which the film's web of intertextuality both reflects and challenges the narrative's assumptions about the ethical power of literature and art. Throughout, Silberman highlights issues of intermediality, a major theme of much contemporary film criticism, looking at how the translation of cultural forms across media point to the limits form places on representation. It is the question of translation that is key to Chapter Eight. Ian Thomas Fleishman examines translation as a function of real and metaphorical 'border crossing' in the film, specifically with regard to the transnational context of the film's consumption. For Fleishman, *The Lives of Others* seeks to create a bridge across geographical and temporal boundaries, translating the experience of life under the SED for audiences situated beyond Germany and after the GDR period. He teases out productive tensions in the film's self-conscious exploration of its own status as both a transnational and *post*national cinematic text. Here he continues a discussion that spans Part II and III on the representational limits of film as a medium, as well as *The Lives of Others'* place within the canon of German national film culture.

Part III (Beyond the Film) broadens the volume's frame of reference still further, extending the exploration of the film's place within contemporary German culture and continuing the project of analyzing *The Lives of Others* using the wide range of tools available to contemporary film scholars but often not employed in the analysis of German cinema. At the same time we look at the way the film plays to current trends in German film production, while also re-evaluating the debate on the nature of this production that the film initially sparked. Lutz Koepnick revisits Fleishman's exploration of intermedial borders, along with the volume's discussion of the limits of cinematic representation, in his investigation of von Donnersmarck's soundscape. Developing the work of Michel Chion, in Chapter Nine, Koepnick positions the film's auditory field as a critically charged space which refuses the straightforward integration of sight and sound generally to be found in mainstream cinema. Specifically, Koepnick challenges the film's description as either an example of heritage or consensus cinema – two mainstays of the mainstream film industry in Germany. Instead, he argues that the complexity of von Donnersmarck's soundscape suggests ways that the film might be placed alongside the type of esoteric filmmaking generally considered to be its antithesis by many cultural commentators. Sabine Hake also looks at the film's location within broader trends in film production, returning to debates about German heritage cinema. Chapter Ten examines the role of production design and material culture in the film, analyzing its politics of representation. However, rather than evaluating the film's politics from the perspective of its presentation of GDR history, Hake's concern is the changing nature of representation in the digital age. That said, she does explore contemporary fascination for the material culture of pre-unification East *and* West Germany, so-called *Ostalgie* and *Westalgie*. This she examines as a manifestations of what Jonathan Bach has termed 'modernist nostalgia', a 'longing for longings once possible' but lost in the post-ideological Berlin Republic, where digital reproduction has the potential to sever any indexical link with the material culture of the past. Chapter Eleven further explores the changing nature of cinematic representation, revisiting discussions begun by Bathrick on the film's place within international traditions of filmmaking, along with its use of genre. Paul Cooke investigates von Donnersmarck's engagement with the aesthetics and representational politics of the auteur-driven Hollywood Renaissance of the 1960s and 1970s. In particular, he explores von Donnersmarck's dialogue with Francis Ford Coppola's *The Conversation* (1974). The role of *The Conversation* as an intertext in von Donnersmarck's film has often been mentioned (not least in Koepnick's contribution to this volume). However, it has not until now been discussed in detail. This connection is then contrasted with the role of Hollywood in von Donnersmarck's second film, *The Tourist* (2010), looking at how the film reflects a broader shift in the relationship of many contemporary German filmmakers to this hegemonic film culture. Finally, in Chapter Twelve, Eric Rentschler draws the discussion of the film to a close by returning to the initial controversy it sparked on the nature of German national film production. He revisits his influential essay of 2000 'From New German Cinema to the Post-wall Cinema of Consensus', exploring, and challenging, the various ways notions of 'consensus' have shaped debates about contemporary German film culture in the decade since its publication. Complementing both Koepnick and Hake's chapters, this discussion he places alongside an examination of heritage cinema as it has come to be defined by cultural commentators across Europe. Rentschler opens up the term, exploring a variety of alternative conceptualizations of the heritage film, as well as film heritage, within the context of German film production. The chapter closes with an examination of *Jahrgang 45* (Born in '45, 1965), which Rentschler offers as a useful counterpoint to *The Lives of Others*, the volume again reminding us of the contribution DEFA made to German film history and the richness of its engagement with life in the GDR before and in the aftermath of unification.

Although each chapter offers a specific approach to the film and can be read in isolation, it is hoped that the volume will also be read as a whole, some of its key questions being debated across several of the contributions. Why was *The Lives of Others* such an international success? How does this success speak to the increasingly transnational modes of production, distribution and exhibition that define the global film industry today? How does this reflect its engagement with internationally understandable genre conventions and to what extent does this, in turn, highlight the shifting contours of mainstream and more avant-garde film production in Germany? What does this say about the limits of cinematic representation? How does the film engage with contemporary historical debates, and how were these considered during the production process itself? Who has the 'right' to represent the past, and how are we to understand the 'value' of film as history? How does *The Lives of Others*, and its attempt to work through the legacy of the GDR, relate to the longer tradition of German *Vergangenheitsbewältigung* (coming to terms with the past) of the Nazi period? Can a popular film text, and in particular the popular heritage film that has played such an important role in German national cinema's recent international visibility, offer new insight into the past? How do these films, with their identificatory narratives focussed on the emotional engagement of the spectator, compare with the often more explicitly self-reflexive, critical history films of the New German Cinema – films that in their day played an equally important role in the international success of filmmakers such as Fassbinder and Schlöndorff –, or the DEFA tradition and the representation of history on the GDR screen? Finally, how does the film's popular and academic reception engage the broader concerns of film studies generally, as well as German film studies in particular? What does its reception say about the state of the discipline and its increasing interdisciplinarity, drawing as it does on methodologies and thematic concerns from areas as varied as cognitive psychology, sociology, economics, literary studies, history, gender and star studies? These are some of the questions this volume attempts to answer.

I. Making the Film

Florian Henckel von Donnersmarck

CHAPTER ONE
Seeing a Film Before You Make It

Introduced by Christopher Young

Florian Henckel von Donnersmarck is a big name – especially when it appears in your inbox. In January 2008, I was thrilled to see it stretch across my computer screen when I opened my email and read Florian's acceptance of our invitation to come to the University of Cambridge to deliver the inaugural X-Changing Lecture on German culture. The event bore the name of the sponsors of the annual Oxford-Cambridge Boat Race, a company whose then CEO, David Andrews, wanted to express his fondness for and admiration of Germany with a generous donation for an occasional intellectual counterpart to the physical exertions on the Thames. The excitement around the various institutions supporting the lecture (the Department of German and Dutch, the Judge Business School and Pembroke College) that took place the following October and the turn-out of several hundred, spilling out into and filling the overflow room, were fitting testimony to von Donnersmarck's standing and the interest his debut feature film had generated in the UK and beyond.

As befitted the largely student audience, von Donnersmarck touched on the importance of his undergraduate and graduate careers in various countries. In general, he has been openly enthusiastic about his time at Oxford, particularly praising 'the visual self-containment of the city, and the fact that you live there within specific aesthetics, as if in a film'.[1] When introducing him in Cambridge I gained myself an easy laugh with the quip that three years in Oxford must have been the perfect preparation for depicting the drab and dreary world of the former East Germany. I had little sense that this casual remark struck at the heart of von Donnersmarck's cinematic vision, as his opening comments would soon go on to show.

The GDR, of course, was no joking matter either. But as Peter Schneider, author of the famous *Der Mauerspringer* (The Wall Jumper, 1984) and member of the jury that awarded von Donnersmarck the Deutscher Filmpreis, noted: 'For a long time, there was a tendency to portray the GDR as a state where no one really

---

1 Annette Maria Rupprecht, 'Florian Henckel von Donnersmarck: XXL', *German Film Quarterly*, 3 (2006), 16–17 (p. 16).

suffered and the Stasi was regarded as something of a joke'.[2] *The Lives of Others* has frequently been read as a corrective to films such as *Sonnenallee* (Sun Alley, Leander Haußmann, 1999) and *Good Bye, Lenin!* (Wolfgang Becker, 2003) in its portrayal of the GDR's totalitarian reality and way the Stasi terrorized millions of East German citizens. It is certainly a masterful piece of filmmaking, one – as historian Timothy Garton Ash comments in the *New York Review of Books* – which 'uses the syntax and conventions of Hollywood to convey to the widest possible audience some part of the truth about life under the Stasi, and the larger truths that experience revealed about human nature. It mixes historical fact with the ingredients of a fast-paced thriller and love story'.[3]

Not everyone, however, would have awarded the film the Oscar. Not everyone would have wished the film to be made in the first place. Dr Hubertus Knabe, historian and director of the museum and memorial at the former Stasi prison in Hohenschönhausen, in fact, refused to allow filming to take place on his premises. Knabe and others such as Anna Funder (the author of *Stasiland*)[4] expressed their concern about the moral relativism of the film, the creeping rehabilitation of the Stasi – and point to the lack of concrete examples of any East German officer undergoing the change of heart that Wiesler does in this film.[5] This is certainly a view, and one that we have to take seriously, but it misses the point.

As a work of art, it is not the job of *The Lives of Others* to serve up answers, but to ask questions and explore solutions. It is important to ask these questions, because the GDR, a country into which 17 million Germans were born but that no longer exists, sits paradoxically between obsession and forgetting. On the one hand, continuities have meant that no other communist dictatorship has been opened up to such intense scrutiny as the GDR has by the Federal Republic. There is no, and nor is there ever likely to be, a KGB *The Lives of Others*. On the other, it is a sobering fact that, as recent research has shown, 50 percent of current school children living in the former East Germany today are ignorant of the fact that the GDR was a dictatorship. The figures are reminiscent of the late 1960s, when the Mitscherlichs wrote about the Federal Republic's inability to mourn.

In his recent book, *Cultural Amnesia. Notes in the Margin of My Time*, Clive James talks about Germany's role in the barbarism of the twentieth century and the danger of American cultural imperialism (themes that resonate with obvious questions about the content and style of a film like *The Lives of Others*): 'We

---

2 Rupprecht, 'Florian Henckel von Donnersmarck: XXL', p. 16.
3 Timothy Garton Ash 'The Stasi on Our Minds', *New York Review of Books*, 31 May 2007.
4 Anna Funder, *Stasiland. Stories from Behind the Berlin Wall* (London: Granta, 2003).
5 Anna Funder, 'The Lives of Others', *Guardian*, 5 May 2007.

Florian Henckel von Donnersmarck at the University of Cambridge, 10 October 2008.

could, if we wished, do without remembering, and gain all the advantages of travelling light; but a deep instinct, not very different from love [again a *The Lives of Others* theme, CY], reminds us that the efficiency would be bought at the cost of emptiness'.[6] It is important for Germany and the world in general that we do not pay that price. *The Lives of Others* – if the pun does not seem too cheap at a time of global austerity – keeps us solvent.

To quote once more from Garton Ash's review: 'The Germany in which this film was produced, in the early years of the twenty-first century, is one of the most free and civilized countries on earth. In this Germany, human rights and civil liberties are today more jealously and effectively protected (it pains me to say) than in traditional homelands of liberty such as Britain and the United States. In this good land, the professionalism of historians, the investigative skills of its journalists, the seriousness of its parliamentarians, the generosity of its funders, the idealism of its priests and moralists, the creative genius of its writers, and yes, the brilliance of its filmmakers have all combined to cement in the world's imagin-

---

6 Clive James, *Cultural Amnesia. Notes in the Margin of My Time* (London: Picador, 2007; corrected edition 2008), p. 7.

ation the most indelible association of Germany with evil. Yet without these efforts, Germany would never have become such a good land. In all the annals of human culture, has there ever been a more paradoxical achievement?'[7]

Art, of course, is the medium of paradox par excellence. It can hold opposites in creative tension that would corrode and destroy each other in reality, and – at its most optimistic – offer hope that the good and beautiful might overcome the malign and ugly. In his talk (given on 10 October 2008) – which is reproduced below with only minor editing to account for the transition from ex tempore delivery to the written page[8] – von Donnersmarck outlines what can best be described as an aesthetics of artistic and human beauty as a response and challenge to political depravity. His achievement is altogether worthy of that good land Germany, but – as his talk clearly illustrates – his achievement is an eloquent reminder that being good and helping others in their own lives to be good requires the artist to strive at all times and without compromise for nothing but the very best.

Seeing a Film Before You Make It

The success or, let's say, acceptance of *The Lives of Others* in England was particularly heart-warming, because I always found it hard to make myself understood in this country – even during the three years I spent at Oxford. It's easy to look at somebody who's 6'9 tall with a name that needs the cinema-scope format to fit it in, as somehow alien. I could never completely break through that, which I regretted, because I knew the fault was mine; and so I'm glad that I was able to reach out to this country through my film. I do feel that films, and art in general, can be a form of exchange – even between countries. It's harder, for example, for two countries to go to war if, through a film, individuals have been able to be a person of the other nationality by identifying with the protagonist. That's the true meaning of the word 'identify'. You become 'identical' with that other person. You become him. Imagine spending two hours identifying with a character on screen, becoming a Stasi officer, and somehow developing sympathy for him. It's much harder then to see even that character completely as an enemy. Film allows us to do that more than other art forms because we can combine so many things.

---

7 Garton Ash, 'The Stasi on Our Minds'.
8 With thanks to Charlotte Lee for her transcription and to the managers of the Tiarks Fund in the Department of German and Dutch in the University of Cambridge for the small grant that supported it.

But at the beginning it was pretty hard to get the film shown in Britain. When Lionsgate first decided to distribute it, their big question was, 'How are we going to get people in this country to go and see this? People are not really open to watching German films'. They went through the relatively short list of German films that had received some attention. There was *Downfall*, which was kind of successful; and *Goodbye Lenin!*, which a few people had seen; *Run Lola Run* wasn't a particular success. You have to go back to *Das Boot* before you find a film that attracted a substantial number of viewers – and that was almost thirty years ago. But finally they had an idea: 'We'll just have to mask the fact that it's a German film. Let's not have any German words or names on the poster or even in the trailer'. (Quite something for a film that's largely dialogue-based!) They didn't go so far as to suggest we dub it: 'In English, you only dub kung-fu and porn films, not normal fiction', I was told. So they spent several weeks trying to edit the trailer without a single word of spoken German in it, to somehow trick people into thinking the film was not really that German after all [*HvD screens the trailer for the audience, showing that it does not contain a single spoken word. The audience laughs*]. You didn't believe me, did you? Well, anyway, that's what they did and it lured more people into the cinemas than any other German film, ever, in the UK.

I have been asked many questions about the film, but the three that recur most often are: first, what was your own experience of the GDR? Second, how did the idea for the film come about? And third, were you surprised by its success? Let me try and give you some honest responses to each of these.

I don't think there's a single journalist who hasn't asked that first question, and I sometimes wonder if, when they meet Ang Lee, who made *Brokeback Mountain*, they always ask, 'Are you gay? Are you a cowboy?' It would be very depressing if you could only make films about your own experience, and in the first interviews I said, 'I don't really have much experience of the GDR, I just researched this and looked into that,' but that's not what journalists want to hear. So I just dug into the very few connections I had to East Germany and talked about those at length. But really, I only visited the GDR a few times as a child when I was eight or nine, when we were pretty much just driving through. I remember my brother and I used to wind the windows down, sing the old German song 'Die Gedanken sind frei!' (thoughts are free) and feel like real rebels. It made a definite impression on me that the people who lived there couldn't leave the country – that would, of course, make an impression on any child. Maybe I picked up on a few atmospheric things at the time, but later that was not the most important part of it for me. I just sensed that this was material that would give a story an interesting visual and emotional background. That might sound a little superficial, but the visual texture of a film can be very important. Oxford, for instance, is such an incredibly beautiful place, but I remember when I visited Cambridge for the first time, in my second year, and saw there was none of the greyness that Oxford has as a town – just the poetry and beauty – I thought 'Oh my God, maybe I made the wrong choice!' I think it makes a great difference to your quality of life if you are in an environment that is completely visually consistent, if things somehow fit together. I spend a lot of time designing my workspace and all that sort of thing; it means a great deal to me, and I've always tried to be in places where I can get that kind of energy. I've spent a lot of time in Venice and St. Petersburg, which are incredibly beautiful places, built very much in a single coherent style . New York, I find, is like that too. When there is a visual universe that allows me to focus on something, I can suddenly breathe and – weirdly – the communist bloc had that. It had a certain world of colours that somehow matched one another.

A chemist once explained to me that this was because the East didn't have access to certain colour patents that were developed in the sixties to create the bright neon-like colours that became so omnipresent in the West. Up until the early sixties, there wasn't actually much difference between the way the East and West looked, then suddenly the West developed all these incredibly bright shining tones and the East got left behind. It could only produce weak colours, but this created a certain kind of beauty. I went to study Russian literature in Leningrad (as it was still called) after my *Abitur* in 1991. I graduated from high school that July, and in August there was the coup against Gorbachev, and only after that failed was it clear that *perestroika* was here to stay. So in September I was able to go to the East as a completely free Western student, and it was a really great experience, entering into this world (it was still the Soviet Union then) of colours and shapes that were all more or less designed by one central organization, the government. It somehow had its own beauty. I remember when I left in 1993, shortly before going to Oxford, the first Western cars started to appear, and it was like a shock, or an insult even. I remember the first Marlboro ad with that red colour, it just really threw me to see it there. This was a universe that I wanted to recreate, and I worked very hard to use the beauty that I learned from Oxford, Cambridge, St Petersburg and create it in the drabness of the GDR. Of course, we always aim for beauty, but I don't think there's ever any excuse for making something less beautiful than it can be. Art should always strive for beauty – it can be found in very depressing things, but these should always be as beautiful as possible.

There was a lot of injustice in the GDR, and injustice is always a fantastic ingredient for a film story. From my earlier life and education I think I understood something about the main factor that led to this injustice: the ideology of communism. Although I never had any strong communist leanings myself, I really understood what these people were trying to say, what they were feeling, and what led to all this excess. When I first met with Prof. Manfred Wilke, a great expert on all things GDR, after I had read up enough to feel I could present my idea to him and seek his advice, he said to me, 'You understand faith. Why do you understand faith?' And I thought this was kind of a weird question, until he said, 'It's really interesting. I don't know many people of your generation who really understand what it is to believe in something religiously. I think this film will be good, because you understand exactly what motivated these people'. And then we talked about what it could be that helped me with that. I think it was that I grew up in an extremely Catholic family – breaking loose from the rigidity of that may have been similar to what Wiesler went through in my film. But it also showed me that it's really not as simple as saying that these people were using this system cynically for reasons of power alone. There can be real faith, and a real desire somehow to do something – to do something *good* through ideology, but sometimes it involves ignoring your feelings more and more, and just following principles that you once understood to be right. But those feelings are still there, and I wondered what would happen if somehow a floodgate were suddenly to open and sweep this man back in the direction of feeling. Those are things that I experienced in some way in my own family and in my own biography, and I think they contributed to my wanting to make the film. I found those ingredients in the history of the GDR, and thought it would be a good setting in which I could tell this story.

As for how the actual idea came about (the journalists' favourite second question) – I still remember that very vividly. I think most people, when they make a film or write a novel or something, can remember when the idea first came to them, because it comes in a flash, it comes very quickly. In the very first semester of my first year at film school, we did a course on film technology. There is this idea at the Munich Film School – it's a very German idea – that you have to be able to build a camera before you can stand behind one as a director. I've actually spent a lot of time since then trying to forget all that technical stuff, but we had ten hours a day of intensive technical lessons, and somehow our creative side had to be kept alive too. So our professor had this homework that he gave us, where he said 'OK, during these first eight weeks you have to develop fourteen completely original film plots, and write them down as an *Exposé* – that's the word they use in the German film world to mean a two- to three-page description of pretty much everything that happens sequentially in a film. And he said, 'If you don't deliver these, you'll be expelled; and if I ever find out that you've recycled something you've used before, you'll be expelled for that, too'. So I felt under such incredible pressure – I don't think I've ever felt under so much pressure in my life – and when I came home from those creativity-stifling technical days, I would think, 'OK, now I have to have a new idea'. I didn't know that the professor's theory was that creativity is like a muscle that needs to be developed. But for him, it wasn't like in bodybuilding where you have to increase the weight by five pounds every month or whatever to make the muscle grow. Instead, you had to jump-start it by overloading it completely, and this overloading was supposed to really get your creativity going. That's what he believed. It didn't feel at all like this then, because we were not supposed to talk to each other about our projects either, and I was just depressed. I thought, 'I've chosen the wrong profession, and I thought I was going to be so good at this'. But then the ideas started coming and I wrote them down; they were so-so to begin with but gradually got better.

I had to finish up in the last two days, little knowing that the professor threw all these pieces straight in the waste paper basket: he never read them, it was really just an exercise to get us going. I'd done twelve, and I remember being so depressed because I thought I had written myself completely dry. There was no aspect of my biography or personal life, or of anything I'd ever read left that I could even vaguely plagiarise. I was living in my aunt's guest room, because you couldn't get an apartment in Munich due to the internet boom. So I was lying there on the floor, thinking about what I was going to do now after investing a year and a half in film, drawing story-boards for commercials and other depressing stuff, and wondering how I was going to get back on track and become a consultant or an investment banker like my friends from Oxford. I put on some music to lift the depression and listened to some Beethoven piano sonatas, including the *Moonlight Sonata*. Really that's something I shouldn't have been listening to any more, because it's been used in so many commercials etc. But it was so beautiful and relaxing, and it shifted my mood pretty quickly. And suddenly it reminded me of something I'd once read by Lenin, who talked to Maxim Gorky about the *Appassionata* (which is not my favourite piece of music, but seems to have had the same effect on Lenin as the *Moonlight Sonata* does on me) in the following terms:

> I know of nothing better than the *Appassionata*, and could listen to it every day. What astonishing, superhuman music. It always makes me proud, perhaps with childish naivety, to think that people can work such miracles. But I can't listen to music very often, it affects my nerves; I want to say sweet, silly things to people and pat their little heads. People living in a filthy hell can create such beauty. These days one can't pat anyone on the head, they might bite your hand off. Hence those little heads must be beaten in, beaten mercilessly, although ideally we are against doing any violence to people.[9]

I hadn't thought about this for a while, and I realized how incredible it is that someone who was so much at war with his own humanity could feel something we would all try to encourage in ourselves but nonetheless say, 'No, because I have decided that something is right, I will not let that feeling into my heart'.

---

9 Maxim Gorky, *Collected Works*, XVII (Moskow: Foreign Language Publishing House, 1950), pp. 39–40.

And then I thought, might there somehow be a way of taking a great man, or potentially great man, like Lenin, and exploring what would have happened if he had been *forced* to listen to the *Appassionata*. If someone had put earphones on his head and he had had to listen to it and wasn't able to shut the music off any more. It probably wouldn't work, I thought, because he would just close off part of his soul – this happens if you're not listening with the right attitude, with your own free will. But what if he were in a situation where he had to listen pretty closely – had to do it by his own free will because he thinks he's listening in on what his enemies are saying, but actually he doesn't really see them as enemies any more? The idea became complicated, and then suddenly I thought, OK, who is this, who listens in on other people? The Stasi, that's what they're known for. Who could this be? And suddenly, really within a few minutes, the whole idea flooded into my head. This can happen from time to time when you work in a creative field, or probably in any field – this sudden flow of new ideas that probably don't come completely *from* you, but bring a feeling of order to what's already *in* you. And suddenly, without looking for it, I had the story, the complete plot. Actually, moving offices a few months ago, I found a copy of the original *Exposé* that landed in my professor's waste paper basket the next morning, and I'd say it contained about eighty per cent of the final plot of the film.

I sat down, wrote it up in about an hour, filed it away and forgot about it. A few years later, when I wanted to make my first full-length feature rather than waste any more time in the world of short films – aspiring filmmakers should avoid short films, they're really an incredible waste of time – I went through my filing cabinet of ideas to see which of them still seemed alive to me. It's amazing how quickly ideas die – they seem really good at the time and then you realize all you were doing was picking up on something in the air, something that seemed modern and was trendy at a particular moment but later turns out to be quite embarrassing. I find it sobering to look through ideas I once thought good enough to file away, because most of them aren't that great. But with this one I thought, no, this doesn't have to be made in a specific time. In a way it was independent of time and fashion. I also thought the historical background would mean it wouldn't be boring for me to spend a year researching, writing and making the film. Little did I know it would take me four and a half to five years to fight for the financing and then make it. It was just an idea, of course, and an idea in itself is really only the beginning – that's something else I came to learn. I think everyone has an idea for a film, even many ideas, but the real challenge is to stick with it over several years and see it through to completion. *Run Lola Run* is the only film I know that turned out great without many years of suffering. People say 'Well, Sylvester Stallone wrote *Rocky* in a few weeks'. Maybe he did, I don't know if that's true or not, but he then had to fight for something like six years before they would allow him to make it on his terms. In any genre, in any direction, it's always incredibly hard to stick with an idea for years and not to be tempted away by other things that seem to offer you easy solutions to your problems. Over the years I spent writing and rewriting this film, going to people and trying to convince them to finance it – and I had one important stipulation, which was that the contract had to give me creative control over the whole thing – I received some pretty alluring offers. An American film distributor was planning to open a branch in Germany and wanted me to help them build it up. This seemed like an interesting project – it was close enough to what I wanted to do, but it wasn't *exactly* what I wanted to do. I was asked by one of the German digital channels to present a children's TV show, which would have been fun and also got me out of having to borrow money from my brother and having my wife pulling much more than her share of the household. But in such cases, you really just have to ask yourself, what is it that I want to do *exactly*? Because there's a great difference between doing exactly what you want to do and doing something pretty close to what you want to do. There's an incredible gulf between them, in fact, even if it's not totally visible from the outset. So I'm more proud of the fact that I stuck with the idea than of the idea itself.

The third question I am always asked is if I was surprised by the success of the film. Journalists actually ask this in a very suggestive way, along the lines of, 'Sir, surely you were incredibly surprised by the success of this film, and it must still feel like an unreal dream?!', and you just have to answer, 'Yeah, yeah, sure, you're right'. But there's one thing I discovered in making films, and that is: you truly have to learn to visualize a film. I have to have seen the film in my head before I can really write it down, and certainly before I can make it. I have to know exactly what it's going to feel like – that world, that Cambridge or St Petersburg world of my film, I have to know that. I have to have a feel for the kind of movements my actors will be making, for the inflections of their voices. I have to have seen all that, what the costumes look like etc. That's why, I think, if you're a director, there's nothing you can't find interesting, because all these things are equal parts of a visualization that you have to be able to make. Anyone can do it; at the beginning, it's an almost painful exercise, it hurts a little. But, imagine a scene you want to see, close your eyes and try to really, actually, see it – it's pretty hard to do, but it's possible; you can get your mind to do it. And after a while, I learned that this was something I could apply to all fields of my life. I learned how to visualize a film, and that really helped me because I knew in my heart that this film was going to be good – if I was not completely deluded. I knew it would work. And I learned that you can also apply this to how you want something to happen, how you want a meeting to go, for instance. It's possible, in a way, to see yourself as the actor in the movie of your life.

The difficult thing with visualization, of course, is that you still have to sell your vision to someone else, and that's never harder than when you're making your first full-length film. Maybe 99 out of 100, or 999 out of 1000, first films are all but unwatchable. They fail completely at the box office and the money that's put into them is completely lost – that's just how it is. In a way, the whole system exists just to find those two or three first films a year, which then make it easy for the budding director to go on and make a second film. So you're talking to financiers who are seeing fifty people a day, and you go into the room and they have this expression on their face – 'Why should I think you're not as deluded as the forty-nine other people I've talked to today?' And all I have is the conviction that I've actually seen the film, I've seen it in my mind. But of course they're not too impressed if all you can tell them is, 'I have this vision'. I had one thing I thought would help them visualize *The Lives of Others* – a short film I had made in film school. Sometimes I wonder, though, whether that short film actually helped or made it much, much harder. The world of short film festivals and presentations is like the world of modern poetry. Apart from maybe graduate students, the only people who read modern poetry are other modern poets. Likewise, the only people who watch short films are other short filmmakers. And it's actually pretty hard to appreciate someone's skill in a short film unless you've seen a lot of them. I was so deeply into that world that I thought it would just be clear to people that this was a great short film, but the financiers were rather perplexed. The film was *Dobermann*, and it's a four-minute story of a man who baits a dog by barking at it through the window of the car it's cooped up in and comes to regret it as the dog breaks free and seeks to take vicious revenge. It's the product of a traditional assignment in the Munich film school, which is to make a short film on 16mm. You're given just a few reels of film, there's no budget, people have to bring their own sandwiches – and dialogue is strictly forbidden, because it's supposed to train you in the visual language of film.

It's actually really hard to construct a situation in which people don't speak. The school has taken on twelve directors per year for the last forty years – people like Wim Wenders, Roland Emmerich, Bernd Eichinger, Doris Dörrie and so on have all done this exercise, and it was really interesting to see what they came up with. But it all had to be done so quickly – we had a couple of weeks to prepare and a week or so for post-production, and only had the equipment for a few days. In my case, the lead actor was actually a friend of mine from school who runs a youth hostel in Berlin, and I just thought that he would be the only person crazy enough to bark back at a dog if it barked at him. The financiers were not amused – they thought, 'How is that guy supposed to play a Stasi agent?' They didn't understand that I didn't want to use the same actor, and that the dog wouldn't be featuring either. (It wasn't even a film dog, by the way, but an attack dog, and

Man (Philipp Kewenig) baits dog, *Dobermann.*

when the trainer, a dangerous looking guy, came onto the set, he said 'I forgot to ask – how have you insured your production?' I said, 'I think the film school's insurance covers this'. 'Good,' he said, 'because I should make this clear: Dobermanns don't bite, they bite *off*'. And it's true, these dogs are so incredibly dangerous, it was quite a life-threatening experience to make that short film.) It was probably harder going to financiers and telling them, look at this, at least I've made a short film, because they didn't understand that this was made on a 16mm, semi-amateur format and that I had only had three days to shoot it. They said, 'What does this have to do with a serious drama about a person finding himself?' So I told them, 'I saw *Dobermann* in my head; I didn't actually write a script, I just made a series of, maybe, 62 drawings for each camera position. I saw that film: it works for what it is, and this one will work for what it is too'. They just thought it was very strange [*screens 4 minute 16mm black and white short film Dobermann. Laughter and applause from the audience*].

So I went to distributors, thinking that if I could find someone who would show the film when it was finished, maybe I could find someone to finance it. But every single distributor turned it down. When I asked them why, they said, 'Even if you pulled this off – and we don't know any actor who could do this – people are not going to want to see a film with Beethoven, Brecht, Lenin, Gorky and all that in it. It's going to be too dark, too intellectual, too German. This is not what people want to see'. The quality of film today is in a very strange downward spiral. This is completely unwarranted. We enjoy the highest level of education we've ever had, yet we don't see that reflected in the films that are being made. This has to do with the fact that distributors go to superhero films or to screenings of films like *Transformers* and try to work out who's there and what films they're interested in. They'll see it's predominantly a very young audience with no interest in cultural things; and so they go back and feel that they have to make films even more specifically for that group. And, of course, when they probe and test the audience at the next film, it's even more apparent, and those people who *do* want to see quality films just stay away from cinemas. But I thought, maybe it would be possible to break through that logic: if I kept the film somehow 'pure', if I assembled a group of people who would go into the project believing in it, maybe *that* would convince them to give me the money. So I decided to start assembling my team and ask them, 'If I can raise the money, would you be willing to work with me on this? And would you put that in writing too?'

I liked the music of *The English Patient*. It was by a brilliant Lebanese composer living in London, and I wrote to him. The reply came from his second assistant, who said that he was very touched by the offer, but was busy working on *Troy*, and that, because they only had a music budget of $6 million, they were having to work round the clock. That music budget was more than twice my total budget, assuming I somehow managed to raise the money. But I just kept writing – like in *The Shawshank Redemption*, you know, where he just writes again and again about that library – and finally I said, 'Could I see you just for ten or fifteen minutes, so that I can explain why I think you are the only person who could do this?' That's kind of hard to refuse, so he said, 'OK, come to London'. And, of course, he went into the meeting thinking, 'I'm going to give this guy fifteen minutes and then tell him to work with one of my students'. But I said to him, 'There is a piece of music in the film that actually helps transform one of the main characters, something that will take the place of the *Appassionata*. Imagine you could go back in time – let's say to 1932 or 1933; Hitler has not committed any of his atrocities yet, and you get to spend one and a half minutes with him; you're not allowed to kill him, or even speak to him; you're just allowed to play him something on the piano, your own creation. What would you write? *That's* what I'm looking for – and you're the only person who can write that for me'. And he said, 'Oh yeah, that's really interesting, but maybe you should talk to one of my students'. I could see his expression, so I said 'Just think about it, think about it. I think you're the only person who can write it, and I think you may have an idea'. And then he said, 'Goodbye,' and continued working on *Troy*. Then, two weeks later, I got a call from him saying, 'I've had this amazing idea for your theme – I'll play it to you'. He put the telephone on the piano and I heard this fantastic piece of music. He said, 'Work with a composer for the other things, but you can use this piece, because I think it's the best idea I've had in a long time'. And I said, 'Well

I'd be really happy to take this, and I think we could also use elements of it for other parts of the film. There is something else I want to do: since a dominant theme in this film is the way people experience love, I would like to develop an almost Wagnerian love theme. It would start between the man and the woman and then make its way into the final scene, where we hear it fully, at the very end, when he opens that book. It would show that, somehow, the true love axis is between these men, who can never be friends, but have a connection. I think it would be very sad to have someone else work from your idea'. – 'I just don't have the time,' he said, 'I'm working on *Troy*'. – 'Well, that's too bad,' I replied, 'I really will have to take it to someone else then'. Two hours later I got a call: 'I'll do it'.

So I had the very best international film composer, and I knew of a production designer who had done some amazing work. She had always worked on low-budget films but had been successful enough to move into a new budget range. Production design is incredibly important: the more budget you have – in theory – the more you can do. She didn't really even want to meet me. She liked the screenplay a great deal, but said 'I can't do another low-budget film'. So I said, 'Look, I just want to present this one idea to you'. – 'It won't make a difference'. – 'I think we have a unique chance with this film'. Normally, the highest level of production design allows you to achieve a completely consistent colour scheme for your film; but that's incredibly expensive to do. I come across this in Los Angeles all the time – you'll suddenly see people spraying an entire street a certain shade of green, or red or whatever, or they'll actually paint the leaves to make the colour stronger. It's amazing the detail and trouble people will go to. Take a film like *Indiana Jones* (the first one, and only the first one): if you think back to that film, you'll remember a universe of colours and texture, where you have the brown of the leather whip and hat, the red of the sunset, the yellow of the sand, and not much else – all the other colours are kind of left out. And that creates a visual universe that you really want to return to – much of the success of that film, I think, is down to that.

Generally, though, when people try that in European films, it seems really artificial. So I said to her, 'I think we would have a chance here to have a consistent colour concept and not be lying, in a way, because there *were* these special colours in the GDR'. – 'But changing every colour to make it look as if it were the East would be incredibly hard to do on our budget', she replied. And then I showed her a series of drawings that I'd made. If I look at the lecture room we're in now, the things that are brightest and most Western are the colours blue – a real blue – and red. I showed her a picture of a normal office that seemed completely normal and Western, and another drawing of the same office where everything red had been replaced with a kind of orange, and everything blue with green. Suddenly, you had the impression that you were in the world of the East. Of course, they had reds and blues – red was the colour of socialism after all – but the *impression* was right. There are a few other things you can do, such as emphasizing slightly edgy shapes – you could really push that. Even when we showed this picture to people who had lived their lives in the East, they would say 'Wow, that's it', because we had left out those incredibly bright, extreme colours. It wasn't actually going to cost much to do this, it was very feasible; and suddenly the designer saw that it would be possible to make a film that would have the universe-value of a huge production. At the end of the meeting, she said, 'My partner is going to kill me, I'm going to kill myself, but I'm going to do it'.

I knew I'd picked up momentum with these great creative people, and so then I went to the actors – the biggest stars in Germany, no question, five of them together in one film. I approached them individually and said, 'I don't have any alternatives for you [because I went to each one individually], I need you specifically, and if you can't do it, this film won't work. I really am going to try for something here, I want us to create something real'. I hadn't known Ulrich Tukur, who plays the Stasi officer's boss, as an actor, but my wife had spent her youth in the theatre watching his performances (he mainly did stage work). But I knew that my wife has fantastic taste in art and I wanted to impress her by working with this guy. So I just wrote to him saying, 'I somehow have the feeling that you would be right for this film, let's find a part for you'. I had just read something really fascinating about Carl Jung's theory of character. Jung says that in each and every one of our souls, all vices, all virtues, all characteristics are present, and our personality is what we choose to display or shine a light on. By extension, the task of an actor is to move that spotlight onto a completely different part of his soul. And I talked to them about how we would never do anything artificial, never do any acting but actually look for the reality of those characters in their soul. It was really interesting – the actors, composers, production designers *wanted* to create something special, and suddenly money was irrelevant. The actors worked for about twenty per cent of what they normally make, everybody else worked for about fifty per cent, and suddenly I had this cast and crew that was just about the very best ever assembled in Germany. At that point, I secured a budget of around € 1.6 million, which is very little for this kind of film – even a regular German film could cost four to five times that, an American film twenty times. But everybody was there, fighting for the project. It was actually a wonderful experience, because nobody was in it for the money, they were all there because they wanted to make something special, and that created a really great atmosphere. The thing developed such a momentum that somehow things just went right.

But not everything went right. One major thing went very wrong after we finished shooting. I wanted the film to be seen in the right way, as a film that makes no compromises. I didn't want to go to one of the usual companies that publish screenplays, for instance. Normally, a published screenplay is a transcript of what you see on the screen – but you don't really need that. It's more interesting for people reading a screenplay to see how things were at the beginning of the shoot and how they evolved on set – because films really do change, through the creativity of the actors as well as the need to fix things that aren't quite right at first. I wanted *The Lives of Others* to be seen as literature and as high culture, not just as a movie. So I went to Suhrkamp, the most venerable publishing house in Frankfurt (they publish Brecht and Hesse, and a lot of the other great modern authors too) and said, 'I really think we should do this together'. They thought this was very weird – why should they publish a screenplay? But I talked to them for a long time, and although I think I got the lowest rate any author has ever had, it was really important to me for the film to be viewed in that context. I also told them that this would be a setting in which Ulrich Mühe, my leading actor, would be willing to speak about his personal connection to the story – which I hadn't known about when I asked him to be in the film, but found out about as time progressed and we worked together and became friends.

Ulrich showed me his Stasi files and told me that he had been under close surveillance from the moment he left high school. They realized he was going to be a big star in the theatre almost before he did; they knew he wasn't quite along their ideological lines and feared that, since he was going to become a famous actor, he might have quite a lot of influence and speak out against them. So they positioned him as a sniper at the Berlin Wall during his obligatory military service. This was actually very unusual, but they wanted to show him who was *am längeren Hebel* (who was boss). He had to sit there with a different partner every day, to whom he wasn't allowed to speak because they didn't want them creating any kind of bond. He was such a sensitive man that, at the age of eighteen, he developed stomach ulcers just at the thought of what he would do if somebody crossed the border – because he was told that if he didn't shoot to kill, he would never be allowed to become an actor. But equally if he did shoot, he knew he would never be able to live with himself. He became so sick that he collapsed on duty and was taken to hospital where they had to remove three-quarters of his stomach. They then excused him from the rest of his stint (i.e. could leave the army) and allowed him to go to acting school, but he remained under very tight surveillance. Whenever he did anything that wasn't politically straight, they would call him back in and say, 'You stay in line or we'll send you back to serve the second part of that military stint' – even though he was a really successful actor – 'and you will die'. Yet, even at the big demonstrations on the Alexanderplatz in Berlin before the Wall came down, he was there, using his power and influence to speak to the people and to say that things had to change in the country. The greatest betrayal and the greatest shock for him came a few years later, when they opened the Stasi archives and he asked for his files. The files stated that his own wife, to whom he had been married for six years – they had divorced not long before, but were still on good terms and had a beautiful daughter who is also a successful actress – had been a Stasi informant all along and had even asked the Stasi for permission to marry him.

That was a real blow to him, and he had never spoken about it. Now he showed them to me, hundreds of pages detailing the most personal things. I said, 'Look, Stasi files are public, especially those on public people; this will all come out when the film is released. Why don't we use the fact that we have a good platform here, with a serious publishing house, which will give us as many pages as we need to talk about this, for you to tell this story in an interview with me, without any interruption or being reduced to the restricted format a tabloid would demand?' And he agreed. I still have the tapes of this five-hour conversation (which ended up being condensed into fifteen pages in the book), where he talks about all these things. From time to time, to give himself strength, he says, 'I want to be able to answer these questions because I'm not ashamed of anything. I'm willing to speak about this if asked, because I have nothing to hide'. But when it was published, and when the film came out and went on to be a big success, the tabloids picked it up. It became a huge story, and the head of Germany's far-left party, Gregor Gysi, who was a lawyer in the GDR, contacted Ulrich Mühe's wife and offered to sue. The court found in favour of Mühe's wife, who denied the charges, claiming that her involvement was a fabrication and the files were a forgery.

Ulrich Mühe and I were sued – he for much more than me and more than I had ever paid him for the film – for speaking about his wife like this without having proof that the Stasi files were not forgeries. The onus of proof was on him. But how could you prove something like that? And suddenly, all the people who were so angry about what our film had shown about the GDR but who had not been able to come out of the woods and attack us because they would have shown their true colours by doing so, had something, somewhere to vent their anger about the film. It was all about Ulrich Mühe slandering his wife 'who had done nothing, who had been a victim of the Stasi herself' and who had also become quite ill at the time, so it was a really big story. When he was still in good health, Ulrich said to me, 'I don't feel I can live with these attacks'. Actors live for applause and love, even more than the rest of us. He lived round the corner from me, I would go round to his house, and every day his answering machine was full of people venting their anger and shouting abuse; it was an organized thing, his whole letter box was full of people saying, 'How could you do this? You're a swine, a traitor, a *Denunziant*'. He would get letters from people, some of them very prominent, attacking him so viciously that – as we travelled with the film as it went international, going to England and America – I could see the disease coming back. It was the same one he had had when he was young, but now he only had a quarter of his stomach and it had developed into stomach cancer. It was crazy, but with the success of the film abroad, the attacks from this group became ever stronger, and he died within a very short space of time. It was an incredibly sad thing. There was never a moment when we could just enjoy the success of our film. While he was at the Academy Awards, his chemotherapy was timed so that he would have those few days, and he didn't want anyone to know – my wife and I were the only people beyond his immediate family that knew. He said, 'I don't want admiration out of pity' – he was a very proud man in his own way. He was someone whose constitution was much weaker than his bravery. This was a very sad final chapter, but he never regretted making the film. We talked right up until two days before the end, and it was interesting to see that the love an artist gets for something that he has made is important even in the moment of death. It meant a lot to him that people had loved his work, and that he had gained acceptance outside his own country, which he had never had before.

Manfred Wilke
Chapter Two
Wiesler's Turn to Dissidence
and the History behind the Film

As von Donnersmarck notes in his contribution to this volume, it was at the start of his time at film school in Munich while recalling Maxim Gorky's memoir of Vladimir Lenin that the director came up with the idea for *The Lives of Others*. In Lenin's well-known statement about his fear of the potential of Beethoven's *Appassionata* to soften his approach to politics – a statement made in the context of the Russian civil war –, the founder of the Soviet Union pointed to the discrepancy between a humanist vision of socialism and the terrorist methods used by the ruling Bolsheviks. This discrepancy was a defining feature of Lenin's political life. However, after his death it was exacerbated still further in the terrorist regime established by his successor Joseph Stalin, a leader who reduced humanist socialism to the mere ideological justification of power. The stark contrast between the supposedly humanist objectives of the state order and the terrorist means communist regimes invariably used to remain in government was never eradicated in the Eastern Bloc, since the parties in power could never give up an ideological commitment to their ultimate communist objective as it served to legitimize their monopoly of power.

As if in a 'trance', as the director puts it, von Donnersmarck drew inspiration from Gorky's anecdote about the impact of music on the Russian revolutionary, the idea becoming the central conceit of the film. He imagined a secret agent of the Ministry for State Security (MfS) listening to a moving piece of music not for fun but while on duty, spying on an 'enemy of his ideas' who is, at the same time, a 'friend of this music', just like him.[1] In the narrative, this music was to act as a catalyst for Gerd Wiesler's refusal to comply with the State's authority – but was this motif really a convincing basis for the film's storyline? The idea behind the narrative, that music has the power to change people's view of the world, defined the cultural environment that the story would be set in. Authors, actors and intellectuals are a 'high risk' group for any form of ideologically-based regime. This was certainly true for the German Democratic Republic, where those in charge knew full well that social change always begins in people's minds. It is for this reason that censorship, linguistic control, along with surveillance by the secret

---

1 Florian Henckel von Donnersmarck, '*Appassionata:* Die Filmidee', in *Das Leben der anderen. Filmbuch* (Frankfurt am Main: Suhrkamp, 2006), pp. 169–70 (p. 170).

police, were an everyday reality in this totalitarian system. From the rulers' point of view, *Kulturschaffende* (creative artists) had to be monitored and controlled particularly thoroughly.[2] The history of academic research and culture in the GDR was characterized by numerous conflicts between academics and artists, on the one hand, and the regime on the other. These historical conflicts would provide the material basis for the story. At this point in the process of conceptualizing his script, von Donnersmarck needed consultants with a detailed understanding of GDR history to advise him further. This was when I became involved with the project; I received a call from the director and met up with him to discuss his ideas.

Von Donnersmarck was only seventeen years old when the Berlin Wall came down and was thus reliant on contemporary witnesses to help him write his script. He was meticulous in his research, interviewing and listening to a large number of contemporary witnesses including former MfS officials. His open attitude allowed a good deal of room for heated discussions and competing views on the detailed content of his script. An initial bone of contention between me and the director was whether the story he had in mind could convey the central idea of his film in a convincing manner. I had my doubts, but felt that it could work if the theme of music was related explicitly to the ideological contradictions that become increasingly obvious in the course of the eavesdropping operation, the so-called 'Operativer Vorgang' (Operative procedure, OV) itself.[3] And this is precisely what the film does, when Wiesler's mission to monitor the writer Dreyman turns his worldview as a communist and secret police officer upside down. As a consequence, Wiesler loses his clear ideological understanding of the enemy. The involvement of leading actor Ulrich Mühe further helped to enhance the authenticity of this plot line. Mühe's acting career began in the GDR, where he himself had been a victim of the MfS. His experience allowed him to portray Wiesler in a cold, yet compelling manner and thus evoke the social climate of the final phase of the GDR in a way that captivated audiences the world over.

---

2 The German term *Kulturschaffende* had been taken over by SED officials as early as 1945 and, probably not accidentally, from Nazi terminology.
3 An 'Operativer Vorgang' was the highest observation level. It was considered a pre-emptive measure to recognise the actions of 'hostile-negative forces' at an early stage. For further discussion see the entry 'Operativer Vorgang' in *Das MfS-Lexikon*, ed. by Abteilung Bildung und Forschung der Behörde des Bundesbeauftragten für die Unterlagen des Staatssicherheitsdienstes der ehemaligen DDR (Berlin: Ch. Links, 2011), pp. 231–32. See also David Bathrick's contribution to this volume.

The Script and its Historical Sources: the Film's Image of the GDR

In order to portray GDR reality convincingly, the film had to show the human conflicts caused by the party's claim to power. For this reason, it focused on the impact of the ruling party, the Sozialistische Einheitspartei Deutschlands (Socialist Unity Party of Germany, SED) and its centralist structures on the film's key protagonists. What the SED expected of 'its' people, both within and without the party, was set out in numerous programmes, plans, directives and interdictions, the ideological basis of which invariably revealed a strictly dichotomous view of the world shaped by the ideas of Marxism-Leninism. International communism was engaged in a class struggle for socialism against imperialism. Domestically, this defined the limits of individual freedom, as codified in the state's Penal Code. It was also reflected in, and enforced by, the division of Germany into two separate states. The Berlin Wall served as a further symbol of division and as the demarcation of the GDR from the Federal Republic and West Berlin, which formed a democratic exclave within GDR national territory. This dichotomous worldview was then further reinforced linguistically, with party officials and their secret police officers able to categorize the activity of its citizens in clear, standardized terms. The creative arts were subject to particular linguistic control, the party wishing to use art for its own ideological purpose while also wishing to oppress human individuality and independence. Thus, the state ideology empowered the MfS both to define and denounce those 'others' who did not live and act according to its draconian rules, turning them into objects of hate, which it could then legitimately arrest and interrogate. Hate was a strong motivation for MfS officials: hatred of present-day enemies was a prerequisite for the future happiness of GDR citizens. In the lecture he delivers at the MfS University in Potsdam-Golm, depicted at the start of the film, Wiesler reminds his students: 'In interrogations, you are faced with the enemies of socialism. Never forget to hate them'.

The script had to find a way to 'translate' a potentially abstract exploration of GDR ideology into a story which illustrated in an understandable and concrete manner the conflicts between the party and 'its' people. My task as a historian was to identify suitable conflicts between the SED and members of the opposition that occurred during the Honecker era (1971–1989) that could be used as case studies for the film script. The film's portrayal of MfS interrogations is based on Jürgen Fuchs's *Vernehmungsprotokolle* (Interrogation Protocols), an account of the GDR dissident writer's detention at the MfS prison in Berlin-Hohenschönhausen from November 1976 to August 1977. Shortly before obtaining his degree in psychology, Fuchs was excluded from the SED and expelled from university in

Jena because of a number of short stories and poems he published. He was sub-sequently arrested for signing the petition against the expatriation of the singer-songwriter Wolf Biermann. After being released from prison, Fuchs was deported to West Berlin. The 'Interrogation protocols' of his imprisonment were then pub-lished later that year in the news magazine *Der Spiegel*, providing an authen-tic documentation of the interrogation methods used by the MfS at that time.[4] Shortly after this, in early 1978, *Der Spiegel* published a further critical analysis of the current situation in the GDR by the historian Hermann von Berg. What both publications had in common was the fact that they could only appear in West Ger-many at that time. In the following, I will look in more detail at the ways in which the basic questions concerning the structure and mechanisms of the GDR dicta-torship to be found in these and other pre-unification publications shape the por-trayal of the state in *The Lives of Others*.

What Evidence is there of Dissenters among MfS Officers?

However, before looking at these broader case studies and their relationship to the film's narrative, let us address the most controversial element in the script, namely the proposition that an MfS officer might refuse to comply with the orders of his superiors. Given the intense debates in Germany since unification on the role of the MfS, the credibility of the film hinged first of all on the answer to a his-torical question: is there any evidence that members of the East German secret police rejected the state's authority? If there were not, the scriptwriter would in-evitably be accused of revisionism with regard to the MfS and its historical role. Von Donnersmarck was very mindful of this, knowing that he would face criti-cism of this kind, despite the obvious differences between a documentary and a fictional film. However, if one examines the historical record, the answer is clear. Yes, there were dissenters within the MfS.

Dissenters exited the organization in a variety of ways. While some were dis-missed or changed sides and started working for a Western secret service, others were killed. The first two Ministers for State Security, Wilhelm Zaisser (1950–1953) and Ernst Wollweber (1953–1956), old communist revolutionaries, dared contra-dict SED party leader Walter Ulbricht. They both lost their posts, and in 1957 Erich

---

4 Jürgen Fuchs, *Vernehmungsprotokolle* (Reinbek: Rowohlt, 1978). See also Jürgen Fuchs, 'Dann kommt die Angst', in *Gefangen in Hohenschönhausen. Stasi-Häftlinge berichten*, ed. by Hubertus Knabe (Berlin: Ullstein, 2007), pp. 268–301.

Mielke was appointed Minister for State Security. Mielke had in fact been involved with the Ministry from its inception in 1950, working for the organization as State Secretary, and he remained at its head until 1989. During his time in office, the MfS nonconformists Major Gerd Trebeljahr (1979) and Captain Werner Treske (1981) were sentenced to death and executed. Werner Stiller – who ran a network of agents from East Berlin among West German physicists engaged in the peaceful use of nuclear energy – fled to the West in 1979 when it was discovered that he had been working as a double agent for the Federal Intelligence Service. Finally, on 9 November 1989, MfS officers Harald Jäger and Edwin Görlitz played an important role in the opening of the Berlin border checkpoint at Bornholmer Brücke. On that day, they were in charge of the passport control unit that determined who could enter or leave the country. Jäger and Görlitz acted against explicit instructions when they decided to open the checkpoint to the protesting citizens of East Berlin at 11:30 p.m.

Mielke showed no mercy to those he defined as traitors to socialism, a fact that he used to emphasize openly: 'We can never be absolutely certain that we have no scoundrels in our midst. But if I were to discover one today, they would be dead by tomorrow. We can show these people no mercy! Because I'm a humanist I have to take this approach'. This he declared in front of his generals in 1982, adding: 'All this waffling about no executions, no death sentences – complete rubbish, comrades. Executions are necessary, and if needs be without a trial!'[5] In order to understand Mielke's position one must also understand his biography. Mielke was born in 1907 and joined the Communist Party of Germany (KPD) in 1927. A member of the *Parteiselbstschutz* (Party Self Protection), he was among those who killed two police officers in Berlin on 9 August 1931. He evaded arrest by fleeing to Moscow, where he completed a training course at the International Lenin School (1936–1939). During the Second World War, he illegally lived in France before returning to Berlin in 1945. From 1947, and with the consent of the Soviet military administration, the SED entrusted him with the establishment of secret-police structures in the Soviet occupation zone and later in the GDR. Mielke was a product of Marxist-Leninist ideology in practice. When, at the age of 75, he threatened traitors with death, Mielke demonstrated that the regime based its power on violence and terror, and yet could still not ignore the need for a humanist rationale to justify its approach.

---

5 Erich Mielke, 'Schlusswort auf der Kollegiumssitzung des MfS vom 19. Februar 1982', quoted by Karl Wilhelm Fricke, *'Schild und Schwert'. Die Stasi* (Cologne: Deutschlandfunk, 1993), p. 28.

The MfS as an Investigative Body and the State's Penal Structure

The film opens with a suspense-packed scene at the main MfS interrogation prison in Berlin-Hohenschönhausen. A detainee is brought into the room. Wiesler is shown to be a conscientious officer who is trying to resolve a case of 'Republik-flucht' (flight from the GDR). After the erection of the Berlin Wall in 1961, the prevention and solution of cases of 'Republikflucht' was one of the MfS's main tasks. The majority of political prisoners in the GDR between 1961 and 1989 were people who had tried and failed to flee the country or who had helped others to do so. Recalling descriptions of the interrogation process in Fuchs's account, Wiesler uses sleep deprivation to force the detainee to reveal the name of an 'escape agent' who helped a fugitive escape over the Berlin Wall. According to Paragraph 213 of the GDR Penal Code, the 'illegal crossing of the border' constituted a 'crime against the state order', punishable by a prison sentence of up to two years. Even merely planning to escape counted as a chargeable offence. The 'escape agent' would be accused of either 'enticement to leave the GDR' or potentially even 'human trafficking'. This conceptualization of human trafficking was enshrined in Paragraph 132 of the same code and led to several West Germans being prosecuted by the GDR authorities. Actively aiding the escape of a person 'abroad' (generally in practice the other part of Germany) was punishable by deprivation of liberty for up to eight years.[6]

The principle of the 'separation of powers', which is at the heart of Western democracy, was diametrically opposed to the principles of the SED's dictatorial rule. The MfS and its network of 'Inoffizielle Mitarbeiter' (unofficial collaborators, commonly referred to as IM) were not only in charge of monitoring the general population. It was also entrusted with ensuring the political 'reliability' of the country's legal authorities. When a state prosecutor or judge was to be appointed to a role that entailed responsibility for MfS matters, the MfS effectively had the right of veto.[7] Its control of process was most visible in the appointment of state prosecutors and committing magistrates in charge of political crimes, one of the most important of which was, as already noted, 'Republikflucht'. Thus, the investigation of such cases was ultimately controlled by the MfS. As Karl Wilhelm Fricke suggests, from its very beginning in the 1950s, the MfS had considerable control over the progress of 'criminal'

---

6 Ministerium für Justiz, *Strafrecht der Deutschen Demokratischen Republik* (Berlin East: Staats-verlag der Deutschen Demokratischen Republik, 1984), p. 327.
7 Roger Engelmann, 'Verhältnis des MfS zur Justiz', in *Das MfS-Lexikon*, pp. 170–71.

investigations, the course of such trials as well as the severity of sentences the guilty would be given.[8]

Party and State Security

Historically, the central role played by the MfS in stabilizing the SED regime is undisputed. It was also very clear to the broader population, who generally considered the party and its secret police to be inextricably interlinked. In order to portray the relationship between the party and the MfS as well as the ways in which the secret police acted with respect to the population, the film needed to emphasize two distinct elements in the narrative. The first was the way power was manipulated in the GDR. The film's milieu is the GDR's cultural industry. Here the SED determined cultural policies, while its secret police was in charge of control and surveillance. Crucially in this regard, the MfS was subordinate to the SED. This hierarchical relationship is highlighted in the film through the interaction of Bruno Hempf, the Minister for Culture and member of the SED Central Committee, with Anton Grubitz, a Lieutenant Colonel at the MfS. As a Minister and, more importantly, party functionary, Hempf has the authority to command Grubitz to instigate an OV against Dreyman: 'Nobody must know about the OV before we have found anything. If you find something to incriminate this guy, you will have a powerful friend in the Central Committee', Grubitz is informed. The party controls everything, including the Stasi.

The second aspect of life in the GDR the film portrays is the day-to-day reality of living and working in the cultural scene for authors, actors and directors. The entire milieu is shown to be subject to the power of the SED and to manipulation by the MfS. In his toast to all *Kulturschaffende* at the beginning of the film, Hempf describes clearly what the party expects of 'its' writers: 'A great socialist (I cannot remember who) once said: "The author is the engineer of the soul"'. The journalist Paul Hauser replies: '"Engineers of the soul" ... It is Stalin whom you have just quoted'. Hempf only smiles and gives an evasive response that does not confirm the authorship of the expression but nonetheless puts the journalist in his place. As a party official, it is Hempf who sets the rules on who is culturally acceptable and who is not. This is confirmed later in the film during an argument with Dreyman, when his partner, the actress Christa-Maria Sieland, laconically describes in more detail the everyday reality that artists subject to this regime are forced to ne-

---

8 Karl Wilhelm Fricke, *Die DDR-Staatssicherheit* (Cologne: Verlag Wissenschaft und Politik, 1989), p. 135.

Wiesler, the Stasi man, instinctively knows when he is being watched, *The Lives of Others*.

gotiate: 'They decide which plays are put on stage, who may act and who may direct'. When she decides to stop having sexual relations with the Minister, he orders her to be arrested and says that he never wants to see her act on a German stage again.

The Minister considers himself to be an important man and demands the 'allegiance' of the actress (specifically sexual compliance), safe in the knowledge that she is reliant upon his favour. The perception of the power relations within the GDR's cultural sphere is identical at the top and at the bottom. The MfS generated fear in order to ensure the obedience of the population to the party and its policies. In the film, one short scene suffices to illustrate this climate of fear. A neighbour witnesses the MfS breaking into Dreyman's apartment. Wiesler, who notices somewhat ironically that he himself has been observed, threatens the woman: 'Frau Meineke, if you mention this to anyone, your daughter Mascha will lose her place at medical school tomorrow. Do you understand?' The woman gives a fearful nod and as a 'reward' for her discretion becomes an unofficial collaborator with the secret police.

The 'Chekist Ideology'

The SED considered the GDR to be constantly under threat of attack by its 'imperialist enemies', which sought to fight the socialist state from beyond its borders and to support 'hostile-negative forces' within them. For this reason the establishment of a powerful secret police force was deemed necessary. Its goal was to secure the road to socialism, and it was socialism that legitimized the terror and repressive measures used by the secret police. This dogmatic conviction shaped the particular *esprit de corps* of MfS officers who proudly called themselves 'German Chekists'. The formation of the Soviet 'Cheka' on 20 December 1917 was one of the first measures taken by Lenin's revolutionary government.[9] The tradition of Soviet security forces set the tone for MfS officers and is reflected well in their self-definition. What might be described as the MfS's 'Chekist ideology' can be characterized by three main elements. First, the MfS considered itself to be the 'shield and sword' of the party. All decisions taken by the Stasi were defined by SED policy. Its full-time employees were usually members of the party. Second, the Stasi legitimized itself as an instrument of the 'Dictatorship of the Proletariat'. This self-image justified the use of violence and repression as a means of waging 'class war' with the purpose of protecting socialism and accomplishing its victory over Western imperialism worldwide. The idea of a global confrontation of ideological blocs led to the cultivation and propagation of the image of the 'imperialist' enemy which was crucial to the way in which MfS officers perceived conflicts within society and between different countries. Third, at the same time, the humanist purpose of their action, as the Chekists perceived it, justified the methods used by the intelligence service in the GDR, namely espionage, the denunciation and persecution of dissenters, the execution of 'traitors' and attacks on 'dangerous' enemies.[10]

This self-image as 'combatants in the name of ideology' against enemies both inside and outside the State borders provided the German Chekists with their personal motivation, based on a strong belief in the value of their cause. They were driven by their hatred of an enemy who wanted to hinder and prevent the establishment of socialism. The interrogation scene that opens the film illustrates the role that this hatred played in the Chekists' work. Such hatred leads to a very nar-

---

9 The name is short for 'The All-Russian Extraordinary Commission for Combating Counter-Revolution and Sabotage'. This organ of 'Red Terror' in the Russian Civil War changed its name several times, becoming the KGB (Committee for State Security) in 1954 and remaining so until the collapse of the Soviet Union in 1991.

10 For further discussion see Jens Giesecke, 'Ideologie. Tschekistische', in *Das MfS-Lexikon*, p. 153.

row view of the suspect who is not seen as an individual with rights, but rather solely as a subject within the State's criminological structures. Even if an individual had not yet been convicted, the mere fact that he or she had been arrested was considered evidence enough that the MfS was dealing with an enemy of the state, or a 'hostile-negative element'. Whenever the 'lives of others' did not meet the expectations of the party, it was the political mission of the MfS to become involved in an active and threatening manner in order to change fundamentally those lives.

Publishing in the West as an Act of Resistance: Dreyman's *Spiegel* Article and the GDR Penal Code

The writer Dreyman is initially considered to be toeing the line by the SED and MfS. However, when he hears about the suicide of his friend, a director who has been banned from working, Dreyman decides to protest by publishing in the West German magazine *Der Spiegel*, writing an article about suicide rates in the GDR, statistics that had been strictly confidential since 1977. The GDR was in a unique position in the Eastern Bloc in that it had a mirror image in the West. People living in the opposing Federal Republic also spoke German, so work by GDR authors did not have to be translated to be published there. Dreyman is able to negotiate the publication of his article directly with a *Spiegel* journalist based in East Berlin. Convinced that his home is not being monitored, he invites the journalist to come to his private apartment. The journalist agrees to publish the article, promising that the author's identity will not be revealed.

Once again we might ask whether there is any historical basis for this element in the narrative. In order to answer this, let us first consider the standard procedure GDR authors had to follow when looking to be published in the West. Such publications had to be approved by the *Büro für Urheberrechte* (Copyright Office) and were consequently automatically subject to state control. In the case of the suicide article Dreyman wishes to publish, permission would never have been granted. Suicide statistics were confidential and their publication would have violated a number of paragraphs of the GDR Penal Code. While the film does not openly mention these laws, it explicitly reflects their existence, in particular the offences of 'espionage' (Paragraph 97) and 'treasonable communication' (Paragraph 99), which were punishable with a prison sentence of 'not less than five years'. 'Espionage' was defined broadly to comprise 'all confidential information and material that is collected, delivered or made available to a foreign power, its institutions or secret service, or to foreign organisations, to the detriment of the German Democratic Republic'.[11] However, not only espionage in this strict sense was punishable. Publishing anything that was deemed to be 'to the detriment of the German Democratic Republic', even information that was not necessarily classified as confidential, was considered to be a 'treasonable communication' (Paragraph 99) and thus a 'crime against the GDR'.[12] Of course, it was not actually necessary to pass information to commit a crime. It was also illegal even to establish contacts with the likes of Western journalists, academics or human rights organizations. Such people were classified as 'illegal contacts' (Paragraph 219) and correspondence with them was punishable with a sentence similar to that issued to people who attempted to escape from the GDR: 'Anybody knowingly contacting organizations, institutions or individuals who pursue objectives that are aimed at undermining the state order of the German Democratic Republic will face a prison sentence of up to five years'.[13] Dissidents and oppositional movements within the Soviet empire had always been of particular interest to *Der Spiegel* magazine. It regularly published work by Soviet dissidents, Polish and Czech civil rights activists as well as essays and interviews by GDR citizens, including Robert Havemann and, as already discussed, Jürgen Fuchs. *Der Spiegel* counted among those enemy organs with which GDR citizens were not allowed to establish 'unmonitored' contact. By working with *Der Spiegel* on his article, Dreyman violates all these laws.

The Historical Model: the Manifesto of the 'Association of Democratic Communists in Germany'

A *Spiegel* publication from 1978, the manifesto of the *Bund demokratischer Kommunisten Deutschlands* (Association of Democratic Communists in Germany), based in the GDR, provided the specific historical impetus for von Donnersmarck's portrayal of Dreyman's Western publication.[14] As its authors, the magazine named 'officers and high officials in the GDR' who, understandably, wished to remain anonymous. After 1989, it was revealed that the main person respon-

---

11 *Strafrecht der Deutschen Demokratischen Republik*, p. 268.
12 *Strafrecht der Deutschen Demokratischen Republik*, p. 272.
13 *Strafrecht der Deutschen Demokratischen Republik*, pp. 487–88.
14 See Günter Johannes and Ulrich Schwarz, *DDR. Das Manifest der Opposition* (Munich: Wilhelm Goldmann Verlag, 1978). All further references to this work will be referred to as (M) in the text.

Cover of *Der Spiegel* from 1978 which published the
Manifesto of the 'Association of Democratic Communists
in Germany'.

sible for this manifesto was Professor Hermann von Berg, a historian who, in
1978, taught at the East Berlin Humboldt University. In the 1960s, he had worked
for the press office of the GDR Council of Ministers. In this role, he looked after
West German journalists when they were in the East and was active in the Federal
Republic as an envoy of the GDR Prime Minister Willi Stoph. At the same time, he
worked as an IM, reporting to the MfS *Hauptverwaltung Aufklärung* (Head Office
of Reconnaissance).[15]

Just a few years later, von Berg had become disillusioned with the SED regime
and passed an article highly critical of the GDR to Ulrich Schwarz, the East German
correspondent for *Der Spiegel*. For a brief period of time, the so-called '*Spiegel* manifesto' generated a heated public debate which involved both the Soviet
newspaper *Pravda* in Moscow and *Neues Deutschland*, the official party news-

---

15 Hubertus Knabe, *Die unterwanderte Republik* (Berlin: Propyläen Verlag, 1999), pp. 31–77.

paper of the SED. The West German government under Helmut Schmidt (SPD) queried the provenance of the article. The executive director of the SPD, Egon Bahr, who had been an influential voice in negotiating the 1972 Basic Treaty with the GDR, also questioned its authenticity, basing his scepticism on the language used in the text. Nobody in the GDR would speak of 'East Berlin', he suggested. 'East Berlin' is always referred to as 'the capital of the GDR' (M, 120). The 'manifesto' did not only damage relations between the two German states, it also led to an internal debate on the position of the West German government towards the division of Germany. The conservative CDU/CSU opposition vociferously expressed their suspicion that the social-liberal government had given up the objective of German reunification completely and instead decided to accept division as a political reality. The CDU Member of Parliament Werner Marx declared: 'Nearly every sentence in this article challenges us to re-think the image of the GDR that the Federal government has constructed. It betrays a despair and anger towards a corrupt elite supported by Moscow. It regards the GDR as a poor man's sixteenth Soviet republic' (M, 127).

The 'manifesto' was indeed highly critical of the Soviet Union, and was understood by some as a declaration of war on the SED: 'The polit-bureaucratic orthodoxy of Moscow has objectively become a reactionary force [...]. It pursues power politics without any consideration of the international labour movement or its so-called socialist sister countries' (M, 16). Stalinism and National Socialism are described as 'twin' terrorist regimes, with GDR reality characterized implicitly through a series of rhetorical questions: 'Why does the German Democratic Republic have some of the highest rates of divorce, suicide and alcohol abuse?' (M, 24). The main target of the 'manifesto' was the 'clique at the top' that was 'damaging the very idea of socialism in Germany and Europe more than any form of so-called enemy propaganda'. The article's attack culminates in the statement: 'Never before has a ruling class in Germany lived on others the way these two dozen families do who consider our country to be their own self-service store [...] Have a closer look at them. Has any one of these self-appointed leaders ever had an idea or written an article, let alone a book, in any academic field, even politics? [...] At the same time, these polit-bureaucrats are pathologically vain. Count the titles: Erich and Co. by the grace of Brezhnev, King of Prussia etc. etc' (M, 26–8). The 'clique at the top' countered the publication of this paper by closing the *Spiegel* office in East Berlin.

Von Berg quickly came under suspicion and was arrested by the MfS. However, he was soon able to resume his academic work. It was only in 1985, after the illegal publication of two books in West Germany, that he lost his chair, quit the SED and was expatriated, leaving for West Germany in 1986. After the expatriation of singer-songwriter Wolf Biermann in 1976, this was the most common method of dealing with critical artists, writers and academics. The SED deported them to West Germany in order to spare itself negative headlines in the international press on political prisoners in the GDR. This was quite different from the situation in Poland, for example, where from 1976 a radical reformism began to emerge amongst intellectuals that openly proclaimed its objective to be the destruction of the Polish communists' monopoly on power. Its representatives, such as Jacek Kuroń and Adam Michnik, were not expatriated but had the chance to organize opposition from within the country. In 1980, the trade union federation Solidarność was founded in Gdańsk which effectively set up a form of co-governance in the country, until the party declared martial law in December 1981, re-securing its control for the following seven years. This contrasted starkly with the GDR. Even those who stayed, such as the chemist and dissident Robert Havemann, remained isolated. While under house arrest in 1978, Havemann nonetheless commented with enormous prescience on the future of his country. He could have left the GDR with immediate effect. Yet he decided to stay and predicted the downfall of the SED state, against all indications within the global political reality of the time or the majority view of intellectuals in the West: 'I do not intend leaving the GDR, where every day I observe the regime losing all its support. Indeed, it has already lost it. All we really need now is some external impetus or event to send the whole Politburo packing'.[16]

As the film script was written fifteen years after the fall of the GDR, von Donnersmarck drew upon these types of contemporary testimony in order to portray authentically the structures and mechanisms of the SED state system. After 1990, the significance of such testimony changed considerably. Initially meant to express their authors' indignation against an all-powerful regime, they came to be seen as historical milestones indicating the decline of the totalitarian power of communism. Geologically, the erosion of stone is a long and subtle process. Similarly, the decay of political orders takes places very slowly and gradually. Only a very few people tend to have a sense of the changes that happen. Havemann had this ability and was courageous enough to oppose the decaying power and reflect upon alternatives to its totalitarian system. Havemann had a long history of such opposition. In 1943, following the Battle of Stalingrad, he organized the resistance group *Europäische Union* (European Union) that aimed to help Jewish citizens who were being persecuted by the Nazis. However, the Gestapo shattered the group, and the 'People's Court' sentenced Havemann and fifteen other group

---

16 For further discussion see *Robert Havemann. Ein deutscher Kommunist*, ed. by Manfred Wilke (Reinbek: Rowohlt, 1978), p. 29.

members to death.[17] As a valued physical chemist, however, Havemann managed to escape execution, instead continuing his research in Brandenburg-Görden Prison. After Red Army troops liberated him in April 1945, he was given a chair at the Humboldt University and joined the SED. In 1964, he made his first public appearance as a reform communist, demanding the combination of GDR socialism with democracy. Accused of being a 'revisionist', he was expelled from the SED, lost his chair and membership of the Academy of Sciences. After the suppression of the Prague Spring in 1968, Havemann became a key but isolated voice for civil rights in the GDR. At this point, he advocated – albeit in vain – the democratic reform of the GDR system. With the ability to predict milestones of change and express his vision, he was courageous enough to counter two totalitarian systems at different points of his life.

Who is the Enemy? From Self-doubt to Dissidence

The film takes place towards the end of the GDR period. When portraying Wiesler's rejection of the state, von Donnersmarck constructs this in quasi-Christological terms as a crisis of faith. On the one hand, within communism, the Christian promise of paradise in the afterlife is reconfigured as the promise of Heaven on Earth. On the other, the way that clerics have abused the power of faith throughout Church history corresponds to what we see of the attitudes of the party elite in the twilight years of GDR communism. At the beginning of the film, Wiesler is portrayed as a loyal communist true to party principles. His oath of allegiance obliges him to 'fight the enemies of socialism, even at the risk of losing my life, and fulfil all duties assigned to me to ensure the security of the state'.[18] When he takes on the Dreyman case, he still has the emotional disposition of a faithful SED communist. Yet, even at this early stage, he seems revolted by the cynical careerism exhibited by many of his Chekist comrades, represented in the film by his superior, Grubitz. To Grubitz, of all people, Wiesler unburdens his heart: 'Don't you also wish sometimes that it was already here – communism?!' 'You think too much', his superior replies. Wiesler yearns for the paradise on Earth promised by his party but which seems a long way off in the grey everyday world of 'real exist-

---

17 For further discussion see Manfred Wilke and Werner Theuer, '"Der Beweis eines Verrats lässt sich nicht erbringen": Robert Havemann und die Widerstandsgruppe Europäische Union', in *Der SED-Staat. Geschichte und Nachwirkungen*, ed. by Hans-Joachim Veen and Manfred Wilke (Cologne: Böhlau, 2006), pp. 91–110.
18 'Fahneneid des MfS', quoted in David Gill and Ulrich Schröter, *Das Ministerium für Staatssicherheit* (Berlin: Rowohlt, 1991), p. 27.

ing socialism'. He begins seriously to lose faith in the party when he discovers that the real reason for the surveillance operation against the writer is due to a private whim of the Minister for Culture. Hempf wants to destroy the romantic relationship between the actress Sieland and Dreyman, so that he might have her to himself. In order to get rid of his rival, Hempf tells Grubitz to initiate an OV against Dreyman. Grubitz, an assiduous MfS carrierist, in turn, draws Wiesler into this on the terms that he himself finds most compelling, promising him a reward if he finds something. He explains to Wiesler that they both have 'a lot to gain ... or to lose from this love story'. However, ultimately Wiesler cannot be motivated by the promise of career advancement. When Wiesler refuses to cooperate further, he does so because he has come to realize that the surveillance of Dreyman has no role to play in the fight against the imperialist enemy of socialism. Although music is a key motif in the film, Wiesler in fact comes to realize this bitter truth before hearing 'Die Sonate vom guten Menschen' (The Sonata of the Good Person), presented to him by his now deceased friend at his earlier birthday party.

It is the moral turpitude of the 'clique at the top', criticized in the '*Spiegel* manifesto', that turns the fictional Dreyman OV into a moral litmus-test for Wiesler. Is this really all about the fight against imperialist 'diversion', as it was described in official party parlance, or is the MfS being abused in order to finish off a love story for the benefit of a high official? Within this context, Wiesler can no longer be guided straightforwardly by his hatred of the enemies of socialism. Indeed, in this specific case, who is the enemy of socialism? Is it the molested actress, or the writer who has not yet spoken out against the system? Or is it the Minister, who represents the party but is motivated by lust? Wiesler is tormented because all of a sudden, the clear distinction between friend and enemy that has always defined his relationship to the state no longer seems viable. At this point in the film, music is used as a catalyst for Wiesler's decision. This is how von Donnersmarck conveys the idealistic notion that anyone who has ever been confronted with real art can no longer be a servant of dictatorship. He believes that music has the power to change people, even to force open the hard shell of an ideological worldview and re-activate individual conscience. However, it is also important to understand that the seeds of doubt were already growing in Wiesler's mind. That said, it is after he listens to the music that he actively begins to work against the authorities.

On the way to his flat one evening, Wiesler breaks with his previous behaviour for the first time. A young boy runs after his ball and comes to ask Wiesler if it is true that he works for the Stasi. Wiesler responds by asking if the boy even knows what the Stasi is. The boy replies: 'They are evil men who put people in prison ... says my Dad'. As a reflex action, Wiesler goes to ask the boy the name of his father, but then pauses in the middle of the sentence and instead asks for the name of the ball. The boy convulses in laughter, unable to understand the grown up's request. Everyone knows balls do not have names. In this scene, Wiesler does not show the normal 'vigilance' that is demanded of him. Members of the MfS had the responsibility to preserve 'socialist legality'. It would consequently have been Wiesler's duty to find out the name of the boy's father. The remark this man made would have been classified as 'public defamation', which was punishable under Paragraph 220 of the GDR Penal Code: 'Whoever publically vilifies the state order, state organs, institutions or social organizations or their actions or ordinances will face a prison sentence of up to three years'.[19] Wiesler also, in fact, contravenes this law himself by his lack of action. When saying good-bye to him, the boy exculpates Wiesler: 'But you're not a bad man'. In so doing, Wiesler steps into the world of GDR illegality but genuine humanist morality.

Reading the Stasi Files

The aim of this chapter has been to demonstrate the degree to which von Donnersmarck grounded his story in historical sources and an understanding of the state's structures. MfS officers were members of the SED. As the 'guards of socialism', and as already noted, they had a particular *esprit de corps* and considered themselves to be part of the country's elite. After 1985, however, when Gorbachev came to power in the Soviet Union, the ideological foundation of the party began to be challenged, even among this group of people. Although SED leaders knew very well the increasing difficulties faced by the GDR population in the 1980s, as the difference in the standard of living between East and West continued to grow, they did nothing to improve matters, choosing instead to ignore reality. In the film, Wiesler withdraws his cooperation with the state when he realizes that even high party officials no longer believe in a communist ideal. By that point in time, overwhelmingly the elite was merely driven by their own personal goals. The authorities were now largely looking to protect their privileges, (relative) luxury and personal influence, and were happy to abuse their power in order to achieve these aims. Wiesler is not strong or determined enough to resist openly. Nonetheless, he refuses to present the observation results his superiors wish to see. This type of covert rejection of the state's authority can be found in the actions of many members of the SED in 1989. In the course of the peaceful revolution, numerous violations of the official party line were committed by SED officials, which in turn made an important contribution towards the success of the revolution. When, on

---

19 *Strafrecht der Deutschen Demokratischen Republik*, p. 489.

9 October 1989, SED leaders and security forces tried to end the 'Monday pro-tests' in Leipzig by violent means, three district party secretaries, along with the composer Kurt Masur, stood up against these plans and signed a petition con-demning violence. The day before, Dresden mayor Wolfgang Berghofer had al-ready met with a group of protesters for talks about the situation in the city. Simi-larly, his colleague in East Berlin invited members of civil rights groups to join the committee charged with the investigation of police brutality against protesters in Berlin on 7–8 October 1989. Thanks to these and other decisions by members of the establishment, the SED rapidly lost its monopoly on power.

Wiesler is a broken figure by the end of the film's main narrative arc. In a very convincing fashion, the film portrays the mechanisms of repression used by the SED system, showing how a devoted communist learns that instead of hunting enemies in the name of a humanist dream, he has in reality been abusing inno-cent individuals who wish to lead an independent life. After unification, Dreyman gains access to his MfS files and reads Wiesler's observation reports. By includ-ing this sequence, the film makes a subtle, yet convincing plea for the necessity to make MfS files accessible to all its victims. After unification, being able to use the files to find out who was really who in the GDR was an important step in the pro-cess of overcoming the legacy of the past. By 1989, the Stasi employed 91,000 full-time officers, 13,000 of whom directed the work of about 170,000 IM. The task of this enormous 'army' was to work towards the SED's ridiculous goal of the total surveillance of all aspects of GDR life. However, von Donnersmarck did not want to produce a film entitled 'Snitches Among Us', analogous to Wolfgang Staudte's famous 1946 DEFA film *Die Mörder sind unter uns* (The Murderers Are among Us). It was not his aim to produce a political plaidoyer on the use of the Stasi files as a means of 'outing' IMs in order to come to terms with the GDR past. He wished, rather, to create a script telling a fictitious story about the SED state, narrated in the style of a thriller, but based on historical material. He wanted his film to be both truly authentic and touching. This he achieved, and the film was, of course, a huge international success, culminating in the Oscar win.

Dealing with the History of the SED Regime in a United Germany

When the career of secret police officer Wiesler is drawing to a close, we see an issue of *Neues Deutschland* in Wiesler's car dated 11 March 1985. 'New General Sec-retary of the Communist Party of the Soviet Union Elected: Mikhail Gorbachev' runs the headline, highlighting the fact that we are in the final phase of Soviet communism. For historians, one of the big questions, even today, is how the collapse of communism in the countries of Central and Eastern Europe could have happened so breathtakingly quickly and in such a peaceful manner. Scholars have suggested numerous factors that contributed to the implosion of these regimes: the challenging economic situation, the regimes' inability to bring in economic and democratic reforms, the technological gap with the West, the desire for national sovereignty in individual Eastern Bloc countries and the increasing disillusionment with communist ideology even among party officials. In actual fact, all of these factors had long existed across the Eastern Bloc as early as 1968, when the Soviet Army stamped out the uprising of reformed communism in Czechoslovakia and re-installed a dictatorship for the following two decades. From a military point of view, there was no reason why this could not have happened in Germany in 1989. The Soviet army would not even have had to invade the GDR, as it had constantly been stationed on GDR territory since 1945. However, it did not. Soviet army forces took no action against protesters in Leipzig in October or when the Berlin Wall came down in November. The Soviet regime instead decided to give free rein to history.

The absolute power of the communists had already begun to erode when Gorbachev became head of state in the Soviet Union and this erosion of power was crucial to the success of the peaceful revolution in the GDR. However, this aspect of the *Wende* faded into the background against the media images of East German self-liberation. The story of MfS officer Wiesler in *The Lives of Others* serves as a reminder of the erosion of communist power that lies behind the images of mass popular protest. It is set in the era of transition, when totalitarian structures and methods were still in place, but more and more people were beginning to question and defy official regulations. This is true for both the writer and the Stasi officer. The communists were no longer willing to enforce a socialist ideology through violence. The SED and its secret police cadres had lost their self-confidence and no longer believed that their cause was invincible. At the end of their reign, all that drove the party elite was the wish to advance individual careers and to maximize the privileges enjoyed by functionaries. These are not goals that people will normally risk their lives for.

After the victory of democracy in East Germany, the SED's secret police was dissolved and morally ostracized. The role of the MfS tended to be characterized in black and white terms, with the Stasi being presented as straightforwardly evil perpetrators of state oppression. Restitution for its victims was mainly conceived of in legal terms, the focus on justice being used as a way of highlighting the political morality of the new unified German democracy. A different perspective was morally and politically unthinkable within the framework of a German memory culture that – then as now – was strongly influenced by the repercussions of National Socialism, the need to acknowledge the suffering of its victims and the broader injustices of the past. Apologists for the SED dictatorship and the MfS could only be found among members of the SED successor party, the PDS (now part of Die Linke), and its corresponding ideological milieu which sought to concentrate discussion on positive aspects of everyday life in the GDR.[20]

Given the parameters of public opinion in Germany, von Donnersmarck clearly broke a taboo by introducing the positive figure of a fictitious MfS officer in *The Lives of Others*. By portraying the mechanisms of the communist dictatorship from the point of view of a Stasi officer, the film provided a stark contrast with the way members of the MfS and the role they played within the system are generally discussed in the media. For this very reason, some former civil rights activists and victims of the SED regime accused von Donnersmarck of telling a 'fairy tale of the good Stasi officer'.[21] Roman Grafe, author of the highly respected *Die Grenze durch Deutschland* (The Border Through Germany, 2002), criticized the film for concealing the true nature and scale of the MfS's destructive influence of society: 'fear, mistrust, hatred, the destruction of individual lives, a quarter of a million political prisoners, torture, abduction, contract killings'.[22] Grafe spoke for many critics of the film, his attack culminating in the allegation that *The Lives of Others* completely ignored the structural violence exerted by the dictators against their victims. However, is this the case?

Societies under the rule of dictators are always far more complex than any model of totalitarian domination can possibly capture. This is certainly true of the GDR. People had to find ways of accommodating the official ideology, its language and norms, on the one hand, while also pursuing their own personal interests on the other. This they did by exploiting inconsistencies in the party's aims and objectives. The straightforwardly dichotomous view of a society that can be divided up into victims and perpetrators neglects the fact that in a totalitarian system, the opposition is as much a part of society as the secret police and party officials. They are all individuals who are, albeit in very different ways, part of the system and who maintain manifold relations with this system. They

---

20 Die Linke (The Left) was founded in 2007 following the merger of the Partei des Deutschen Sozialismus (Party of Democratic Socialism, PDS) – the successor of the SED (from 1989) – and Arbeit und soziale Gerechtigkeit – Die Wahlalternative (The Electoral Alternative for Labour and Social Justice, WASG).

21 Roman Grafe, 'Wohlfühldichtung für Mitläufer: Das Lügenmärchen vom guten Stasi-Mann', in *Die Schuld der Mitläufer. Anpassen oder Widerstehen in der DDR*, ed. by Roman Grafe (Munich: Pantheon, 2009), p. 175–85.

22 Grafe, 'Wohlfühldichtung für Mitläufer', p. 175.

are constantly confronted with the successes or failures of the party. Individuals can change when circumstances change. They remain individuals; they are not genetically programmed, and thus can re-evaluate their lives. It is, essentially, this view of individuality that is at the heart of *The Lives of Others*. It is undoubtedly the case that there were individuals in the GDR ready to make a stand against the party's monopoly on power, despite the personal risk they ran of prosecution and repression. The history of the GDR contains numerous stories of opposition and resistance. However, it is important to remember that some of this opposition came from within the state's own institutions. The distinction between SED membership and opposition could be rather fluid at times, as can be seen in the cases of Havemann, Fuchs and von Berg discussed in this chapter.

However, Grafe, along with many others, reduces the complexity of GDR society to a simple dichotomy of perpetrators and victims. His perception of society somewhat resembles that of the communist rulers: whoever did not fight the regime is seen as a *Mitläufer* ('fellow traveller'), and every *Mitläufer*, because s/he did not resist, is to blame for the regime's survival. Given his background and past experience, Grafe's standpoint is understandable. It is, moreover, a specifically German one, shaped by the debates about the National Socialist past that have defined Germany since the Second World War as a country seeking a new sense of cultural and political identity. One aspect of the debate about German postwar *Vergangenheitsbewältigung* (coming to terms with the past) with regard to the Nazi period that it is important to remember when considering the GDR is the question of agency. If the majority of Germans had not followed Hitler – for whatever reason – neither the Nazi regime, nor the war of extermination against Poland and Russia, nor the genocide of the European Jews would have been possible. The GDR, however, is a rather different case. The people did not choose to live under this dictatorship. It was a consequence, rather, of the unconditional surrender of the German Wehrmacht at the end of the War. The regime was installed by Soviet occupation forces and perished in a peaceful revolution when the global political constellation underwent a fundamental change.

Grafe's moral verdict that von Donnersmarck made a film for the followers of the SED dictatorship is wrong. Such criticism neglects the fact that conformity with a given society and its political system is a common phenomenon in human communities. Finally, it does not do justice to the director's intentions. It was never his aim to produce a film for, or about, GDR *Mitläufer*, or to depict a process of self-conscious *Vergangenheitsbewältigung* for the GDR. His aim was to make a great film. For such an endeavour, it would not have sufficed merely to condemn the former regime, not least because he was also looking to illustrate the GDR's mechanisms and structures for an audience that has little detailed historical knowledge of the GDR. Thus, echoing the words of the *Spiegel* journalist in the film, von Donnersmarck wished (and managed) to 'show, to the whole of Germany, the true colours of the GDR'.

Translated by Christine Henschel

Randall Halle
Chapter Three
The Lives of Others, the New Matrix of Production and the Profitable Past

Central to the immediate discussion generated by *The Lives of Others* was the work of the images on the screen, their visual language and potential to convey a touching drama that offers insight without nostalgia into life in a totalitarian state. This essay, however, will turn our attention away from the screen and instead consider the production phase. In asking how this story came to the screen, we hope, ultimately, to offer further insight into the nature of the history produced. There are many rumours behind *The Lives of Others*: in the US, based on stories he heard about the production history of the film, neo-conservative film critic John Podhoretz speculated that the film had a hard time finding funding as a result of its confronting the horrors of communism.[1] Such assertions are pointedly false speculation based on a lack of knowledge about the German film industry and about the vicissitudes of German politics. Rather than think of the film as having had a hard time in its passage through pre and post-production, we should consider that the opposite is actually the case. We should question instead, how it was possible that the film received the funding it did.

The production history of *The Lives of Others* does not attest to a conspiracy of silence or a systematic attempt to block the film, rather it reveals a great faith in the talents of a rising star. Florian Henckel von Donnersmarck was, as he began the project, a young filmmaker barely out of film school, working on his debut as a feature length filmmaker. Yet this relatively unknown character was able to gain enough trust from the funding mechanisms to amass a limited but significant enough budget in order to produce one of the most highly acclaimed films of the Berlin Republic to date.

---

1 John Podhoretz, 'Nightmare Come True: Love and Distrust in the East German Police State', *The Weekly Standard*, 12 March 2007 (http://www.weeklystandard.com/Content/Public/Articles/000/000/013 /360jfrwt.asp).

West Germans Recounting East German History

Considering the conditions of production, we may rather ask why it is that no art-ist who grew up in the former East Germany, who is personally familiar with it, has had such success with a film that offers a serious reckoning with the GDR. Indeed, in the critical reception of *The Lives of Others*, one aspect that seems to have compelled much of the negative assessment of the film, especially by those who lived in the GDR or have studied the terrors of the system of 'real existing socialism', was von Donnersmarck's West German background. To be sure many identified the film as an improvement on Wolfgang Becker's earlier 'GDR block-buster film,' *Good bye, Lenin!* (Becker, 2003), yet they questioned why West Ger-man directors like Becker and von Donnersmarck gained funding to produce stories about the GDR while those who lived through the system have not.

We should offer a critical corrective immediately. In this comparison there is an expectation that the personal experience of East German directors could allow them to make films with more historically unimpeachable insights. However as Leander Haußmann's *Sonnenallee* (Sun Alley, 1998) shows, an East German back-ground guarantees neither accuracy nor reality. Haußmann's film was an ener-getic farce that sought with colourful songs and comedic elements to satirize the police state of the GDR. Its visions of youth rebellion through popular culture never sought to represent life authentically or realistically. In its use of genre con-ventions to appeal to mass audiences, it never claimed to offer a history 'as it really was'. Birth and background do not determine depictions or define knowledge.

Nevertheless we can take seriously the question of West versus East German representations as a general consideration of the condition of filmmakers from the former GDR. Why have the successful films about the GDR been made as positive stories, light-hearted farces or redemptive melodramas, and those largely by West German filmmakers? Ralf Schenk added poignancy to this question when he noted:

> What has been missing for quite a while with respect to the GDR and its consequences are films by important former DEFA directors. Egon Günther, Rainer Simon, Roland Gräf, Lothar Warneke, Evelyn Schmidt, Jörg Foth, Herwig Kipping have not been able to realize any film projects for quite some time. Will German cinema have to accept the accusation that it forced especially these voices into silence, and thereby missed an important chance for Ger-man-German reflection and reconciliation?[2]

---

2 Ralf Schenk, 'Go, Trabi, Go – DDR-Vergangenheit, Wende und Nachwende in Deutschen Kino-filmen zwischen 1990 und 2005', *Filmportal.de* (2005). (http://www.filmportal.de/thema/ go-trabi-go-ddr-vergangenheitwende-und-nachwende-in-deutschen-kinofilmen-zwischen-1990-und-2005).

Schenk's observation appeared in 2005 on *Filmportal.de,* a web-portal produced by the German Film Institute and sponsored by various state and industry organizations. From this prestigious platform, Schenk made his observations precisely at a time that allowed him to note the release of *The Lives of Others* but he was also looking back on a history of films like *Good bye Lenin!, Sonnenallee, Go, Trabi, Go* (Peter Timm 1990), *Go, Trabi, Go 2: Das war der wilde Osten* (That was the Wild East, Wolfgang Büld und Reinhard Klooss, 1992), *Helden wie Wir* (Heroes Like Us, Sebastian Peterson, 1999), *NVA* (Haußmann, 2005).

His essay overall paints a fairly differentiated picture of postwall filmmaking. He acknowledges the directors who trained in the GDR like Haußmann, Carsten Fiebeler, Andreas Kleinert, or Andreas Dresen among others who have proven able to produce films about the East. Importantly though, Schenk's list of silenced filmmakers belongs to the generation preceding Dresen and colleagues. Schenk's critical observation, even indictment of the current system, indicates that a whole generation of acclaimed *and* critical directors, individuals who had an if not antagonistic relation to the old system certainly an agonistic one, have ceased to work in film altogether. Haußmann, Fiebeler, Kleinert, or Dresen create a contrast, belonging to the last generation of filmmakers of the GDR, a generation of filmmakers whose real debut work began in the new postwall republic. And further, their films achieved greatest success when they strove to emulate the general light-hearted entertainment qualities of German popular film and avoided too dark and locally specific stories, what Schenk defines as the 'concentrated tragic tone' of the older generation.[3]

Schenk incites us to question what happened to the previous generation. Unlike the character Dreyman in *The Lives of Others* who seems able to find his way easily in the new united Germany, the reality of that generation of GDR film directors is quite the opposite. They are not only not making films about the GDR; they are not making films at all. This silence is not simply a matter of a generation of filmmaking communist ideologues being swept aside by the entry into democracy and capitalism. Highly acclaimed GDR filmmakers, filmmakers with established system critical credentials, saw their careers come to an absolute standstill after the fall of the Wall. And it is not for lack of material or effort on their parts. Reinhild Steingröver has identified extensive holdings at the archives in Potsdam of film scripts and treatments by former GDR filmmakers from the period of the *Wende* already about the GDR past, films that have never received funding.

The very real desires of these filmmakers to come to terms with 'their' GDR past in film came into confrontation with what they frequently describe as the

---

3 Schenk, 'Go, Trabi, Go'.

new censorship of the market. The filmmakers Schenk identifies complain that the West German funding agencies and production companies did not have any interest in picking up their projects. Even Andreas Dresen, a successful filmmaker who belongs to the last generation of the DEFA studios, echoes some of the same concerns as his more senior colleagues. In a recent high profile article in *Film-Dienst*, Dresen suggests that at the point of unification, he benefitted because he was just beginning his career, unlike the 'middle generation' before him, that is those directors Schenk identified who had persevered in the system or in spite of it and had begun to make a name for themselves.[4] Dresen described how this generation, marked by its experience of DEFA, appeared tainted to their West German counterparts.

Lest these reflections appear as paranoid conspiracy theory, we should recall that Volker Schlöndorff, upon his assumption of his position as manager, announced prominently 'the word DEFA will hopefully disappear; I find that it doesn't smell good'.[5] Shortly after the *Wende*, the DEFA studios experienced a rapid decline, dropping from 2400 employed professionals in various divisions to roughly 750. At the time that Schlöndorff made the statement about the 'smell' of DEFA, the studios had been reduced to a maintenance crew of around 400 employees.[6] Under Schlöndorff's tenure a further purging took place and the studios in Babelsberg became increasingly a service-providing site. Work was undertaken increasingly in outsourced form by people who came from West Germany.

While I do not want to discount the animus of a number of well-placed West German individuals in directorship positions, like Schlöndorff, vis-à-vis their East German contemporaries, I would encourage a resistance to conspiracy. Of general concern here is the introduction of *a new matrix of production*. It is this matrix that East German directors identified as the censorship of the market. The DEFA studios and the centralized system of controlled production in which they were embedded fell away with the end of the GDR. In other Eastern European countries a reform and privatization of the old system set in during the 1990s and this process incorporated and transformed old institutions. Acclaimed directors like Andrzej Wajda, István Svabó, Jiří Menzel continue to work into the present. In the new Federal Republic of Germany a different condition obtained. It is not simply a question that the DEFA studios were privatized and in the transformation into Studio Babelsberg the majority of artists and artisans were laid off. Fundament-

---

4 Andreas Dresen, 'Die Bilder der Anderen', *Film-Dienst*, 62.22 (2009), 32–34 (p. 33).
5 Ralf Schenk, 'Zwischen Fangschuß und Unhold: Volker Schlöndorff wird am Sonntag mit dem Konrad-Wolf-Preis der Akademie der Künste geehrt', *Berliner Zeitung*, 4 December 1997.
6 Randall Halle, *German Film After Germany. Toward a Transnational Aesthetic* (Urbana: University of Illinois Press, 2008).

ally the system of production, the state-based methods of funding and distribution disappeared with the collapse of the GDR. New systems did not replace these old methods, as happened in the rest of Eastern Europe and the Soviet Union with more and less success. In the united Germany, the already existing West systems of production remained intact. Those who were in that system before the *Wende* remained in it, in leading positions, while the former citizens of the GDR suddenly found themselves competing for entry into unfamiliar mechanisms. In this condition, new to them, the well-established filmmakers of the former GDR entered into competition for production support alongside new up and coming filmmakers fresh out of film school. It was a condition in which Kleinert and Dresen's generation actually had a sudden advantage over their onetime teachers and mentors at DEFA.

Returning to Schenk's observation on the potentially missed opportunity of German-German reflection, we can consider this matter a question primarily of material conditions. In the twenty years since the *Wende* the system of film production in Germany has changed radically, nevertheless no effort was made at the time truly to unify the filmic talent and cultural potential of both Germanies; subsequently no affirmative action has taken place to reintegrate excluded and demoralized talents into the current system. The end result of this material exclusion of a significant generation of talent that had direct experience in the GDR has meant that, as Dresen notes, 'Today the filmic reworking of GDR history is undertaken mainly by artists from the former West – with very mixed results. On television such work is almost quotidian'.[7] He identifies inane 'event' movies and retro shows as the primary result but also a few serious projects. For his own part, Dresen underscores that up to 1997 he did produce films that engaged with GDR history, but with no success. Perhaps the stories did not attract an audience in the West out of a lack of sympathy and understanding. However, he also notes that they did not find an audience in the East, which he views as the result of a lack of desire to recall the painful sides of the East German past. Dresen does not even question if whether now, twenty years since unification, there might not be an audience for such film work by East German directors.

---

7 Dresen, 'Die Bilder Der Anderen', p. 33.

The New Matrix of Production in the Berlin Republic

To consider the matrix of production in which West German filmmakers are able to tell tales about East Germany with relative ease, we can step back and place *The Lives of Others* in a history of developing production mechanisms. Rather than accept a clear distinction between East and West, we can distinguish between a critical direction characterized by a locally specific focus and typically tragic or at least dark ending, and a popular direction typically with a universalizing perspective and a light-hearted quality or at least a positive redemptive ending.

As already noted, Haußmann's *Sonnenallee* belongs to this latter direction. And at this point it is worth exploring more closely how this director and film emerged. Haußmann, the same generation as Kleinert and Dresen, moved quickly to the West after the fall of the Wall. His work on the stage brought him in contact with a number of West German actors, artists, and directors, including Christoph Schlingensief and Detlev Buck. The East German Haußmann in many ways paralleled the career and profile of West German Schlingensief, becoming a sort of enfant terrible and provocateur in his own right. Buck, though, supported most directly Haußmann's introduction to the West German film networks. Buck was ideally suited to play this role. Buck's career had begun in the Comedy Wave of the 1990s at a point in time when the West German film industry was in a state of real crisis. In this moment of crisis Buck directed a number of films that drew record audiences and he was able to set a new direction and tone in German film production. His directorial successes supported his establishment of a production company, Boje Buck. And in this role he has been one of the leading directors and producers of successful German popular films: comedies, touching social problem films, and even children's films. With the production support of Boje Buck, Haußmann rapidly integrated into this new matrix of production, a matrix defined by West German networks. Haußmann orientated *Sonnenallee* within those networks to a popular appeal that crossed West and East German divisions via catchy tunes, cool nostalgia, and youthful slapstick.

Wolfgang Becker's hit *Good Bye, Lenin!* (2003) offers, however, a different case study. The film is a foil to both *Sonnenallee* and *The Lives of Others*. It represents precisely a major breakthrough story told by a West German about East Germany. In effect, it represents the emergence of a West German ability to speak about the East German past in a *historical subjunctive* and not in the historical indicative: a tale told as 'what if', i.e. what if it had been this way in the GDR, characterizes the

Leander Haußmann (r) and Detlev Buck (l) on the set of *Sonnenallee.*

film's critical direction. The success of *Good Bye, Lenin!* derives largely from the production strategy developed by the collective X-Filme Creative Pool. X-Filme arose as a filmmaking collective in the 1990s, joining together at that time young directors Tom Tykwer, Dani Levy, and Wolfgang Becker along with producer Stefan Arndt with the goal of supporting each other in the production of a new kind of film. They wanted to break with the model of the Comedy Wave, current in Germany at the time and in which Buck was a key player. X-Filme sought from the start 'to create German films that are both challenging and yet appealing to the audience', and that were also aimed at a transnational market.[8] The first major success of X-Filme was, as is well known, Tom Tykwer's *Lola rennt* (Run Lola Run, 1998), appearing the same year as *Sonnenallee*. It was a film that broke box office expectations and drew global attention back to German film.

Between *Lola rennt* and *Good bye, Lenin!*, X-Filme went through a phase of minor films. Thus to recapture some of the momentum from their first big film, Arndt and Becker began work on *Good bye, Lenin!* with a carefully orchestrated production strategy that was to stretch over years and recreate the model of *Lola*

---

8 See the company philosophy, http://www.x-filme.de/html/philosophie.html.

Christiane (Katrin Saß) looks on as the GDR is dismantled, *Good Bye, Lenin!*

rennt's success. The plan included the small budget art film *Heide M.* (Michael Klier 2001) as a vehicle for Katrin Saß. Saß, who was slated to play the central role of the mother in Becker's film, had not performed in front of the movie camera for a number of years, and *Heide M.* was understood as a practice piece. While the film was not intended to be a major success, Arndt gave it full support in marketing. Although it did not find a general distributor, it offered Arndt the chance to develop and expand the networks of the recently established X-Filme distribution.

The work on *Good bye, Lenin!* began in 2001 after the release of *Heide M. Good bye, Lenin!* thus entered into a tested system of production stamped with the brand of one of Germany's most dynamic film production units of the period. Initial resonance began when it was taken up for the competition at the Berlin Film Festival in 2003. While *Lola rennt* had to be given over to Prokino Filmproducers to find distribution, in the case of *Good bye, Lenin!*, X-Filme distribution was able to retain primary control while joining up with the larger and more forceful Bavaria Media Marketing, a unit of Bavaria Film oriented precisely toward bringing smaller budget films into a higher profile distribution. Altogether the pre and post-production strategy allowed X-Filme to retain primary control over the film, garner the profits, and reinvest them in the various branches of a growing network with a global orientation.

The Lives of Others as a Student Debut Film

These considerations of the condition of GDR filmmaking after German unification and the productions of *Sonnenallee* and *Good bye, Lenin!* within complex and elaborated post-unification matrices of production offer both a background and a foil to *The Lives of Others*. In the case of *The Lives of Others*, a central aspect of the development of the film derives from the training von Donnersmarck received at film school in Munich. The film school training offers not just an opportunity to develop skills but also brings the student into contact with existing networks. Of all the film schools in Germany, Munich has the reputation as the most entertainment industry-oriented school, although at this point all film schools have broken with the auteurist model of training and offer students certifications in the various specializations of filmmaking from cinematography and editing to producer training. Munich as a film school could offer von Donnersmarck the opportunity to work out ideas with young student colleagues but also entrée into an increasingly elaborated network and support system. It is this form of entrée that senior filmmakers from the GDR lacked. Furthermore, von Donnersmarck's decision to go to film school coincided roughly with the first major successes of X-Filme, a time when film-industrial networks in Germany and Europe were rapidly expanding.

Exposure to these networks is of course not a guarantee of success in the industry and many students, even those with clear vision and talent, fail to make the transition from film school to a secure career as filmmaker. Born in 1973, von Donnersmarck began film school in 1997, slightly older than his colleagues and with an already broad set of experiences. As discussed in the introduction to this volume, he grew up as a polyglot through the international settings in which he was raised. He studied in the Soviet Union and in London, receiving training both in the humanities, languages and literatures, and the social sciences, especially economics. Industrial film production of the sort taught in Munich may be understood as offering a direction that combined the facets of this background. Moreover, it should be considered that although von Donnersmarck was raised extensively in the US and could have oriented himself toward film schools there with the goal of a direct path to the Hollywood industry, his move to Munich represented an immediate localization to the German and European film industry.

Von Donnersmarck's first film projects in film school were films that could be categorized as action-adventure and fantasy, experiments with entertainment strategies of visual storytelling. It is perhaps revealing of his orientation that in an interview with the London-based *Sunday Telegraph*, he identified Jean-Paul Belmondo in his action roles as having a great influence on him as a child.[9] Further, he described as his two favourite films François Truffaut's *La Sirène du Mississippi* (Mississippi Mermaid, 1969) and Harold Ramis's *Groundhog Day* (1993). He ascribed to the latter film a profound but accessible philosophical message. 'It's a very deep and philosophical film; the great thing is you don't notice immediately. It's not one of those in-your-face philosophical films, but it's a film that manages subliminally to get the message across that the only way you can change the world is by changing yourself'.[10] These curious identifications of filmic influence may be signs of a savvy ability to speak to the popular press in an accessible fashion, but they may also be taken as signs of von Donnersmarck's points of reference between popular and European art-house film. Certainly they also indicate an interest in more complex storytelling, Truffaut designating an interest in an European strategy of storytelling. His interests in accessible philosophy, action and drama also can be taken as signs of a distance from experimental and art cinematic genres.

Certainly von Donnersmarck's early work indicated talent in its visual style and storytelling strategies. Already with one of his first films, *Dobermann* (1999), von Donnersmarck received a great deal of attention. The story follows a man on a walk in the city reading *Bild*, the epitome of sensationalist German press. Anticipating the film's narrative, he reads an article about a man mauled by a pit-bull just as he steps into a dog pile on the sidewalk. Passing a barking Doberman in a parked car, the man taunts the animal, blowing cigarette smoke at it through a crack in the car's window. In a peal of breaking glass the dog breaks the window and the man's taunting laughter turns to sounds of fear and desperation as he begins to run. The majority of the film then tracks the attempt to flee the dog, who proves a resourceful and even avenging juggernaut. Shot in black and white and with no dialogue, the film relied on a history of chase scenes and a number of genre conventions around suspense and retribution. In many ways the film could pass as a low-grade slasher film but it also indicated a clear sense of continuity editing, ability to manipulate genre expectations, convey story through visual language, and maintain a sense of pacing to carry spectator interest. The film won

---

9 Florian Henckel von Donnersmarck, 'My Favourite Movies: Director Florian Henckel Von Donnersmarck', *The Sunday Telegraph*, 16 September 2007.
10 von Donnersmarck, 'My Favourite Movies'.

prizes at short film festivals in Würzburg, Dresden, and most importantly the short film prize at the Max Ophüls Festival for young film talent that takes place annually in Saarbrücken. The success of *Dobermann* led to the ability to put together a larger budget for his next film.

Der Templer (The Crusader, 2002) really initiated von Donnersmarck's career, garnering a series of prizes starting with its debut at the Internationale Hofer Filmtage 10.2002 where it won the Eastman Förderpreis für Nachwuchs-Regisseure. It won further prizes from the Filmbewertungsstelle in Wiesbaden: Short Film of the Month December 2002; The Short Film Prize: Friedrich Wilhelm Murnau Prize; and then the Special Prize of the Producers' Jury: Student Film Festival Potsdam. The script was written by von Donnersmarck's brother Sebastian Henckel von Donnersmarck. The story is a simple one of a disillusioned crusader who on his way home comes across a witch burning. Having lost faith in God and the Devil, he fights to free the young woman as the flames of the stake rise higher. He slaughters the soldiers and clergy and drives off the townspeople, but both are wounded as they make to flee the town. Lying in the woods together bleeding the next morning, she tells him that they do not need to die if he will collect the ingredients for a balsam she can prepare. When it is almost finished she informs him that the missing ingredient is his heart, which, upon turning into a demon, she rips out. The final scene shows her drinking the potion, recovered and more beautiful than ever.

Politically, an exchange between the crusader and a corrupt monk in the town's inn offers an opaque allusion to the First Gulf War and the War in Afghanistan. The monk tries to sell him a tail feather of the Holy Spirit, certified authentic by the Bishop of Trier. The knight identifies such corrupt certifications as part of the methods the Church uses to whip up the frenzy necessary to inspire misadventures like the Crusades. The monk responds by identifying his cynical faithless character as the reason why Jerusalem had not been captured. If we take seriously the political allusions the film makes, then the twist at the end proves the disillusioned knight wrong. There is a God and a Devil and the battle for Jerusalem both did matter and did fail because of people like him.

A very artful use of tracking shots characterizes both films, although in *Der Templer* the crane shot is particularly deftly deployed, allowing for a more complicated camera motion. Likewise in that film, the setting and costuming prove impressively exact, recalling a Breugel painting and foreshadowing the setting and scenery work in *The Lives of Others*. Pacing in both films speaks well to genre conventions, alternating action and pauses in order to build intensity. Close up shots alternating with far shots provide a clear sense of identification with characters and yet a sense of continuity and coherency in the action. The atmosphere and pacing of *Der Templer* seems to bespeak more an existentialist Bergmanesque art film à la *The Seventh Seal* (1957). All these qualities point directly to the skills that will develop their art fully in *The Lives of Others*.

However, if we are to consider the subsequent success of *The Lives of Others* as growing out of this work, I want to return to the point made earlier that it is less the particulars of the films as much as it is the contacts that they facilitated. *Der Templer* represented the first collaboration between von Donnersmarck and his film school colleagues Max Wiedemann and Quirin Berg who were establishing their own production company. Perhaps most important though was the contact with Claudia Gladziejewski, head of the Short and Debut Film division of Bavarian Television, the Bayerischer Rundfunk (BR). Gladziejewski works extensively with film schools and festivals to find new talents and mentor them into the establishment. Having seen promise in him with *Dobermann*, Gladziewjewski worked together with von Donnersmarck on *Der Templer*. She served as the executive producer for the film. Importantly and suggestively, she described the film as belonging to a genre which she herself does not particularly appreciate, nevertheless in von Donnersmarck's film she could recognize a fundamental talent in the visual language deployed.

With BR involvement, the project could easily gain support from ARTE, the transnational French-German television station. Here the story of *The Lives of Others* actually begins. Gladziewjewski has introduced various mechanisms for developing film material in Germany, including importing a practice of *Drehbuchaufstellung*, or script development from Hollywood, a practice that remains relatively unknown in Germany still. Gladziewjewski, in addition to her many other roles, established the company Script Doctors to promote this practice.[11] In these meetings, an author, director, producer or other industry professionals have an opportunity to pitch their stories. A number of films have been fostered in this way to successful completion, receiving intricate feedback on figures, strengths of relationships, believability, sequencing of scenes, audience engagement, dynamic of plot and subplots, among other aspects of the script. Script Doctors can strengthen possible projects and bring them into connection with interested backers.

In the case of von Donnersmarck, Gladziejewski was able to approach him after the success of *Der Templer* and ask him if he had any ideas for a feature film. She invited him to a *Drehbuchaufstellung*. After much encouragement he presented a simple idea. At that session he set forward the core idea that he has described on numerous occasions: the image of a man as agent of a totalitarian apparatus hearing a piece of music that transforms him fundamentally. Instead of

---

11 Claudia Gladziejewski, 'Script Doctors', (http://www.script-doctors.com/de/home/index.php).

spying on the couple he was set to observe, the man has an epiphany and is transformed. As is discussed elsewhere in this volume, the image derives not from considerations of the GDR specifically but more directly from an anecdote that von Donnersmarck heard, presumably while studying in Russia; Maxim Gorky's famous conversation with Lenin regarding Beethoven's *Appassionata*.[12] Von Donnersmarck was fascinated by the question of what would have happened to the violence of the Russian Revolution and its totalitarian outcome if Lenin had indeed chosen instead to listen to music. Here the key elements that would become elaborated in *The Lives of Others*, a tale of redemption via a voyeuristic triangle, a spy in an attic room and a tragic couple, found their first positive formulation. In effect, von Donnersmarck left this brief pitching session with incentive to move his attention away from fantasy and action genres to a much more contained drama. From this point it took four years to write the script and draw the cast and crew together. Interestingly, in interviews von Donnersmarck remarks periodically on *Good Bye, Lenin!* as influence, sometimes filmic foil. Indeed, the pre-history of *The Lives of Others* is almost bookended by popular GDR films; von Donnersmarck began film school with the appearance of *Sonnenallee* and the original pitching of the concept for his film coincided roughly with the debut of Becker's film. The subsequent development of the story unfolded under the shadow of the success of that film.

Part of the narrative of the film alluded to above, the writing of the script, entailed von Donnersmarck undertaking an extensive period of research.[13] This commitment to an understanding of the historical conditions in the GDR is often presented as a counterpoint to the limitations of the feel-good story *Good Bye, Lenin!* provided. Von Donnersmarck spent a year and a half undertaking research including at the Stasi archives. Furthermore, he conducted interviews with victims of the state security system of the GDR as well as with members of the Stasi. He read widely and he was assisted by various experts, including Manfred Wilke, the West German sociologist at the FU who had long studied the East German Communist Party and state apparatus. During this phase von Donnersmarck moved to Berlin and lived in *Mitte* not far from the Volksbühne where the characters of his film, Christa-Maria Sieland and Georg Dreyman, would work as actor and director. At this point, the story of the genesis of the film takes a romantic turn, when, for the writing phase, von Donnersmarck retreated to the Heiligen-

---

12 Maxim Gorky, *Collected Works*, XVII (Moskow: Foreign Language Publishing House, 1950), pp. 39–40.
13 Kevin Lally, 'Spies & Lies: Florian Henckel Von Donnersmarck Examines Recent German History in Drama About Artists and Stasi Agents', *Film Journal International*, 110.3 (2007), 12 and 28.

kreuz Abbey in Austria where his uncle lives as a monk. There in solitude he set about writing the script.

Having completed the script, von Donnersmarck sought contact with larger established production companies who reacted with interest but lack of enthusiastic engagement. Gladziejewski advised him to look for young producers who would demand less pay but also have access to support from public financing sources that established producers did not. As noted earlier, Max Weidemann and Quirin Berg both had studied at the Munich School for Film and Television alongside von Donnersmarck and in the separate track for producers in which they had actually served as the producers for *Der Templer*. As students, Weidemann and Berg worked together to foster the projects of their colleagues at the school and they did this with great success, garnering multiple prizes for the numerous films they oversaw. Weidemann and Berg proved particularly adept at drawing together larger than typical budgets for film-school productions and successfully gaining access for their films in competitions. Nevertheless they had had relatively little experience with anything other than short films when they took on the role of producers for *The Lives of Others*. Two popular entertainment films for television were all they had on their résumé.

Weidemann and Berg were among the youngest producers in Germany when they took on the project. The production money for the film they drew together began as subsidy funds from the regional and federal film boards, financing which derived largely from the debut status of the participants in the project. BR became the first funding source to sign on to the film. In the configuration of typical funding it could be understood as a sign of Eastern recalcitrance that MDR, the Eastern German television station, rejected the project for support. However the support of BR did further facilitate the relationship to ARTE. Proceeding in this fashion, Weidemann and Berg were able to bring together a budget of € 1.5 million. This budget was certainly substantially more than the typical student debut film, but also remarkably little for the high production values and professional quality of the film, a point worth considering as part of the art of this particular work.

Although budgets for filmmaking in Europe have been steadily rising, by comparison to films produced in a Hollywood network of production, Europeans produce mid to low budget films, more in line with US independent films. Of course the numbers are relative if we consider that the current level of audiovisual financing is such that the budget for *The Lives of Others* was twice as much as that of *Die Ehe der Maria Braun* (The Marriage of Maria Braun, Rainer Werner Fassbinder, 1979) at approximately $2 million versus $1 million. Certainly it is necessary to adjust for inflation. However, the comparison reminds us that von Donnersmarck as a student filmmaker working on his debut film had available to him production funds that one of the most significant directors in the history of

New German Cinema barely had available at the height of his career. Yet when such a film enters into global competition it does so against Hollywood block-buster films that can amass budgets that rival the GDP of some countries in the developing world.

The story of the film develops further around the question of the strategy von Donnersmarck, Weidemann and Berg pursued to maximize the professional potential of the budget. After his careful research and work on the script, von Donnersmarck continued to engage the project with a certain amount of micro-managing. Paralleling the work of New German Cinema directors in some ways, von Donnersmarck developed the film as quasi-auteur attending to all of its aspects. Von Donnersmarck took over the significant work in casting and describes repeated and extensive contacts with the actors before he convinced them to sign on. In the casting he exhibited a certain grandiose orientation, pursuing big name actors and producers. This he did with such passion that the actors were willing to work with an unknown director at a fraction of their normal salaries. Von Donnersmarck has described the first meeting with Ulrich Mühe as an exam situation in which not the director but the actor was the examiner. Von Donnersmarck describes how Mühe tested him about his aesthetic, theatrical and historical understanding and when satisfied agreed to join the project. Von Donnersmarck atypically pursued a star cast even into the smaller roles, seeking out many actors who, like Ulrich Mühe, were born in the GDR and had their own history of confrontation with the state apparatus: Thomas Thieme, Hans-Uwe Bauer, Charly Hübner, Volker Michalowski, Martin Brambach, among others. In general, von Donnersmarck described being able to convince his highly skilled cast of the importance of the film and that for them the shooting would allow them to push their own acting skills.

He also sought out crew members according to similar criteria. Likewise he signed on former citizens of the GDR to work behind the camera, contributing to and supporting the sincerity of his quest for accuracy and authenticity. And in his desire to create an accurate environment he sought out authentic devices as props, like the listening devices that play such an important role or the letter steamer that appears briefly but has an important symbolic function.[14]

Given the centrality of the *Appassionata* to the conception of the film though, von Donnersmarck pursued with a singular purpose Gabriel Yared as composer for the film.[15] Yared has written scores for over 100 films, starting with Godard's

---

14 Diane Carson, 'Learning from History in *The Lives of Others*: An Interview with Writer/Director Florian Henckel Von Donnersmarck', *Journal of Film and Video*, 62.1–2 (2010), 13–22; John Esther, 'Between Principle and Feeling: An Interview with Florian Henckel Von Donnersmarck', *Cineaste*, 32.2 (2007), 40–42.
15 Jörg Gerle, 'Das Leben der Anderen', *Film-Dienst*, 59.7 (2006), 42.

Sauve qui peut (Every Man for Himself, 1980). He has won multiple awards including the Oscar. Yared represented for von Donnersmarck an important mediator between film and demanding classical music and he pursued contact with great and necessary persistence. Although in interviews von Donnersmarck underscores his awestruck approach to Yared as a certain recklessness, it is clear that Yared has an interest in young talent. One of Yared's accomplishments, which establishes a lasting legacy for Yared, is his founding of the Pléiade Academy, oriented toward supporting young talented composers. Nevertheless, Yared accepted like the other members of cast and crew to work at a fraction of his typical budget. This generous contribution was certainly crucial to the success of a film in which music is key to the plot and in which the budget is limited.

The limited budget expresses itself in the images on the screen both through the setting and the camerawork. Upon examination one notes a relative lack of far and establishing shots. Such shots would have required more elaborate setting. Keeping the frame close insured an ability to crop out any details in the locations that might have indicated the elapse of time since 1984, the year of the film's diegesis. The film is in many ways thus a chamber piece playing in a relatively limited space that reduced strategically the need for elaborate sets. The tight frame worked ultimately to the film's advantage, infusing the images with an affective connection to the characters. On the other hand, a central expense of the film was the insistence on working with 35mm film stock. This was necessary because von Donnersmarck and his cinematographer Hagen Bogdanski, with whom he had also already worked while in film school, sought to match the film to the colour scheme of the GDR itself. They aimed for a more subdued hue along the line of the famous pastels that characterized GDR design. Red and blue are absent, while browns, greens, yellows, and greys dominate. With 35mm this manipulation of colour could take place in production and not as a postproduction digital effect on the film material.

Media Controversy, Distribution and Reception Circuits

The considerations of the film's matrix extend here into the post-production phase of distribution and screening. Even before its release the film had acquired an industry 'buzz', because the premiere proved difficult and controversial. Frequently cited as a sign of opposition to the film, it was submitted to the Berlin Film Festival but was turned down. The refusal to include *The Lives of Others* in the competition was criticized extensively later, with many understanding it as an ideological and not aesthetic decision. It was not a question that the Berlinale was closed to German productions, as has often been the complaint about other festivals, Cannes especially. That year the competition at the Berlinale included four German films and four co-productions comprising almost a quarter of the films up for awards. Reviewing the selections made, of the German productions *Requiem* (Hans-Christian Schmid), *Elementarteilchen* (Atomised, Oskar Roehler), and *Der freie Wille* (The Free Will, Matthias Glasner) received awards but all of the films in the competition, including *Grbavica* (Grbavica: The Land of My Dreams, Jasmila Zbanic), the co-production that won the Golden Bear, proved less successful at the box office and received less overall acclaim than von Donnersmarck's film. This disparity in reception does suggest that purely aesthetic criteria were not at work in the selection committee's decision.

Oksana Bulgakowa surmised that Dieter Kosslick declined the film because he did not want his festival to become a platform for an antagonistic German-German polemic. This reasoning is highly unlikely because the Berlin Film Festival has thrived on controversy in the past.[16] More likely is the consideration that *The Lives of Others* was only a debut film from an unknown film school student. This rationale is born out by the rumour that the Festival offered von Donnersmarck the opportunity to premiere the film in one of the many other and highly respected venues, such as the Panorama. Kosslick, since assuming the directorship of the Berlinale, has been plagued by the difficulty of attracting major films and especially Hollywood works to premiere at the festival. The A-list status of the Berlinale depends on the competition being reserved for films premiering there. Glamour, perhaps more important to the status of the festival than critical acclaim, depends on the ability of its director to bring big name stars and directors to Berlin. Panorama, Forum, and Perspective German Cinema are frequent venues for high profile student debuts. And indeed a few years later when the student debut film *Shahada* (Burhan Qurbani, 2010) did premiere in the competition at the Berlinale, independent of the merits of the film, the press identified this event negatively as a sign of the failure of Kosslick and the demise of the festival. However at this earlier point, when Kosslick refused to address publicly the decision to turn down the student film *The Lives of Others* for the competition, a controversy arose in the media. What is certain at his moment is that, as Bulgakowa also noted, the rejection offered the film the best publicity for its launch.[17]

The film, as product of a Munich Film School student and recipient of Bavarian funding, had been submitted to the Bavarian Film Prize, the results of which

16 Oksana Bulgakowa, 'Das Sehen der Anderen', *Film-Dienst*, 60.11 (2007), 14–16 (p. 15).
17 Bulgakowa, 'Das Sehen der Anderen', p. 15.

were announced just shortly before the start of the Berlinale, drawing further attention to the decision to decline the film. Whatever was behind the decision of the Berlinale, a politicization of the film clearly did take place when the conservative politician Bernd Neumann, then the Bundeskulturminister, Representative of the Federal Government for Culture, invited the members of the German parliament to a special screening. At roughly the same time as the film was sent off for consideration by the juries of the Bavarian Film Prize and the Berlinale, it was also sent to the German Film Academy. The film was nominated in 11 categories and the nomination for the German Film Award, the Lola. It may be worth noting that this award is funded by Neumann's office. The Lola was handed out just a few months after the Berlinale and the trend that had begun in Munich continued. It swept the awards with seven out of eleven nominations, a success that could be understood as a comment on its aesthetic quality, as a response to the Berlin Film Festival, even as a sign of the privileged position it had been given by the conservative Minister of Culture.

Weidemann and Berg's strategy was to orient the film to a market that went immediately beyond Germany, beginning with submissions to international festivals and high profile film awards from the start. Although they had a difficult time finding a distributor, the film's eventual distributor supported this market orientation. Part of the function of the film festival is not just to present a film to an audience but to showcase it to potential distributors. Without the contacts available through the Berlinale, the film had to be marketed directly. German distributors responded negatively, seeking works that were comedic and lighthearted as offering a promise of profitability in the German market. A student debut film on a serious topic, albeit one with a positive and even redemptive ending, did not hold a clear promise of profit. It was the German subsidiary of Buena Vista that picked it up and, paralleling the development of *Good Bye, Lenin!*, Buena Vista Deutschland brought the film into the larger networks of the Disney system, orienting it quickly toward a market beyond Germany and Europe.

For all of its awards in Germany, the film was not immediately successful at the German box office. In the year of its general release, *The Lives of Others* achieved only the sixth place on the list of German Film Hits compiled by the German Federal Film Board.[18] *The Lives of Others* was preceded on the hit list by the German British French co-production *Das Parfum: Die Geschichte eines Mörders* (Perfume: The Story of a Murderer, Tom Tykwer) in first place, the documentary of the German team in the soccer World Cup games *Deutschland, ein Sommermärchen* (Germany, a Summer's Fairytale, Sönke Wortmann) in second place, and

---

18 Filmförderungsanstalt, 'Filmhitliste: Jahresliste (deutsch) 2007', (http://ffa.de/).

in places three, four, and five respectively the parody *7 Zwerge – Der Wald ist nicht genug* (7 Dwarfs: The Forest is not Enough, Sven Unterwaldt), the teen comedy *Die wilden Kerle 3* (The Wild Guys 3, Joachim Masannek), and *Hui Buh* (Sebastian Niemann), a fantasy/comedy ghost story. A comparison to the German International Hit List likewise confirms that while 2006 was an impressive year for the market percentage of German films, nevertheless audience preferences in Germany followed the trends of mainstream audiences globally with comedies, fantasy-adventure, and children's films topping the list. Importantly though, the national market played a qualified role here. International success of German films is not predicated on box office success in Germany. Actually, *The Lives of Others* is one of the many German films for which success outside of Germany led to success in Germany. Consider that *The Lives of Others* remained on the Hit List the following year in eleventh place after the awarding of the Oscar brought renewed interest in Germany for the international German hit.

Ultimately though, the success of the film for the German film industry was the ability of a German film to achieve more on less. This success has larger overall ramifications for German films. That a German debut film could achieve such international acclaim attests that German, and European films in general do not face off with Hollywood directly, blockbuster against blockbuster. Rather German and European films enter into expanded transnational markets within the circle of distribution for independent films. European films compete against US independents, mid to low-budget against mid to low-budget films. In this condition of competition and profitability, expanded budgets for film school projects and debut work is a tricky matter. It is positive as a development for debut work, but it also represents a trend towards smaller budgets and to a reliance on film school films. For Florian Henckel von Donnersmarck, the budget for *The Lives of Others* was the highest budget he had experienced to that date and he used it artfully. For established German filmmakers used to larger budgets still, *The Lives of Others* presents them with the challenge of a downsizing of their budgets. Due to this film's success, they are challenged to be like von Donnersmarck and likewise to make more with less.

That 'Difficult' German Past and Audience Appeal

The discussion of the film's matrix of production underscores that the success of the film is not simply a matter of the images, but of considerations of orientation already reached in the pre-production phase: popular orientation, historical setting, clear moral issues, positive parable, a reliance on genre conventions that allow for a universalizing appeal. This orientation is fostered of course by a funding and production milieu that determines success based on size of box office, number of spectators, Oscar nominations. These criteria for success determine funding for future projects and the possibility of careers. This matrix of production attracts and influences film school students and the most established of filmmakers alike. As opposed to the period of transition following the fall of the Wall, this matrix characterizes now the general system in Germany but also across Europe.

In conclusion there is one final aspect worth noting regarding what we could identify as the cultural and historic specificity of *The Lives of Others*. If its success in Germany was predicated on its success abroad, it bears questioning more closely what aspects of the film appeal to international audiences. What function does the quality stamp 'made in Germany' leave on the film? Derek Elley, writing for *Variety*, suggested that the film benefitted from 'growing offshore awareness of well-crafted German dramas inspired by recent history'.[19] His allusion to recent history may be referring to the GDR past. However, it is just as likely that Elley is including there the critical and box office success of films about the Third Reich like *Sophie Scholl – Die letzten Tage* (Sophie Scholl – The Final Days, Marc Rothemund, 2005), or *Der Untergang* (Downfall, Oliver Hirschbiegel, 2003). In that connection, discussing the film for *Cineaste*, Christina White blithely and problematically condensed representation of the Third Reich with that of the GDR; she noted that *The Lives of Others* follows *Schindler's List*, as a kind of 'Schindler light' in its focus not directly on the victims of the system but on the redemption of one of the perpetrators.[20] This condensation of Third Reich and GDR into one system indicates that the success of *The Lives of Others* but also of *Good Bye, Lenin!* and others occur in part because international critics and spectators appear prepared to add an interest in GDR historical narratives to the interest in the Third Reich. That 'difficult German past' becomes a profitable resource for the international success of contemporary German cinema.

---

19 Derek Elley, 'Film Reviews: Cannes: *The Lives of Others*', *Variety*, 403.5 (2006), 40.
20 Christina White, 'The Lives of Others', 32.2 *Cineaste*, (2007), 58.

Jaimey Fisher

CHAPTER FOUR
A Historical Sort of Stardom: Casting, Ulrich Mühe, and *The Lives of Others'* Authenticity Problem

To begin, I would like to offer three moments circulating in and through the cultural and political phenomenon of *The Lives of Others*. First, in writing about *The Lives of Others*, the director Andreas Dresen argues something searingly critical that is hard to deny. Dresen, unlike *The Lives of Others'* director Florian Henckel von Donnersmarck, is from the former East Germany, and in assessing von Donnersmarck's blockbuster, he writes 'this film has about as much to do with the GDR as Hollywood with Hoyerswerda. [... T]he film tells, quite effectively, the fairy tale of the good person who resides in each of us, even in the worst Stasi collaborator. This kind of thing is popular, not least because it is so wonderfully reassuring. But it does not help us to get at the truth'.[1] Dresen's statement underscores what one might call the truth or authenticity problem of *The Lives of Others*, a problem persisting despite, or perhaps exacerbated by, the film's enormous success. One hardly requires reminding that the story of a Stasi officer lying to protect subjects of surveillance is, if not a lie, then at least highly, even misleadingly, rare. Most of the criticism of *The Lives of Others* relates to this problem, the notion that the film could find truth in a plot that is not only fictional, but that also clearly distorts the vast majority of historical cases.[2] In this essay, I would like to address how the film's casting, particularly of the celebrated actor Ulrich Mühe, helped von Donnersmarck address this authenticity problem in powerful, although also controversial ways.

Second, and resonating with Dresen's invocation of Hollywood versus Hoyerswerda, let us look at a press photograph from the week after Ulrich Mühe died in 2007.[3] This seems to me revealing about *The Lives of Others'* unique place in post-1989, even postwar, German cinema. The film, as has already been noted (see the Introduction to this volume), is one of the highest grossing post-1989 Ger-

1 Andreas Dresen, 'Ost-West Film: Der falsche Kino-Osten', *Die Zeit*, 31 July 2009.
2 See Jaimey Fisher, 'German Historical Film as Production Trend: European Heritage Cinema and Melodrama in *The Lives of Others*', in *The Collapse of the Conventional. German Film and its Politics at the Turn of the Twenty-First Century*, ed. by Jaimey Fisher and Brad Prager (Detroit: Wayne State University Press, 2010), pp. 186–215.
3 'Cruise: Abschied von Mühe', *Berliner Morgenpost*, 3 Sept 2007.

Von Donnersmarck and Tom Cruise at the funeral
of Ulrich Mühe. *Berlin, Morgenpost*, 3 September 2007.

man film in terms of US box office, almost doubling even *Lola rennt's* (Run Lola
Run, Tom Tykwer, 1998) impressive haul of $7.3 million. Its status was affirmed
when von Donnersmarck was the upset winner of the 2007 Oscar for Best Foreign
Language Film, overcoming the heavy favourite, Guillermo del Toro's *Pan's Laby-
rinth*. On stage to receive the surprise honour, von Donnersmarck thanked a
number of participants in the film, but his ode to Mühe (who was present but apparently already quite ill with the stomach cancer that would kill him) is perhaps
the most memorable: he declared Mühe the 'greatest artist' and 'don't let anyone
tell you otherwise'. It is hard, though undeniably amusing, to imagine what impact such a declaration would have on a roomful of Hollywood-sized and -based
egos, but this surprising superlative, offered at ground zero of the global film industry, is a telling remark that invites an analysis of acting and stardom in von
Donnersmarck's film.

Finally, as one contemplates *The Lives of Others'* global success, it is notable
that the three German-language films that have won the Oscar since 2000 have all
been historical dramas, or even, as discussed elsewhere in this volume, heritage

films. In his book-length study of the heritage system, Andrew Higson offers a telling image from *The Guardian*, an image in the form of a mock recipe with both ingredients and directions to a commercially successful heritage film.[4] Entitled 'Modern Recipes: No 21 – Costume Drama', it lists such tongue-in-cheek ingredients as '1 classic text/1 large tub whimsy/ 3lbs. mixed anachronisms'. For its ultimate ingredient, the recipe calls for '1 Helena Bonham Carter (or own-brand equivalent)', with whom the heritage-cinema dish is to be 'garnished'. Here Higson foregrounds casting, a central aspect of heritage cinema that goes, as it does quite often, largely neglected in film studies, especially German film studies. Even more than *Nirgendwo in Afrika* (Nowhere in Africa, Caroline Link, 2001) or *Die Fälscher* (The Counterfeiters, Stefan Ruzowitzky, 2007) – the two other recent Oscar winners from German-speaking Europe – *The Lives of Others* became identified with one actor in particular, Mühe, and, even though one cannot claim for him a global heritage-industry fame à la Helena Bonham Carter, his varied career does invite reflection on both his role in the spectacular success of *Lives of Others* as well as casting in German historical drama in general.

A Stellar *Sonderweg*? The German Way of Stardom

In addressing casting and the undisputed star of *The Lives of Others*, I take up a distinction in star studies that Erica Carter has convincingly made in the case of Germany: that star studies in the German literature tends to break down into two basic groups, those engaging the Anglophone scholarship on stars versus those featuring what I would call a kind of German *Sonderweg* of the star, with the particularities and even peculiarities of Germany's quasi-star system in the foreground.[5] I agree with her that we should not dispense with either of these approaches, and I would like to unfold herein how the German *Sonderweg* of stardom can make a significant contribution to the dominant theories of stars as they have emerged and evolved in Anglophone scholarship. A possible third-way between Hollywood-style stardom (and theories of it) and a German *Sonderweg* is a sensitivity to the international market in art-house cinema, something that moves the historical and memorial functions of the star into the foreground. Both of these aspects – the global market in art-house cinema and the role of historical memory in stardom – constitute important contexts for Mühe's status before and

---

4 Andrew Higson, *English Heritage. English Cinema* (Oxford: Oxford University Press, 2003), p. 33.
5 Erica Carter, 'Stars: Introduction', in *The German Cinema Book*, ed. by Tim Bergfelder, Erica Carter and Deniz Göktürk (London: BFI, 2002), pp. 59–62.

in *The Lives of Others*. Such a third way is localized in the casting, in the historical experience, and even in the very body of Mühe.

Ulrich Mühe was born in 1953 in Grimma, Saxony, near Leipzig, where he did his theatre training after apprenticing in construction (he told one interviewer in the mid-1990s he could still build a chimney if he had to) and then military service that included a stint as a border guard before being discharged for stomach problems. In 1979 he first appeared on the stage in then Karl-Marx-Stadt (today's Chemnitz), but, in 1982, was brought to Berlin by the celebrated dramatist and director Heiner Müller for his Volksbühne production of *Macbeth*. This began his long and formative association with Müller. In 1983, he joined the ensemble of the Deutsches Theater, so by age 30 he had, by his own admission, reached the pinnacle for actors in the GDR and was not even really sure what else he should be seeking (he said, perhaps portentously, 'Deutsches Theater was the [GDR] actors' Olympus, and after that there was only the Wall').[6] His theatre roles in this period at the Deutsches Theater included Goethe's *Egmont* and, perhaps most memorably, Hamlet in Heiner Müller's eight-hour production of *Hamlet/Hamlet-Maschine*, which premiered in February 1989. In the period after the fall of the Wall in November 1989, he had, according to one newspaper article, six on-going roles at the Deutsches Theater.[7]

Mühe had an unusually high-profile role for an actor in the events of the autumn of 1989, at a time when he was already celebrated as one of the GDR's best-known and most accomplished actors. Moreover, he had, by that point, acquired something of a profile in the West for his role in Bernhard Wicki's *Das Spinnennetz* (The Spider's Web, 1989) with Klaus Maria Brandauer and Armin Mueller-Stahl. The production took him, at the age of 33, for the first time to West Berlin, about which more below. With this profile, precarious but also protecting him, he was surprisingly public in his dissent toward certain GDR policies, if not toward the state itself. In October 1989, he read on the stage of Deutsches Theater from a banned book, *Schwierigkeiten mit der Wahrheit* (Troubles with the Truth), by dissident author Walter Janka, and on 4 November he participated in a large and important demonstration on Berlin's Alexanderplatz organized by intellectuals and artists (David Bathrick has called it the 'crowning event of East Germany's [1989] October Revolution'[8]). In front of an estimated one million assembled

---

6 Christian Schröder, 'Von Kunst mag er nur selten sprechen: Ulrich Mühe, ein Schauspieler der bei Rollenangeboten äußerst geschmäcklerisch ist', *Süddeutsche Zeitung*, 20 March 1993.
7 Ursula Meves, 'Die Geschichte der Atombombe: Dramatischer Stoff für einen Spielfilm', *Neues Deutschland*, 12 May 1990.
8 David Bathrick, *Powers of Speech. The Politics of Culture in the GDR* (Lincoln: University of Nebraska, 1995), p. 1.

Ulrich Mühe taking part in the protest on Alexanderplatz
with actor and director Johanna Schall, 4 November 1989.

people, Mühe read a short speech that declared 'the claim to power of a party
should not be mandated by a law'.[9]

This biographical context and trajectory serve as backstory for the way historical memory informed Mühe's career as one of the postwall stars of German
cinema, a mechanism and dynamic that can illuminate our understanding of *The
Lives of Others* as well as theories of stardom and casting in Anglophone scholarship. Before arguing in this direction, however, it makes sense to recall how German film casting and – if one may term them such – stars differ from Hollywood's.
Germany's system was probably closest to the classical Hollywood-studio cultivation and control of stars during the Nazi era, but, since then, it has differed
significantly, not least due to relatively weak domestic box office and the fairly
decentralized character of German cinema. Moreover, as the 'Kino-Debatte' (Cinema Debate) of the 1910s and the Weimar era suggested early in German cinema
history, this also has to do with the role of culture (that is, *Kultur*) in German
society, which has long estimated theatre more artistically accomplished and
therefore more highly than film.

The acting talents of theatre actors who also perform in the cinema serve as a
means of distinguishing German actors – and cinema more generally – from
the competition provided constantly, and usually overwhelmingly, by Hollywood
and its global stars. In von Donnersmarck's Oscar speech, for instance, he tellingly declared Mühe the greatest artist, not the greatest actor, in the world. What-

---

9 Christian Schröder, 'Von Kunst mag er nur selten sprechen'.

ever one thinks of the acting talent of Hollywood stars, it is notable that German discussions of its actors in relation to Hollywood tend to emphasize both the the-atre-honed acting skills of German stars as well as the strong theatrical system that distinguishes Germany from the US (where stars are at least minted, or 'dis-covered', with commerce foremost). As Claudia Fellmer notes in her discussion of Armin Mueller-Stahl, another star from the former East, Mueller-Stahl consist-ently regards himself as a character actor more than a star (which he sees mobi-lizing movie goers en masse – an essentially commercial understanding). In his German press coverage, there is more of an acceptance of his commercial appeal. Nonetheless, this is invariably linked to his presentation as a star who is also, indeed foremost, a credible actor.[10]

East Germany had its own particularity around its celebrated actors. In the 1940s and 1950s, East Germany developed a parallel but different kind of star sys-tem to that which functioned in West Germany. As far as back as the period of the rubble films, discourse about everyday character actors versus stars helped dis-tinguish DEFA cinema from West German cinema.[11] During the 1950s, however, DEFA and East German cultural officials started to cultivate a kind of alternative star system to the West, one that has been described as a system favouring the 'Publikumsliebling' or 'audience favourite' over the Hollywood-oriented dis-course of the term 'star'.[12] 'Publikumsliebling' emphasizes the relationship of the actor to the audience, underscoring the importance of the people they serve and therefore, in the discourse about star and celebrity, their ordinariness over and against the extraordinariness of the Western counterparts. Press accounts of Mühe into the mid-1990s referenced him as a 'Publikumsliebling' in his GDR years, making him, it might be noted, an unusual transitional figure within the discourse of German stardom.[13]

By the time Mühe was making his mark in the GDR system of the 1980s, the era of the antifascist star was largely over, and East German cinema was reacting to developments in film, and in casting, brought about in the FRG by the success of the New German Cinema. Mühe's first celebrated film role came in a kind of literary heritage film about Hölderlin, *Hälfte des Lebens* (Half of Life, Herrmann Zschoche, 1985), which can be viewed as a dual reaction to the New German Cin-

---

10 Claudia Fellmer, 'Armin Mueller-Stahl: From East Germany to the West Coast', in *The German Cinema Book*, ed. by Tim Bergfelder, Erica Carter and Deniz Göktürk (London: BFI, 2002), pp. 94–95
11 See Jaimey Fisher, *Disciplining Germany. Youth, Reeducation and Reconstruction after the Sec-ond World War* (Detroit: Wayne State, 2007), pp. 213–15.
12 Fellmer, 'Armin Mueller-Stahl', p. 91.
13 Ulrich Mühe and Christian Schröder, '"Bin ich nicht mitgeschwommen?" Ulrich Mühe und die geschlossene Gesellschaft eines U-Bootes', *Tagesspiegel*, 21 March 1993.

ema, both in its literary orientation and in its casting of Mühe, a rising theatre star. As Thomas Elsaesser outlines, New German Cinema saw the rise of a number of new, younger stars, many of whom had previously created a name for themselves in the theatre world and who then crossed over to become the kind of character-actor star that would be a mark of distinction in many films of the time. Several of these figures went on to enjoy a level of international renown that would foreshadow Mühe's worldwide appeal (such as Bruno Ganz or, even better known internationally, Hanna Schygulla). As Elsaesser also notes, this era was marked not so much by the establishment of a certain image for a given actor, but rather was 'intertextuality sufficiently stable enough to give the impression of a coherent fictional universe although sufficiently variable to inhibit typecasting'.[14] Against the US system of stardom, which thrives on typecasting (e.g. Arnold Schwarzenegger or Jack Nicholson), in German cinema in the West, and from the 1980s increasingly the East, there was an emphasis on 'high-visibility character actors' who had crossover appeal from theatre. Mühe was part of this trend.[15]

The 1990s witnessed a change in this mode of cinema and a subsequent shift in the nature of Germany's highest profile actors. As Malte Hagener has argued, the trajectory of the casting and star system in the 1990s followed the general turn in the industry toward commercial concerns. Discussing the emergence of a stronger system of professional agents after 1994, Hagener regards the cultivation and promotion of stars like Til Schweiger in line with increasing talk of 'US-script manuals', 'plot points and box office returns'[16] – all of which were drivers of a postwall cinema of consensus, as Eric Rentschler has influentially termed it.[17] Schweiger was a typical star of the 1990s German cinema of consensus, not least for his association with producer Bernd Eichinger, who consciously staged his discovery of stars, largely for marketing reasons. Although Schweiger did have some theatre training (in Cologne) and some stage experience (in Bonn), he embodied a shift from the theatre-based, character-actor stars of the New German Cinema to a conceptualization of stardom based on the increased integration of the television and film industries.[18] Having started on a fairly minor stage far away from Berlin's historically celebrated theatres, Schweiger garnered his first sub-

---

14 Thomas Elsaesser, *New German Cinema* (New Brunswick: Rutgers University Press, 1989), p. 286.
15 Elsaesser, *New German Cinema*, p. 286.
16 Malte Hagener, 'German Stars of the 1990s', in *The German Cinema Book*, ed. by Tim Bergfelder, Erica Carter, and Deniz Göktürk (London: BFI, 2002) pp. 98–106 (p. 99).
17 Eric Rentschler, 'From New German Cinema to the Post-Wall Cinema of Consensus', in *Cinema and Nation*, ed. by Mette Hjort and Scott MacKenzie (New York: Routledge, 2000), pp. 260–77.
18 It is notable that, in December 2011, Schweiger, although he is one of German cinema's biggest 'stars', agreed to return to the television series *Tatort*.

stantive attention on the long-running TV show *Lindenstraße* (1985-). Perhaps unsurprisingly, this shift also impacted performance style. Hagener emphasizes the more casual style of Schweiger's acting, along with that of his contemporaries such as Moritz Bleibtreu or Katja Riemann, far removed from the work of German actors from the preceding decades: Schweiger's 'physical presence', he suggests, is relaxed to the point of negligence'.[19] Hagener regards this in stark contrast to the 'stilted and even histrionic' style of theatrically based German actors, which is, of course, not entirely fair to Mühe at least, as his restrained performance in *The Lives of Others* shows. As evidenced by the box-office success of *Keinohrhasen* (Rabbit Without Ears, 2007) – both directed by and featuring Schweiger as lead –, Schweiger remains an enormous star in Germany. Yet his peculiar bitterness towards the industry upon Eichinger's death in early 2011 demonstrates how the mode of commercial cinema signified by the likes of Eichinger and Schweiger is still contentiously debated in the country's wider cultural landscape. Indeed, as a number of scholars have argued, German cinema has changed since the early and mid-1990s, when genre films seemed ascendant and then dominant.[20] I want to argue that the rise of Mühe as star (and the resurrection of a different mode of stardom itself) in German cinema of the 2000s reflects further shifts in German film away from the 1990s cinema of consensus to a more serious, deliberative cinema. This shift is also reflected in a largely unexplored aspect of stardom, namely its historical-memorial function, a function that is particularly central to certain conceptualizations of many star personae in Germany.

Star-Theories: Of Social Types and Historical Memory

The more serious, post-1989 mode of Mühe's stardom allows us to nuance star studies as it has developed in Anglophone scholarship: the vagaries of the German *Sonderweg* of stardom can elucidate aspects of casting and stardom that have not garnered much systematic attention. While my approach here is certainly indebted to the most influential scholarly work on stars, Richard Dyer's

---

19 Hagener, 'German Stars', p. 99.
20 Paul Cooke and Christopher Homewood, 'Introduction: Beyond the Cinema of Consensus? New Directions in German Cinema since 2000', in *New Directions in German Cinema* (London: Tauris, 2011), pp. 1–20; Jaimey Fisher and Brad Prager, 'Introduction', in *The Collapse of the Conventional*, ed. by Jaimey Fisher and Brad Prager (Detroit: Wayne State University Press, 2010), pp. 1–38.

1979 work of that name, I also try to address German specificity, particulary as it is inflected by German history and what I term the 'memorial function' of the star in domestic film production. With the case study of *The Lives of Others* and Mühe's role in it, I would like to consider how Germany's national cinema can illuminate aspects of the global system of stardom on which Dyer does not so much focus.

In his book *Stars*, Dyer combines sociology and semiology to break away from the text-based, psychoanalytic approaches of much 1970s film studies, a foreshadow of, as well as indelible influence on, the 1980s and 1990s turn to cultural studies and historical context. He attends not only to a film or even series of films, but also to promotion and publicity surrounding the star, especially advertisements and reviews that help construct a star's image extra-filmically. Dyer highlights how stars often stand in a contradictory relationship to their broader socioeconomic constellation, both confirming and transcending the context around them, conceptualized around dual axes of 'ordinariness' versus 'extraordinariness'.[21] This is fundamentally a sociological analysis, defining the star as one of a variety of social types, the concept itself viewed as an important social phenomenon operating within, and constructed by, a specific ideological context.[22]

The Lives of Others, however, raises equally intriguing and largely neglected questions about the star and how it intersects not only with society, but also history and historical events. Of course, the society and social discourse to which the star stands in contradictory relation is always already historical, but it is telling that this historical aspect is often obscured by the star themselves – indeed, one of the star's social functions seems to be to negate the unpleasant aspects of the passing of time and thus our shock at seeing a star age. But what if an actor can serve, in a different mode, not so much as a social, but rather a historical type? In such a model, the actor, and the casting of that actor, might serve not only a social function, but also a historical function, even operating as a memorial to a past age. In these cases, casting choices of a given star would be informed not only by the social type relating to his or her iconography and performance, nor solely by the commercial concerns normally evoked in discussion of stars, but also by their (constructed) historical or memorial value. This mode of stardom, it should be noted, is not limited to Germany. To take one moment in film history, there seems to have been, in Germany and beyond, an explosion of self-consciously historical or memorial casting of films in the 1960s and 1970s. In his *Last Picture Show* (1971), for example, Peter Bogdanovich insisted on casting Ben Johnson, an old

---

21 Richard Dyer, *Stars* (1979; London: BFI, 1998).
22 For further discussion of the star as sociological phenomenon see Edgar Morin, *The Stars* (Minneapolis: University of Minnesota Press, 2005).

cowboy type associated mainly with John Wayne's Westerns.[23] Revealingly, this casting choice had to negotiate historical conditions and generational change of the late 1950s and early 1960s. Famously, Johnson did not want to take the role if he would have to put up with too much swearing around him. Bogdanovich ultimately prevailed upon him, and his presence in the film, just by his very casting, helps register within the plot the fundamental historical change that underpins the project.

Within a German context, the way a star can be endowed with memorial value takes on added significance given the trajectory of German history since the invention of cinema and the emergence of the star system. In ways that have hitherto been little explored, casting choices sometimes cross well-known historical caesurae. One example about which I have written elsewhere is the first post-Second World War star vehicle in Germany, the US-licensed ... *und über uns der Himmel* (The Heavens Above, Josef von Báky, 1947). This deliberately, but controversially, cast the biggest male star from the Nazi period, Hans Albers. Albers's iconography and extra-filmic discourse display the standard social contradictions for a celebrated star, with his happy-go-lucky image and the fetishization of his baby face and especially blue eyes. But his coding also intersected a specific historical moment, given his reputation, on the one hand, as someone who had enormous success during the Nazi time and yet, on the other, manifested (at least rumoured) resistance to the worst of Nazi crimes. Of course any such resistance had to be a matter primarily of conscience and not action, as he continued to be a high-profile figure throughout the regime.[24] The casting choice of a happy-go-lucky, conscientiously if not overtly objecting star seems an over-determined deployment for the first US-licensed film of the postwar period. However, such a historically-informed casting choice could help postwar audiences negotiate both the rampant nihilism the omnipresent rubble seemed to exude and tricky questions of complicity that their favourite cultural figures, and by extension they themselves, might need to face. To recast Dyer's ordinary-and-extraordinary binary historically, Alber's was indeed a historical story of extraordinary success during the Nazi time yet (putatively) ordinary internal resistance to the Nazis, a story that would serve clear historical and memorial functions for postwar audiences.

---

23 Peter Biskind, *Easy Riders, Raging Bulls. How the Sex-Drugs-and-Rock'n'roll Generation Saved Hollywood* (New York: Simon & Schuster, 1998), p. 121.
24 See Fisher, *Disciplining Germany*, pp. 213–44.

Mühe as GDR Star in the 'Normalizing' 1990s

If a star embodies a social type – as Dyer and others have suggested – German stars can also embody certain historical types, especially figures important at specific moments of historical transition, of which Germany has had more than its share across the history of cinema. The importance of this aspect of stardom in Mühe's case would vary the sort of New-German-Cinema-influenced stardom important early in his career and, I argue, will also end up reflecting changes in the mode of stardom that became important in the 1990s with actors like Schweiger or Riemann. In 1992, Mühe ended his full contract at the Deutsches Theater, and, as he suggests in interviews, this departure signalled a deliberate decision to dedicate himself to film work 'for the next ten years'. Throughout the mid-1990s, amid theatrical stints in Vienna (including at the Burgtheater) and Hamburg, he accepted a wide range of film and television roles, including comedies such as *Schtonk!* (Helmut Dietl, 1992) and *Peanuts: Die Bank zahlt alles* (Peanuts: The Bank Pays Everything, Carlo Rola, 1996), the memorably titled children's film *Rennschwein Rudi Rüssel* (Racing Pig Rudi Snout, Peter Timm, 1995), three films by Michael Haneke (*Benny's Video*, 1992, *Das Schloss* [The Castle], 1996, *Funny Games*, 1997) and a series of historical dramas. Given the diversity of work he took up in this period – not least, as he admits, for financial reasons because: 'I learned fast that capitalism is no fun unless you have some money'[25] – and the dominance of historical drama within German film production, it is perhaps not a surprise that he appeared in a number of historical films.[26] However, within the context of this present discussion, it is interesting to note it is his work in historical drama, more than the comedies, television series, or even his work with Haneke, that were repeatedly the focus of his coverage in the media, such films invariably being tied to his own biography.

Of particular focus in his persona as it was created in the media at the time was his experience of the last stages of the GDR and the 1989 'Veränderungen' (or 'changes' as he usually called them in interviews, seeming deliberately to avoid the word '*Wende*', as one piece in the *Süddeutsche Zeitung* noted).[27]

---

25 Thomas Thieringer, 'Das Kapital: Ulrich Mühe rettet seinen Erfahrungsschatz aus der DDR. "Nicht der Schauspieler ist das Zentrum, das Zentrum ist die Figur"', *Süddeutsche Zeitung*, 10 March 1993.

26 Among others: *Der kleine Herr Friedemann* (The Little Mr. Friedemann, Peter Vogel, 1990), *Jugend ohne Gott* (Godless Youth, Michael Knof, 1991), *Ende der Unschuld* (End of Innocence, Frank Beyer, 1991), *Das letzte U-Boot* (The Last Submarine, Frank Beyer, 1993), *... nächste Woche ist Frieden* (... Next Week is Peace, Peter Schulze-Rohr, 1995), *Nikolaikirche* (Frank Beyer, 1995).

27 Schröder, 'Von Kunst mag er nur selten sprechen'.

Although only one of these historical dramas (all of which were made for TV, two also having theatrical releases) was about the end of the GDR, the press connected all of them to Mühe's own experiences in 1989/1990, perhaps also because three of them were directed by Frank Beyer, the celebrated DEFA director. Two concerned the end of the Second World War and the confusion bred of such transitional moments in history. In Beyer's *Das letzte U-Boot* (The Last Submarine, 1993), Mühe played the commander of a submarine that was carrying plans for an atomic bomb to Japan when the crew learns of the German surrender. Mühe's character has to decide whether to carry on with the mission after the end of the regime, the various options open to him being represented by the various views of those in the sub, including a resistance-oriented German general, some officers committed to the 'Endsieg' (final victory) and two Japanese officers who favour delivery. Mühe recounts in multiple interviews that he understood the Second World War commander's frame of mind from his own experience of the end of the GDR. This was an individual, he suggests, who had some control and power in a fragile situation, but also wanted to be careful to protect himself – a position that also forces him to question what he did throughout the newly defunct and discredited regime.[28]

In 1995, he made another film set in 1945 ... *nächste Woche ist Frieden* (... Next Week is Peace, Peter Schulze-Rohr), in which a radio producer who has up to this point survived the regime by keeping a low profile, decides in the last weeks of the War to hide a Jewish woman. In interviews, Mühe again tied this act to his own experience. While offering the obvious caveats about comparing these two very different historical periods, he cites the essential parallels of living in a dictatorship and his experience of having to negotiate individual ethical action without getting 'burned' by the authorities.[29] It is telling that both of these films are set in the historically liminal time at the end of the War, when the stranglehold grip of the regime suddenly unravelled. Although qualifying the comparisons, both interviewers and Mühe nonetheless draw somewhat problematic parallels with the end of the GDR. However, for better or worse, such statements, made in multiple interviews in some of Germany's most prominent newspapers, underscore his status as a star with a strong historical dimension to his persona.

---

28 Schröder, 'Von Kunst mag er nur selten sprechen'; Ulrich Mühe and Christian Schröder, '"Bin ich nicht mitgeschwommen?" Ulrich Mühe und die geschlossene Gesellschaft eines U-Bootes', *Tagesspiegel*, 21 March 1993.
29 Ulrich Mühe and Thomas Klug, '"Menschlichkeit bewahren": Ulrich Mühe über seine Rolle in ... *nächste Woche ist Frieden*', *Berliner Zeitung*, 25 April 1995.

Two other works from this period linked Mühe explicitly with the GDR, not only in their marketing but also in their narratives. Given his later casting in *The Lives of Others*, it is also interesting to see how these films position him vis-à-vis questions of Stasi surveillance and GDR state violence. In *Der Blaue* (The Blue One, Lienhard Wawryzn, 1993–94), Manfred Krug plays Otto Skrodt, a Brandenburg veterinarian who has successfully made the transition from East Germany to the post-*Wende* era, now running a successful equestrian centre and having become a member of the Bundestag. At this post-*Wende* moment of triumph, however, Mühe's Kalle Kaminski appears from out of Skrodt's GDR past. Kaminski is Skrodt's former best friend (and lover of his daughter) on whom Skrodt informed for the Stasi. During the GDR period, Kaminski had attempted to flee to the West on an inflatable raft, but was somehow discovered and then spent three years in prison for reasons – or rather, due to a betrayal – he could never fathom. Mühe's Kaminski thus appears as a kind of GDR ghost that upsets Skrodt's plan to move ahead and up in the new Germany, where the latter has become friends with a federal cabinet minister and stands to become a deputy minister (*Staatssekretär*). Skrodt contacts his former Stasi handler because he decides that he has to be rid of Kaminski to clear the way for his future. The film is full of Stasi files, steaming open letters and betrayals of friendship, but here Mühe plays the victim of the Stasi throughout. He is at the centre of a web of friends and lovers that otherwise blurs the lines between perpetrator and victim, a constellation that would be engaged, but also simplified, in *The Lives of Others*.

The last of Mühe's mid-1990s historical dramas with Beyer, *Nikolaikirche* (1995), explicitly references the recent events of 1989 and similarly foreshadows von Donnersmarck's theme of the Stasi. The story of East German dissent and conformity is mapped onto fictional siblings, Astrid and Sascha, played by West-German actors Barbara Auer and Ulrich Matthes. Mühe plays a pastor at the eponymous Leipzig church that was involved in the famous Monday demonstrations of 1989. Astrid and Sascha's father was a general in the GDR security services, and Sascha has followed in his ideological footsteps by becoming a Stasi officer. Astrid, on the other hand, is disgusted with, and increasingly resistant to, the regime. Although the film focuses on tensions within the family, Mühe's role is key to this film's broader historical dimension, Pastor Ohlbaum giving memorable sermons to the growing congregation at the Nikolaikirche, crowds that reached some 70,000 by October 1989. Moreover, Mühe played an important role in the marketing of the film. Once again, his work in a film about the dilemmas and decisions faced by individuals in transitional times was linked to his own personal experience. In this case, the political function of this religious figure was presented as a mirror image of his conceptualization of his job as an actor in the GDR, which he saw performing a similarly political function at the time.[30]

Millennial Shifts and the Lead up to *The Lives of Others*

Mühe's late 1990s and early 2000s career was also shaped by television, which, as already noted in our discussion of Til Schweiger, played a particularly important role within German conceptualizations of stardom in the 1990s. In 1997 Mühe committed to a leading role in the television series *Der letzte Zeuge* (The Last Witness, 1998–2006), in which he played an idiosyncratic and sardonic forensic doctor.[31] If, in the US star system, television is generally considered a sort of minor league out of which stars are sometimes promoted and to which they might be demoted once again, Mühe's choice demonstrates how television was more interwoven with film in Germany at the time, evident not only in the 'cinema of consensus' but also in the growing predominance of private television in the German media landscape.[32] When Mühe was asked why such a well-known and accomplished actor would agree to a recurring television role, he cited the inconsistency of the German film industry, both in terms of the roles on offer and the quality of specific scripts. It was not an industry that he could rely on.[33] He also complained that decent roles for more mature actors were growing ever more rare, contrasting the German film industry to that of the US. Consequently, he felt, an actor like himself is well advised to take a recurring television role in order to stay present for the young film directors who now dominate the scene. This is why, in the early 2000s shortly before his casting in *The Lives of Others*, this former theatre star's highest-profile media presence was a recurring TV role.

While this choice of a TV role is in some ways contiguous with the 1990s interweaving of popular television with consensus-driven genre films, Mühe's cast-

---

30 Ulrich Mühe, 'Mann mit Botschaft. Ein Gespräch mit dem Schauspieler Ulrich Mühe', *Stuttgarter Zeitung*, 15 May 2001.

31 In many reviews and interviews, it was emphasized that in Germany such doctors are not allowed to undertake criminal investigations. Instead this was an expansive conceit taken from US television.

32 Although *Der letzte Zeuge* was shown on ZDF (a public television station), the main public stations (ARD and ZDF) have themselves been irrevocably transformed by the growth of private television over the past three decades.

33 Ulrich Mühe and Harald Heinzinger, '"Wir sind zarte Wesen". Ulrich Mühe wieder als Dr. Kolmaar im ZDF – Ein Gespräch', *Stuttgarter Zeitung*, 30 April 2002.

ing was nonetheless also, once again, linked to his GDR past and, in particular, his place as a theatre star. Even ten years after the fall of Wall and his many different roles, his historical experience was still a central aspect of his stardom: his presence on a primetime television series still evoked historical memory of the two Germanys and the changes that ended them. Many of the interviews about *Der letzte Zeuge* emphasize how many former GDR-theatre people were working on the show. In fact, one interview refers to the veto-power (*Mitspracherecht*) of Mühe over the show and suggests that he only agreed to the series because he was able to hire a group of colleagues and acquaintances from his time in the GDR, especially from the pre-*Wende* Deutsches Theater – production conditions that Mühe did not deny. In fact, aside from his complaint about the German film industry, the other major factor he cited in his taking the role was that he was offered a 'package deal' to work with people with whom he wanted to collaborate.[34] The show employed, and brought to prominence, the writer Gregor Edelmann, whom Mühe had met through Heiner Müller (how many primetime TV shows can credit someone like Heiner Müller as their matchmaker?). The series also employed the director Bernhard Stephan and the actor Jörg Gudzuhn, both of whom Mühe had worked with at the Deutsches Theater.[35] To underscore his camaraderie with Gudzuhn, multiple interviews mention a game that he and Mühe regularly played during takes, a game of trying to get in the last word, each improvising (as they often did) additional dialogue until the director finally said cut. The image offered here of the popular and critically acclaimed show, then, was one of fun and games for cultural producers identified with the former GDR and with the entire theatre world that had been lost with it.

This lost theatre world of the GDR is another recurring topic in interviews and profiles from the late 1990s right up to 2004 when Mühe was cast in von Donnersmarck's film. Although Mühe emphasizes his playful delight about working with colleagues from the GDR, he is also clear that he does not think much of television, which he regards as fundamentally a 'consumer-medium'. Affecting indifference to the show, he pretends that he has forgotten plot points about which interviewers ask and refers repeatedly to 'needing to pay the rent' (an observation softer than his earlier, abovementioned comment: 'Capitalism is no fun unless you have some money'). Suggesting a dynamic but at times vexed relationship between film, theatre and television, interviews consistently ask him how he, as an accomplished theatre actor, ended up leaving the ensemble of Germany's most

---

34 Ulrich Mühe and Iris Schmid, 'Kein Alter Ego: Ulrich Mühe über seine Rolle im *Letzten Zeugen*', *Stuttgarter Zeitung*, 31 March 2005.
35 Mühe and Schmid, 'Kein Alter Ego'.

celebrated theatre in 1992. His responses are revealingly different to those answers he gave in the mid-1990s, shortly after he had left the Deutsches Theater and when he had repeatedly referred to his understanding of theatre as political and acting as a kind of political career. These post-2000 interviews and profiles foreground instead the social, rather than political, function of theatre and his confusion before a changing audience – as with his line about the rent, he seems to have learned a certain idiom of post-unification discourse.[36] Looking back from the early 2000s, he admits that by the early 1990s, he 'did not know what kind of audience he was performing in front of' at the Deutsches Theater, and was not happy with the direction of the theatre because he had always considered it a moral and didactic institution that could intervene in social debates.[37] The theatre in Germany of the 1990s had no way, he felt, to address the issues of the day.[38] Mühe's stardom from this time suggests the continued importance of television in the public understanding of his persona. Nonetheless, it is very different to the way television functions in the stardom of a figure like Til Schweiger. For all its centrality to the actor's continued visibility within the German cultural landscape, theatrical 'high culture' remains of paramount importance, even as Mühe discusses a television role. Moreover, it anticipates the post-2000 careers of another generation of cinema stars such as Nina Hoss and Ulrich Matthes – two marquee names now tending not so much to blockbusters as to art-house films who also both belong to the ensemble of the celebrated theatre Mühe left the decade before. This mode of mixed stardom, revived from the New German Cinema in Mühe's career and alive in Hoss and Matthes reflects or, at least parallels, broader developments in the cinema landscape since 2000.

Leading up to his casting in *The Lives of Others*, Mühe continued this kind of post-1990s balancing act. For instance, in an interview given shortly before the premiere of *The Lives of Others* at the 2005 Munich Film Festival and before it went on to win the audience prize at the Locarno Film Festival in August 2005, Mühe emphasizes the diversity of his on-going work, giving only cursory mention to von Donnersmarck's film. The fiftieth episode of *Der letzte Zeuge* was about to be broadcast and he said he was open to more. At the same time, he informs us that he was about to leave for the Avignon Theatre Festival to perform in a play by the British playwright Sarah Kane (*Blasted*) and that he would soon be shooting a film about an adventuring archaeologist, based on what he called a 'Harrison-

---

36 Mühe and Schmid, 'Kein Alter Ego'.

37 Mühe and Heinzinger, 'Wir sind zarte Wesen'.

38 Ulrich Mühe, '"Ist doch toll": Ulrich Mühe über sein Leben im Niemandsland aus Fernsehen, Film und Theater', *Tagesspiegel*, 16 April 2000.

Ford dramaturgy'.[39] One wonders if this last project was tied to the envy he mentioned of available, quality roles for middle-aged and even senior actors in the US, including Harrison Ford. This was a career interwoven with his GDR past that remained a central part of his stardom over fifteen years after the fall of the Wall, but it is also symptomatic of the complex, unfolding dynamic of German stardom across television, film and theatre.

Given his historically informed and inflected stardom, it is certainly not a surprise, then, that von Donnersmarck would turn to Mühe, or that Mühe would be initially sceptical of accepting this role from a young German from the West (by way of the US). He was sent, he recounts, many scripts about the GDR past and tended, with the exception of *Nikolaikirche* and *Der Blaue*, to avoid them, even as he worked extensively in the German media's heritage industry. But *The Lives of Others*, playing as it does in the theatre world of the 1980s, certainly seemed relevant to his experience as well as to his stardom, and after quizzing von Donnersmarck on his knowledge of the Stasi milieu – gained by reading his own file – Mühe seemed convinced. I would underscore, however, how the role that would come to define his legacy would both continue and extend the kind of historically-based stardom I sketch above. In interviews and profiles from the late 1990s and early 2000s, there was hardly any mention of the Stasi. Certainly, there was an awareness of the brutality of the regime (as suggested in the parallels he drew between his experience of the GDR and National Socialism in discussions of his historical dramas) and he avoided any engagement with the *Ostalgie* wave. But he did not foreground his own experience of the Stasi until *The Lives of Others*.

This connection is made in the volume published by Suhrkamp to accompany the release of the film, the longest contribution to which, besides the 100-page script, is an extended interview with Mühe, highlighting the film's self-identification with the discourse around its biggest star. One moment in his interview with Christoph Hochhäusler and von Donnersmarck is particularly telling, both about Mühe's past and how that past functions for the two interviewers and for the authenticity problem of the film discussed above. Hochhäusler and von Donnersmarck are both directors a generation younger than Mühe, both were teenagers from West Germany when the Wall fell; Hochhäusler is, of course, a celebrated director in his own right, a founder of the journal *Revolver* and one of the key figures of the Berlin School. The interview has a trajectory that is telling: it arcs from discussion of the details of Mühe's involvement in the project to making

---

39 Ulrich Mühe and Carla Woter, '"Grauenhaft. Das würde ich ablehnen": Schauspieler Ulrich Mühe über Homestorys, Schmerzgrenzen und 50 Folgen als TV-Pathologe,' *Tagesspiegel*, 1. April 2005.

him a kind of historical native informant about the Stasi, one that lends the film a very useful authenticity. This represents a shift from his stardom of the mid-1990s when the media coverage of the heritage works discussed above did bring up his past (contra von Donnersmarck's statements), but tended to focus on the behaviour of an individual negotiating a moment of transition time – finding echoes of his own experience with the transitional, heroic individuals, invariably ahead of their historical time, he plays in these films.

When Hochhäusler and von Donnersmarck ask Mühe about his personal experiences with the Stasi, Mühe initially demurs, saying that he does not want to highlight his own experience, since he was not one of those who really suffered. Even if he had been under surveillance since his military service (when he wrote a letter to a friend critical of the army that was intercepted by the Stasi and landed in his file), Mühe says he still regards himself as someone who ended up on the 'sunny side' of the regime, able to do what he wanted – namely act – and, indeed, at the highest level. Von Donnersmarck and Hochhäusler, however, press him to repeat an anecdote he apparently told von Donnersmarck when they were shooting *The Lives of Others*, about a moment when, at a highpoint in his GDR career and a few years before the Wall fell, the state authorities once again made their powerful presence known to him. Mühe initially resists recounting it in the interview, again arguing that he was not someone who had really suffered. However, Hochhäusler suggests that precisely because this kind of show of force seems quotidian, even minor, to Mühe, it is important that he share it with a younger (and in particular Western) generation that can have no idea of what life was really like in the GDR. Mühe then recalls that in 1986, as noted above, he was cast in *Das Spinnennetz*, with Bernhard Wicki as director. This was a role that brought him an international profile. He was given a passport and visa so that he could cross over to Wicki's shoot, but which he also used to go to the theatre and visit with friends. One day, at the age of thirty-three and already well established as one of East Germany's best known actors, he received a draft notice ordering him to a doctor to see if he were fit for military service. When he reminded the doctor that he had had a stomach operation that had seen him discharged from the NVA, the doctor listened and then declared him fit for duty. Called before the draft board, he listened to them remind him that they could call him back to serve at any time. He recounts in the interview that, sitting powerless before them, he wanted to cry, but fought not to in front of them. As soon as he was out, however, he curled up in a corner and wept. The day after this disquieting meeting, he told Dieter Mann, the artistic director of the Deutsches Theater, about the episode, and Mann said to let him see what he could do. He came back ten minutes later from his office and informed him that it was taken care of. They would not bother him anymore. With this apparently happy end to the anecdote, Mühe then loops back to something the three had discussed earlier in the interview – he says at precisely that moment, the nature of a dictatorship was clear to him, not so much that he could have been called in by the state authorities, who were clearly committed to reminding him of their hold over him, but that a single phone call by the director of the theatre could solve any such problem. It reminded him of the privileges he had, privileges arbitrarily created, revoked, and granted anew by the state.[40]

This anecdote, told to two of Germany's most prominent young directors, seems especially relevant to my present discussion because it links the East German state authorities to the global film industry of which they are also a part – Wicki was after all one of the few internationally known directors and film figures from the German-speaking world before New German Cinema. The intimidation by the East German authorities seems geared to keep Mühe from the world industry of international art-house cinema, with which he was clearly enjoying working during the making of *Das Spinnennetz* and to which he initially returned post-1989 in his work with Haneke.

Mühe's anecdote to Hochhäusler and von Donnersmarck also demonstrates how, despite his initial resistance, Mühe could now be deployed discursively as a victim of the regime, something that he had generally avoided in earlier interviews and profiles. This foreshadows the protracted legal fight he would subsequently face with his ex-wife Jenny Gröllmann, who is alleged to have informed on him for the Stasi. These allegations emerged at around the same time as the film was to be released, and, in fact, the interview from which I quoted above was substantively cut due to the Gröllmann lawsuit. There is no evidence (as some of Mühe's critics have alleged) that he deliberately foregrounded these allegations for marketing purposes.[41] The details of Gröllmann's alleged work for the Stasi

---

40 Ulrich Mühe, Florian Henckel von Donnersmarck and Christoph Hochhäusler, '"Es hat schon viele viele Versuche gegeben, die DDR-Realität einzufangen": Ein Gespräch mit Ulrich Mühe', in Florian Henckel von Donnersmarck, *Das Leben der anderen. Filmbuch* (Frankfurt/Main: Suhrkamp, 2006), pp. 182–200.

41 Mühe and Gröllmann met each other during the making of *Hälfte des Lebens* (Half of Life, Herrmann Zschoche, 1984), in which she starred opposite Mühe, and they were married from 1984 until 1990. Around the time of the release of *The Lives of Others*, Mühe publically stated his bitterness concerning Gröllmann's work with the Stasi, about which he apparently found out only post-2000 from a magazine. Stasi files linked to her included information about Mühe, although there is some controversy as to whether she actually reported the material attributed to her – there are cases in which Stasi officers lied about and exaggerated the information gained from informants, certainly a much more common form of mendacity than lying to protect subjects, as in von Donnersmarck's script. Gröllmann died of cancer in the summer of 2006 and Mühe in the summer of 2007, but the controversy continued well past their deaths. In 2008, a Gerare very murky and probably will never be known, but they are not essential to Mühe's casting or the success of his performance in *The Lives of Others*. As I have tried to argue in this chapter, it was clear well before *The Lives of Others* or the revelations about his ex-wife that Mühe, as one of unified Germany's best known and most celebrated actors, enjoyed a stardom that was thoroughly interwoven with his GDR past. His extra-filmic notoriety illuminates an aspect of stardom that has been largely been missing from Anglophone studies of the star. In the cases of actors like Hans Albers or Ulrich Mühe, this historical aspect of stardom – the star not so much, or not only as, a social type, but also a historical type – is certainly relevant to their careers and, textually speaking, to the caesura-bridging, epoch-spanning films they made. Whether or not this historical-memorial aspect of the German *Sonderweg* to stardom will continue to be relevant in the present age of normalization, only time, or rather history, will tell.

---

man book on defamation appeared that cast Gröllmann as the victim of the controversy and accused Mühe of using her to promote *The Lives of Others*, underscoring the complexity of victim and perpetrator in matters Stasi. The controversy received much press in the German public sphere, although most of it after *The Lives of Others*' success. Given the popularity of the film, many tied the case of alleged spousal betrayal to its plot, although also acknowledging that the reality was considerably more complex than this fiction. For a good overview, see Frank Pergande, 'Die Schauspielerin, Ihr Mann und Ihr Liebhaber. Die Geschichte von Jenny Gröllmann und Ulrich Mühe klang ohnehin wie *Leben der Anderen*. Neuester Dreh. Ein postumer Rufmord', *Frankfurter Allgemeine Sonntagszeitung*, 2 March 2008; as well as Uwe Müller, 'Die verlorene Ehre des Ulrich M', *Berlin Morgenpost*, 16 January 2008. The importance of this story for von Donnersmarck, along with the controversy to which it gave rise, is also clear from its retelling in the director's contribution to this volume.

II. Re-positioning the Film

Andrea Rinke
CHAPTER FIVE
Fear and (Self-)Loathing in East Berlin: Gender and Melodrama in *The Lives of Others*

The Lives of Others has been read variously as a thriller,[1] a heritage film and a melodrama, as von Donnersmarck himself stressed in an early interview: 'I am making a melodrama with thriller elements, for which the closed system of the GDR offers an excellent background – like all totalitarian regimes. One just has to think of *Casablanca*'.[2] The term 'melodramatic' in everyday usage tends to connote an 'excess of sensation and sentiment, a manipulation of the heart-strings that exceeds the bounds of good taste'.[3] On the face of it, *The Lives of Others* does not look like a melodrama. The film is notable for its pronounced representational and performative restraint – a style conventionally associated with the concept of 'realism' or art-house cinema. The impassive performance of its central figure, Wiesler, and a muted visual colour scheme shape the sombre and understated mood of the film, evoking the overwhelming sense of oppression that dominated GDR society during the mid 1980s. However, in its ability to provoke strong emotions among a wide range of audiences, along with its narrative of redemption and moving musical score, *The Lives of Others* is a typical melodrama. And indeed, as Owen Evans and Jaimey Fisher have convincingly shown, the phenomenal international appeal of this low-budget debut film owes much to von Donnersmarck's skilful orchestration of universally understandable melodramatic conventions.[4]

---

1 Matthew Bernstein, '*The Lives of Others*: An emotive surveillance Thriller set in Communist East Germany', *Film Quarterly*, 61.1 (2007), 30–6; Eva Horn, 'Media of Conspiracy: Love and Surveillance in Fritz Lang and Florian Henckel von Donnersmarck', *New German Critique*, 35 (2008), 127–44.

2 Von Donnersmarck in an interview with Philipp Lichterbeck, 'Die innere Wahrheit der DDR. Die Stasi-Falle. Wie in Mitte gerade ein Film über die Angst im Sozialismus gedreht wird', *Tagesspiegel*, 5 December 2004. And indeed von Donnersmarck's film contains an homage to *Casablanca* (Michael Curtiz, 1942) in the name of the surveillance process, 'Operation Laszlo'.

3 Linda Williams, 'The American Melodramatic Mode', in *Playing the Race Card. Melodramas of Black and White from Uncle Tom to O.J Simpson*, ed. by Linda Williams (Princeton and Oxford: Princeton University Press, 2001), pp. 10–44 (p. 11).

4 Owen Evans, 'Redeeming the demon? The legacy of the Stasi in *Das Leben der Anderen*', *Memory Studies*, 3 (2010), 164–77; Jaimey Fisher, 'German historical Film as Production Trend: Euro-

A primary characteristic of melodrama is its appeal to pathos through the emotions of a suffering female character – indeed so much so that by the 1980s the term was used in academic discourse as a synonym for the 'woman's film'.[5] In *The Lives of Others*, it is the desire of three male characters for the female protagonist that drives the narrative and contributes to the film's affective impact. And it is the actress Christa-Maria Sieland (played by Martina Gedeck) – her fear and self-loathing, and the sympathy her suffering engenders with the audiences – who is the focal point of the melodramatic mode which permeates this film. Drawing on theories of melodrama and on Murray Smith's concept of 'engaging characters,' this chapter explores the ways in which the character of Sieland contributes to the film's appeal to pathos, inviting an emotional response from its audience.[6]

In *The Lives of Others*, all three main characters struggle with emotional and moral dilemmas revolving around questions of loyalty and betrayal. However, Sieland's dilemma is arguably more grave than those faced by Dreyman and Wiesler (a choice between Party loyalty and dissidence), and takes on a truly tragic dimension. Whereas the men's decision to resist state power is made in secret and therefore, in Dreyman's case, remains unpunished, the outcome of Sieland's choice between her love for Dreyman and her love for the stage is very much in the public domain – bound up with the decision to accept or to spurn the advances of one of the most powerful men in the country. There is no solution to these two mutually exclusive lines of action other than her death. Nevertheless, as this chapter aims to show, because the spectator is aligned to her situation and feels a strong allegiance to this character, her death is felt as a devastating shock. As Scott Holloran puts it, 'unlike *Life is Beautiful*, *Downfall*, *Munich* or any other variety of movie that trivializes evil, this story calculates a logical culmination of life under dictatorship [...]. The wrenching, violent climax [Sieland's death] is still moving beyond words'.[7]

The melodramatic combination of pathos and action in *The Lives of Others* seems largely divided into conventional male and female roles, in that Sieland,

---

pean Heritage cinema and Melodrama in *The Lives of Others*', in *The Collapse of the Conventional. German Film and its Politics at the Turn of the Twenty-first Century*, ed. by Jaimey Fisher and Brad Prager (Detroit: Wayne State University, 2010), pp. 186–215.

5 For a discussion of melodrama as a genre, see *Home is where the heart is. Studies in melodrama and the woman's film*, ed. by Christine Gledhill (London: BFI, 1987).

6 Murray Smith, *Engaging Characters. Fiction, Emotion and the Cinema* (Oxford: Oxford University Press, 1995).

7 Scott Holleran, 'German Movie Indicts Altruism by Implication', boxofficemojo (http://www.boxofficemojo.com/reviews/?id=2263&p=.htm).

for much of the film, represents the suffering victim who is eventually defeated, and Wiesler and Dreyman, while also suffering to some extent, are able to persevere as active heroes and ultimately win the moral battle between good and evil. Not surprisingly perhaps, the role of Christa-Maria Sieland has drawn scathing criticism from some quarters. Claudia Lenssen regrets that 'the woman at the apex of the drama remains passive, compliant and emotionally unstable'.[8] In a similar vein, Thomas Lindenberger critiques the 'banal misogyny' of the film: 'The female leading figure has to take the part of the weak, seduced, and guilty character, who, driven by her drug addiction and yearning for male recognition, fails in an exemplifying way'.[9]

However, this chapter aims to offer a more 'negotiated reading' of *The Lives of Others* to use Stuart Hall's term.[10] While acknowledging that the gender relations in the film can indeed be deconstructed from a feminist point of view, I argue that the female protagonist is more ambiguous than it might appear; and that a reading of her character within the parameters of melodrama offers a more positive interpretation which goes beyond the cliché of the vilified sexual femme fatale. Moreover, the success of the film owes much to its appeal to pathos (through the female protagonist), engaging its spectators in a more complex fashion than some critics have suggested. Gary Schmidt for instance, maintains that the film constructs hierarchical masculine/feminine binarisms that ascribe to the feminine qualities associated with materiality and corporeality, namely: temporality, corruptibility, and death.[11] However, such neat categorizations and sweeping generalizations can lead to descriptive inaccuracies and explanatory simplifications in the discussion of the rhetoric of this film, and the way in which the spectator engages with it.[12]

---

8 Claudia Lenssen, 'Die Rezeption des Films von Florian Henckel von Donnersmarck in Deutschland', *Verband der deutschen Filmkritik* (2007) (www.vdfk.de/137-schwerpunkt-2-rohrbach-und-die-folgen).

9 Thomas Lindenberger, 'Stasiploitation – Why Not? The Scriptwriter's Historical Creativity', *German Studies Review* 31.3 (2008), 557–610 (p. 562).

10 Stuart Hall, 'Encoding/decoding' in *Culture, Media, Language,* ed. by Stuart Hall, Dorothy Hobson, Andrew Lowe and Paul Willis (London: Routledge, 1980), pp. 128–38 (p. 137).

11 Gary Schmidt, 'Between Authors and Agents: Gender and affirmative Culture in *Das Leben der Anderen*', *The German Quarterly*, 82 (2009), 231–49 (p. 233).

12 For example, Hempf and Grubitz are very much associated with qualities Schmidt associates with femininity, i.e. 'materiality, corporeality and corruptibility'. Equally, Jerska, a male character, is associated with 'temporality' and 'death' by virtue of his suicide.

Spectator Engagement

In my exploration of the film's affective impact, with particular focus on the role of the female protagonist, I will be drawing on Murray Smith's theories of spectator engagement with fictional characters. Focusing on narrative analysis, he rejects psychoanalysis as too blunt an instrument and grounds his approach instead in analytic philosophy and cognitive anthropology.[13] In his book *Engaging Characters. Fiction, Emotion and the Cinema* he proposes that the spectator can respond to characters on three distinct but interrelated 'levels of engagement', which he calls 'recognition', 'alignment' and 'allegiance' and which together comprise the 'structure of sympathy'.

On the most basic level, the spectator 'recognizes' characters in terms of constructing these on the basis of previous knowledge of the genre and his or her own 'real life' experiences: 'While understanding that characters are artifices [...] we assume that these traits correspond to analogical ones we find in persons in the real world'.[14] On the second level, *textual* mechanisms 'align' the spectator with a specific character by letting us experience parts of the story through this figure. In other words, we as spectators are placed in 'alignment' with characters if the film gives us access to their actions, knowledge, thoughts and feelings. This can be achieved with narrative and filmic devices, such as our spacio-temporal attachment to the characters, their dialogue and performance, the camera work including optical point-of-view shots, the mise-en-scène and the film's musical score. The concept of 'allegiance' refers to the ways in which we choose (or refuse) to associate imaginatively with characters based on our evaluation of the moral values they embody.[15] In *The Lives of Others* the structure of alignment is centred predominantly on Wiesler whose perception (optical and aural) and imagination are our main conduit for the information the film provides. Relatively few instances of alignment with the other characters are offered to us, including Sieland. However, on the third level of 'allegiance' within the framework of the melodramatic mode, *The Lives of Others* also locates moral and affective power in the Sieland character. As the innocent, and hence virtuous victim, her character can function to provoke the spectator's disgust and moral indignation against her persecutors – contributing to the film's retrospective condemnation of the totalitarian regime in the GDR.

---

13 Smith, *Engaging Characters*, p. 5.
14 Smith, *Engaging Characters*, p. 82.
15 Smith, *Engaging Characters*, p. 75.

The choice of the GDR as 'background' for von Donnersmarck's 'universal story' of villainous abuse of power seems an obvious one, considering that he had firsthand experience of Stasi bullying during his childhood, a fact he has been keen to point out in interviews.[16] Some of his mother's relatives had stayed in East Germany, while her part of the family left before the Wall was built. Hence his mother, Anna Maria von Berg, was considered a traitor to the socialist cause, and was on one occasion held for hours to be strip-searched. This utterly shocked the young von Donnersmarck: 'That people would have the right to undress my mother! She seemed so powerful to us [...] The experience taught me an important lesson about the very nature of totalitarianism'.[17]

Spectator 'Recognition' – the Tragic Fall From a Great Height: Gedeck, Marta, Sieland

This memory of his mother, a dignified aristocratic lady, being humiliated by agents of the GDR regime may well have contributed to the conception of the film's female protagonist. The director's choice of actress, Martina Gedeck, is telling in this context: a tall, elegant and highly respected character actress, as well as one of the most popular female film stars in Germany, she embodies exactly the kind of charisma and star image von Donnersmarck envisaged: 'the Meryl Streep of Germany [...] a beautiful and impressive woman [...] perfect for this part'.[18]

The photos, interviews and other press releases posted on Gedeck's homepage tend to 'manufacture'[19] a star image of sensuality and glamour while at the same time highlighting the pride and vulnerability of the 'real person' Martina Gedeck.[20] The female protagonists Gedeck plays are often wilful, creative women who live (and suffer) passionately for their professional vocation – much like Sieland in *The Lives of Others* – including the gourmet chef *Bella Martha* (Mostly Martha, Sandra Nettelbeck, 2002), Gedeck's international breakthrough feature, and the acclaimed GDR writer Brigitte Reimann in *Hunger auf Leben*

---

16 Von Donnersmarck in an interview with Nina Freydag, 'Es braucht zehn Jahre, um über Nacht berühmt zu werden', *Brigitte,* March (2007), 104–5.

17 Florian Henckel von Donnersmarck, 'Thirteen Questions with Florian Henckel von Donnersmarck, Writer and Director of *The Lives of Others*', *The Lives of Others Press Booklet* (Sony Classic Films, n.d.) (http://www.sonyclassics.com/thelivesofothers/externalLoads/TheLivesof Others.pdf).

18 Donnersmarck on his DVD commentary.

19 Richard Dyer, *Heavenly Bodies. Film Stars and Society* (London: Routledge, 2003), p. 7.

20 For instance, references recur to her suffering after the suicide of her partner of many years.

(Hungry for Life, Markus Imboden, 2004), an award winning TV-biopic.[21] For German audiences in particular, the experience of *The Lives of Others* would have been enriched by their knowledge about Gedeck's star image. And for these viewers, seeing her in a screen role that very much resembled her own as a glamorous, sensitive and popular actress, the subsequent humiliation and destruction of her character would surely have carried a strong emotional impact.

There are a number of small but significant deviations in Gedeck's performance from von Donnersmarck's instructions in his screenplay, which seem to suggest some measure of influence in making her role more ambiguous than it appeared in the director's original concept – that is, dignified as well as desperate.[22] While von Donnersmarck initially seems to have wanted a straightforward melodramatic expression of ('feminine') hysteria – suggesting in the script that Sieland should 'implore' Dreyman in one scene (p. 67), should 'bury her face in her hands sobbing silently' in another (p. 85), or should express 'panic' (p. 112) – Gedeck's Sieland neither begs, cries nor panics in these scenes. Rather, she acts with great restraint, revealing mere glimpses of her inner turmoil under a mantle of dignified composure, thereby making the impact of her suffering much more poignant. Gedeck sublimates emotions into facial expressions, often captured in close ups on her eyes, and subtle gestures. For example, when Grubitz, during her first Stasi interrogation, asks her who wrote the subversive *Spiegel* article, she does not 'laugh hysterically' as the script suggests, but delivers a subdued, muted and more ambiguous response veering between a suppressed sob and a knowing smile.[23]

Gedeck stresses in an interview how important it is for her to have an emotional connection with her roles.[24] In *The Lives of Others* it was Sieland's sense of identity as an actress and the need to continue working at all costs that resonated particularly strongly with Gedeck herself:

---

21 She went on to play other women who were passionate about their 'calling', including the Romantic composer and wife of Robert Schumann in *Geliebte Clara* (Clara, Helma Sanders-Brahms, 2008) and the terrorist Ulrike Meinhoff in *Der Baader Meinhof Komplex* (The Baader Meinhof Complex, Uli Edel, 2009).

22 See von Donnersmarck's published screenplay *Das Leben der anderen. Filmbuch* (Frankfurt/M: Suhrkamp Verlag, 2006).

23 Von Donnersmarck, *Das Leben der anderen*, p. 123.

24 Gedeck in an interview with David Baum, 'Disziplin heißt ja nicht, daß man sich zu etwas zwingt', *Quest* (2006), 130, available on Martina Gedeck's homepage (www.martinagedeck.com).

> There is one thing I can relate to: if you want to call yourself an actor you have to prac-
> tise your profession permanently [...] We engage with and shape the unformed, testing the
> powers of imagination. We create a reality that would not otherwise exist. This is something
> you have to do regularly otherwise you lose the ability.[25]

The sensational pathos and action typical of melodrama operate to tap into our
need for 'moral legibility,' according to Peter Brooks.[26] Questions of moral justification – the basis of 'spectator allegiance' – are crucially related to the character
of Sieland and her tragic dilemma. Did she really need the Minister? Should she
have resisted his brutish advances more forcefully? Did she really need to reveal
the hiding place of the typewriter?

Due to Gedeck's nuanced performance, many viewers have tended to 'recognize' the Sieland character as 'true to life.' For instance, A.O. Scott of the *New York
Times* remarks:

> And even as they are, to some extent, enacting a morality play, the actors [in *The Lives of
> Others*] also seem like real, vulnerable people forced into impossible choices. This is es-
> pecially true of Ms Gedeck, whose natural nobility, her height, her carriage, the strong line
> of her jaw, makes Christa-Maria's half-hidden fragility all the more poignant.[27]

Sieland as Marta:
the Strong Socialist Heroine

Significantly, *The Lives of Others* first introduces Sieland in her professional role as
a performing artist in Dreyman's new play *Gesichter der Liebe* (Faces of Love). She
plays the factory worker Marta, whose passion, charisma and luminous beauty
dominate the screen (highlighted in close ups). However, like Sieland herself, the
character Marta is also a tragic heroine. She is cursed with prophetic visions of
death, in this case another worker's husband being crushed by an ominous 'giant

---

25 Gedeck in an interview with Christiane Peitz, 'Wenn es gut geht, tanzen wir miteinander', *Tagesspiegel*, 21 March 2007.
26 Peter Brooks, *The Melodramatic Imagination. Balzac Henry James, Melodrama, and the Mode
of Excess* (New Haven: Yale University Press, 1976), p. 64.
27 A.O. Scott, 'A Fugue for good German Men', *New York Times*, 9 February, 2007. Martina Gedeck
was – perhaps understandably – annoyed that von Donnersmarck did not invite her, as the female
lead, to attend the 2007 Academy Award ceremony but took his wife instead. Martina Gedeck
in an interview with Kathrin Buchner, 'Keine Einladung zur Oscar Feier', *Stern.de* (http://
www.stern.de/kultur/film/martina-gedeck-keine-einladung-zur-oscar-feier-582425.html).

machine'. Marta's vision on stage is thus very subtly linked to the rest of the film, as it foreshadows Sieland's own inevitable demise: she will be crushed by the Stasi machine.

Three separate scenes from the play are compiled in a montage that serves to characterize Marta, and by implication Sieland. The first sequence echoes Sieland's role as a popular performer: Marta is seen (through Wiesler's eyes) animatedly telling an amusing story while female workers crouch at her feet listening and smiling adoringly. In the second, we see a feisty Marta fending off a male worker's advances, grabbing him by the scruff of the neck and pushing him to the ground. In the third, Marta is shown dancing an energetic waltz with another female brigade member in an exuberant and comical performance which earns her Dreyman's smile and the audience's applause. All three sequences bear an uncanny resemblance to DEFA *Frauenfilme* –, films centred on female protagonists – in particular the national award winning *Alle meine Mädchen* (All my Girls, Iris Gusner, 1981) – and to these films' critique of male chauvinism in the workplace, where the main decisions are made by men in positions of power. Thus, the montage sequence in *The Lives of Others* shows Marta embodying the socialist ideal of the strong, emancipated woman, which Sieland plays with great gusto. Later in the film, this utopian ideal is contrasted with Sieland's abject off-stage position as the victim of male power abuse. The film seems to suggest that under 'real existing socialism' in the GDR, a society in which gender equality was proclaimed an accomplished fact, women could still find themselves at the mercy of the ruling male elite.[28]

Sieland: Expulsion from Paradise

The affective impact of Sieland's destruction is all the more powerful because she falls from a great height. Rather than being portrayed as weak from the outset of the film, she is first introduced as a self-assured and graceful woman. While Gedeck clearly plays her character as a highly strung, sensitive, and ultimately vulnerable artist, initially she also comes across as confident and strong – both in her role as a celebrated stage diva and in her loving relationship with Dreyman. The narrative cause-effect chain suggests that her spirited character is systemati-

---

28 Walter Ulbricht proudly proclaimed in 1968: 'If this [the emancipation of women] was the one and only achievement of socialism, it would suffice to prove its historical superiority' quoted in Andrea Rinke, *Images of Women in East German Cinema 1972–1982. Socialist Models, Private Dreamers and Rebels* (Lampeter: Edwin Mellen Press, 2006), p. 20.

cally crushed by totalitarian state power embodied by Minister Hempf: his relentless pursuit forces her into deceiving her lover, the inner conflict of which drives her to (illegal) anti-depressants.[29] These make her an easy target for arrest, interrogation and enforced compliance.

Drawing on Peter Brooks, Linda Williams posits that the narrative in melodrama 'usually begins when the villain intrudes upon an idyllic space'.[30] When Sieland is first introduced off stage at the post-premiere party, she is indeed presented as inhabiting a 'space of innocence', which the film celebrates by showing her dancing solo with Dreyman – enjoying her success and her love.[31] Previously, during an interval in the play, the spectator has seen her (through Wiesler's eyes) visit Dreyman's box for a clandestine romantic moment, smiling and kissing. Consequently, we 'recognize' her as a passionate, impetuous and carefree woman in a happy relationship. These moments of Sieland at the 'height of her game' are contrasted later in the film with her gradual descent into despair, as the Minister tightens his grip on her – laying waste to her innocence until it decays into guilt.

Much like the classical melodramatic villain, Hempf, the politician, intrudes upon the 'space of innocence', the artists' private party. As Sieland seems unaware of, and unconcerned by, the Minister's intense stare, he makes it known both to her and his rival that he will be ignored at their peril: he forcibly interrupts the live music and the couple's loving union. The villain proceeds to claim his fresh prey verbally and physically – with a toast and proprietary gesturing towards the actress: 'Christa-Maria Sieland. She is the most beautiful pearl of the GDR. I will not have anyone dispute this'. Cynically asking Dreyman's permission, but without waiting for a response, he grabs her by the shoulders and kisses her on both cheeks. The convergence of political and sexual coercion in this film is anticipated when his veiled threat ('the Party needs the artist but the artist needs the Party much more') cuts to a close up of his hand touching Sieland's behind. She is taken aback by his impudence, declines his offer to dance and hastily leaves the party with barely suppressed embarrassment.

We see Sieland next (in an extreme long shot from Wiesler's point of view) exiting from what turns out to be Hempf's car. As the film aligns us with Wiesler, we have no access to Sieland's thoughts and feelings. However, based on the cause-effect logic of the film's narrative, we might infer that Hempf's display of power at the premiere party the previous night – a combination of flattery, veiled

---

29 The film shows her taking a pill for the first time after her first private encounter with Hempf, and the second time after he has forced himself on her in his car. The narrative logic thus links her dependence on anti-depressants (called Aponeuron) to her sexual abuse by Hempf.
30 Williams, 'The American melodramatic mode', p. 21.
31 Brooks, *The Melodramatic Imagination*, p. 69.

threats and sexual harassment – has led to this encounter. We might also infer, based on Gedeck's performance in this scene, that she has done nothing ('morally') wrong at this early stage: she is seen striding across the road purposefully with her head held high.

Hempf's violation of the second, more private 'space of innocence' (by means of 'Operation Laszlo') is more clandestine. Dreyman and Sieland's spacious but cosy flat is experienced by Sieland (and Dreyman) as a safe haven from the outside world. The preparations for Dreyman's birthday party, with Sieland hanging up flower garlands, and the post-party love making scene can be read as an homage to the DEFA film *Die Legende von Paul und Paula* (The Legend of Paul and Paula, Heiner Carow, 1973), another celebration of a couple's (doomed) love, which von Donnersmarck admired: 'Carow was by far the greatest director of the GDR' and '*Die Legende von Paul und Paula* is one of the most beautiful love films of all time'.[32]

Sieland's party preparations are accompanied by the popular 1980s (GDR) song 'Versuch's mal mit Champagner' ('Why don't you try it with champagne') sung by Angelika Mann.[33] The female singer's words, in particular the refrain 'Drink champagne like life!' in this upbeat song about living life to the full, externalize Sieland's feelings and align us to her effervescent, confident mood. This effect is enhanced by the mise-en-scène and the dialogue before and after the birthday party. She is positioned above Dreyman, standing on a chair, while he hugs her legs like a little boy would his mother's; she teases him about his inability to bind a tie and about his appreciation of the – in her view – tacky birthday presents, and she initiates sex after the party. Their passionate feelings for each other during the ensuing love making sequence are expressed (non-diegetically) by Gabriel Yared's musical 'love theme' leitmotif that recurs later in the film.[34] The sequence thus contributes to the spectator's recognition of the Sieland character as a happy, confident woman before 'the fall', that is, before the regime, embodied by Hempf and Grubitz, knocks her down. The motif of the social order violating these private 'spaces of innocence' – as symbolized by the officers' knives brutally penetrating sofa cushions during the first flat search – converges with the motif of its violation of the innocent woman.

---

32 Donnersmarck, DVD commentary.

33 The songs are available on the soundtrack CD *Das Leben der Anderen*. Their lyrics are available at *ostmusik* (http://www.ostmusik.de).

34 On the soundtrack CD of *Das Leben der Anderen*, this tune is entitled *Gesichter der Liebe*, which is also the title of the play within the film starring Sieland. The music is thus linked to both the love she feels for Dreyman and her strong performance as Marta.

Spectator Allegiance with Sieland: Moral Indignation

Sieland's first sexual encounter with Hempf, filmed in a way that suggests rape, harks back to the earliest manifestations of the melodramatic mode.[35] These early works, as Thomas Elsaesser points out, featured a 'thoroughly corrupt yet seemingly omnipotent social class' who abused their 'superior political and economic power invariably by sexual aggression and attempted rape, leaving the heroine no other way out than to commit suicide'.[36] Von Donnersmarck is not the first to adapt the generic conventions of the 'Bürgerliches Trauerspiel' (Bourgeois Tragedy) to the socio-political context in the GDR. In fact the narrative of *Die Verfehlung* (The Mistake, 1992) by Heiner Carow, von Donnersmarck's favourite DEFA director, bears some resemblance to *The Lives of Others*.[37] Also a melodrama set in the GDR in the 1980s, *The Mistake* revolves around Elisabeth (played by Angelica Domröse) – the object of desire for two men at opposite ends of the political spectrum – who, like Sieland, is sexually assaulted by the man in power and punished for rejecting him.

The GDR in the 1980s, as Mary Fulbrook shows, was not a classless society but rather was ruled by what she calls a 'communist court', a small but highly privileged power elite.[38] *The Lives of Others* critiques not merely that power elite but also the fact that unequal – gendered – power relations still structured this allegedly 'egalitarian' society. Hempf is introduced as a Minister in the Cultural Department of the SED Central Committee – a position very close to the top of the political elite. Moreover, he used to be a powerful figure in the MfS who had artists such as Jerska, Dreyman's former stage director, blacklisted, and is hence a well-known and feared figure in Sieland's circle. His determination to have Sieland to himself and to fulfil his desire by any means necessary is further highlighted when he tells Grubitz to fabricate evidence against Dreyman: 'Find something. I wouldn't want to advise my worst enemy to disappoint me. And now beat it'. Minister Hempf's air of entitlement – of the right to take and treat a woman any

---

35 Owen Evans also points out the striking parallels in Minister Hempf's conduct and that of those early melodramatic villains. See Evans, 'Redeeming the demon?'.

36 Thomas Elsaesser, 'Tales of Sound and Fury: Observations on the Family Melodrama', in *Imitations of Life. A Reader on Film and Television Melodrama*, ed. by Marcia Landy (Detroit: Wayne State University Press, 1991), p. 68–91 (p. 70).

37 For a broader discussion of the relationship of the Bourgeois Tragedy tradition to the film see Marc Silberman's chapter in this volume.

38 Mary Fulbrook, *The People's State. East German Society From Hitler to Honecker* (New Haven and London: Yale University Press, 2005), p.180.

way he wishes – seems symptomatic of the powerful 'clique at the top' in the GDR at the time,[39] who treated their country like a 'Selbstbedienungsladen' (self service store).[40]

Rather than portraying Sieland as 'seduced' and therefore 'guilty', as Lindenberger claims,[41] *The Lives of Others* shows her first sexual experience with Minister Hempf to be dominated by fear – a stark contrast to her playful, sensual and passionate lovemaking with Dreyman. When she tries to walk away from Hempf's car, ignoring his first invitation, he changes his tone to a deep, menacing bark: 'Get in!' and warns her: 'You don't know what's good for you', blatantly threatening her with his power over her career, before he proceeds to force himself onto her. In the face of her total lack of response, he insists 'don't tell me that you don't need it, too, one word and I'll let you go at once'. Jennifer Creech interprets Sieland's silence (i.e. not taking this 'opportunity' to say 'no') as sexual weakness and political complicity with the GDR regime, offering a scathing condemnation of her character as 'whoring herself out to the Minister'.[42] Similarly, Schmidt accuses the figure of Sieland of 'collaboration with power and failure to resist it'.[43] And Ute Wölfel, too, interprets this scene as Sieland's 'first betrayal of their [her and Dreyman's] mutual love'.[44] These readings suggests an element of free will and choice on Sieland's part. However, this is not borne out by the way in which this scene is constructed cinematically.

Crucially, this is also one of the few instances in the film where narrative information is not filtered through Wiesler's eyes, ears or visualizations, which creates a sense of greater immediacy, and gives the spectator access to Sieland's subjectivity. The information is provided by the camera as omniscient narrator through a static two shot. During this long take we have access to both characters' feelings through their performance: that is, we are placed in alignment with both Hempf and Sieland. However, the spectator is positioned to feel allegiance (which does not depend on the use of optical POV shots) with Sieland, as she is contrasted here with a morally unscrupulous and unsympathetic villain. Moreover, the close

---

39 Fulbrook, *The People's State*, p. 180.

40 For further discussion see Manfred Wilke, 'Wiesler's Umkehr' in *Das Leben der anderen. Filmbuch*, pp. 207–10.

41 Lindenberger, 'Stasiploitation', p. 562.

42 Jennifer Creech, 'A few good Men: Gender, Ideology, and narrative Politics in *The Lives of others* and *Good Bye, Lenin!*' in *Women in German Yearbook. Feminist Studies in German Literature & Culture*, 25 (2009), 100–126 (p. 105).

43 Schmidt, 'Between Authors', p. 233.

44 Ute Wölfel, 'Inverting the Lives of "Others": Retelling the Nazi past in *Ehe im Schatten* and *Das Leben der Anderen*', *German Life and Letters*, 64 (2011), 601–18 (p. 617).

framing of the two characters visually highlights her sense of entrapment in the back seat of Hempf's car and his utter indifference to her feelings. Gedeck's muted but powerful performance conveys Sieland's repulsion: at first she makes herself stiff to resist his pull, letting her arms hang down limply like those of a puppet. Then she writhes in his grip as if having to force herself not to push him away.

Deviating from the screenplay, Gedeck's body in this sequence is 'inscribed', to use Brooks's term, with the emotional message of her barely suppressed disgust.[45] The director's stage directions ask 'Or does she also feel something? Then she turns her head away; whether she does this in order to refuse him her lips or to offer him her neck is not clear'.[46] By contrast, in the film, Gedeck's performance conveys her character's loathing of being groped by the Minister quite unambiguously, which she endures only because she has no choice. Hence, the critics' references to Sieland 'being seduced' into becoming Hempf's 'mistress' and going to a 'rendezvous' – both of which have romantic connotations – seem quite misplaced. Rather than suggesting Sieland's sexual compliance, her silent endurance of forced sexual intercourse is born out of total powerlessness. This interpretation is underlined later in the film when she does pluck up the courage to spurn Hempf, and he retaliates with an order to have her blacklisted, ultimately setting in motion the process of her destruction. The spectator is invited to recognize that Sieland – rather than being seduced – is sexually coerced. Through the moral indignation at this brutal abuse of male power, the spectator's allegiance is drawn to the (innocent) female victim of a patriarchal totalitarian regime.

The emotional impact Sieland's suffering engenders is enhanced by the fact that we experience it predominantly through Wiesler's *sympathetic* eyes, ears and visualizations. And as we are, for a large part of the film, aligned with Wiesler's point of view, we are invited to 'see' her through his eyes, in other words to share his infatuation with and empathy for her. In a key sequence, Wiesler listens to Sieland's helpless attempts to clean herself in the shower after her semi-rape, metaphorically trying to wash off her defilement. The appeal to pathos in this sequence is created by placing the spectator in a position of alignment with Sieland, based on a spacio-temporal attachment to her actions (we saw what happened in Hempf's car which Wiesler did not), and on the highly emotive score expressing her distress. The spectator gains access to Sieland's feelings in this scene through Gedeck's performance and the mise-en-scène: she collapses in the shower uttering a stifled sob, clutching her knees and revealing a bruise on her

---

45 Brooks, *The Melodramatic Imagination*, p. xi.
46 Von Donnersmarck, *Das Leben der anderen. Filmbuch*, pp. 64–5.

Rape, not rendezvous, *The Lives of Others*.

upper arm. Finally, Dreyman finds her curled up on the bed in a regressive fetal pose asking to be held.

In this sequence the non-diegetic musical score functions as a sound bridge linking the feelings of Sieland (in the shower) with those of Wiesler eavesdropping in the attic above, thus enhancing the powerful moment in the film when his emotional bond with Sieland is established. Wiesler is puzzled at first by what he hears. He had believed Sieland to be a consensual adulteress and initially had wanted to hurt Dreyman by exposing her infidelity; now he is moved by (aurally) witnessing Sieland's pain and the compassion with which Dreyman responds to her situation. As the film cuts from the couple on the bed to Wiesler in the attic one last time in this sequence, we see him cradling himself. With his eyes closed, he sits in relaxed abandon, his torso turned slightly sideways, mirroring the spooned bodies of the couple downstairs, and clutching the tape recorder cable as if it were an umbilical cord – the poignant image of his emotional 'birth' is expressed visually through an 'embodied simulation' of his (imagined) embrace of Sieland.[47] The seed is planted for Wiesler's gradual change of heart – and change of political sides.

---

47 Diana Diamond, 'Empathy and identification in von Donnermarck's *The Lives of Others*', *Journal of the American Psychoanalytical Association*, 56.3 (2008), 811–32, (p. 811).

Spectator Alignment with Sieland's Motives: the Actress

Due to Sieland's role within the melodramatic narrative, as an object of desire for three male characters, she is represented predominantly through the male gaze (of Hempf, Dreyman and Wiesler). However, her character is not entirely reduced to a sexualized object. Significantly, the spectator gains access to her subjectivity in scenes linked to her identity as a working actress. Again recalling an important aspect of DEFA *Frauenfilme*, Sieland's *work* is the one aspect of her identity that crucially informs her sense of identity, motivating three of her decisions that drive the plot towards ever more melodramatic climaxes.

Firstly, she continues to see Hempf against her will because without her acting career her life would be meaningless and might as well end, as she stresses in a bitter outburst to Dreyman:

> I don't need him, do I? I don't need this whole system? [...] But you are sleeping with them, too [...] because they determine what is performed, who is allowed to act and who can direct. You don't want to end up like Jerska. And I don't either! And that's why I'm going now.

The film cuts to Wiesler in the middle of her monologue ('they determine – ') to which he is seen listening with a troubled expression. The intensity of his connection with her, and the emotional impact her damning indictment of the regime has made on him, is further highlighted by him rushing out of the attic, holding on to the door outside, pausing to breathe heavily.

Consistent with the construction of the Sieland character as a passionate artist, her second major resolution, the decision to spurn Hempf, is not only motivated by personal reasons (her commitment to Dreyman). It is also (significantly) taken on the basis of her sense of identity as an actress. Wiesler, posing as an adoring fan on their first encounter in a bar, helps her to make this decision, albeit with feigned, manipulative naiveté. Alluding to her star persona as a gifted artist who plays strong female characters, he suggests that her loving public would expect her to be as strong in private as she comes across on stage: 'I have seen you on stage. There you were more how you are than how you are now. [I know because] I am your audience'. In an attempt to establish an ironic distance to the 'true self' Wiesler claims to know, Sieland shifts to the third person, projecting her dilemma onto her star persona: 'So, you know her well, this Christa-Maria Sieland. What do you think, would she hurt someone who loved her more than anything? Would she sell herself for art?' Wiesler retorts without hesitation and with absolute conviction: 'Sell herself for art? She already possesses that, doesn't she?'

It is one of the tragic ironies of this melodrama that the two men who love Sieland the most, Dreyman and Wiesler, unwittingly contribute to her downfall. They trigger her demise by fatally misjudging the dependency of the (female) art-ist on the (patriarchal) state in a totalitarian system. Dreyman's insistent plea to Sieland: 'You don't need him [Hempf]' is politically naïve, as he is in a less vul-nerable position than Sieland, not only on account of his social status but also his gender. As a man, he is not likely to be sexually coerced by members of the ruling elite, who were almost exclusively male. Wiesler, too, underestimates the deter-mination of his superiors to abuse their power, by misguidedly convincing Sie-land that her talent as an artist will suffice to keep her in the job.

The narrative information about Sieland's subsequent actions is again me-diated through Wiesler's (sympathetic) eyes, ears and imagination. We see what he visualizes (as a flashback) on the basis of his sleeping assistant's report: Sie-land's joyful return to Dreyman, flying into his arms and making love. The entire sequence is underscored by Yared's soaring emotional adagio tune *Faces of Love*, recalling the earlier love making scene after the birthday party, and thus signal-ling a glimpse of hope for a return to a former 'space of innocence'.

A little later, in a key montage sequence all three protagonists are shown trying to do the morally right thing, their words being drowned out by the (non-diegetic) song 'Stell dich mitten in den Regen' (Stand in the middle of the rain) with its refrain 'und versuche, gut zu sein' (and try to be good), performed by the East German band Bayon.[48] The film cuts from Dreyman writing his dissident article to Wiesler writing a fake report to protect the couple, and finally to Sieland in bed with Dreyman, committing fully to him instead of meeting Hempf, with the instrumental part of the song cued to her promise: 'Now I am wholly yours'. Thus, the song linking a number of spatially separate scenes includes Sieland in the protagonists' shared transformation. As Rick Altman argues, the insertion of a pre-composed song often over-determines the meaning of the film sequence it accompanies through its dependence on language, to the extent that 'non-die-getic popular song lyrics provide a unique opportunity to editorialize and to focus audience attention'.[49] The lyrics of the song provide comment – much like a voice over – on the brave decisions all three characters have taken, encouraging them in their endeavour even if it means risking being burnt, drowned, or swept away (by fire, rain, or storm in the song's lyrics). This sequence strongly suggests,

---

48 'Stell dich mitten in den Regen' was first performed by Bayon in 1972 to the lyrics of a poem by Wolfgang Borchert, entitled 'Versuch es' (Try it).
49 Rick Altman, 'Cinema and popular song. The lost tradition', in *Soundtrack available. Essays on Film and Popular Music*, ed. by Pamela Robertson Wojcik and Arthur Knight (Durham and London: Duke University Press, 2001), pp. 19–30 (p. 26).

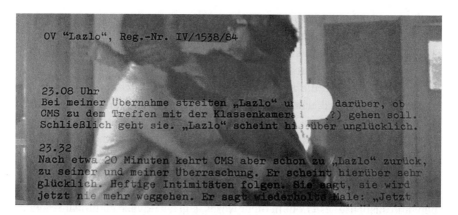

'Stand in the middle of the rain', *The Lives of Others*.

contrary to some critics' claims, that it is not solely the male characters who are shown willing to change and transform. Sieland, too, is trying to be 'good' by rejecting the powerful Minister. However, in her case – and in marked contrast to the fate of the two male characters – the triumph of virtue can only be a fleeting moment. In true melodramatic mode, the woman's desire for self-fulfilment is in conflict with a corrupt, oppressive society and hence must be repressed.

Sieland's harassment and manipulation into cooperation by the agents of a totalitarian system stands, as Wölfel points out, in the melodramatic tradition of two lovers threatened with separation.[50] However, within the cause-effect logic of the narrative of *The Lives of Others,* her final major decision to reveal the hiding place of the typewriter is – again – motivated by her need for self-preservation as a working actress. Her initial attempt to save Dreyman – 'there is no evidence. There is no typewriter. I made that up' – is dismissed by Wiesler's claim that Dreyman's cause is lost, his fate is sealed. Her continued silent resistance is only broken when Wiesler appeals to her sense of self as a stage actress: 'Think of your audience [...] Tonight you will be back on stage, in your element, in front of your audience'. The spectator is aligned with Sieland's feelings through Gedeck's muted but powerful performance, very subtly conveying Sieland's shock, fear and confusion, as well as through the long close ups of her face and nervous body language. Grubitz had warned Wiesler that this was his last chance: 'Your future depends on this', and the spectator recognizes Sieland as the betrayed victim, a female pawn in the men's power game. The appeal to pathos in this sequence

---

50 Wölfel, 'Inverting the Lives of "Others"', p. 613.

is enhanced by its cinematography and mise-en-scène. Wiesler's interrogation is observed by Grubitz through a one-way mirror which frames the crouched figure of Sieland (wearing a white, fluffy jumper which highlights her vulnerability) like a trapped animal in a particularly cruel experiment.

In conclusion, I would argue that *The Lives of Others* does not represent Sieland as a 'bad woman', who deserves to be punished – as some critics suggest – quite the opposite in fact. Within the framework of the melodramatic mode, her tragic death can be read as the unjust fate of a 'virtuous' victim. It follows her courageous deed of spurning the villain and committing to Dreyman – jeopardising her career, her safety and eventually her life. Melodrama's recognition of such a virtuous (self-)sacrifice involves a combination of a fear of loss with the excitement and suspense of action, in other words, a give and take of 'too late' and 'in the nick of time'. As Linda Williams explains, 'the effect is to propel events into the future while insisting on the continued reminder of the past pathos of "too late"'.[51] She calls this 'an intensely rhythmic tease whose core question is melodramatic: will we ever get back to the time before it is too late?'[52] Wiesler's and Dreyman's last-minute embraces of Sieland's body just before she dies provide such moments of melodramatic tension. This tension is enhanced by the previous parallel montage of Grubitz breaking open the threshold that he assumes holds the incriminating evidence and Sieland running away from the scene. Although a rapid succession of shots gives the effect of events happening extremely fast, the parallel cutting between Grubitz and Sieland actually retards the ultimate duration of the event, building up to an intense, emotional climax. The image of the dying heroine lying on the hard asphalt, barefoot and vulnerable in her fluffy white dressing gown, affects the spectator not only because it combines pathos (of her suffering) with action (Dreyman's failed rescue) but also because Sieland's flight into the street is a suicidal self-punishing gesture. Arguably, she is melodramatically redeemed through the pathos of her previous sexual and political victimization. Most poignantly, her dying scene is staged in an iconic fashion, with Dreyman holding her dead body in a pose recalling the *Pietà* with all its religious connotations.[53]

---

51 Williams, 'The American Melodramatic Mode', p. 33.
52 Williams, 'The American Melodramatic Mode', p. 35.
53 On the DVD commentary von Donnersmarck points out that he 'tried to work with that symbolism to make that scene stronger'. He has also mentioned in numerous interviews that he wrote the film script during a reclusive month in a monastery run by his uncle (the abbot) where he would have been surrounded by religious imagery. The connotation of bodily suffering with virtue is, of course, a topos of western culture that goes back to Christian iconography. Hence, the character Christa-Maria Sieland (whose name connotes a female saviour) has been read as

The character Christa-Maria Sieland is no triumph for feminism, to be sure. But the critics' polemical comments about her sexual compliance, political complicity and selfishness quoted above seem to oversimplify the more complex and ambiguous character that the film constructs. Sieland is portrayed on a downward narrative trajectory typical of the classical tragic heroine: from a proud and celebrated actress to the timid victim of sexual abuse; from a vivacious, confident lover to a secretive woman paralysed with fear and self-loathing. What really victimizes Sieland is not simply her 'emotional fragility' or the personal villainy of Hempf and Grubitz but, the film seems to suggest, a patriarchal state that allowed men in position of power to prey upon its vulnerable (female) citizens.[54] Von Donnersmarck skilfully uses the melodramatic mode to convey Sieland's victimization and – via the complex orchestration of a 'structure of sympathy' – aligns the spectator with the Sieland character during key moments in the film, engendering allegiance with her in the form of moral indignation with the system. Confronted with the impossible choice between submitting to sexual abuse and betraying her lover, or being blacklisted for the rest of her life (a virtual suicide for someone as committed to her art as Sieland), she has no way out. Christine Gledhill observes that 'part of the excitement of the [melodramatic] mode is the genuine turmoil and timeliness of the issues it takes up and the popular debate it can generate when it explores controversies'.[55] *The Lives of Others* has certainly sparked popular debates about the representation of the GDR in the post-unification era – debates which hinge not just on von Donnersmarck's choice of a Stasi officer as a 'good man' in a redemption story but also on his alleged vilification of his female protagonist. This chapter is intended as a contribution to that debate.

---

the bearer of all sins who must die, in the quasi-Christian moral agenda underpinning *The Lives of Others* (see, for example, Lindenberger, 'Stasiploitation', p. 562).

54 Lenssen, 'Die Rezeption'.

55 Gledhill, *Home is where the Heart is*, pp. 18–19.

David Bathrick

CHAPTER SIX
Der Tangospieler: Coming in from the Cold Once and for All? *The Lives of Others* as Cold War Spy film

Another way of reading Florian Henckel von Donnersmarck's *The Lives of Others* would be to frame it as the first post-89 blockbuster Cold War spy film. Indeed its very closure could be seen to suggest that the conversion of Stasi Captain Wiesler from Marxist-Leninist villain to a guardian angel of Western democratic values might even have accelerated the fall of the Wall as well as the process of political and moral rehabilitation. At the generic core of the Cold War spy novel and film lie fundamental questions concerning values and tactics basic to the binarial opposing systems often staged as democracy versus totalitarianism. This was the case regardless of whether it be a James Bond film, the novel (1963) and film (1965) versions of John Le Carré's classic *The Spy Who Came in from the Cold,* or the post-wall attempts by German fimmakers from the old and new *Bundesländer* (federal states) to deal cinematically with the Stasi.

Hence my reading of *The Lives of Others* as spy film chooses to situate it within two comparative memory frameworks: the first in light of changes occurring generically within the spy novels and films that appeared during the period of the Cold War (1949–1989). Here I will sketch the dominant architecture of the Cold War spy genre in Ian Fleming's James Bond novels and the James Bond films and then look at John Le Carré and director Martin Ritt's attempted deconstruction of that very architecture in the film version of *The Spy Who Came in from the Cold.* My second comparison considers *The Lives of Others* in relation to the post-wall DEFA film *Der Tangospieler* (The Tango Player, Roland Gräf, 1991) for what it might tell us about differing modes of East German cinematic coming to terms with the Stasi past immediately following the fall of the Wall.

Brief History of the Stasi

Given that since the end of the Cold War the Stasi has often been remembered ahistorically as an icon for universal evil, I find it important at the outset to emphasize that the organizational formation that I will be focusing on – and that *The Lives of Others* claims to be depicting – consists of Section (Hauptabteilung) XX, subsection 7 of the MfS (Ministry for State Security) as it was functioning during the last decade of the GDR's existence (1980–1989). This temporal designation is particularly significant in that such a framing seeks to acknowledge the extent to which the thoroughly 'modernized' Stasi of the 1980s had very little in common with the goals and practices of the ministry that was bequeathed to the fledgling GDR by the Soviets in the early 1950s at the outset of the Cold War. The fact that between 1956 and 1989 the MfS grew from 16,000 to 91,000 official employees, in addition to 175,000 IMs (unofficial collaborators),[1] was put forth by the Stasi itself as but one indication of their oft made claim to have achieved maximum penetration, 'flächendeckend' (absolute coverage) in Stasi parlance, of the entire social body of the GDR. Important as well is that this vastly expanded Stasi be also seen historically as a paranoid pre-emptive response by the intelligence services to the structural changes that were occurring within the Eastern bloc under the rubric of detente starting in the early 1970s.

The various non-proliferation treaties (Salt I, 1969–1972, and Salt II, 1972–1982), the Helsinki accords (1975), begrudgingly signed by the GDR due to their commitment to human rights issues and freer movement across borders, and finally, Willi Brandt's *Ostpolitik* were all quite rightly viewed by First Party Secretary Erich Honecker and the Stasi's Director General Erich Mielke as a threat to the very existence of the East German state.[2] Within the literary public sphere, rapidly growing Stasi paranoia subsequent to the expatriation of Wolf Biermann in 1976 in turn led to major adjustments in their modus operandi to bring about an even more 'flexible system of control'.[3] Mielke himself summed up the new direction referred to as 'operative Zersetzung' (operational decomposition) in the following manner: 'You know that for political as well as for operational reasons, we cannot immediately arrest all our enemies, although the purely legal prerequisites do exist for that. We know these enemies, have them under control and know what they are always and ever planning'.[4]

The operable phrase in that blunt assertion is 'have them under control', which viewed through the Stasi inflected prism of 'kontrollieren' suggested multitude forms of containment such as 'überwachen' (monitor), 'überprüfen' (scrutinize), 'decken' (cover) and finally 'beherrschen' (absolutely control). What it could no longer mean for political and diplomatic reasons, as Mielke also reminds us, was immediate incarceration. The resulting search for 'softer' or what Huber-

---

1 Jens Gieseke, *Miele-Konzern. Geschichte der Stasi 1945–1990* (Stuttgart: Deutsche Verlagsanstalt, 2001), p. 70.
2 David Childs and Richard Popplewell, *Stasi. The East German Intelligence Service* (London: Palgrave, 1996), pp. 174–77.
3 Mike Dennis, *The Stasi. Myth and Reality* (London: Pearson Education, 2003), p. 112.
4 Quoted in Dennis, *The Stasi. Myth and Reality*, p. 112.

tus Knabe has called 'quiet repression' led to procedural and institutional inno-
vations.[5] One example of this would be the increasingly widespread use of 'Operative Personenkontollen' (OPKs, operational personal checks). If initial OPK
enquiries revealed indications of 'hostile-negative' attitudes or illegal behaviour
that infringed upon the GDR's highly elastic Penal Code, then an 'Operativer Vorgang 1' (OV1, operational case 1) could be launched to spy on and blackmail, followed up by an OV2 to harass and destabilize, and finally, only in extreme cases,
an OV3 to arrest or deport.

Clearly what we see depicted in *The Lives of Others* is an extreme, if not cari-
catured version of an operational personal check as confirmed to us by the OPK
stamp on Dreymann's file during his visit to the Gauck-Behörde at the end of the
film, which in turn became an OV1 when Wiesler was sent into the attic. Whether
the version of a new, modernized Stasi depicted above was more or less Orwellian
than its predecessor is hard to say. What does become clear comparatively is that
the undifferentiated depictions of good and evil that drive the characterological
and narrative machinery of *The Lives of Others* do not even begin to resemble
the 'quiet repression' and ethical grey zones brought into play by the immense
and complicated presence of the IMs. The ruthless Captain Wiesler undergoes a
weakly motivated, born again epiphany enhanced by the accidental overhearing
of a moving piano sonata and the reading of Bertolt Brecht's well known early
love poem 'Erinnerung an die Marie A.' (Remembering Marie A.), both of which he
is introduced to while spying on Dreyman and his actress partner Christa-Maria
Sieland. The only IM in the film, Sieland, 'atones' for her own and everybody
else's sins with a deus ex machina suicide.[6]

---

5 Hubertus Knabe, 'Strafen ohne Strafrecht. Zum Wandel repressiver Strategien in der Ära Honecker', in *DDR. Recht und Justiz als politisches Instrument*, ed. by Heiner Timmermann (Berlin:
Dunker und Humboldt, 2000), pp. 91–109 (p. 94).
6 See Thomas Lindenberger, 'Stasiploitation – Why Not? The Scriptwriter's Historical Creativity', *German Studies Review*, 31.3 (2008), 557–66. Lindenberger emphasizes that '[J]ust by name
she is marked as the bearer of all sins, and so she must be sacrificed. The sacrifice connotation is
staged highly visibly through the Pietà-like posture in which Dreymann is holding his dying lover
in his arms' (p. 562).

The Cold War Spy Genre

And how does all of this link up with the Cold War spy genre? It is no secret that the emergence of the Cold War in postwar Europe provided, already in the 1940s, a potential feeding ground for would be spy novelists.[7] There are a number of compelling reasons for starting my treatment of what I call the dominant paradigm of the Cold War Spy genre with the name James Bond. The first certainly is the significant commercial success of Ian Fleming's twelve James Bond novels and three short stories, almost all of which were turned into even more financially successful films at the box office. In my research for this chapter I twice ran across the preposterously bogus assertion that 'half the population of the world has seen a James Bond film'.[8] That notwithstanding, although Ian Fleming died in 1964, the James Bond moniker continued its prolific output cinematically, some of the films based on Fleming's twelve Bond novels, plus two volumes of collected stories, and others not. The Bond movie series at the moment totals twenty-five films featuring six different actors playing Bond. With the success of *Skyfall*, starring Javier Bardem and Daniel Craig, in 2012, it would seem there are still no signs of closure.

Yet more important for my purposes of tracing Cold War medial memory is the extent to which the popularity of the Bond subgenre offers us a virtual treasure trove for locating global fantasies and neuroses of Cold War culture, particularly during its initial decades. As Jeremy Black, the author of *The Politics of James Bond,* has argued, the Bond series drew on contemporary fears in order to 'reduce the implausibility of the villains and their villainy', while also presenting potent images of national character, 'exploring the ambivalent relationship between a declining Britain and an ascendant United States', charting the course of the Cold War while offering an 'ever changing but also ever adapting absolutist demonology'.[9]

While initially a quintessentially British creation, with a lifestyle oriented toward sophisticated British mores, Bond's move into American financed films frequently had him involved in saving the United States. In *Dr. No*, the first Bond film made in 1962, the hero thwarts a Soviet backed attempt to bring down American rockets, the West Indies serving as a Cold War battlefield that makes Britain

---

7 For a review of the genesis of the Cold War Spy novel see Robert Lance Snydor, '"Shadow of Abandonment", Graham Greene's *The Confidential Agent*', *Texas Studies in Literature and Language,* 52.2 (2010), 203–26.
8 Jeremy Black, *The Politics of James Bond. From Fleming's Novels to the Big Screen* (Westport: Praeger. 2001), p. ix.
9 Black, *The Politics of James Bond*, pp. ix-xii.

relevant to the US. A sense of America under threat is also central to the narrative of *Goldfinger*, where, with the help of the 'super woman' Pussy Galore, Bond prevents the Fort Knox Gold reserves in Lexington Kentucky from being rendered radioactive. Although the national ethnicities of the enemy vary over the years in accordance with assignments and the needs of the tourist industry, our sexually active defender of Western values, and his ontologically evil communist adversaries, remain steadfast signifiers in an unending variety of Cold War stand-offs. And while it is also true that the narrative scale and cinematic pomposity of the Bond series would seem to have little in common with the severity of pace and bleakly narrowed focus of *The Lives of Others*, these two films do share important structural and diegetic components: by virtue of their mastery of the regnant ideological Cold War codes as articulated at the level of their formal and aesthetic organization, both succeeded in situating themselves as blockbusters in a transnational memory system.

To sum up my argument in terms of Cold War memory culture, what is generated generically in the reception of films like the Bond series as well as *The Lives of Others*, are co-existing reception processes of global and local memory feeds; films that potentially speak, simultaneously yet in remarkably varying ways, to local, regional and transnational audiences. When Maurice Halbwachs first defined the term collective memory, it was used to designate groups sharing and experiencing the same spatial and temporal arena, such as families, believers of a religion, social classes or, at the farthest reach, members of a single nation.[10] In her work on memory, Aleida Assmann helps us go beyond the exclusivity of a social or collective memory that is bound only to temporal or shared remembrance. She does this by drawing a distinction between what she calls communicative memory, which emerges in an environment of 'spatial proximity, regular interaction, shared life styles and shared experiences', and, on the other hand, 'cultural memory'.[11] Cultural memory, as she and Jan Assmann have theorized it, translates the experienced memory of witnesses into a temporally long term or spatially distant memory culture that expands its geopolitical and generational borders with the help of educational institutions, data banks, archives, the internet and various global media systems, such as film and television.

The relevance of cultural memory for understanding the reception of *The Lives of Others* is this: in a Germany still divided very powerfully at the level of re-

---

10 Maurice Halbwachs, *On Collective Memory*, ed. and trans. by Lewis Coser (Chicago: Chicago University Press, 1992).

11 Aleida Assmann and Ute Frevert, *Geschichtsvergessenheit/Geschichtsversessenheit. Vom Umgang mit deutschen Vergessenheiten nach 1945* (Stuttgart: Deutsche Verlaganstalt,1999), p. 36.

membrance, a successfully Hollywoodized recollection with carefully constructed moments of identificatory 'authenticity' is bound to call up, as one saw in subsequent *Feuilleton* reviews, discrepant, even conflicting modes of reception. On the one hand, historians such as Jens Giesecke were relentless in pointing out the countless errors in von Donnersmark's 'moralistic' depiction of Wiesler, which he summed up in the following way: 'The over idealization of this brooding sensitive intellectual had nothing in common with the real Stasi's much more banal combination of subalternism, anti-intellectualism and power hunger in which traditions of the *Obrigkeitsstaates* (authoritarian state) are wedded in a very ugly way with the worst of Stalinism'.[12] Opposing this view, and as is discussed in the Introduction to this volume, both the dissident songwriter Wolf Biermann[13] and Joachim Gauck of the Gauck-Behörde found the film absolutely authentic.[14]

Looking at the global picture, *The Lives of Others* had in general an extremely positive reception outside of Germany, in part because its finely crafted aesthetic codes, the classical Hollywood model, were much more familiar to audiences than was their contingent knowledge of 'real existing socialism' in the GDR. Typical of reviews both in Great Britain and the United States, A. O. Scott of the *New York Times* called it 'a supremely intelligent, unfailingly honest movie [...] that illuminates not only a shadowy period in recent German history, but also the moral no man's land where base impulses and high principles converge'.[15] This combination spy and German totalitarianism Cold War thriller enabled foreign viewers to see and even feel 'East German reality', many for the first time, while at the same time leaving them blind, for example, to the banality that was such a part of the Stasi's own investment in the terror that they employed. Cultural memory, simply as global mediatized memory, always risks getting and losing parts of the same puzzle. *The Lives of Others* was just such a film precisely because its signifying system also drew on latently familiar stereotypes at the very heart of transnational Cold War culture.

Turning again to earlier models of Cold War Spy films, I now consider a subgenre thereof that grounds its epistemological starting point precisely as a counter to the dominant paradigm by depicting the intelligence services of both the Eastern and Western nations as practising the same expedient amorality in the name of a national security. The novelist John Le Carré's *The Spy Who Came in*

---

12 Jens Giesecke, 'Stasi goes to Hollywood. Donnersmarcks *The Lives of Others* und die Grenzen der Authentizität', *German Studies Review*, 31.3 (2008), 580–88 (p. 581).

13 For Wolf Biermann see Christina Tilmann, 'Wer ist Florian Henckel von Donnersmarck', *Tagespiegel*, 25 February 2007.

14 Joachim Gauck, '*Das Leben der Anderen*. "Ja, so war es!"', *Stern.de*, 25 March 2006.

15 A.O. Scott, 'A Fugue for Good German Men', *The New York Times*, 9 February 2007.

Leamas and Perry negotiate the banal reality of the Cold War spy, *The Spy Who Came in from the Cold*.

from the Cold of 1963 was followed two years later by a screen version directed by Martin Ritt and starring Richard Burton as Alec Leamas, whose antidote to the cartoonish antics of James Bond renders a deeply morose portrayal of a burnt out, disillusioned, semi-alcoholic agent, who long since has abandoned any notion that he was working for the better cause. Asked toward the end of the film by his girlfriend Nan Perry (Claire Bloom) for whom and for what he was doing this, in short 'what are the rules?', Leamus offers an answer that could stand as the underlying credo of Le Carré's entire work:

> There is only one rule here – expediency. What the hell do you think spies are? Moral philosophers measuring everything they know against the word of God? Or Karl Marx? They are not, they are just a bunch of seedy, squalid bastards like me. Little men – drunks, pansies, henpecked husbands, civil servants playing cowboys and Indians to brighten up their rotten little lives [...]. How good does a cause have to be before you start killing your friends?

Leamus's soliloquy comes as he and Nan are preparing to climb over the Berlin Wall to leave the East, he having accomplished his duty of protecting the despicable ex-Nazi British double agent Hans-Dieter Mundt (Peter van Eyck) at the lethal expense of a relatively innocent East German spy, the Jew Fiedler (Oskar Werner). Half way up the Wall they are shot and killed from the Eastern side, but also more indirectly, from the Western side as well. London knew what it was doing when they sent Alec Leamus 'back into the cold'. Sadly, the ever-tortured Leamus surely knew it at some level as well.

Le Carré's deconstruction of the Bondian Cold War spy paradigm – he more recently labelled James Bond a 'neo-fascist gangster, who would ply his trade for any country provided he could get a plentiful supply of beautiful women and dry martinis'[16] – consisted of ingredients that were to be shared by a select group of authors and filmmakers starting in the early sixties. Also prominent in this regard was Len Deighton, the author of *The Ipcress file* of 1962, which in its 1965 film version, directed by Sidney Furie, launched the career of Michael Caine as Harry Palmer. Palmer has been described by Richard Bowden as a 'short sighted, class-ridden, form signing petty criminal co-opted into the spy service to avoid a year in jail'.[17] Put next to Leamus as well as Le Carré's ubiquitous and iconic George Smiley (who was once characterized by Le Carré as 'one of the London meek who do not inherit the earth'[18]), what we find articulated epistemologically via spy as anti-hero is a narrative that arises from a 'disequilibrium between the individual and the regime within whose ideology the spy lives and from which he dissents';[19] an ethical grey zone, where questions of culpability, perpetration and, yes, evil can apply to one's own colleagues just as well as to the so-called other side. Robert Lance Snyder went so far as to laud the early 1960s as the 'Golden Age' of espionage fiction, when we 'thus find the genre stamped by a resolute cynicism regarding all competing ideologies and their supporting apparatus associated with the Cold War period.'[20]

DEFA and the Stasi

Following up on my discussion of the Cold War Spy film, I turn now to Roland Gräf's postwall DEFA film *Der Tangospieler* based on a story by Christoph Hein with the same title. As noted in the Introduction to this volume, there has been a plethora of critical discussion as to whether von Donnersmarck's *The Lives of Others* served as an antidote to *Ostalgie* in films such as *Good Bye, Lenin!* (Wolfgang Becker, 2003) or *Sonnenallee* (Sun Alley, Leander Haußmann, 1999) or whether it was itself simply another scarier version of *Ostalgie*. My view is that neither is the case, sharing the notion of those who would argue that collective memory cultures are simply too heterogeneous and complex as to be reduced and

---

16 Anita Singh, 'James Bond a Neo-Fascist Gangster', *The Telegraph*, 17 August 2010.
17 Richard Bowden (http://www.democracyforum.co.uk/television-film-radio/86193-ipcre).
18 Anthony Lane, 'I SPY. John Le Carré and the rise of George Smiley', *The New Yorker*, 12 December 2011.
19 Alan Hepburn, *Intrigue. Espionage and Culture* (New Haven: Yale University Press, 2005), p. 8.
20 Snyder, 'Shadow of Abandonment', p. 223.

thereby condemned to a singular modality. By that I mean that it is possible to be appalled by the negative aspects of growing up in a dictatorship and still hold certain tender life memories of events that occurred therein.

My reason for focussing on a DEFA film is this: while there have indeed been a number of postwall German films other than *The Lives of Others* that have dealt with the Stasi – Volker Schlöndorff's *Die Stille nach dem Schuß* (The Legend of Rita, 2000) and Christian Klemke and Jan Lorenzen's documentary film *Das Ministerium für Staatssicherheit: Alltag einer Behörde* (The Ministry of State Security: The Daily Routine of an Agency, 2003) represent two of the best – there has been relatively little discussion devoted to the DEFA Stasi films that appeared after 1989. Here we would mention, in addition to *Der Tangospieler*, films such as *Der Verdacht* (*The Suspicion*, Frank Beyer, 1991), *Abschied von Agnes* (Farewell to Agnes, Michael Gwisdeck, 1994), and the documentary *Verriegelte Zeit* (Imprisoned Times, Sybille Schönemann, 1990). Certainly one of the reasons for such neglect stemmed from a political environment emanating from the postwall West that proved powerfully antithetical to any notion that East German artists, writers or intellectuals would be up to dealing with their Stasi past.

Here I should also briefly point out that the aforementioned postwall Stasi films were not the first Cold War Spy films to be made by DEFA. An extremely successful film called *For Eyes Only – Streng Geheim* (János Veiczi, 1963) appeared during those 'golden years' of spy films, perhaps as an intended antidote to the influx and dominance of the genre in the West during the same period. In *For Eyes Only*, the Stasi has successfully planted a mole named Hansen (Alfred Müller) into an American Military Intelligence Division (MID) located in Würzburg, West Germany, that is fronting as a trade commission called *Concordia*. The year is early 1961 and the Americans are depicted scheming as part of a larger operation led by NATO and the *Bundeswehr* (code name 'DECO II') to take over the GDR on 'day X'.[21] After much complicated romancing and scheming in his new quarters, Hansen succeeds in absconding with a copy of the plans, the publication of which brings an end to the Americans' operation as well as an unspoken justification for building the Wall a few months later. Not surprisingly, it is the ugly Americans who end up executing two of their top officers, Major Collins (Helmut Schreiber) and Colonel Rock (Hans Lucke), for failing to discern what was going on, whereas the 'loving father and husband' Hansen returns as a hero to his happy family in

---

21 Bernd Stöver, "'Das ist die Wahrheit, die volle Wahrheit". Befreiungspolitik im DDR-Spielfilm der 1950er und 1960er Jahre', in *Massenmedien im Kalten Krieg. Akteure, Bilder, Resonanzen*, ed. by Thomas Lindenberger (Cologne, Weimar, Vienna: Böhlau Verlag, 2006), pp. 49–76. It is estimated that in the month of August 1963 alone 650,000 saw this film. It was also shown throughout the Eastern Bloc.

East Berlin. There are no questions here as to who are the evil adversaries in this arraignment of values.

Christoph Hein's novel *Der Tangospieler* was published in March 1989, simultaneously in the East and the West. Plans for a DEFA version of the story commenced in 1989 as well, under conditions hardly conducive to a measured, dispassionate *Aufarbeitung* (working through) of the Stasi's immediate past, as noted by director Roland Gräf.

> I wrote the script under pretty insane pressures. As I was writing people were leaving the GDR in massive numbers. I had a sudden impulse: you have to make this film, you have to expose everything so that the people will want to stay here. But my problem was, I couldn't write as fast as they were leaving. The events of the day simply ran me over. And then suddenly it was no longer a question as to whether we could make the film, but rather the question as to whether it was even worth making.[22]

Gräf's words delineate emblematically the political position of many of the older generation dissident intellectuals in the GDR before, during and beyond the events of November 9. Whether Volker Braun, Christoph Hein, Heiner Müller, Stephan Hermlin, Stefan Heym or in this case Roland Gräf, they all shared Christa Wolf's publicly expressed 'dream' – on the occasion of the 4 November 1989 demonstration on the Alexanderplatz – of building a socialism where 'nobody runs away' ('stell' Dir vor, es ist Sozialismus und keiner geht weg').[23]

The film version of *Der Tangospieler* adheres closely to Hein's narrative, as it tells the story of Hans-Peter Dallow (Michael Gwisdek), an historian at the University of Leipzig and part-time piano player, who has spent 21 months in jail for having played a politically incorrect Tango in a cabaret. A student band at the university had asked Dallow at the very last minute to replace their ailing piano player without informing him that the lyrics for one of the songs that evening had been rewritten as a stinging satire of First Party Secretary Walter Ulbricht, which in turn got them all thrown in jail for the next two years. *Der Tangospieler* finds its starting point diegetically in Spring of 1968 with Dallow's release from prison, and focuses subsequently on his complete inability to readjust to the status quo during the next five months. Devoured by his own rage, Dallow finds it impossible to locate or even desire employment; or, for that matter, to sustain almost any relationship with those around him, whether it be old or new.

---

22 Roland Gräf, *Der Tangospieler* (http://filmmuseumpotsdam.de/de/446–1484.htm).
23 *4. November '89. Der Protest. Die Menschen. Die Reden*, ed. by Annegret Hahn (Berlin DDR: Propyläen, 1990), p. 172.

However, it gradually becomes clear that there are reasons other than just his self obsessions that are responsible for Dallow's bizarre behaviour and repeated failures; reasons emanating from his immediate environment that are less easily decipherable and as such contribute to creating an epistemological grey zone of undecidability, halfway between hallucination and genuine threat. For example, at three different times he is forced into meetings with two bizarre male figures named Schulze (Peter Sodann) and Müller (Rainer Heise), who turn out to be Stasi agents offering to get him his job back at the university in return for his working as an IM in the history department. Although Dallow categorically dismisses them each time, he nevertheless begins to attribute his failure to gain employment to the intrigues of these 'two clowns', as he calls them, and not just to his own self-pitying, abject refusal to take himself seriously, as his temporary girlfriend Elke (Corinna Harfouch) tells him directly as they part ways. Whether Schulze and Müller actually did intervene elsewhere is never confirmed, in part because their interactions with Dallow come to have less of a narrative function and more one of signification, in this case as part of the uncanny mise-en-scène; as only one benign variant of a complex system of observance and control all of us now have come to call security. Drawing on Wolfgang Iser, one might also read Schulze and Müller as a visual 'gap' in the text allowing, if not forcing, the viewer to fill in his or her own meaning, similar to a floating signifier. Certainly the non-diegetic music and moments of comic *Verfremdung* (distanciation) that are introduced incrementally throughout not only add to a prevailing sense of the banality of this evil, if it be evil; it also, in Iser's words, 'activates our own faculties, enabling us to recreate the world it presents'.[24]

Other variants of state intervention are initially not quite as visible, but gradually become so the more our anti-hero simply refuses to work. For instance, on several occasions in his odyssey, Dallow 'accidently' runs into another duo, mostly in bars, in this case his defence lawyer Herr Kiewer (Gunter Schoß) and Dr. Berger (Hermann Beyer), the judge who sentenced him to 21 months in prison. The fact that these supposedly adversarial players in the justice system turn out to be drinking buddies says all Dallow and the viewer need to know about this ever expanding zone of postponed accountability. In the end, Dallow lands a temporary job as a seasonal waiter on the Baltic Island of Hiddensee, from whence he works his way psychically and politically back into the mainstream so as to resume his job at the university.

---

24 Wolfgang Iser, 'The Reading Process: A Phenomenological Approach', *New Literary History*, 3 (1972), 279–99 (p. 285).

Dallow with his 'two clowns', *Der Tangospieler*.

As might be expected, the reception of the *Der Tangospieler* in immediate postwall Germany was mixed. On the one hand, it was chosen as a competition film for the Berlinale in 1991 (as opposed to the rejection at the Berlinale of *The Lives of Others* fifteen years later), won a number of European film prizes,[25] and was praised by Michael Althen of the *Süddeutsche Zeitung,* and numerous other critics, for telling its story without 'maudlin sentimentality and an attitude of the know it all' ('ohne Larmoyanz und Besserwisserei'), with 'precision of memory and remarkable exactness in its reconstruction'.[26] The *taz* review, on the other hand, called it 'disingenuous nostalgia' and went on to elaborate that *Der Tango-spieler* presents us with the 'predictable hot topics of the day such as Stasi, prison, Russian tanks in Prague; nor are we spared images even more predictably dreary, such as run down houses and miserable apartments, all filmed in grubby tones of grey'.[27] *Der Spiegel* described it as a typical DEFA film where 'the filmmaker has

25 1991 Deutscher Filmpreis: Lola, Filmband in Silber, Best Film; 1991 Deutscher Filmpreis: Best Actor (Michael Gwisdeck); 1991 Bergamo (Italy) International Film Festival, Best Film.
26 Michael Althen, '*Der Tangospieler*', *Süddeutsche Zeitung*, 22 February 1991.
27 Oksana Bulgakowa, '*Der Tangospieler*', *tageszeitung*, 18 February 1991.

turned a bitter parable about the absurdity of the narrow-minded into a condensed film about the eternally lasting inner crisis of the soul'.[28]

In taking issue with some of the negative responses to the film, and as a conclusion to this paper, I move now to summarize a reading of *Der Tangospieler* that seeks to tease out the ways it might serve as an alternative, if certainly not an antidote, to a blockbuster Cold War Spy film such as *The Lives of Others*. Interesting to me in this regard is that the only review that looked at the film in a generically similar way to my view was Stephan Holden of the *New York Times*, who began his very positive November 1993 review by saying that 'movies and spy novels have so relentlessly portrayed life under Communism as a paranoid adventure fantasy that a drab little film like Roland Gräf's *Der Tangospieler*, which is set in East Germany in 1968, stands as a revealing corrective to the adventure fantasy cliché'.[29]

In my discussion of spy films that have served as antidotes to the James Bond model, I have drawn on a theoretical paradigm known as 'the grey zone' that finds one of its sources, as is well known, from writings about the Holocaust; and which I will elaborate on now for my discussion of *Der Tangospieler*. Primo Levi coined the phrase to describe the dilemma of prisoners in Nazi concentration camps where relationships 'cannot be reduced to the two blocks, victims and perpetrators [...] The grey zone possesses an incredibly complicated internal structure within itself enough to confuse our need to judge'.[30] It was a zone in the camps where survival often occurred as a result of some form of collaboration, or complicity. Just one of the myriad examples of a grey zone as narrativized in *Der Tangospieler* is Dallow's relationship to his Judge, the oily Dr. Berger. Having sentenced him to 21 months and in his serial subsequent meetings having refused to acknowledge any wrong doing or even doubt about the excessive sentence he imposed, Berger is suddenly attacked and nearly strangled to death on his way home one night by a totally deranged Dallow. Instead of levelling retribution, Berger becomes the enforcer of Dallow's salvation by threatening to have him arrested within three days time if he fails to find employment; and, once Dallow does find a job as a waiter, Berger is the one who pressures the university into giving him an even better position than he had before in the history department.

In contrast to *The Lives of Others*, this is not a story of heroic resistance or hallowed redemption, but rather their opposite. Dallow's nihilistic war against the world around him is engendered by a psychic but also visceral revulsion towards an environment steeped in surveillance and mendacity. On two occasions of im-

---

28 *Der Spiegel*, 'Letzter Tango', 9 (1991), 264.
29 Stephen Holden, '*Der Tangospieler*', *New York Times*, 3 November 1993.
30 Primo Levi, *The Drowned and the Saved* (New York: Vintage, 1989).

plied threat and semi-harassment, he simply bolts from the scene convulsively in order to vomit in the nearest toilet and then returns. Yet it is precisely his refusal to work that renders partly visible the webs of multiple surveillance that with the increasing deployment of IMs have expanded the possibilities for what the 'modernized' MfS spoke of with pride as 'flächendeckend'. At the conclusion of the film, neither he, nor we, is sure about the moral or political status of almost any of those with whom he is involved; or for that matter, the status of Dallow either.

Although staged as a minor triumph, Dallow's return to the history department must ultimately be viewed as surrender by our anti-hero to an unalterable status quo. How do we know this in a maze of undecidability? I see two clues; there could be more. The first is rooted in its historical contextualization: Dallow's release from prison occurs in March of 1968 and his five month odyssey is henceforth linked visually and aurally as non-diegetic white noise in the form of voice radio, television footage, newspaper headlines, and daily fragments of public conversation to the events of the Prague Spring during the same period. This is not to suggest that Dallow ties his fate to those momentous happenings. On the contrary, to the extreme consternation of many of his dissident friends who identify with the attempted reforms, Dallow, the historian, steadfastly insists he has absolutely no interest whatsoever in it. Nor should it be surprising that the tragic crushing of Dubcek and his regime on 22 August occurs simultaneously with Dallow's first day back on the job at the university.

This suggested double defeat is in turn backed up by a second ironic hint to the effect that Dallow's return is a return of the same. The concluding scene of the film opens with Dallow walking down a long hallway at the university on his way to sign a contract. At the other end of the hall walking toward him we see by means of a Dallow point-of-view shot a tall figure in a suit that looks increasingly like the nefarious Müller of 'Schulze and Müller' the closer it gets. From the shot-reverse-shot way they look at each other as they pass each other by we are given no further information. Yet the very fact that Dallow and the Stasi agent Müller occupy the same domain as part of a quotidian collegiality says all that one needs to know about the workings of what Gräf himself labelled disparagingly as 'der gewöhnliche Sozialismus' (everyday socialism).[31] What better end to a 'drab little film' that refuses closure.

Thus what bothered many postwall Western critics most about *Der Tangospieler* was its seeming lack of a critical stance toward the GDR. 'Gräf's treatment of the subject is so tentative', wrote Wolfram Schütte in the *Frankfurter Rund-*

---

31 Roland Gräf, '"Der gewöhnliche Sozialismus". Interview mit Axel Geiss', *Filmspiegel*, 5 (1991), 8–9.

schau, 'that you would think he still had Comrade Mielke looking over his shoulder on the set'.[32] Alfred Holighaus is even more explicit in a rebuke stating that '*Der Tangospieler* resembles a folksy trip down memory lane to a time in the past when things were particularly hard in the GDR. The film does not deal sufficiently harshly with the former state, with its lackeys and fellow-travellers'.[33] Roland Gräf's response to this and similar critiques starts with a reminder that both the book and film versions of *Der Tangospieler* were conceived and, in the case of the film, for the most part carried out before the Wall came down. But rather than apologize for not having 'judged' the system in tones of black-and-white or good and evil, what Gräf sought to portray in Dallow was precisely a 'hero' who 'against his better knowledge and despite terrible experiences nevertheless makes his peace with the system. That was the issue that interested me most. An attitude, I think, that was very prevalent in the GDR'.[34]

What in 1989–1991 Gräf (or anyone else) could never have been able to accomplish in the GDR of the *Wende*, namely a fundamental exposure of Stasi barbarism, pushed him (and Christoph Hein) in turn into an important focus on what Gräf calls 'ever new variations of conformity'.[35] In so doing, we are offered a brilliant micro portraiture of the myriad grey zones of an everyday socialism that under the mantle of 'softer forms of repression' brought into being webs of surveillance by ever increasing numbers of Stasi IMs of their fellow citizens and even family members.

All of which brings us back to our comparison with *The Lives of Others*. In his review of the film, Timothy Garton Ash quite rightly suggests that '[when] negotiating the treacherous moral maze in evaluating how people behave under dictatorships, one characteristic mistake is the simplistic, black-and-white, Manichaean division into good guys and bad guys. X is an informer so he must have been all bad, Y was a dissident so she must have been all good'.[36] We have addressed above how the two paradigms of Cold War films emerging in the post war periods could likewise be distinguished according to strategies of characteriz-

---

32 Wolfram Schütte, '*Der Tangospieler*', *Frankfurter Rundschau*, 21 February 1991.

33 Alfred Holighaus, quoted in Detlef Gwosc, 'Social Criticism in the Films of Roland Gräf', in *DEFA. East German Cinema, 1946–1992*, ed. by Seán Allan and John Sandford (New York and Oxford: Berghahn Books, 1999), pp. 245–66 (p. 251).

34 Gräf, 'Der gewöhnliche Sozialismus', p. 9. Gräf's use of the term 'Der gewöhliche Sozialismus' is a clear reference to the classical Russian documentary film entitled *Der gewöhnliche Faschismus* (Michail Romm, 1965). Here Romm focuses on 'everyday', seemingly normalized dimensions of Nazi barbarism.

35 Gräf, 'Der gewöhnliche Sozialismus', p. 9.

36 Timothy Garton Ash, 'The Stasi on Our Minds', *The New York Review of Books*, 31 May 2007.

ation that differed between black-and-white figures, on the one hand (James Bond films), and grey, that is to say complicated ones (John Le Carré/Martin Ritt *The Spy Who Came in from the Cold*), on the other. In *The Lives of Others*, we find a preponderance of black-and-white, offset by two characters that trouble the scheme, but still lack complexity.

Clearly, the two main perpetrators are quintessentially evil. One is not surprised to discover that the actor playing Colonel Grubitz, Wiesler's sinister superior, is Ulrich Tukur who was well known for his many iconic performances as SS and Stasi Officers on stage and screen.[37] In fact, one might also argue that it is precisely the visual suffusion of his brown Stasi uniform with hints of Prussian-SS grey that further enables *The Lives of Others* to serve ominously as a German totalitarianism film *tout court*. An equally severe caricature of evil is the salacious minister of culture Bruno Hempf (Thomas Thieme), who wants to get rid of the playwright Georg Dreyman so he can pursue unimpeded an affair with Dreyman's partner Sieland. Thus, writes Slavoj Žižek, 'the horror that was subscribed into the very structure of the East German system is relegated to a mere personal whim. What's lost is that the system would be no less terrifying without the minister's personal corruption, even if it were run by only dedicated and "honest" bureaucrats'.[38]

The 'good' people on the other side of the ledger are not really plausibly so, hence they leave us with questions rather than answers. In the case of Wiesler, we are asked by the filmmaker to believe that within an extraordinarily abbreviated amount of time the impact from reading a Brecht poem and listening to 'Die Sonate vom guten Menschen' (The Sonata of the Good Person) could actually undo half a lifetime's socialization into the banality of a bureaucratic GDR security apparatchik. Of course, such a thing is possible, although highly improbable; just as a semi-fascistic Stasi colonel, who marches his bully underlings stomping en masse in and out of apartment buildings in broad daylight is also possible.

But in the GDR of 1984, that is no longer the way the system actually worked. The manner in which this 'real existing socialism' had been reorganized in order 'to protect itself' during the period of détente and 'soft repression' entailed as its starting point an excessive recruitment of IMs living or working within the immediate vicinity of various targeted 'enemies' – IMs (friends, neighbours, col-

---

37 Tukur made his theatre debut in 1984 playing SS Officer Kittel in Joshua Sobel's *Ghetto; Mutters Courage* (My Mother's Courage, Michael Verhoeven, 1995), *Nikolaikirche* (Frank Beyer, 1995), *Der Stellvertreter* (Amen, Constantinos Gavras, 2002), *Eichmanns Ende* (Eichmann's End, Raymond Ley, 2010) are a few of the films in which Tukur played SS Officers or a Stasi Officer.
38 Slavoj Žižek, 'The Dreams of Others', *In These Times*, 18 May 2007 (http://www.inthese-times.com/article/3183/).

leagues, even family members, etc.) who were willing to observe and report on the activities of the 'object' of an OPK, sometimes on a daily basis. One former IM estimated that in the 1980s one in every eight persons in the country was formally involved in the effort to generate Stasi files, and that perhaps 'a third of the population, more or less, had at one time or another worked for the Stasi'.[39] In *The Lives of Others*, Sieland is the only figure nominally an IM, but the brutalizing rape sessions in the back seat of Minister Hempf's limousine, as well as her violent suicide as an act of shame and/or redemption mark her more as a tragic victim than a perpetrator.

While considerably more modest in scope and message, Roland Gräf's *Der Tangospieler* situates its anti-hero in a grey zone marked by personages and events not to be easily deciphered or evaluated by him; or for that matter, by the spectator of the film. For this Gräf was taken to task by a number of critics, who in the political climate of the *Wende* were not in a frame of mind to tolerate what was read by many as an unwillingness to call a spade a spade. What they were looking for, it would seem, is precisely the film that did appear some sixteen years later made by a young West German. Be that as it may, the long term value of *Der Tangospieler* may well lie in its courage to provide us with an updated, perhaps more modernized version of an Orwellian universe where Big Brother has been transmogrified into considerably more banal, yet even more horrifying minions of little brothers and sisters. Which of course would include Dallow himself, as Gräf suggests when he describes him as someone who, although victim of a situation that enabled him to see clearly the horrors of the system, nevertheless reveals himself as 'one of those, who despite knowing better and despite terrible experiences, in the end make their peace with that same system'.[40]

39 See Irena Kukutz and Katja Havermann, *Geschützte Quelle. Gespräche mit Monika H. alias Karin Lenz* (Berlin: Basisdruck, 1990), p. 57. Cited in Robert Gellately, 'Denunciations in Twentieth Century Germany: Aspects of Self-Policing in the Third Reich and the German Democratic Republic', *Journal of Modern History*, 68.4 (1996), 931–67 (p. 955).
40 Gräf, 'Der gewöhnliche Sozialismus', p. 9.

Marc Silberman
Chapter Seven
The Lives of Others: Screenplay as Literature and the Literary Film

The German cinema has a long tradition of artists and performance films, more specifically of films focusing on writers. Classic poets such as Goethe, Schiller, Hölderlin and Büchner have been favourite film protagonists almost since the beginnings of film production in Germany.[1] Literary bio-pics as well as films about fictional writers and the writing process have traditionally offered filmmakers pertinent characters, issues and situations for self-reflexive investigations and commentaries on their métier. While reviewers and scholars have variously characterized Florian Henckel von Donnersmarck's *The Lives of Others* as a thriller, spy film, historical drama, fairy tale, melodrama and psychodrama, and focused almost exclusively on the story's presentation of the systematic surveillance by the Stasi in the GDR, in this essay I consider it from the perspective of a fictional literary film. The filmmaker himself emphasizes in the distributor's official press booklet this context of the film being about the art of film making:

> Because, at the end of the day, although I spent much time researching this topic, my true passion is films, dramaturgy, actors, psychology, not the Stasi or communism. I am not a preacher, nor a historian or politician but a filmmaker, a storyteller. I enjoy thinking and talking most about how to help actors live their art to the fullest, I spend my free time philosophizing about colours, shapes and beauty. Of course, the Stasi is an interesting topic, but the story was there first. And that's what the film is really about.[2]

Taking this claim at face value most obviously focuses attention on the figures of Georg Dreyman, a successful dramatist, and his partner, the stage actress Christa-Maria Sieland, but it also allows us to consider the protagonist, Stasi agent Wiesler, in his role as performer (in the classroom) and performance spectator (surveillance operative) who himself becomes at a crucial turning point in the

---

1 On history of German 'poets' films and films about German poets/writers, see Sigrid Nieberle, *Literarhistorische Filmbiographien – Autorschaft und Literaturgeschichte im Kino. Mit einer Filmographie 1909–2007* (Berlin: De Gruyter, 2008), especially chapter 4: 'Literaturgeschichte vor der Kamera'.
2 'Thirteen Questions with Florian Henckel von Donnersmarck, Writer and Director of *The Lives of Others*', *The Lives of Others Press Booklet* (Sony Classic Films, n.d.), p. 12. (http://www.sonyclassics.com/thelivesofothers/externalLoads/ TheLivesofOthers.pdf)

plot a writer-dramatist, penning the beginning of a play about Lenin as a cover for Dreyman's illegal journalistic activities. Moreover, focusing on *The Lives of Others* as a literary film reveals several other relevant dimensions that may not be so obvious, for example, the film as a backstage drama, explicit and implicit literary references to writers such as Bertolt Brecht and G. E. Lessing and the screenplay itself – authored by von Donnersmarck – as a text with literary pretensions. This will lead me to conclude that the prize-winning, box office success is in the first place a film about the filmmaker and the art of film making, even a manifesto about how von Donnersmarck believes art, and his art of film making, can contribute to reconciling a fractured and controversial German past. From this perspective his film has less to do with GDR reality than with the fraught present of post-2000 Germany in which conflicting memories of pre-unification Germany in East and West remain unresolved. The focus on writers and artists may accurately reflect the importance of cultural life in the GDR and the crucial function of the theatre in particular as an alternative public sphere, and hence the disproportionately strong interest of the Stasi in this demographic, but it should not deflect attention from more general and familiar issues in postwar Germany: complicity, guilt and (lack of) resistance.[3] How does von Donnersmarck, a representative of the younger generation of filmmakers emerging in the 1990s, imagine 'coming to terms with the past' vis-à-vis what he considers to be the (new) shameful German past of the GDR?[4] Attending to the literary aspects of both the screenplay and film helps us to recognize the strategies he employs.

The Lives of Others as Screenplay

Florian Henckel von Donnersmarck authored the screenplay of *The Lives of Others*, for which he garnered major prizes, including the Bavarian Film Prize for best screenplay (January 2006), the German Film Prize for best screenplay (May 2006) and the European Film Prize for best screenplay (December 2006). The printed version appeared as a paperback at the prestigious German publishing

---

3 See Mary Beth Stein, '*Stasi* with a Human Face? Ambiguity in *Das Leben der Anderen*', *German Studies Review*, 31.3 (2008), 567–79 (p. 569). For a more general study on GDR literature as an alternative public sphere, see David Bathrick, *The Powers of Speech. The Politics of Culture in the GDR* (Lincoln: University of Nebraska Press, 1995).

4 The director explicitly criticized what he considered to be the dominant rewriting of history in nostalgic television shows and comedies about the GDR, not naming but referring most likely to films such as Peter Timm's *Go, Trabi, Go* series (1990, 1992), Leander Haußmann's *Sonnenallee* (Sun Alley, 1999) and Wolfgang Becker's *Good Bye, Lenin!* (2003). See 'Thirteen Questions', p. 13.

house Suhrkamp Verlag in Spring 2006 to accompany the opening of the film in March and included also short contributions by the screenwriter, the actor Sebastian Koch (Dreyman) and the historical consultant Manfred Wilke, as well as an interview with actor Ulrich Mühe (Wiesler). This first edition (Suhrkamp Taschenbuch 3786) came out in at least four printings, but because of statements in Mühe's interview about Jenny Gröllmann (his estranged ex-wife) cooperating with the Stasi, she sued, and the publisher was enjoined by a court to blacken several passages because they compromised her privacy rights (pp. 200–204). A second, 'revised and shortened' version of the interview appeared in the updated edition (Suhrkamp Taschenbuch 3908), published in 2007 with the extra-judicial material expunged.[5] This in itself was a remarkable marketing initiative, considering that the publisher is best known for modernist literature and cutting edge scholarship. The institutional status or cultural capital guaranteed by the Suhrkamp name invites us, then, to recognize the aura of von Donnersmarck's 'original screenplay' and to evaluate its literary nature and quality. In fact, screenplay writing in Germany is considered by some to be the stepchild in movie production, and compared to the USA, Britain, France or Italy, published screenplays are the exception rather than the rule. Despite the strong tradition established in the German film industry during the 1920s – one thinks of Carl Mayer's screenplays for canonical Expressionist films or Thea von Harbou's screenplays for Fritz Lang – the art of screenplay writing diminished during the Third Reich, when pre-production censorship and the prohibition of film reviewing created institutional obstacles to their publication. The dominance of *Autorenkino* (authors' cinema) among New German Cinema directors in West Germany during the late 1960s and 1970s meant that the film director, defined as the film's author, rather than the screen writer (who was often the director in any case) became the genius or the authority behind the film. Moreover, the general lack of talented screenplay writers led to a strong reliance at least in the New German Cinema on adaptations of literary texts.[6] Hence, instead of published screenplays we tend to find re-releases of novels or plays adapted for the cinema and marketed upon the

---

5 Florian Henckel von Donnersmarck, *Das Leben der anderen. Filmbuch* (Frankfurt am Main: Suhrkamp, 2006). Note that in contrast to the German film title, the screenplay title does not capitalize 'anderen'. All page numbers in parentheses in this chapter refer to the screenplay in the 2007 paperback edition, from which I have translated passages into English.

6 On adaptations of literary texts in the German cinema, see *German Film and Literature. Adaptations and Transformations*, ed. by Eric Rentschler (New York: Methuen, 1986); *Literaturverfilmungen*, ed. by Franz-Josef Albersmeier und Volker Roloff (Frankfurt am Main: Suhrkamp, 1989), esp. Part 1; *Interpretationen. Literaturverfilmungen*, ed. by Anne Bohnenkamp (Stuttgart: Reclam, 2005).

respective film's release as 'film books' (referred to in German as 'das Buch zum Film').

The published screenplay of *The Lives of Others* was, according to von Donnersmarck, the fifth and last version prior to the shooting script.[7] As quoted above, the director invested quite a bit of time in researching the background to his story, generally claiming one and a half years for that effort, before actually writing the first version of the screenplay, which was undertaken in a monk's cell at a twelfth-century Cistercian abbey outside of Vienna and completed in this preliminary form in six short weeks.[8] Elsewhere he has explained the idea that inspired the screenplay years before that: while listening in the early months of his studies at the Munich Film School in fall 1997 to a recording of pianist Emil Gilels playing Beethoven's *Appassionata* (No. 23 in F minor, Op. 57), he remembered Russian writer Maxim Gorky's anecdote about Lenin, who loved this piece of music but believed such beauty would undermine a commitment to revolutionary violence: 'Lenin had chosen one extreme: all principle, but in a way, his statement was also a beautiful testament to the humanizing power of Art'.[9] We will return later to the 'humanizing power of Art', but the powerful music led von Donnersmarck to imagine then and there what might have happened if Lenin had been forced to listen to Beethoven's piano sonata for the sake of the Bolshevik revolution, and with that the image of a man with headphones listening to music in an empty room triggered within a few moments the entire structure for what became the film.[10] Within three hours he had outlined the story, and then he needed another one and half years to work out the full screenplay after completing his research.[11]

Meanwhile, von Donnersmarck had finished his film training in Munich, where he apparently was introduced to handbooks and guides for writing screen-

---

7 See the director's running commentary on the German DVD edition of the film (Munich: Buena Vista Home Entertainment, 2006).

8 The Cistercian abbey Stift Heiligenkreuz was under the administration of Abbott Gregor Henckel-Donnersmarck. See the article on von Donnersmarck's more recent film *The Tourist* (2010) by Lars-Olav Beier, 'Unter Genieverdacht', *Der Spiegel*, 49 (2010), 140–45 (p. 142).

9 'Thirteen Questions', p. 8.

10 Florian Henckel von Donnersmarck, '"Appassionata": Die Filmidee', in *Das Leben der anderen. Filmbuch* (p. 170). Jennifer Creech points out that the director selectively remembered the Gorky reminiscence of Lenin, who drew a very different conclusion from the anecdote about listening to beautiful music. See Jennifer Creech, 'A Few Good Men: Gender, Ideology, and Narrative Politics in *The Lives of Others* and *Good Bye, Lenin!*' *Women in German Yearbook*, 25 (2009), pp. 100–26 (p. 110).

11 'Thirteen Questions', p. 8.

plays and had learned some of their key lessons.[12] If we accept its autonomy or independence vis-à-vis the completed film, then reading the screenplay as text allows us not only to identify its 'literariness' but also to gain some insight into the process of filming, since we can recognize those passages not transformed into visual images. Thus, it is helpful to distinguish between the terms screenplay and (shooting) script, which do overlap in meaning and function and sometimes are even used interchangeably. The former presents the narrative with commentary on how it is to be converted into visual art, while the latter actually transforms this into dialogue, story flow, camera instructions, lighting set-ups and set description.[13]

Von Donnersmarck's screenplay follows many of the conventions of popular genre cinema, which draw on Aristotelian rule-bound aesthetics of classical drama, including characteristics such as a three-act structure with beginning, middle and end (exposition, conflict, resolution); a causal scene arrangement in which each scene is connected to the previous one; and a closed form, often with a happy end and a clearly articulated moral lesson. This particular screenplay employs familiar conventions from the realist theatre as well. Dramatic irony, for instance, helps create closure when Minister Hempf's early, cynical statement to Dreyman that, despite the writer's firm belief in the changeability of people, they never do change (p. 34), becomes precisely the source of both Hempf's personal denouement and that of his government. The development of dramatic tension is another such theatrical convention. The strategic withholding and revealing of information from the star-crossed figures serves to trigger expectations and anxiety in the viewer, as becomes clear at the dramatic highpoint when the characters come together to witness the opening of the hiding place where the contraband typewriter should be, but then discover that it is empty (pp. 141–42). The screenplay also includes a familiar meta-theatrical device, the play-within-a-play, or here more accurately an intermedial device, the play-within-a-film. The repetition of the same staged scene from Dreyman's drama at the beginning (1984, with Christa-Maria Sieland playing the lead) and in the epilogue (1991, with the lead played by a black actress) thematizes the very idea of prophecy, as the Cassandra-like figure relates her vision of a catastrophic death (p. 25 and p. 146). Finally, the stylized language of realist drama rather than the everyday naturalism of many popular films dominates the dialogue, for example, in Wiesler's question to Grubitz: 'Don't you sometimes yearn that it were already

---

12 For example, the director is familiar with the screen writing 'rules' for building a plot based on turning points. See 'Thirteen Questions', p. 11.

13 Note that the film credits attribute the (shooting) script to Matthias Junge.

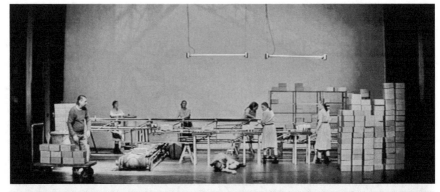

Staging Dreyman's play (a) in 1984 with Christa-Maria Sieland in the lead role, and (b) post-unification in 1991, *The Lives of Others*.

here – communism?' (p. 35). In some significant ways, however, the screenplay *The Lives of Others* deviates from conventional dramatic structures. The first scenes are dominated by long dialogues aimed at creating the oppressive atmosphere rather than signalling the coming plot trajectory (not unlike a chamber drama with a limited number of characters in a closed space). The protagonist Wiesler, moreover, is not established from the outset as the figure of positive identification for the viewer; on the contrary this happens gradually and is recognized as such by the viewer only retrospectively (beginning when Wiesler 'rings' the doorbell so that Dreyman discovers Sieland's infidelity with Minister Hempf, p. 66). In fact, the protagonist in his role as observer remains relatively passive and guarded throughout the film rather than confronting his antagonists, a type of behaviour that one could expect from an undercover Stasi officer. Finally, the film's epilogue, after the resolution in which Wiesler is able to save Dreyman but must sacrifice Sieland, is unusually long (over 15 scenes), although it still serves the interests of conventional dramaturgy by resolving open questions and delivering poetic justice.[14]

A closer look at the screenplay as literary text indicates that the author (von Donnersmarck) employs an omniscient, third-person narrator who intervenes in ways that are characteristic for realistic literary fiction. For example, on the stylistic level there is a striking use of qualifying adjectives to describe the environment ('a sickly plant without blossoms' in the interrogation room, p. 14; or 'hostile [surveillance] equipment' in the attic, p. 76), and the prose is peppered with similes (Sieland gets into Hempf's limousine 'as if she were climbing the gallows', p. 64; and she exits it later 'like a chewed up bone', p. 66). Also, a rhetorical use of repetition signals intensification through the accumulation of phrases. When she returns to the apartment from the encounter in Hempf's limousine, the stage direction reads: 'Christa goes directly into the bathroom, locks the door, washes herself, wants to clean herself, can't, collapses in sobs under the shower' (p. 67); or later when she decides not to come to another tryst with Hempf, we read: 'Very unhappy ["tieftraurig"] the Minister sits on a chair next to a large double bed in an East Berlin hotel room. He realizes that she will not be coming, that she will never again come. That it's over' (p. 113). On the level of narrative voice frequent interpretive and speculative passages, sometimes with a question mark added, reveal a self-conscious narrator – not transformed into a voice-over in the actual film. In a scene that was ultimately not shot, the narrator comments on Wiesler after he has denounced three young people: 'Three people ["Existenzen"] destroyed. Not an unusual end of a day for Wiesler' (p. 38). Or after Sieland exits from the Minister's limousine, the narrator reflects: 'She is paralyzed. Or does she feel something?' (p. 64). In other passages the italicized stage directions comment on the behaviour of the film figures, possibly intended by the author as advice to the film actors. When Wiesler is interrupted in his attic lair by his sidekick, for example, the narrator remarks: 'He has no idea what an effort it is for Wiesler to give him the headphones' (p. 83). These are only a few of the many examples one could point to in the published screenplay as evidence for its status as an autonomous literary text. While usually these details are translated visually through the camera and editing, they demonstrate how von Donnersmarck conceived of his screenplay as something more than a mere script by drawing on specific devices

---

14 Daniela Nagel's study *Das Drehbuch. Ein Drama für die Leinwand? Drehbuchanalyse am Beispiel von Florian Henckel von Donnersmarcks 'Das Leben der Anderen'* (Marburg: Tectum, 2008) presents a systematic review of the screenplay; I am indebted to her careful analysis and paraphrase here some of her conclusions.

of literary fiction that reveal the context and the inner life of his figures at crucial points in the story.[15]

The Lives of Others as Backstage Drama

If *The Lives of Others* has a strong connection to the tradition of literary fiction films, it also shares genre characteristics of the cinematic backstage drama.[16] The prototype is the backstage musical that became popular with the introduction of sound by Hollywood studios, peaking in popularity during the late 1920s and 1930s. *Broadway Melody* (Harry Beaumont, 1929) marked the beginning of an entire series of such backstage romances, and *42ⁿᵈ Street* (Lloyd Bacon, 1933) – presenting the behind-the-scene view of a musical production from casting call to opening night – counts as the paradigm for a trend that peaked in the 1950s with romantic comedies such as *Kiss Me Kate* (George Sydney, 1953) and *There's No Business Like Show Business* (Walter Lang, 1954). Meanwhile the backstage drama, which continues to produce compelling films such as *Black Swan* (Darren Aronowsky, 2010), traces the trials and tribulations of struggling artists in the various performing arts, including the concert world (composers and singers), dance (chorus girls and ballerinas), opera (divas) and the live theatre (directors and actors). Von Donnersmarck is not only well versed in Hollywood film history but also consciously strives to adapt the entertainment and production values of American popular cinema in his films. Yet there is also a national tradition of the 'backstager' in Germany, the 'Revuefilm' or dance and music extravaganza, which became a staple of cinema entertainment during the Third Reich in the 1930s and 1940s and in postwar East and West Germany during the 1950s. One thinks of box office hits like *Hallo Janine!* (Hello Janine!, Carl Boese, 1938) and *Es leuchten die Sterne* (Stars Are Shining, Hans Zerlett, 1938), the West German feature *Schwarzwaldmädel* (Black Forest Girl, Hans Deppe, 1950) and the East German musical feature *Meine Frau macht Musik* (My Wife Makes Music, Hans Heinrich, 1956). Yet already prior to the Third Reich backstage classics were produced: E. A. Dupont's silent feature *Variété* (Jealousy, 1925) was the first of a long series of romantic dramas treating love, risk and injury under the circus tent and in the circus wagons, and Josef von Sternberg's *Der blaue Engel* (The Blue Angel, 1930) introduced the

---

15 Nagel, *Das Drehbuch*, p. 99.
16 Rick Altman distinguishes between genres and cycles and suggests that the 'backstager' is a cycle rather than a genre in 'Reusable Packaging: Generic Products and the Recycling Process', in *Refiguring American Film Genres: Theory and History*, ed. by Nick Browne (Berkeley: University of California Press, 1998), pp. 1–41 (p. 22).

seedy backstage intrigue that would become a staple of the German cinema with powerful features by the likes of Detlev Sierck (*Zu neuen Ufern* [To New Shores], 1937), the East Germans Kurt Maetzig (*Ehe im Schatten* [Marriage in the Shadows], 1947) and Konrad Wolf (*Solo Sunny*, 1980) and the West German Rainer Werner Fassbinder (*Lili Marleen*, 1980). The backstage genre codifies several typical elements relevant to *The Lives of Others*. Beyond the physical setting and the cast of figures, conflicts generally arise in a parallel or mirror situation that contrasts on-stage and backstage encounters, public and private desires. This in turn provides a quintessentially and potentially self-reflexive cinematic structure in which the pro-filmic theatre audience and the virtual film viewer both watch staged performances with overlapping but different knowledge and expectations.

As already mentioned, *The Lives of Others* frames the story with stage performances of a scene at the Gerhart Hauptmann Theatre (identified by name in the screenplay, pp. 22–30 and pp. 146–50, Hauptmann being a major German dramatist who lived from 1862 until 1946), and other film figures besides the playwright and actress hail from the theatre, including the side-lined director Jerska, who commits suicide, and the director Schwalber, who turns out to be a Stasi mole with the cover name of Max Reinhardt, as we read in the screenplay (p. 11, Reinhardt being the name of a famous German theatre director and manager who lived from 1873 until 1943). Von Donnersmarck complicates the theatre dynamic, however, by embedding his characters within a different kind of performance space. Much of the film action is situated within the apartment inhabited by Dreyman and Sieland, which becomes a stage observed by the Stasi surveillance team sitting above in the building's attic space. The apartment contains a number of design elements related to the artistic careers of its inhabitants: posters on the wall document well-known GDR theatre productions (Peter Hacks's *Omphale*, Peter Weiss's *Der neue Prozess* [The New Trial]); a marionette on the wall is framed behind Sieland during the crucial dialogue in which she and Dreyman argue about her dependence on the Party (p. 82); and when the Stasi searches the apartment, we see GDR magazines like *Film und Fernsehen* and *Theater der Zeit* on Dreyman's writing desk.[17] Not only does Wiesler sketch out the apartment's spatial configuration with chalk on the attic floor as a kind

---

17 Jerska's room also has a theatre poster of a famous GDR production of Schiller's *Die Räuber* (The Robbers) hanging on the wall. In an interview von Donnersmarck has stated that he prefers more abstract design elements, like the generic books in Dreyman's overfilled bookcases that suggest an intellectual's study, and expressed his hope that the 'clearly visible posters [had] a letter size that is really too small to read' so as not to be distracting for the viewer. See Diane Carson, 'Learning from History in *The Lives of Others*: An Interview with Writer/Director Florian Henckel von Donnersmarck', *Journal of Film and Video*, 62.1–2 (2010), 13–22 (p. 16).

Christa-Maria Sieland is framed next to a marionette hanging on the wall as she and Dreyman discuss their relationship to the Communist Party, *The Lives of Others*.

of map for blocking the movements of his charges below, but parallel cutting between the apartment and surveillance centre above configures spying itself as a theatrical relationship between observer and observed, spectator and actor, listener and speaker. Thus, Wiesler sits in the theatre and watches the play in the film's opening performance, but he also observes through binoculars the audience, including Dreyman in his loge and Minister Hempf in his orchestra seat. As one astute critic notes: 'The various parallels that are drawn between the voyeurism of the audience in the theater, the cinema, and the Stasi in the attic, point to the complexities inherent in the exercise and control of power'.[18] This extends even further, if we consider the film's interrogation scenes, first in Wiesler's lecture at the beginning of the film narrative when he presents excerpts from a taped interrogation to his students at the Stasi training school, and later when he himself interrogates Sieland at the Stasi prison. In both scenes the figures' masks (that is, the roles of interrogator and interrogated) as well as the interplay of looks conveyed by the camera and editing reinforce the power dynamics of voyeurism inherent in the practice of surveillance. As a consequence, the tropes of seeing/being seen and watching/being watched dominate the entire film, from the lecture on interrogation techniques that ends with Grubitz's applause for Wiesler's rhetorical 'performance' to the performance of Dreyman's play about prophetic visions to various tools used for spying (binoculars,

18 Mareike Herrmann, 'The Spy As Writer: Florian Henckel von Donnersmarck's *Das Leben der Anderen*', *Gegenwartsliteratur. Ein germanistisches Jahrbuch*, 7, ed. by Paul Michael Lützeler and Stephen K. Schindler (Tübingen: Stauffenburg, 2008), pp. 90–112 (p. 94).

cameras, television monitors) and the peephole in the entry door of Dreyman's neighbour.

Von Donnersmarck implements these tropes to structure the relations of power and control represented in the film, and this becomes nowhere more densely 'performed' than in the face-to-face encounter between Wiesler and Sieland in a desolate corner bar. She is trying to decide whether to meet Hempf again that evening, and Wiesler – who had eavesdropped from his surveillance centre in the attic on her intense conversation with Dreyman moments before she left the apartment – approaches her and, like Dreyman, wants to convince her not to give in to Hempf's sexual blackmail:

> Wiesler: Frau Sieland.
> *Christa looks up automatically.*
> Sieland: Do we know each other?
> Wiesler: You don't know me. But I know you ...
> He has her attention. Staggering slightly, he sits down at her table.
> Wiesler: Many people love you ... only because you are how you are.
> Sieland: An actor is never how he is.
> Wiesler: But you are.
> *She stares at him with a questioning look.*
> Wiesler: I have seen you on stage. There you were more how you are than ... how you are now.
> *Christa smiles at the helpless formulation and the statement, which pleases her.*
> Sieland: (*smiling, trying to be ironic*) You know how I am?
> Wiesler: Yes, I am your audience. (p. 86)

As Gary Schmidt has written, Wiesler assumes a position here of looking while not being seen. He knows her predicament, but she does not know that he spies on her as a Stasi agent:

> Wiesler knows the intimate details of Sieland's life, whereas he is completely unknown to her; Wiesler is an agent of the Stasi, whereas Sieland is an actress dependent on the good will of the state that Wiesler represents in order to practise her profession. Yet these unequal positions of power and knowledge are framed positively in this exchange, which offers both Wiesler and the viewer a fantasy of sovereign authorial power not only to create meaning through narrative scripting, but also to clearly define the role for those who participate in the production and dissemination of meaning.[19]

---

19 Gary Schmidt, 'Between Authors and Agents: Gender and Affirmative Culture in *Das Leben der Anderen*', *German Quarterly*, 82.2 (2009), 231–49 (p. 238).

The double import of Wiesler's statement that he is Sieland's audience and knows her true self better than she is lost on her but not on us, the cinema viewer whose point of view has gradually become aligned with that of Wiesler through the cinematography and editing. The cinema viewer comes to identify with the spying operation as a positive form of knowing and in this case intervening in the life of the other, the object of surveillance. This is one of the most striking aspects of *The Lives of Others*, its ability to position the viewer to share in a Stasi agent's power and to identify with his desire to manipulate her, to write her script for her, so to speak.[20] Yet it is important to emphasize that if both espionage and theatre aim at influencing their respective audiences, there is a difference. In the former, surveillance and staged interrogations by operatives are opaque procedures for those being watched but felt by them to be a pervasive threat, whereas actors in the theatre know they are masked figures on stage and being watched by their audience in the service of entertainment and enlightenment.

Literary Allusions in *The Lives of Others*

The imbrication of visibility and self-identity with the agent/actor's mask brings us to Bertolt Brecht and to von Donnersmarck's explicit appeal to his 'sponsorship' of the film's message about the transformative nature of art. Although the filmmaker has expressed his admiration for the grandness of Art by opera composer Richard Wagner and writer Thomas Mann, both of whom Brecht criticized harshly and repeatedly for their politics and aesthetics, he 're-functions' Brecht as a weapon for the 'humanizing power of Art'.[21] In a film set in the GDR theatre environment the reference to Brecht is not surprising, after all he is one of the most important German-language writers, poets and dramatists of the twentieth century, a communist sympathizer who played a significant role among exile German intellectuals and artists in the anti-Hitler, anti-fascist effort. After being called to testify before Joe McCarthy's House Un-American Activities Committee in 1947, Brecht immediately left the USA for Switzerland and settled in East Berlin in 1948, where the communist leaders invited him to establish his own theatre, the Berliner Ensemble, where he produced plays until his death in 1956. As a non-dogmatic, internationally recognized Marxist who championed artistic

---

20 In a psychoanalytic approach to the film Diana Diamond calls this effect 'embodied simulation', see 'Empathy and Identification in Von Donnersmarck's *The Lives of Others*', *Journal of the American Psychoanalytic Association*, 56.3 (2008), 811–32.
21 See Baier, 'Unter Genieverdacht', p. 140.

experimentation, he had a tense relationship with the government authorities but represented for many East German artists and intellectuals a reasoned voice in support of modern art and a staunch critic of orthodox socialist realism.

What is Brecht's function, then, in *The Lives of Others*? His name arises during Dreyman's birthday party when his close friend Jerska, who avoids the other partygoers, retreats into a corner with a volume of poems by Brecht.[22] Later Wiesler steals this very volume from the apartment, with its distinct yellow binding, and we see him lying on his sofa, while we hear a voice-over, Dreyman's voice, as he reads the first strophe of Brecht's famous love poem 'Erinnerung an die Marie A.' (Remembering Marie A.). Most apparently Brecht functions on the story level first as a representative of the kind of high art to which Wiesler never before had access but which he now discovers through his gradual sympathy for and identification with Dreyman. So Brecht becomes a measure if not even a motivation for Wiesler to change sides; it is the first step of his 'moral education' that will succeed by means of the humanizing power of Art, be it a piano sonata, a novel or a poem. That he reads this particular poem (well known to the German viewing audience) and fantasizes Dreyman reading it to or for him further underscores the depth of feeling he has developed for the playwright, one that will later be reciprocated by Dreyman writing a novel dedicated to him. Indeed, von Donnersmarck has even pointed out that this short scene suggests how the 'real axis of love' is between these two men (rather than between Dreyman and Sieland).[23] Less apparent, because we only hear the first of three strophes is the poem's message. Brecht's initial title for the 1920 poem was 'Sentimental Song No. 1004', indicating its characteristic critique both of sentimental love songs and the repetitive nature of this type of poem. And indeed the first strophe introduces a series of sentimental clichés such as the September moon, the pale girl in his arms, etc. But the two following strophes, which we do not hear, invert this sentimentality, producing a parody of the traditional love poem, because here the lyrical I, years later thinking back on the encounter with his lover, has forgotten what she looked like and can only remember the passage of time and the huge white

---

22 The screenplay notes that Jerska reads a poem at this point, one of Brecht's children's poems from the collection *Kleine Lieder für Steff* (Little Songs for Steff, 1934, pp. 52–53), but von Donnersmarck remarks in the director's commentary on the German DVD edition that the Brecht heirs (that is, Barbara Brecht-Schall) refused to allow him to include it in the film. Years later in the film, when Dreyman reads his Stasi files, he comes across a note about that poem, read in a voiceover now by Wiesler: 'Jerska reads "Lazlo" [Dreyman] a poem by B. Brecht. Because of its counterrevolutionary content probably from a West German edition' (p. 154). Again this pointed irony was not included in the film.
23 See the director's running commentary on the German DVD edition.

cloud he happened to have noticed while embracing her. As Gary Schmidt has argued in his sharply critical essay about the film's misogynous gender relations and what he calls its masculine aesthetics, the dematerialization of the female lover's body in the poem (she is replaced by the cloud and a sense of fleeting time) corresponds to the death of Christa-Maria Sieland that will ultimately enable the writer Dreyman to discover in Wiesler his protective 'angel' and begin writing again. In a visualization of that final image of the cloud in the poem, Schmidt writes:

> As Wiesler speeds away from the street in which Christa-Maria lay dying just minutes before, the camera cuts to an image of moving clouds; shot from the perspective of a moving vehicle, the clouds offer a fleeting vision, which, like in Brecht's poem, becomes more real than the vanished woman: with Christa-Maria barely dead, the film already transports the viewer back into the ostensibly transcendent realm of masculine aesthetics.[24]

The transcendence of problematic female corporeality is realized in the masculine written word, a form of communication between writer and reader, Dreyman and Wiesler, that takes place triumphantly now in a novel rather than on the stage through the embodiment of the female actress.[25] Brecht's ironic stance toward the sentimental affirmation of a spiritual union is turned on its head by the conclusion of the film.

There are other more oblique references to Brecht as well. The title of Dreyman's play, *Gesichter der Liebe* (Faces of Love), may bring to mind Brecht's play *Die Gesichte der Simone Marchard* (The Visions of Simone Machard), a story set in 1940 France around the prophetic visions of a Jeanne d'Arc-type character that he worked on in exile from 1941 until 1943.[26] The musical score that Jerska presents to Dreyman at his birthday party also alludes to Brecht. This is 'Die Sonate vom Guten Menschen' (The Sonata of the Good Person), which Dreyman later plays on his piano upon learning of Jerska's suicide, while Wiesler eavesdrops in the attic, ever more fascinated and moved by the music he hears. At this point Dreyman expresses the idea noted above that sparked the entire film story for von Donners-

---

24 Schmidt, 'Between Authors and Agents', pp. 243–44.

25 Roger Cook reads this privileging of Brecht's poem as the first step in Dreyman's gradual repudiation of the theatre and implicitly of Brecht's politics; see Roger Cook, 'Literary Discourse and Cinematic Narrative: Scripting Affect in *Das Leben der Anderen*', in *Cinema and Social Change in Germany and Austria*, ed. by Gabriele Mueller and James M. Skidmore (Waterloo, ON: Wilfrid Laurier University Press, 2012), pp. 79–95 (p. 82).

26 Note that this title *Gesichter der Liebe* does not appear in the screenplay but we do see a brief image of the theatre program with the playwright's name and the title. Actor Ulrich Mühe calls the play by this name in his running commentary on the German DVD edition. Also, the commercially marketed CD with the film music by Gabriel Yared includes the cut called *Gesichter der Liebe*.

marck: Lenin's conviction that one cannot appreciate beautiful music and also fight for the revolution: 'Can someone who has heard this music, really heard it, still be a bad person?', Dreyman asks Sieland (p. 77). Wiesler really hears the music, conveyed visually by the close up of his head with the earphones as a tear slowly roles down his cheek. This marks the definitive shift from Wiesler's emotional detachment to empathy with Dreyman, and after this scene he is referred to as the eponymous 'good person' three times in contradistinction to the widespread reputation of Stasi operatives as 'bad people': first in his encounter with the young boy in the elevator (p. 79), then in his conversation with Sieland in the bar (p. 87) and finally in the last sequence when he discovers Dreyman's just published novel titled 'Die Sonate vom Guten Menschen', dedicated to him personally with his agent's code name HGW XX/7 (p. 158).

The good/bad person dichotomy resonates, of course, with Brecht's play *Der gute Mensch von Sezuan* (The Good Person of Sezuan), one of his most performed plays worldwide, written in Scandinavian exile between 1938 and 1941 and first staged in Switzerland in 1943. Many critics have commented on the film's intertextual reference to Brecht's split figure Shen Te/Shui Ta, identifying variously Sieland, Wiesler and/or Dreyman with the dilemma Brecht thematized of maintaining goodness in a world shaped by self-interest and exploitation of power.[27] As in the case of the poem above, the filmmaker appropriates Brecht in this context for a symptomatically un-Brechtian purpose. Whereas the play and Brecht's views on art generally insist on the need to change society so that the goodness of individuals like Shen Te will not be perverted, von Donnersmarck inserts Brecht into his own aesthetic 'system' that assumes great art must remain apolitical in order to humanize a bad person like Wiesler, who can then change the world: 'I really don't believe there is such a thing as politics. It's all about individuals. [...] So I tried to focus on individual psychology in the film. Rather than tell a political story, I show how people make the politics and how that affects people.'[28]

---

[27] Eva Horn, 'Media Conspiracy: Love and Surveillance in Fritz Lang and Florian Henckel von Donnersmarck', *New German Critique*, 103 (2008), 127–44 (p. 142), points to the contrasting ethical value assigned to goodness and politics in Brecht's comedy and the tragic film story; Mary Beth Stein, '*Stasi* with a Human Face?', pp. 576–77, examines the masks that Dreyman and Wiesler assume in their attempts to be subversive but good; Mareika Herrmann, 'The Spy As Writer', pp. 106–8, pursues a parallel reading of the power dynamics engaged by the dissimulation of Shen Te in the play and Wiesler in the film; Jennifer Creech, 'A Few Good Men', p. 111, compares Christa-Maria Sieland to Brecht's split character; and Gary Schmidt, 'Between Authors and Agents', p. 244, sees the respective messages about the possibility of goodness in a dehumanizing society in the play and the film as irreconcilable.

[28] John Esther, 'Between Principle and Feeling: An Interview with Florian Henckel von Donnersmarck', *Cineaste*, 32.2 (2007), 40–42 (p. 40).

In short, both writers, indeed even the film's fictional writer Dreyman, are committed to art as a means of changing the world, but there is a fundamental difference in how they see change coming about. Brecht's Shen Te, a sympathetic figure with whom the viewer identifies, learns that as a good person she cannot survive under the social and material conditions of capitalism, but she also dons the mask of the ruthless and contemptible Shui Ta when her generosity is no longer sustainable.[29] Thus, the play's open end leaves her facing the audience with no solution, that is, demanding from the viewer – who now understands her predicament – to find a solution. Von Donnersmarck, on the contrary, structures a story around the viewer's gradual identification with the protagonist Wiesler, who appears initially to be a bad person but then undergoes a moral transformation through listening to music and reading a poem by Brecht. The film viewer is asked to recognize the domain of art as a means of self-transformation and redemption, no matter what the social or political contingencies; capitalism and communism from this perspective are both equally oppressive and, as far as art is concerned, the individual, not society, needs to be changed.

The echo of Friedrich Schiller's idealist aesthetics is not accidental and points to a larger program of aesthetic restoration that von Donnersmarck projects for post-unification Germany. Schiller articulated the classical function of theatre as a moral institution aimed at aesthetic education and self-improvement in his essay 'Die Schaubühne als moralische Anstalt' ('The Stage as Moral Institution', 1785). Brecht, an informed but critical reader of Schiller, rejected this humanistic line of reasoning based on the transcendent power of art to attain higher, universal truths. While he shared Schiller's goal of changing the world, his own views on the relationship of art to social transformation emphasized the material and contingent nature of experience, and his notion of pleasure ('Vergnügen') in the theatre aimed to displace Schiller's sentimental pathos that von Donnersmarck reintroduces through the melodramatic structure of his film.[30] Thus, *The Lives of Others* (mis)uses Brecht for a purported aesthetics of resistance

---

29 A further literary reference within the context of 'goodness' is to writer Wolfgang Borchert (1921–1947) whose poem 'Versuch es' (Try It) contains the refrain 'und versuche gut zu sein' (try to be good). These are the lyrics of the music played at the party after the opening of Dreyman's play where he and Sieland encounter Minister Hempf. The song, 'Stell Dich mitten in den Regen' (Go Right into the Rain), based on the Borchert poem, was by the GDR band Bayon.

30 On Schiller, see Cheryl Dueck's brief comment in 'The Humanization of the Stasi in *Das Leben der Anderen*', *German Studies Review*, 31.3 (2008), 599–608 (p. 606) and Gary Schmidt, 'Between Authors and Agents', p. 232. On Brecht's critique of Schiller, see, for example, §3 in 'A Short Organon for the Theatre', in *Brecht on Theatre*, ed. and trans. by John Willett (New York: Hill and Wang, 1964), p. 180–81.

to the Stasi's secrecy and moral corruption but then implements un-Brechtian strategies of emotional identification with individual suffering that confirm an inner freedom only to be achieved through the transformative power of art. This is the melodramatic structure of identity and empathy already examined above in Wiesler and Sieland's brief encounter in the bar.

The Hollywood melodrama is a powerful model for the kind of thematics von Donnersmarck pursues. Historian Manfred Wilke, credited as a scholarly consultant to the film project, advised the filmmaker already while he was writing the first version of the screenplay with the intention of producing a film that would fulfil Hollywood expectations ('den Ansprüchen von Hollywood genügen').[31] Film melodrama is an expansive concept referring variously to a genre, a style or even a theme, but a basic definition includes strong appeal to the emotions in a story that opposes character aspirations to institutional contexts, personal freedom to repressive social constraints. Critics did not need the corroboration of the 2007 Oscar for Best Foreign Language Film to recognize *The Lives of Others*' adept use of Hollywood formulas, and some have sketched out in detail how the film uses a melodramatic narrative to achieve moral legibility through the representation of undeserved victimhood in inhuman times (that is, in the GDR).[32] More relevant than Schiller, let alone Brecht, may be in this context the connection to G. E. Lessing's concept of the bourgeois tragedy as reference frame for von Donnersmarck's fictional portrayal of individual emancipation based on the shared values of humanism, a connection that is not far removed from the tradition of melodrama.[33]

In the play *Emilia Galotti* (1772) and the programmatic theatre reviews collected in his *Hamburgische Dramaturgie* (Hamburg Dramaturgy, 1767), Lessing proposed a counter theatre practice to that of the dominant tragic mode with its

---

31 Manfred Wilke, 'Fiktion oder erlebte Geschichte: Zur Frage der Glaubwürdigkeit des Films *Das Leben der Anderen*', *German Studies Review*, 31.3 (2008), 589–98 (p. 591). See also Wilke's contribution, 'Wieslers Umkehr', in von Donnersmarck, *Das Leben der anderen. Filmbuch*, pp. 201–13, as well as his contribution in this volume.

32 See Daniela Berghahn, 'Remembering the Stasi in a Fairy Tale of Redemption: Florian Henckel von Donnersmarck's *Das Leben der Anderen*', *Oxford German Studies*, 38.3 (2009), 321–33, and Jaimey Fisher, 'German Historical Film as Production Trend: European Heritage Cinema and Melodrama', in *The Collapse of the Conventional. German Film and Its Politics at the Turn of the Twenty-First Century*, ed. by Jaimey Fisher and Brad Prager (Detroit: Wayne State University Press, 2010), pp. 186–215, as well as Andrea Rinke's contribution in this volume.

33 On the relation of the bourgeois tragedy to stage melodrama, see Lothar Fietz, 'On the Origins of the English Melodrama in the Tradition of Bourgeois Tragedy and Sentimental Drama: Lillo, Schröder, Kotzebue, Sheridan, Thompson, Jerrold', in *Melodrama. The Cultural Emergence of a Literary Genre*, ed. by Michael Hays and Anastasia Nikolopoulou (New York: St. Martin's Press, 1996), pp. 83–101.

aristocratic heroes and values. His model of the bourgeois tragedy, conceived at a time when the bourgeoisie was just beginning to assert its autonomy in German political and cultural life, cultivated a specific moral-emotional disposition or sensibility by representing the quotidian bourgeois experience under the regime of absolutism. Two aspects are especially noteworthy in our context of film melodrama.[34] Lessing's hero/ine is defined as a moral rather than a social being, whose heroic character emerges from personal convictions, not from social grievances. External or political conflicts are internalized and reflected back as moral conflicts, and the individual is responsible for his/her actions while objective, material conditions merely trigger the individual's fate. Hence, in Lessing's view not historical authenticity but the dramatic figure's internal coherence takes priority, reflecting the Enlightenment ideal that the active individual is master of his destiny. Second, Lessing reinvents the function of sentiment or emotion, arguing that sympathy can be mobilized in the theatre audience only by something on the scale of the individual, friend or family but not on the level of the abstract state. Through identity and empathy with the bourgeois hero/ine, the viewer ideally achieves a higher stage of moral education. One reviewer went so far as to qualify *The Lives of Others* as the *Emilia Galotti* of German reunification, referring to the play's staging of the conflict between the bourgeois heroine's sense of propriety and the arbitrary exercise of power by the aristocracy.[35] If the film, as I propose, is a regressive fantasy that equates the emancipation from GDR state socialism with the emancipation of the bourgeoisie from feudal class relations in the Enlightenment (or the historical emergence of the bourgeois subject) and with the redemption of a Stasi officer from the opportunism of the GDR's nomenclatura, this makes sense! Yet, while Lessing wrote the script, so to speak, for the social upheaval that would come about through the French Revolution, anticipating by 15 years the momentous shift in class relations it brought about, von Donnersmarck reaffirms 15 years after the 'peaceful revolution', undertaken in 1989 by the collective actions of the people of the GDR, a specific tradition of German idealism in which individual agency is invested with the power to change history.

This brings me back to the initial claim that *The Lives of Others* is not about the GDR but rather gives voice to a contemporary, post-unification desire for reconciliation of and with the schizophrenic Cold War German past. Analysing the literary dimensions and allusions in the screenplay and film reveals that von

---

34 See Gotthold Ephraim Lessing, 'Das 14. Stück' and 'Das 23. Stück', in *Hamburgische Dramaturgie*, ed. by Klaus Berghahn, rev. edn (Stuttgart: Reclam, 1999), pp. 77–81 and 121–25.
35 Oksana Bulgakowa, '*Das Leben der Anderen* – Rückschau auf einen deutschen Erfolgsfilm', *Film-Dienst*, 60.11 (2007), 15–16.

Donnersmarck suggests resolution can be achieved by restoring the humanity of someone who seems least likely to deserve redemption, a Stasi officer who enjoys verbally tormenting his victims.[36] From this perspective the film fits within a larger context of memory politics in Germany, where the representation of victims and perpetrators has a sophisticated history anchored in controversial discussions about German shame for the genocide of the Jews and responsibility for crimes against humanity in the Second World War. Beginning in the 1960s in both East and West Germany the cinema became a privileged medium for reflecting and revealing changing attitudes about this past. As witnesses with their lived memories of that history pass away, their children and children's children begin to tell their own stories, and historical scholarship intervenes with other narratives and documentary evidence. In the new millennium, as Germany becomes more integrated into Europe and more confident of its 'normality', both the cinema and television have increasingly featured stories about this past that seek to humanize, psychologize and 'understand' individual perpetrators, bystanders, resisters and victims. In fact, the very definition of victim and victimization is being renegotiated.[37] *The Lives of Others* focuses on another, more recent German past that also raises issues of shame and responsibility, and von Donnersmarck's thematic and aesthetic choices, which turn this past into moving images, share many strategies with the longer tradition of coming to terms with the Nazi past. As we know from that discourse of *Vergangenheitsbewältigung* (coming to terms with the past), memory practices are engaged in the production of meaning, and these practices, like the film itself, are historical in nature and open to counter narratives.

---

36 Other literary allusions I have not pursued in this chapter include in the screenplay a characterization of Jerska's apartment as 'Faust's study' (p. 45) and a reference to Lady Macbeth when Dreyman's fingers have traces of red ink from the ribbon in the contraband typewriter (p. 109), as well as in the film the copy of dissident Soviet author Alexander Solzhenitsyn's novel *The First Circle* (1968), found by the Stasi when they search Dreyman's apartment, and the bust of writer Maxim Gorky on his desk.

37 For examples of such media entertainment and further discussion, see the introduction and articles in *Screening War. Perspectives on German Suffering*, ed. by Paul Cooke and Marc Silberman (Rochester, NY: Camden House, 2010).

Ian Thomas Fleishman

CHAPTER EIGHT
International 'Auditorism': The Postnational Politics of Interpretation of von Donnersmarck's *The Lives of Others*

Although one might not notice it immediately, Florian Henckel von Donnersmarck's first full-length feature film – *The Lives of Others* (2006) – begins with a border crossing. The opening sequence portrays, in part, an unnerving interrogation undertaken by the film's protagonist-to-be, Stasi captain Gerd Wiesler, who is shown impassively extracting information from his unfortunate source, an acquaintance of someone who has successfully defected to the West. The traversal – or rather, in this case, transgression, *going over* – of the national frontier is thus a precondition for the film's beginning and the origin of a central tension to be played out over the course of the work's narrative, namely: the simultaneous construction of and challenge to distinct national identity. Initially an impediment to the free exchange of bodies and ideas across imposed national divisions, Wiesler's empathetic education (what Ute Wölfel has called an 'aesthetic education') will ultimately make of him a martyr to the cause of crossing a variety of borders – an attitude ironically implicit to his idiosyncratic and intrusive reading strategy throughout.[1] Formally, *The Lives of Others* registers this readerly approach by blurring the border between sight and sound, rendering the Stasi spy's sonic experience visual in a manner to be elucidated in this chapter.

Presenting taped audio excerpts of this initial interrogation to a class of aspiring Stasi agents – slightly later in the same sequence – Wiesler insistently reminds his students that the escaped defector and his captive friend are enemies of the East German state; but at stake here, more globally, is a danger to the status of the nation-state as such. After all, one might rightly regard the fall of the Berlin Wall (with which the film concludes) as the decisive beginning of the phenomenon of mature globalization. William Outhwaite and Larry Ray, for instance, contrast today's ostensibly '"borderless" world'[2] to the Cold War 'world of borders *par excellence* – both physical borders epitomized by the Berlin Wall and sym-

---

1 Ute Wölfel, 'Inverting the Lives of "Others": Retelling the Nazi Past in *Ehe im Schatten* and *The Lives of Others*', *German Life and Letters*, 64.4 (2011), 601–18 (p. 615).

2 William Outhwaite and Larry Ray, *Social Theory and Post-Communism* (Oxford: Blackwell, 2005), p. 117.

bolic borders of "us" and "them" in which crossing a land frontier involved the frisson of transgression'.[3] 1989 then marks the birth of what might be understood as 'more porous' national divisions 'subject to repeated panics over migration and "asylum"'.[4] Under protection during the opening interrogation of *The Lives of Others* is not merely an exemplary national border, but the very *possibility* of the same. And in this manner – considering the ultimate collapse of the nation-state being defended – Wiesler's anxiety regarding border crossing in this first sequence is pertinent not only to the historical conditions in which the film's narrative is to be set, but, perhaps more importantly, also to the political conditions in which it ends: the postwall Europe in which the film is to be produced and received.

Seen from the perspective of a panic about borders, a new light is shed on von Donnersmarck's film – which chronicles a political history concluding with this very phenomenon: German unification and the definitive dissolution of the ultimate border between East and West. This is of particular importance for the postnational politics of *The Lives of Others* if we follow Jürgen Habermas's intimation in *Die postnationale Konstellation* (*The Postnational Constellation)* that the problematic postwall unification of Germany largely parallels current concerns with postnationalism[5] – a set of concerns especially relevant to *film* as an international art form and as a purportedly postnational emissary of national heritage. Here, then, I propose to examine how the filmic form itself inevitably complicates the implicitly nationalizing project of the film's protagonist and an international understanding of this film as a supposed monument to life in the German Democratic Republic. Reading von Donnersmarck's debut from the angle of the postnational, I intend to expose how *The Lives of Others* negotiates an East German national identity for an international audience. After outlining the parameters of national cinema in a contemporary globalized environment, I will examine key sequences from the film in order to demonstrate how *The Lives of Others* thematizes and problematizes these concerns both as a matter of plot and, more subtly but just as importantly, also on a formal level.

---

3 Outhwaite and Ray, *Social Theory*, p. 1.
4 Outhwaite and Ray, *Social Theory*, p. 1.
5 Jürgen Habermas, *Die postnationale Konstellation* (Frankfurt am Main: Suhrkamp, 1998).

(Post)national Cinema

The transcendence of national boundaries is central both to the subject of the film and to its intended audience, for, as one of Germany's most recent international blockbusters, *The Lives of Others* must simultaneously be addressed to a spectatorship sharing this collective past and destined for another, broader audience attracted by its Hollywood appeal. As Timothy Garton Ash has put it in the *New York Review of Books*, the film 'uses the syntax and conventions of Hollywood to convey to the widest possible audience some part of the truth about life under the Stasi'.[6] In a recent chapter on the historical thriller, Jaimey Fisher examines this 'Hollywood syntax' in greater detail, treating von Donnersmarck's debut as both a German heritage film[7] and Hollywood melodrama, highlighting the difference between cinematic works intended to be blockbusters within Germany and those, like von Donnersmarck's, targeted also, or even primarily, at an international audience. In Fisher's view, it is precisely this procedure that positions von Donnersmarck's film as a cultural ambassador of German national identity: 'German historical films would seem to constitute German national cinema, at least as it performs national discourses for international audiences' and 'as it tries to find a niche, both domestically and internationally, in a market dominated by Hollywood product'.[8] *The Lives of Others* is thus a fundamentally *transnational* text,

---

6 Timothy Garton Ash, 'The Stasi on Our Minds', *The New York Review of Books*, 31 May 2007. Ash's position is quoted by a number of scholars as an important point of departure for aspects of their analyses of the film, including Cheryl Dueck, 'The Humanization of the Stasi in *The Lives of Others*', *German Studies Review*, 31.3 (2008), 599–608 (p. 604); Mareike Hermann, 'The Spy as Writer: Florian Henckel von Donnersmarck's *The Lives of Others*', *Gegenwartsliteratur. Ein germanistisches Jahrbuch*, 7, ed. by Paul Michael Lützeler and Stephen K. Schindler (Tübingen: Stauffenburg, 2008), 90–112 (p. 90); Mary Beth Stein, 'Stasi with a Human Face? Ambiguity in *The Lives of Others*', *German Studies Review*, 31.3 (2008), 567–79 (p. 568); and finally Jaimey Fisher, 'German Historical Film as Production Trend: European Heritage Cinema and Melodrama in *The Lives of Others*', in *The Collapse of the Conventional. German Film and Its Politics at the Turn of the Twenty-First Century*, ed. by Jaimey Fisher and Brad Prager (Detroit: Wayne State University Press, 2008), pp. 186–215 (p. 187).
7 This term was first introduced to the study of German cinema in two essays by Lutz Koepnick, who uses it to identify easily digestible films focusing on the German past and most predominantly the history of the Nazi era. See Lutz Koepnick, 'Reframing the Past: Heritage Cinema and Holocaust in the 1990s', *New German Critique*, 87 (2002), 47–82; and Lutz Koepnick, 'Amerika gibt's überhaupt nicht: Notes on the German Heritage Film,' in *German Pop Culture. How American Is it?*, ed. by Agnec C. Mueller (Ann Arbor: University of Michigan Press, 2004), pp. 191–208.
8 Jaimey Fisher, 'German Historical Film as Production Trend', p. 190. The (in)accuracy of *The Lives of Others* as such an historical fiction has been treated widely in the scholarship on the film. Hermann largely writes off this entire debate, concluding that 'objections to the historical improbability of a Stasi captain's protecting one of his subjects echo recurring debates about the

with political concerns as relevant to today's global environment as to its isolated historical and geographic setting.

As an internationally successful cinematic work examining and presenting this particular national past largely for foreign eyes – indeed, *exclusively* for foreign eyes, if one considers the fact that the nation in question no longer exists – von Donnersmarck's *The Lives of Others* necessarily invites reinvestigation of the very concept of national cinema.[9] A wealth of recent studies on German film and

---

authenticity of the representation of historical material in narrative film and may be considered as predictable reactions to an artist's creative treatment of a historical period that is still fresh in the minds of many former GDR citizens and survivors of the regime's terror'. Mareike Hermann, 'The Spy as Writer', p. 92. Daniela Berghahn agrees that 'the authenticity discourse is something of a red herring when it comes to explaining a film's success' and thus addresses to what degree *The Lives of Others* continues in the successful tradition of marketing Germany's dark past to global audiences: '*The Lives of Others* resonates with [...] all-too-familiar depictions of Germany's tainted and traumatic past in cinema [...] to invoke the subconscious Nazi-Stasi association which, arguably, plays an important role in the film's international success'. Daniela Berghahn, 'Remembering the Stasi in a Fairy Tale of Redemption: Florian Henckel von Donnersmarck's *The Lives of Others*', *Oxford German Studies*, 38.3 (2009), 321–33 (p. 323). Thomas Lindenberger would disagree, insisting that 'in the case of *The Lives of Others*, "authenticity" matters in a particular way, insofar as the claim to achieve it was crucial for its successful marketing'. Thomas Lindenberger, 'Stasiploitation? Why Not? The Scriptwriter's Historical Creativity in *The Lives of Others*', *German Studies Review*, 31.3 (2008), 557–66, (p. 558). Jens Gieseke, whom Lindenberger cites, judges the numerous historical inaccuracies of von Donnersmarck's historical imagination more harshly than perhaps any other critic, to some extent condemning the genre of historical cinema on the whole: 'The genre of the historical film is without a doubt useful for sparking curiosity. At the same time, however, such films contaminate our memory with a flood of aesthetic images or even with a faux-historical narrative'. Jens Gieseke, 'Stasi goes to Hollywood: Donnersmarcks *The Lives of Others* und die Grenzen der Authentizität', *German Studies Review*, 31.3 (2008), 580–88 (p. 585). More recently, Owen Evans argues that although 'it purportedly lacks authenticity in its depiction of the Stasi, or at least the conversion of Hauptmann Gerd Wiesler, the film nevertheless possesses what we might call an authenticity of affect. Despite its perceived flaws, therefore, it remains a valuable contribution to ongoing discussions about the legacy of the MfS'. Owen Evans, 'Redeeming the Demon? The Legacy of the Stasi in *The Lives of Others*', *Memory Studies*, 3.2 (2010), 164–77 (p. 165). Revealing a greater affinity than previously acknowledged between *The Lives of Others* and the kinds of *Ostalgie* films it sought to supplant, Paul Cooke provides both a thorough overview of the authenticity debate – as well as the possibility of moving past it – concluding that the film's self-consciously 'complex view of GDR historiography' permits it to 'engage critically with contemporary debates on the historical appraisal of the GDR'. Paul Cooke, 'Watching the Stasi: authenticity, *Ostalgie* and history in Florian von Donnersmarck's *The Lives of Others* (2006)', in *New Directions in German Cinema*, ed. by Paul Cooke and Chris Homewood (London: I.B. Tauris, 2011), pp. 111–27. (p. 117, p. 127).

9 One of the foundational and most commonly cited attempts to redefine this term is in Andrew Higson, 'The Concept of National Cinema', *Screen*, 30.4 (1989), 36–47.

European film, more generally, has interrogated the (im)possibility of the persistence of what one might still call national cinema in a presumably postnational, globalized environment – most coming to the conclusion that the two terms are, at the very least, not entirely antithetical, if not, in fact, ultimately engendered one by the other.[10]

In their introduction to a collection of essays from 2007 – *The Cosmopolitan Screen. German Cinema and the Global Imaginary, 1945 to the Present* – Stephan Schindler and Lutz Koepnick argue, for instance, that,

> Rather than erasing the local, the reality of globalization leads to an unprecedented dynamic in which the local and the global exist in mutual interdependence. One here simultaneously needs and produces the other without requiring the mediation of the national or the nation-state's institutional mechanisms of regulating the political, legal, economic, and cultural aspects of everyday life.[11]

Local identity can only be defined by and in opposition to what is outside of it, which is to say that the delineation of national cinematic traditions is a definition by difference that can, today, only be accomplished within a global context. Such a context is undoubtedly what Thomas Elsaesser has in mind when he contends, 'The label national cinema has to be conferred on films by others, either by other national or "international" audiences, or by national audiences, but at another point in time'.[12] This is precisely the position occupied by *The Lives of Others*, which resuscitates an extinct national history for the viewing pleasure of an audience that will always be removed from it, be it temporally, geographically, or both at once.

It is for this reason that Randall Halle, most recently, in his *German Film after Germany. Toward a Transnational Aesthetic* (2008), can conclude that 'Transnationalism does not undo national cinema'.[13] While acknowledging the merits of

---

10 Randall Halle provides a succinct historical-economic argument for the same – reversing the traditionally assumed historical trajectory from the national to the global – when he contends that 'cinema emerged as a medium for a global market, and only later became bound to national audiences'. Randall Halle, *German Film after Germany. Toward a Transnational Aesthetic* (Urbana: University of Illinois Press, 2008), p. 10.

11 Stephan K. Schindler and Lutz Koepnick, 'Against the Wall? The Global Imaginary of German Cinema', in *The Cosmopolitan Screen. German Cinema and the Global Imaginary, 1945 to the Present*, ed. by Stephan K. Schindler and Lutz Koepnick (Ann Arbor: The University of Michigan Press, 2007), pp. 1–21 (p. 12).

12 Thomas Elsaesser, *European Cinema. Face to Face with Hollywood* (Amsterdam: Amsterdam University Press, 2005), p. 40.

13 Halle, *German Film after Germany*, p.26.

a postnational perspective,[14] Halle rejects the term to some degree, preferring instead the notion of the *transnational*, and arguing that 'the transnationalization of Europe preserves a national cinema, even as it recontextualizes that cinema, creates a break, and radically changes its significance'.[15] The current chapter seeks to expose how *The Lives of Others*, as an historical heritage film, endeavours to define a national sense of self both domestically and for foreign audiences.

As the German Ministry of the Interior asserted in 1996, 'Film is the expression of the cultural identity of a country vis-à-vis its own citizens as well as foreign countries'.[16] And, to this extent, the film itself is comparable to the clandestine essay central to its plot – a piece of journalism published in West Germany, thus crossing borders, intended as an envoy meant to convey to the whole of the country some kernel of truth about living under state surveillance. The precise medial history of this text involves an extensive degree of transnational movement, insofar as the essay will be typed on a small East German typewriter fabricated solely for export and then smuggled back into the country from the West and hidden – throughout the film – underneath a loose doorsill, which is to say: on an unsteady threshold. Moreover, the text requires a certain measure of *translation*, as the visiting *Spiegel* editor insists, while debating his intended revisions with the author, claiming that he only wants to ensure that the essay will be correctly understood in West Germany as well as East. Like the film itself, the essay must adopt an arguably somewhat foreign idiom in order to make its illustration of life in the German Democratic Republic comprehensible abroad.

---

14 As Halle has it, 'Within the context of this debate, some critics, maintaining what could be described as a *postnational* position, have argued forcefully against the label of national cinema altogether. Behind this position is the fact that in the context of transnationalism, it has become increasingly impossible to invoke a transparent, self-evident relationship between the nation and state. Those participants who fundamentally challenge the term 'national cinema' have brought forward particularly astute observations on the permeability of national production and consumption'. Halle, *German Film after Germany*, p. 25. Nevertheless, Halle insists emphatically that one not too readily mistake the transnational (which still contains the possibility for national identity) for the postnational (which would, in a sense, eradicate it entirely).

15 Halle, *German Film after German*, p. 7.

16 Quoted in Halle, *German Film after Germany*, p. 24.

International 'Auditorism'

With an eye to such translation, here I would like to propose an examination primarily of the *medial* manifestation of this dissolution of borders. The presentation of Wiesler's experience of eavesdropping – as we shall see – is emphatically filmic, and both scholarship and popular reviews of von Donnersmarck's debut have tended to defend the film's discursive depth by accentuating the voyeuristic surveillance constituting its plot as an allegory en abyme for the filmic medium itself.

Nicolas Beaupré, for instance, praises the treatment of this 'voyeuristic relationship' as a 'reflective consideration of the cinematic medium that is as engaging as the film's actual subject'.[17] And Eva Horn analyzes Wiesler's transformation from pure medium into a 'good person' in order to demonstrate the complicit role that media themselves can play in surveillance.[18] But such interpretations overlook a central lack: the film's protagonist – a Stasi spectator *qua* eavesdropper – is deprived of the most crucial element of the meta-discursive (filmic) mode, to wit: *vision*. Noting this discrepancy, Mareike Hermann appears to intimate its importance – giving the first early hint of a debate burgeoning in the present volume – when she notes that von Donnersmarck 'offers us visual images to complement the audio Wiesler overhears, which lets us, the peeping Toms in the audience, spy on the couple even more completely than Wiesler, the master spy'.[19] The film's story then turns not on voyeurism per se, but rather on an insufficient and problematic 'auditorism' which must then be complemented for the viewer by the addition of the visual register.

A careful consideration of this transposition (or transcription) of the auditory onto the visual will reveal that von Donnersmarck's film comes to advocate its own peculiar politics of reading with significant implications for the appropriate *inter*national reception of (East) Germany's unique national history.[20]

---

17 Nicolas Beaupré, 'L'enfer des autres', *Vingtième Siècle. Revue d'histoire*, 91 (2006), 163–64 (p. 163).
18 Eva Horn, 'Media of Conspiracy: Love and Surveillance in Fritz Lang and Florian Henckel von Donnersmarck', *New German Critique*, 103 (2008), 127–44 (p. 142).
19 Mareike Hermann, 'The Spy as Writer', p. 94.
20 This general claim can be contextualized in terms of other studies of *The Lives of Others*. In a similar vein, examining the soundtrack of the film, Lindenberger speaks of a transposition from the pure fantasy of the spy moved by the music into the memory discourse of historical fiction. See Thomas Lindenberger, 'Stasiploitation? Why Not?', p. 561. This is also comparable to Alison Lewis's thesis that the film performs a blending of 'communicative' and 'cultural' memory. See Alison Lewis, 'Contingent Memories: The Crisis of Memory in Florian Henckel von Donnersmarck's *The Lives of Others*', in *Limbus 1. Erinnerungskrise/Memory Crises*, ed. by Franz-Joseph Dieters, Axel Fliethmann, Birgit Lang, Alison Lewis and Christiane Weller (Freiberg: Rombach Verlag, 2008), pp. 147–63 (p. 151).

The willing, even careful conflation of visual and acoustic information will come to serve as the chief medium of the global viewer's understanding of the peculiarities of the defunct East German nation and of nationhood as such – which is to say that the portrayal of the very surveillance intended to limit and delineate nationhood ironically serves to deconstruct the arbitrariness of any such delineation.

This precarious dynamic can be observed already in the film's initial shots – the depiction of the interrogation to which I alluded by way of introduction. Von Donnersmarck foregrounds the nascent tension between the auditory and visual registers in his film by beginning with the sound of footsteps in a hallway – as the prisoner is ushered to the interrogation room – before any corresponding visual image is projected. The spectator is thus first required to interpret textual material based on auditory cues alone, initially positing and only later having their imagined visual components supplemented and confirmed. This relationship between sight and sound is then reinforced by the very first line of dialogue: the guard's terse command that the prisoner avert his eyes so as not to see the faces of another pair of individuals passing at the far end of the hallway. Deprived of vision, experiencing the footsteps of his double only acoustically, the prisoner himself is thus in the same situation as the film's viewer.

And this readerly position will itself become the object of an implied mise-en-abyme with the appearance of a tape recorder hidden in the desk of the interrogation room as Wielser turns it on – thus beginning the acoustic documentation to which we, as spectators, have apparently been playing witness for some seconds already. From the outset, our experience of this filmic reality exists only in a playfully liminal space insofar as it is fundamentally unclear to what extent the sound here is intended to be a diegetic rendering of what is captured by this tape recorder. For if initially this interrogation is unframed, it is soon to be contextualized by a flash forward to Wiesler's presentation of the recording in the classroom, marked by the symmetrical introduction of another recording device, spooling back the selfsame tape as Wiesler (qua professor) comments and elaborates on it.

To the onscreen audience of students, only the auditory aspect of this material is presented, thereby postulating an imaginary or mnemonic space – again, beginning, notably, even before the tape recorder is turned on – in which, for the film's spectator, the crosscutting between the classroom and interrogation serves as commentary and explication. Spooling forward, we witness the success of Wiesler's interrogation and his exhortation that his students learn to listen carefully in order to interpret (it is implied) based on auditory information alone.

This insistence is most emphatic at the moment the professor twice demands absolute silence from his students and quizzes them to determine if anyone among them can identify the sound of scraping screws as he (in the flashback) extracts the scent sample from the seat where the prisoner had been repeatedly instructed to place his palms. As the only available hint enabling interpretation of these tactile and olfactory elements, the auditory is established as the inter-rogator's dominant modality. As Eva Horn has noted of Wiesler in his function as an interrogator and eavesdropper, 'He too is a medium – [a] listening device'.[21] Moreover, the predominance of hearing is implied by the very word that Wiesler uses for interrogations: 'Verhören' ('hören' means to hear). The habitual hegem-ony of the visual seems, however, simultaneously uprooted and re-established by the film insofar as the visual supplement of the flashback is required for the viewer's understanding of this scene.

That this, precisely, is the procedure of the film itself will be intimated only a moment later via the intermediary of the theatre. Wiesler finishes his lecture to the unexpected and ironic applause of an intruding senior officer who invites him to a play that same evening – the subject of the following sequence. And as Her-mann has observed: 'The dramatized staging of Wiesler's perfect interrogation, in which his students, as well as the film's viewers, become the audience, and of his performance as a teacher, observed by his superior, serves to underline the paral-lel between Wiesler's job and the task of the actor'.[22] Yet, this parallel between in-terrogation, classroom and theatre – all liminal spaces allowing an observation of the lives of others – will be extended further to the cinematic experience at hand by the belated intertitle first announcing the name of the film, which immediately precedes the opening of the stage curtains. And, again, this title is layered over the sounds of theatregoers shuffling in their seats before the audience or stage is ever pictured on screen. The film's explicit practice will be to visualize what is otherwise, or at least initially, only heard.

Already *The Lives of Others* seems to present the fundamental irony of its pro-tagonist's project. The interrogator is attempting to *restrict* mobility, to establish *impermeable* borders, as it is on such strict proscription that the discrete iden-tity of his nation depends. But the ostensibly objective politics of observation that characterize the passive medial quality of recording are inevitably rewritten by the supplement of the visual, which acts to integrate (in part) the observer's subjectivity – thereby revealing the very disregard for borders (medial, interpre-tive, spatial) underlying these intrusive acts of surveillance and their conflation

---

21 Eva Horn, 'Media of Conspiracy', p. 138.
22 Mareike Hermann, 'The Spy as Writer', p. 97.

of private and public space. And if this surveillance is indeed to be regarded as a mise-en-abyme of the medium of film, in this context, the capacity of *cinema* to bring together distinct spaces appears to render it inherently transnational. The appropriation of the meta-discursive apparatus (of the visual component of the filmic mode) then operates to corrupt the nationalizing endeavour of the film's protagonist.

This is perhaps nowhere more evident than at the moment of the film's apparent ethical apotheosis: the unsubtle establishment of 'Die Sonate vom guten Menschen' (The Sonata of the Good Person) as the central musical and moral motif of Wiesler's transformation from pure medium into a kind of active author. Now roughly halfway through the film, we have witnessed Wiesler bug and monitor the Berlin apartment of playwright Georg Dreyman and his actress girlfriend, growing increasingly enamoured with their artistic existence. If the immediate inspiration for the playing of 'Die Sonate vom guten Menschen' is the (professionally and politically motivated) suicide of the friend and colleague who had given Dreyman the score, the larger context is perhaps more illuminating for the present purpose.

Read closely, the grand and somewhat saccharine epiphany is doubly placed within the broader concerns of border crossings by the two scenes that precede it: a discussion between Dreyman and his girlfriend of the travel ban inflicted upon the outspoken author Paul Hauser followed by a shot of Wiesler at home. Upon learning that Hauser has been denied a travel permit for a lecture tour in the West, Dreyman finds it only natural, asking if the regime can really be expected to allow such a vocal dissident to travel abroad. And, in the attic above, Wiesler's unwanted and incompetent assistant duly notes this as an assenting opinion in his typewritten report. The chief role of this bumbling eavesdropper may appear to be pure comic relief, but he also operates as Wiesler's own contrasting foil, inasmuch as his presence as an inept interpreter highlights the senior officer's readerly prowess.

The discussion of Paul Hauser and his travel ban will then conclude with Dreyman wondering where he has misplaced a certain book – which, as we are to discover momentarily, has been borrowed by another Stasi spectator. For in counterpoint to the restriction of Hauser's movement, Wiesler – initially content merely to listen in on the apartment below – has crossed the line, physically infiltrating the private space of these living quarters and returning, in orphic fashion, to his own with the cribbed collection of Brecht poetry that the viewer finds him reading on the couch. An unwitting self-critique, this quasi-colonization and pillaging is perhaps akin to von Donnersmarck's own project, if we follow Thomas Lindenberger in his assertion that *The Lives of Others* 'can be seen as a classical case of an "exploitation film"' that enacts a '*West* German projection' onto the

East German other.[23] Significantly, this image of Wiesler reading at home is the only instance in the film of direct crosscutting between these two domestic spaces: the distinction between 'us' and 'them' is beginning to break down. Moreover, it is not – in this instance – Wiesler's voice providing the interior monologue for his reading of Brecht, but *Dreyman's* own: the sonic surveillance has gone so far as to appropriate the subjectivity of the other under observation.[24]

Another sonic cue – the background music – bridges into the moment Dreyman learns of Jerska's death. The soundtrack subtly transcends both time and space as the pensive, melancholic music continues softly under the loud ringing of the telephone in Dreyman's apartment. Von Donnersmarck then cuts to Wiesler, now back in the attic, flipping a switch and lifting a receiver to double the author as he answers the telephone below. Throughout the conversation, von Donnersmarck crosscuts between the author and the Stasi officer: that Dreyman's interlocutor is never pictured visually emphasizes that the important dialogue here, albeit wordless and one-sided, is in fact between Dreyman and Wiesler. Receiving the unexpected news of his friend's suicide, as Wiesler overhears, Dreyman stumbles forward to the piano bench and sits, but does not begin to play until *after* the new background music (which will itself turn out to be the piano sonata, 'Die Sonate vom guten Menschen') has begun to be heard, at which point he retrieves the gifted score from a stack of sheet music atop his Rönisch baby grand.

In perfect parallel to the film's opening sequence, the originally still extradiegetic piano music is first layered over the image in another sound bridge introducing the next shot. Present initially as an auditory manifestation without corresponding visual representation, this use of nonsimultaneous sound elevates the musical motif to an extra-narrative niveau existing in a realm neither purely diegetic nor non-diegetic – a coupling of a consummate constructedness and incidental authenticity that is the hallmark of the cinematic experience itself. The

---

23 Thomas Lindenberger, 'Stasiploitation? Why Not?', p. 557. As noted in the introduction to this volume, von Donnersmarck is keen to defend his treatment of the subject with recourse to his parents' East German origins, noting that his family made frequent visits to the German Democratic Republic during his childhood and thus claiming firsthand experience with the Stasi. As a polyglot who grew up internationally, one might, however, make the argument that von Donnersmarck is a particularly 'postnational' individual. Berghahn rallies a defence for von Donnersmarck, choosing to see his 'cosmopolitan upbringing' and looser ties to East Germany as an advantage. In her view, his is a 'prosthetic memory' that 'permits him to look back in empathy, not anger – and to seduce his audience into doing the same'. Daniela Berghahn, 'Remembering the Stasi', p. 323.

24 For Ute Wölfel, 'this demonstrates Dreymann's redeeming force as a "Künstler"'. Wölfel, Inverting the Lives of "Others", p. 616.

steady motion of the pan from right to left that then encircles Dreyman and his lover at the piano will continue, as if uninterrupted, into the next shot of Wiesler listening above them. Moreover, the quality of the sound does not change in the slightest, despite the entirely distinct spatial setting. In the same manner as the crosscutting that preceded it, this formal consistency between the two shots not only implies a shared space of sorts,[25] it also allows the off-screen sound once more to exist both as the variety of mood music typical of Hollywood melodrama and as internal diegetic sound – the music as it is heard by Wiesler.[26] Existing only in the imaginary, the space presented, then, is both borderless and textual, which is to say: it is cinematic.

As indicated by the admittedly bromidic dictum immediately tacked on by Dreyman – that only a decent human being could *truly hear* this music – this moment is meant to mark the Stasi spy's full transformation into a good person. Wiesler has, so to speak, gone native. However, as a transformation from pure medium into *Mensch*, Wiesler's metamorphosis will also prove his worth as a good reader. Patently, the rather cheap aesthetic bliss of this key moment is meant to model a response for the film's audience: like the students in his classroom as they learn to *listen*, Wiesler's enraptured, tearful response to the sonata here is clearly meant to mould our own. Ironically, it is his intrusive and imaginative spectatorship – his skill as an interrogator for instance – that has permitted him to become an ideal reader: one capable of empathy. On a larger level, this personal evolution portends a greater transformation, as Matthew Bernstein has established when he writes of Wiesler: 'people do change. So do countries. That change – life in Eastern Berlin after the wall comes down – is shown in the coda of *The Lives of Others*'.[27] It is this very sort of empathy, the film appears to imply, that permits the postnational spectator to engage with the universal truths of the German Democratic Republic's atypical political past.

---

25 As Paul Cooke notes, 'the parallel montage seem[s] to suggest that the Stasi officer is somehow watching as well as listening to his target'. 'Watching the Stasi', p. 122.

26 Indeed, Fisher takes this musical moment as a chief example of what constitutes the melodrama of the film – which he sees, in a somewhat different manner, as at odds with the political: 'Von Donnersmarck's original conceptualization shows, with surprising clarity, how the mute mode of melodrama, in its music, is opposed in the film to the political. Von Donnersmarck does not argue with Lenin or Wiesler but plays them, as he does for the viewers throughout the film, music to melt the heart, an approach common to the melodrama mode'. Jaimey Fisher, 'German Historical Film as Production Trend', p. 202.

27 Matthew H. Bernstein, '*The Lives of Others*: Matthew H. Bernstein on an Emotive Thriller Set in Communist East Germany', *Film Quarterly*, 61.1 (2007), 30–6 (p. 35).

Von Donnersmarck's film thus comes to espouse a certain ethics of reading qua authorship: not only is the spectator required to supplement auditory experience with his or her own interpretation but Wiesler also ultimately begins to improvise by falsifying documentation, writing fictions rather than recording events as they happen. At the moment of the greatest dramatic tension, we will even discover that he has secretly confiscated into his own possession the incriminating typewriter, the very emblem of authorship.[28] His metamorphosis from mere medium into human being, from passive observer into active reader, is also implicitly a transformation from reader into writer: yet another appropriation of the identity of the individual whom he has been observing. But if the readerly comportment that *The Lives of Others* would appear to advocate is an astoundingly active one, Wiesler's first act of authorial agency will instead be of passive neglect, as he resolves to let Paul Hauser escape across the border – a definitive reversal of his position in the opening interrogation, as I will examine in the concluding pages of this chapter.

Broken Borders

If hearing the piano sonata marks an essential turning point in Wiesler's evolution – the genesis of his becoming an author – this is no less the case for Dreyman.[29] Motivated to political action by his friend's death, the dramatist will resolve to write a covert literary essay on the suppressed statistics of suicide in the East German state: an essay tellingly intended necessarily and exclusively for a West German audience. And even the title of the essay, 'Von einem, der rübermachte' (By Someone Who Crossed Over), recasts many of the film's key themes in terms of this disintegrating border: it is firstly Jerska's suicide, of course, that is compared to a successful escape from East Germany, but also, one might argue, Dreyman's switching sides and becoming politically active against

---

28 In fact, as Hermann highlights, while Dreyman and the others only pretend to write a play in celebration of the fortieth anniversary of the founding of the German Democratic Republic, Wiesler, in his fabricated reports, will be obligated to outline one himself. See Hermann, 'The Spy as Writer', p. 104.

29 As Hermann again notes, 'Both Wiesler and Dreyman are personally transformed as a result of pursuing a deeper truth through their writing: the former goes from recorder and disseminator of overheard dialogue to being a protector and inventor of dramatic discourse, while the latter, who had been an opportunistic creator of abstract dramatic texts, turns instead to the recording and disseminating of previously hidden truth via journalistic discourse'. Hermann, 'The Spy as Writer', p. 93.

the state. As the origin and inspiration for Dreyman's newly politicized (and newly international) authorship, the acoustic experience of the sonata thus represents not only a novel point of complicity between Wiesler and Dreyman, but also between Dreyman and Hauser, whom the former author approaches as a co-conspirator for his anticipated project.

It is the planning of this essay that first alerts Dreyman to the possibility of Wiesler's presence, to the notion that he might be under observation (Hauser's lecture tour was blocked, as he informs the other, because he naïvely rehearsed its subversive material at home and was therefore overheard by the Stasi). In order to determine whether Dreyman's apartment is indeed unmonitored, as they hope, and thus a safe space for open discussion, the two authors stage the preparation of an invented border crossing, loudly plotting how Paul supposedly will hide beneath the backseat of his West Berliner uncle's distinctive gold Mercedes in order to escape his homeland.

As Wiesler listens in on Dreyman and his accomplices hatching this fabricated plot for Hauser's flight – really just a ruse to discover if they're being overheard – they are filmed in a medium-long shot from a high angle, as if from the eavesdropper's acoustic perspective in the attic. Dreyman turns his head, looking towards the camera, and almost yells up his question regarding which checkpoint Hauser and his uncle intend to use, as if intuitively aware of his invisible observer (and would-be interlocutor's) position. Later, bewildered and relieved by the success of Hauser's fictive escape, Dreyman will spread his arms, cock back his head and again shout towards the ceiling – this time an expression of mockery toward the state security apparatus that, unbeknownst to him, is installed directly above his apartment. Such glances consequently operate in the same manner as an eyeline match, putting the following shots of Wiesler gazing down disconcertingly into a kind of shot-counter-shot, establishing the semblance of direct dialogue.

Again we witness Wiesler picking up his telephone receiver, even dialling the border control to inform them of the attempted emigration, before deciding to stay silent and allow this one transgression as a tribute to his evolving one-sided amity for Dreyman. The news of Paul Hauser's successfully staged crossing also comes by telephone, and again von Donnersmarck crosscuts between Dreyman holding a telephone receiver and Wiesler holding his. But whereas the previous telephone conversation was notable for the absence of any visual depiction of Dreyman's actual interlocutor, here the Dreyman-Wiesler duo is supplemented by the image of the third party: Hauser's uncle standing in a phone booth in West Berlin. The filmic visualization of Wiesler's acoustic surveillance has permitted him – perhaps obliged him – to penetrate the very border he had always sought to render impermeable.

Wiesler looks downwards while eavesdropping (a) as Dreyman looks up towards the attic, as if performing on a stage (b), giving the impression of an eyeline match, *The Lives of Others*.

But in an important sense this border crossing is, of course, merely a fictive one: a ploy that has been invented by Hauser himself in order to determine whether Dreyman's apartment is bugged. Hauser, as if required by his surname to remain domesticated, has stayed put. Existing only in that imaginary space where the sonata had been heard – between Dreyman's apartment and Wiesler's attic, between auditory information and the visual imagination – this triumph of transnational movement is truly cinematic. Wiesler temporarily misinterprets this potentiality, ignoring the subjunctive in the telephone call from West Berlin announcing, 'Paul *wäre* drüben' (Paul *would* be across). But the realization of this potential is left entirely to the cinematic imagination. As a wired telephone conversation, the border crossing exists only medially. Equally significantly, the fall of the Berlin Wall will never be directly shown on screen: instead the news is overheard on headphones, on the radio, mediated by the self-same apparatus as Wiesler's earlier surveillance. The definitive disintegration of what might well be the world's most emblematic national border is, by this point, only so much noise.

Globalizing Film

If *The Lives of Others* sells itself in no small way as a document on an East German past addressed to a global audience, it inevitably also becomes a commentary on today's post-*Wende* (hence 'postnational') reality. And, by the same token, despite the potentially nationalizing project of representing this distinctly East German imaginary post facto, the film's own extended emphasis on *mediality* ineluctably transcends the temporal and spatial boundaries of its politically specific subject – as boundaries of this type are utterly insignificant to the *medium* of film.

The very process of creating cinema would appear to involve the transcendence, even the eradication, of space. Indeed, our experience of film always offers us, in some small way, an escape from our domestic space, our home. As Schindler and Koepnick wonder in their introduction to *The Cosmopolitan Screen*:

> Though cinema has often fostered narrowly nationalist causes and fuelled the viewer's exoticist desires, the medium's formal syntax [...] qualifies film as an ideal catalyst and training ground for developing what we might want to call a cosmopolitan vision. To be and become other, to experience the essential contingency of how we constantly draw and redraw boundaries around and between us, to probe different ways of looking at things – isn't all this cinema's innermost promise? [...] Do we not inevitably enter a world of global orientations and cosmopolitan deterritorialization whenever a film's first image leads our senses to places never visited before as such, no matter whether or not our objects of pleasure seek to endorse sedentary homes and strictly bounded existences?[30]

Redefining borders, appropriating the experience of another, indeed, himself *becoming* other and ultimately becoming global, Wiesler's experience, despite its initially nationalist intent, is exemplary of such 'cosmopolitan deterritorialization' and such a 'cosmopolitan *vision*'.

---

30 Stephan K. Schindler and Lutz Koepnick, *The Cosmopolitan Screen*, p. 14.

That *The Lives of Others* is intended largely as a paean to the political power of art is no secret: in addition to the central role of the sonata, this is made manifest by Wiesler's fascination with Dreyman and Sieland, as well as by his own evolving artistry, and suggested even by the very fact that the depicted literati of East Germany are singled out for such strict state control. Questions of historical authenticity aside, and regardless of the kind of exploitation of which the film has been accused, perhaps *The Lives of Others* offers less an attempted justification for its appropriation of the German Democratic Republic's distinct national heritage than a celebration of the inherently globalizing tendencies of the medium that makes such an appropriation possible.

III. Beyond the Film

Lutz Koepnick
CHAPTER NINE
The Sounds of Others

Throughout the last decade, German film studies has largely drawn on two related paradigms in order to assess the aesthetic shapes and political investments
of commercial filmmaking in postwall Germany. The first model, driven by the
notion 'cinema of consensus',[1] has been predominately employed to describe
how romantic comedies of the 1990s provided user-friendly fantasies of reconciliation, thus at once containing and obscuring underlying antinomies of unified
Germany after 1989. Whereas the normative task of this first model was to challenge crucial blind-spots in German popular cinema's newly found hunger for the
present, the second model hoped to provide an analytic able to expose the way in
which German filmmakers in the second half of the 1990s began to package images and sounds of German history, in particular those of the Nazi period,
into profitable items of consumption. Centred around the concept of heritage cinema,[2] the critical mission of this second paradigm was chiefly to address how German filmmakers redressed painful pasts in terms of international expectations;
and how German studios recast the traumas of German twentieth-century history into self-contained stories whose impressive production values and alluring
musical soundtracks invited trouble-free entertainment on a global scale.

It is little surprising that German film critics and scholars quickly took recourse to the consensus and heritage films of earlier years when approaching
Florian Henckel von Donnersmarck's *The Lives of Others*. Von Donnersmarck's
explicit obsession with atmospheric detail – be it a question of interior design,
political structure, or technological equipment – is surely reminiscent of the logic
of heritage cinema. It not only seems to picture the past as a display case for nostalgic attractions, a sight audiences cannot but love to hate, but also, like the Mer-
chant-Ivorys of international heritage cinema, render German national history
easily readable for global audiences. As importantly, similar to the entertainment
fare of the 1990s, *The Lives of Others*, in its effort to draw distinct lines between

---

1 Eric Rentschler, 'From New German Cinema to the Post-Wall Cinema of Consensus', in *Cinema and Nation*, ed. by Mette Hjort and Scott MacKenzie (Routledge: London, 2000), pp. 260–277.
2 The term was initially developed in the context of British film studies; for an overview, see An-
drew Higson, 'The Heritage Film and British Cinema', in *Dissolving Views. Key Writings on British Cinema*, ed. by Andrew Higson (London: Cassell, 1996), pp. 232–248. For its application to German postwall cinema, see Lutz Koepnick, 'Reframing the Past: Heritage Cinema and Holocaust in the 1990s', *New German Critique*, 87 (2002), 47–82.

good and bad Germans during former times of dictatorship, appears to offer viable experiences of consensus for postwall German audiences. Some evil Stasi officers may live on as successful capitalists, but how can we not read the publication of Georg Dreyman's book at the very end of the film – 'Dedicated to HGW XX/7, in gratitude' – as a sign of historical reconciliation? How can we not understand Dreyman's final gesture as a gesture of absolution declaring the dead of the past to be dead and encouraging the German present to learn how to shake hands harmoniously again?

While many signs might point to the contrary, the following pages argue that von Donnersmarck's *The Lives of Others* categorically exceeds the templates of both consensus and heritage cinema and in so doing should remind German film studies to apply greater caution with the normative underpinnings of some of its most central recent concepts. The focus of this essay will be on the film's images of audio surveillance: its choreography of listening and seeing, its framing and unframing of acoustical properties, its – in variation of Jacques Rancière's phrase – distribution of the audible.[3] My principal claim might at first be an obvious one: some of the most essential aspects of *The Lives of Others* are played out on the level of the acoustical, or more precisely, along the uneven border between the visible and the audible, between embodied and disembodied sounds. But in discussing how *The Lives of Others* echoes earlier films that revolve around audio surveillance such as *The Conversation* (Francis Ford Coppola, 1974) and *Das Testament des Dr. Mabuse* (The Testament of Dr. Mabuse, Fritz Lang, 1933), this essay also seeks to show the extent to which von Donnersmarck unsettles some of the central exigencies of consensus and heritage filmmaking, in particular their definition of the cinematic screen as an unproblematic threshold to diegetic meaning and spectatorial pleasure. The ultimate issue of *The Lives of Others*, I argue, is neither a political nor a historical one, it is a theological and metaphysical one; and in order to do justice to the film's complexity – its inconclusive story of guilt, confession, and absolution – we need to expand our critical vocabulary rather than force the film's images and sounds into a corset of existing concepts and expectations.

Though postwall consensus and heritage films could often not be more different in subject matter, they both share a similar politics of the cinematic frame, namely an explicit need to construct a self-contained diegesis in which sound must continually be drawn out of the off and become embodied on screen in order not to destabilize the viewer's act of consuming the image. The acoustical prop-

---

3 Jacques Rancière, *The Politics of Aesthetics. The Distribution of the Sensible*, trans. by Gabriel Rockhill (London and New York: Continuum, 2004).

erties of consensus films are largely vococentric; these films feature the travails of very vocal middle-class couples or intricate triangles, and they by and large resolve their conflicts by establishing unproblematic terms of reciprocity, between their protagonists as much as their formal registers.[4] To be sure, dialogue alone may often fail to produce the desired outcome. In many instances, in fact, and in line with the generic demands of romantic comedy, speech here seems to prolong rather than overcome friction and thereby delay narrative consummation. Yet whenever it does so, the consensus film shows considerable eagerness to mute discordant voices in bodies that are in full display, i.e., to embody silence on screen and thus integrate, through its very denial, the acoustical into the visual. The voice, even when finally muffled, must be seen in the frame of the image to warrant these films' rhetoric of consensus, their desire to suspend the fractured spaces and conflicting temporalities of a nation less unified than it was fervent to claim after 1990. Image and soundtrack need to be wedded into firm matrimony in order to allegorize the nation's promise of bonding its citizens in and to the present.

An analogous process of framing sound can also be seen at work in the heritage film, a genre not only driven by melodramatic intensities, but – according to the genre's constitutive template – by the sudden rise and fall of melos, of melody, of musical properties.[5] Heritage films often rely on neatly choreographed orchestral soundtracks, enveloping what can be seen and heard from the non-diegetic space-off. In many cases, however, the heritage film's musical soundtrack wanders freely between the non-diegetic to the diegetic in order to ensure the consumability of the past in the present. Gramophones help to situate a film's musical score within the image itself; the songs of famous vocalists can be heard both inside and outside the image; nostalgic radios transmit historical sounds and atmospheric values that seem to nestle the spaces of fiction into the larger soundscapes of the past. Though its location may often be mobile and unpredictable, very little about the use of sound in the heritage film is ever meant to destabilize the frame and threaten the way in which spectators are invited to enter the film like a tourist entering the splendour of a historical hotel lobby through a revolving door. No matter how traumatic the history depicted in the heritage film, the heritage film's principal aim is to use the power of the cinematic frame to fold

---

4 Think of films such as, among many others, *Der bewegte Mann* (Maybe ... Maybe Not, Sönke Wortmann, 1994), *Stadtgespräch* (Talk of the Town, Rainer Kaufmann, 1995), *Rossini* (Helmut Dietl, 1997), and *Knockin' on Heaven's Door* (Thomas Jahn, 1997).
5 Think of films such as *Comedian Harmonists* (Joseph Vilsmaier, 1997), *Aimée & Jaguar* (Max Färberböck, 1999), *Viehjud Levi* (Jew-Boy Levi, Didi Danquart, 1999), *Gloomy Sunday – Ein Lied von Liebe und Tod* (Gloomy Sunday, Rolf Schübel, 1999), *Gripsholm* (Xavier Koller, 2000), and *Marlene* (Joseph Vilsmaier, 2000).

sounds and images into a neat package, to contain the past's auditory field in such a way that audiences can indulge their fantasy to own the past in each and every of its moments.

'In cinema', writes Michel Chion, 'the notion of the auditory field is completely a function of what appears on screen. In other words, in film there is no autonomous auditory field; its real and imaginary dimensions are created in collaboration with the image, and at the same time sound is always overflowing and transgressing it'.[6] While consensus and heritage films seek to render sound's transgressive qualities entirely manageable, von Donnersmarck's *The Lives of Others* pictures the auditory field as one critically charged with unruly energies, with deceptive potentials and hidden loopholes – as something no one can ever fully control or contain, yet whose ambivalences and transgressions we might, temporarily, utilize to our advantage. A superficial viewing of *The Lives of Others* might consider the film a document exposing the way in which GDR authoritarianism, precisely by eavesdropping on its citizens, produced the very opposition and rebellion it hoped to contain. Strategies of acoustical surveillance, however, are only one aspect of the film's acoustical regime, the other aspect of which is the deliberate fabrication, performance, and distortion of sonic presence as a means of rubbing against the operations of the state apparatus, of playing out the seen against the heard, of creating alternate realities and allowing fiction to disturb the real. This second aspect not only results in an on-going fracturing or compartmentalization of diegetic space that makes *The Lives of Others* relatively useless for the purposes associated with consensus and heritage filmmaking, their overdetermined drive toward synthesis and integration as much as their definition of the filmic screen as a self-effacing membrane connecting past and present. As importantly, it also situates the relation of sound and image in *The Lives of Others* as something that, all things told, goes far beyond the parameters of a political tale about repression and resistance, and instead defines the film's central concern as being about the limits of knowledge and the reliability of sensory perception, about the borders of what can be known, done, and sensed in a fully secularized, albeit far from truly enlightened, age.

---

6 Michel Chion, *Film. A Sound Art*, trans. by Claudia Gorbman (New York: Columbia University Press, 2009), p. 249.

Wiesler's Dream

Three decades prior to *The Lives of Others*, Francis Ford Coppola's *The Conversation* told a story of moral confusion and psychic disintegration caused by what turns out to be an act of misperception. Equipped with state-of-the-art tools of eavesdropping, Harry Caul (Gene Hackman), in his obsessive search for truth, misconstrues a line spoken by his objects of surveillance – 'He'd kill us if he had the chance' –, and instead of protecting his employer allows him to be murdered by the adulterous couple. In the figure of Stasi officer Gerd Wiesler, Caul's fateful act of mishearing experiences a curious reversal without sparing the film's protagonist from a number of dire consequences. Rather than to misinterpret the data of his technologically expanded auditory field, Wiesler ends up actively misrepresenting it. Rather than to despair over his inability to establish and recognize the truth, Wiesler's trade in the second half of the film is to fabricate fiction and protect the audible from larger circulation. And rather than to descend into a state of utter paranoia and self-destructive suspicion, Wiesler's interventions engender fear and trepidation in his objects of surveillance, whether we think of Christa-Maria Sieland's committing suicide or of Georg Dreyman dismantling – like Caul in the final minutes of Coppola's film – his apartment in search of invisible surveillance equipment.[7]

And yet, in spite of these inversions and transpositions, what von Donnersmarck's film shares with Coppola's is nothing less than a protagonist haunted by both a profound loss of orientation (spiritual in the case of Caul, ideological in that of Wiesler) and the paralyzing effects of tragic guilt. Unable to maintain professional distance, both Caul and Wiesler enter, or better: desire to enter, the very field their equipment is meant to map from afar. While Caul misreads and Wiesler misrepresents the dynamic of the real, they both – precisely by trying to intervene in the course of action and protect their objects of surveillance – help cause unspeakable havoc: the beastly killing of the husband in *The Conversation*, the painful demise of the star actress in *The Lives of Others*. To move into and reshape the auditory field of surveillance, in both films, thus describes a fall from grace. It betrays existing bonds of loyalty and casts the surveillance expert, who in the later film turns out to be the deceiver and in the earlier one the deceived, into a state of radical isolation. It may aim at doing good, but it comes at catastrophic costs, a causing of death for which repentance can only be found in gestures of resigned silence.

---

7 For further discussion of the relationship between these films see Paul Cooke's contribution to this volume.

The perhaps single most important shot capturing Wiesler's changeover, his path into both fabrication and guilt, directly succeeds the first direct transgression of his mandate, i.e., Wiesler's remote ringing of the doorbell, intended to draw Dreyman's attention to Sieland's affair with state minister Bruno Hempf and thereby to bring into play the disruptive force of 'bitter truths'. What we see is Wiesler on the left side of the frame, shot from the waist of his body upwards. He is sitting on his chair in the surveillance centre above Dreyman's apartment. Yet contrary to what we have seen before, he is no longer located in front of the various control panels, but somewhere in the middle of the empty attic, in one of the at once imaginary and real rooms he had drawn earlier onto the floor in order to map out the space of surveillance. His body posture is strangely contorted; he is hunched slightly forward and over to his left, with the ear phones over his head, both hands holding onto the extension wire that connects his listening device to the audio transmitters. The blue light of a monitor faintly glows in the distance, unseen by Wiesler, for Wiesler's eyes are wide shut. We might be tempted to consider the Stasi officer as fast asleep, exhausted from prolonged eavesdropping and reporting. But when his subordinate enters the attic a few seconds into this shot and Wiesler instantly reprimands him for being tardy, we see the contortion of Wiesler's earlier posture in a different light. In retrospect, it becomes readable not as the slackness of a sleeping body, but as the outward expression of utter attentiveness, of rapture, of someone being in two places at once, of someone being all ears in order to communicate with or in fact touch upon a distant reality brought up close due to the mediation of electronic gadgets. Though seemingly mute and completely turned inward, Wiesler's contorted body speaks volumes. We can no longer see him as a cool and detached observer; ontological boundaries here start to collapse as much as the separation of the visual and the auditory, off- and onscreen sound.

But what, we cannot but ask ourselves, does Wiesler actually hear in this shot? What kind of images, what kind of sensory sensations, occupy the inner screens of this expert listener while his hands clasp to the wire of his headphones as if it were an umbilical cord? A quick answer to the first question would be to say: none; and to the second: Sieland's tormented, yet in all its torment, attractive body. The last we saw of Dreyman's apartment, before cutting to the hunched figure of Wiesler, was Sieland crouched in bed, her face and body turned to the camera, her mind clearly seeking solace from the earlier encounter with Hempf. Dreyman approaches her from behind, ready to engage his lover in a conversation about the affair, yet then simply yielding to Sieland's request to remain silent, to 'Just hold me'. The camera cuts to a medium close-up of both Dreyman and Sieland, his face resting next to hers in a horizontal position, no words being uttered at all, before we then cut to the image of Wiesler, his head positioned in almost

Wiesler's expression of rapture (a) as the boundaries between vision and sound start to collapse (b), *The Lives of Others*.

the same position as Dreyman's. The sequencing of cuts and events leaves the viewer with some uncertainty whether the latter shot wants to suggest synchronicity of action, or whether we are meant to read Wiesler's strange posture as a sign of a prolonged act of absorption, an intensity of displacement that by far outlasts what had caused it in the first place. In any case, what matters most about the choreography of cuts in this sequence is the fact that Wiesler emulates Dreyman's pose of mute comfort, that Dreyman here seems to serve as a direct extension of Wiesler's organs and senses, even though not a single word and sound has travelled upstairs after Sieland's request. What matters most about the sequence is that Wiesler's desire to be other – to slip into Dreyman's body, to collapse all spatial distance, and hence to find a physical avatar in the world he is ordered to investigate from a position of detached power – unfolds in a vacuum of diegetic sounds and therefore in the absence of what allows Wiesler to connect to the lives of these others to begin with. It is Wiesler's very lack of both vision and hearing, we might therefore want to conclude, that causes him to enter the realm of the imaginary and, in violation of the repressive mandates of his job, interface with and bond to the body of surveillance. The virtual here briefly overtakes the real, not only to mark a distinctive turn in the film's narrative, but also to document the inner frailty of any repressive system, its ultimate failure to contain each and every aspect of the imagination.

But maybe things are more complicated than they appear at first and we should administer more caution when answering the above questions. Consider the fact that the image of Wiesler's hunched-over posture defines a critical watershed, a kind of aesthetic pivot point, in how von Donnersmarck arranges the relationship of sounds and images when cutting between attic and apartment and hence tracking the process of surveillance. Up to this moment, the cinematic staging of eavesdropping relied on a tight division of visible and invisible sounds. Repeatedly, we see Wiesler or Udo situated in front of their electronic equipment, with headphones over their ears, while off-screen sounds from the apartment will solely gain presence in the attic through acts of additional translation and symbolization: conversations between eavesdroppers about what they have heard; shots showing the conversion of spoken dialogue into typewritten text; Udo's adolescent gestures mimicking sexual activity below. After Wiesler, within the course of a few minutes of screen time, first draws chalk marks on the floor of the attic, then rings the doorbell, and finally daydreams about becoming and being other, von Donnersmarck's choreography of on- and off-screen sounds changes significantly. For from now on, as if the airtight wall between visible and invisible sounds had suddenly crumbled, we can at once peruse the image of Wiesler and hear the voices of Sieland, Dreyman, and Dreyman's collaborators; we can attend to musical sounds travelling easily from apartment to attic as much as from non-diegetic to diegetic spaces. Whether Wiesler in the sequences to follow has his earphones on or not, for the viewer sound suddenly appears liberated from the spaces of its origin; it becomes audible in the image even if Wiesler, due to his headset, is pictured as a privileged and solitary listener.

Chion's concept of the acousmatic might be helpful in order to explore this reversal of relations (even though, as I will argue in a moment, it fails to illuminate the entire problematic at hand here). Acousmatic sounds, for Chion, are sounds whose sources are hidden from the viewer's view. They can reside in or emanate from what lies beyond the frame of the image; or they can resound from non-diegetic spaces, a film's musical soundtrack and the voice-over of a disembodied filmic narrator being the most common examples. In Chion's view, the use of film sound is at its most productive when sounds begin to shift their status, in particular when they undergo what he calls a process of de-acousmatization, that is to say, when invisible sounds suddenly wander across and pierce the frame of the image – be it that they enter the visible from another space of the diegesis or from the non-diegetic off – and forfeit some of the constitutive omni-directionality of the acoustical, yet in return suddenly redefine our point of view and reshape our understanding of and relationship to the integrity of the cinematic frame.

It is tempting to think of Wiesler's contorted posture as an expression, not simply of at once silent and uncanny empathy, but also of a disruptive desire for de-acousmatization. Whereas the success of conventional audio surveillance seems to rest on a categorical division of the visible and the audible, the absence of diegetic sound here enfigures and energizes Wiesler's hope to tear down what separates sound and image; to touch upon distant realities and bodies within the space of the attic; or, conversely but analogously, to gain physical presence in Dreyman's apartment. Wiesler's dream, in this sense, would not be to liberate voices and sounds from their sources and allow them to roam freely, that is to say, without physical or material restrictions. It instead would be to pin sounds to their bodies and experience the voice, not simply as one among different modalities of *representing* a human being (near or far), but as something that should be seen as an inseparable element of the other's identity and body. And to be and rest in silence, for Wiesler, would mean to hold on to the promise of a better future in which voices could return safely to their bodies and not fear punishment by the mandates of dictatorial power.

It does not take much, however, to realize that Wiesler's quest for de-acousmatization produces as much disaster as it intends to avert, and that the ensuing course of narrative action therefore belies Wiesler's act of daydreaming. Rather than to set Sieland free from the grip of totalitarian power and control, it is Wiesler's very hope of pinning voice and words to the actress's body that gets her killed: his desire to touch upon her life results in nothing other than Sieland's suicide. And rather than to move through silence beyond it, Wiesler himself will be the one first muted by the Stasi and later, in his role as a minimal-wage distributor of advertising material, by the new economic conditions of unified Germany, his real name in the dedication of Dreyman's book at once covered and effaced by his old code name – HGW XX/7. In savouring the absence of sound, Wiesler's posture on the chair wants to hold on to narrative cinema's innermost dream, namely to show voice and body in perfect harmony. Yet what he fails to realize is the fundamental ambivalence of this dream, the fact that acoustical embodiment might foster a flourishing of life as much as it can come to represent and produce death.

Perhaps the bitterest truth in all of this is that Wiesler, when indulging the promise of what at first appears to us as a rebellious vision of de-acousmatization and vocal incorporation, secretly feeds into the very systems he is about to defy. For surveillance in the GDR was never solely about tracking the voices, writings, thoughts, movements, and actions of citizens deemed dangerous to the state and its ideology. As stipulated in a set of internal guidelines of January 1976, Stasi operations of surveillance were to include active interventions aimed at creating or amplifying tensions within oppositional forces so as to 'fragment, paralyze, de-organize, and isolate their hostile-negative activities'.[8] Contrary to what Wiesler believes and teaches in the opening of the film, surveillance operations in the GDR were not simply designed to observe and – with cold scientific methods – to produce strategically useful truths and insights. They instead were intended to beat the opposition at its own game, that is to say, choreograph the very sights and sounds deemed as enemy expressions in the first place. In dire need of a foe to stabilize its tenuous legitimacy, the state's surveillance measures stage-managed resistant voices so as to prove its own power in containing them. Wiesler might understand Hempf's personal motives in launching the observation as a violation of what Wiesler believes to be the Stasi's mission. In actual fact, however, these motives reveal the truth of what drove surveillance all along, namely a purely formalistic or existential need to invent firm distinctions between friend and foe independent of substantial reasons and ideological beliefs.

All this is to indicate the complex dynamic at stake when we see Wiesler silently hunching over his chair, a shot that – in true film noir fashion – blurs the lines between framer and framed and thereby has the potential Split in the viewer's relationship to the role of knowledge and identification within the diegesis. Marxist historical materialism had once suggested that material conditions precede and structure consciousness, but both Stasi surveillance methods and Wiesler's daydreaming rely on a momentous introduction of fiction to the real, i.e., the thought that different interpretations of the world indeed have the power to change it. Yet, as we know from the rest of the story, whatever power of the imagination will allow Wiesler to reshape the physical spaces of Dreyman and Sieland's lives will also take these away from him again. For now, let me therefore suggest that Wiesler's subversive dream of de-acousmatization rests on and results in a dual misunderstanding. The first misunderstanding is that Wiesler loses faith in a system whose tasks and methods he had misconstrued in the first place. Because Stasi surveillance was always already commissioned to invent the very reality it was meant to observe, Wiesler's acts of fictionalization in the second half of the film put him on par with the logic of the system itself; to reinvent the relation of voices and bodies means to engage the system on its own terms rather than to establish a new and categorically different order of things. The second

---

8 'MfS-Richtline Nr. 1/76 zur Entwicklung und Bearbeitung Operativer Vorgänge (OV) vom Januar 1976', reprinted in Marianne Falck, *Filmheft. Das Leben der Anderen* (Bonn: Bundeszentrale für politische Bildung, 2006), p.18.

misunderstanding is that Wiesler, as he dreams of a unified state of voices and bodies, anticipates a possible gain in presence and agency that no actual descent from his detached position of observation can ever grant. Wiesler's dream is to exchange detached inspection for embodied co-presence and interaction. Yet to do so means to forfeit the very power and insight that triggered this dream to begin with.

As I argue in the remaining pages of this essay, we cannot sufficiently understand the structure of this dual dilemma if we read *The Lives of Others* exclusively in terms of what most critics have seen as the political aspirations of the film. At heart, Wiesler's dilemma is a metaphysical one. His dream of de-acousmatization symptomatically expresses a profound crisis of knowledge, meaning, and faith; it is indicative of an acute dialectic of rationality within a disenchanted world that denies any attempt to understand the film solely as a tale of complicity and resistance, as a cinematic vehicle to produce political consensus or consumable heritage.

Producing Transparency

The rise of omnipresent electronic media and social networks over the last two decades has placed considerable pressures on framing normative arguments about the ever-increasing presence of surveillance technologies in contemporary society.[9] If we, as citizens of an inclusively networked age, have little qualms about exhibiting the most intimate details of our lives to larger audiences, why not allow state and economic agents to register each and every of our moves, amass useful data, and turn our exhibitionism into an effective tool of power and consumption? Shot in the midst of a time witnessing the complete breakdown of constitutive barriers between the public and the private, von Donnersmarck's *The Lives of Others* clearly recalls an earlier moment in the modern history of surveillance – one in which the private sphere still seemed to harbour energies able to disrupt the public order of things and was therefore eager to protect itself from seamless inspection, but one also that had lost its faith in how modern society since the seventeenth century had hoped to engineer the resources of individual integrity and communal integration by erasing the obscurity – the beliefs, myths, enigmas, and unspeakable secrets – of premodern times.

---

9 Peter Weibel, 'Pleasure and the Panoptic Principle', in *CTRL [SPACE]. Rhetorics of Surveillance from Bentham to Big Brother*, ed. by Thomas Y. Levin, Ursula Frohne and Peter Weibel (Cambridge, MA: MIT Press, 2002), pp. 207–23.

Michel Foucault has famously identified modern discourses of surveillance as an integral part of the vocabulary of the Enlightenment, its hope not only to erase ignorance and foster knowledge, but also in doing so to improve the conditions for a good life. The Age of Enlightenment, in Foucault's perspective, was motivated by the dream

> of a transparent society, visible and legible in each of its parts, the dream of there no longer existing any zones of darkness, zones established by the privileges of royal power or the prerogatives of some corporation, zones of disorder. It was the dream that each individual, whatever position he occupied, might be able to see the whole of society, that men's hearts should communicate, their vision be unobstructed by obstacles, and that opinion of all reign over each.[10]

For Foucault, the panoptic prison designs of English philosopher and legal scholar Jeremy Bentham best exemplified the way in which the Enlightenment hoped to couple individual reform and social transformation to increases in transparency. As envisioned in the last decades of the eighteenth century, Bentham's plans for modern penitentiaries situated wards and inmates in a self-contained system of total visibility that was aimed at encouraging the prisoners' self-control and moral development as much as it was devised to transfer power effectively from unpredictable individuals to reliable institutional structures. A little more than a hundred years earlier, similar ambitions had already energized the enormous listening systems suggested by German Jesuit scholar and poly-scientist Athanasius Kircher. In Kircher's mannered fantasy, huge architectural tubes, caverns, whispering arches, and echo membranes were to transport sound from the court's public spaces to the ear of the Prince, thus encouraging the state's subjects to speak (and think) well at all times, yet also making the singular ruler accountable to higher standards because he could no longer claim ignorance about the voice of his people.[11] In both Kircher and Bentham's visions, the quest for transparency (visual or auditory) not only was part of a modern project of secularization which equated gains in knowledge with growth in power. It was also driven by the hope that in radically erasing zones of ignorance modern society could define power as something structural rather than personal and precisely thus enable the modern subject to explore the resources for responsible moral action in him- or herself. The discourse of modern surveillance, in this sense, wanted to bring

---

10 Michel Foucault, 'The Eye of Power', in *Power / Knowledge. Selected Interviews and Other Writings 1972–1977*, ed. by Colin Gordon (New York: Pantheon Books, 1980), pp. 146–65 (p. 152).
11 Dörte Zbikowski, 'The Listening Ear: Phenomena of Acoustic Surveillance', in *CTRL [SPACE]*, pp. 38–41.

God down from heaven to earth, yet less in order to relocate God's omnipresent powers simply to the hands of one singular political ruler, than to build worldly architectures of unencumbered knowledge in whose context each and every member of society could ideally live up to what was considered the shared traits and public expectations of a good life. According to the Enlightenment's discourse of surveillance, modern secular society would be at its best whenever individual subjects knew perfectly well that rulers knew everything about them. For to be aware of being observed meant to leave those who observe with special obligations to rule well and govern their subjects with the same kind of steadfastness and benevolence God had formerly dedicated to worldly matters.

The opening sequence of *The Lives of Others* presents Wiesler as an interrogation expert deeply committed to this discourse of secular surveillance. Wiesler's examination procedures are based on the application of cold scientific thinking and methodological rigour – a specialized thirst for knowledge, disenchantment, and transparency that leaves no room for lies or inaccuracies. 'Science today', Max Weber wrote in the early twentieth century, 'is a "vocation" organized in special disciplines in the service of self-clarification and knowledge of interrelated facts. It is not the gift of grace of seers and prophets dispensing sacred values and revelations, nor does it partake of the contemplation of sages and philosophers about the meaning of the universe'.[12] Wiesler perfectly embodies Weber's vision of the modern scientist. He has no personal stakes in what he does. Nor does he understand public life as a stage on which ultimate values and transcendental meanings are brought to the fore. For Wiesler, state authorities have assumed the former power of priests, sages, and philosophers to ensure that people will not be misguided by false idols and metaphysical beliefs. As Wiesler lectures in the film's first minutes to a group of future police agents, he leaves little doubt that police interrogations, in their effort to unlock all possible secrets, serve their cause best whenever they go about their business *sine ira et studio* – without anger or prejudice, hate or affective zealousness; and with discipline, consistency, and professional attention to detail. To know and to know it all is all it takes, not only to find one's place in the moral fabric of a post-metaphysical society, but also to define the state apparatus's legitimacy in steering this society into the future. To reveal what is hidden will help even those who do the hiding and allow them eventually to return to the bosom of the secular collective.

---

12 Max Weber, 'Science as Vocation', in *From Max Weber. Essays in Sociology*, ed. and trans. by H. H. Geerth and C. Wright Mills (New York: Oxford University Press, 1946) pp. 129–157 (p. 152).

Wiesler, as grand enunciator (a), shuttles his audience between past and present with the help of a reel-to-reel tape player (b), *The Lives of Others*.

It is important to note in this context that von Donnersmarck, in the opening sequence of *The Lives of Others*, introduces Wiesler as a grand enunciator of (mediated) sounds and sights, confidently managing the realm of the sensible, of what can be heard and can be seen. Though the film's narration seems to start in the midst of an interrogation procedure at the Stasi prison of Hohenschönhausen, soon the viewer is to learn that what we see in the opening sequence is nothing other than what a group of students is hearing at the Stasi Academy in Potsdam-Eiche, played to them by their commanding lecturer Wiesler with the help of a reel-to-reel tape player. As he presses the play and pause buttons, Wiesler shuttles his diegetic audience back and forth between past and present, historical document and critical commentary, index and interpretation. His audience is shown to be all ears, equally absorbed in Wiesler's lecture as it is in the drama of truth finding – of producing transparency – unfolding on the tape recording. But Wiesler's directorial power clearly exceeds his command over his students as this opening sequence situates him as a diegetic narrator and showman with the power to arrange the order of narrative time and the relationship of images and sounds for the non-diegetic audience as well. Facilitated by mechanical reproduction, yet entirely controlled by Wiesler's presence, sound here – for us – is shown as being able to authorize narrative images. Wiesler, in this opening, makes us see with his students' ears; he not only dictates the relation of past to the present, his mode of telling time is grafted straight onto the way in which the mechanical passing of filmic time imprints itself onto our own sense of temporality as viewers. If Dr. Baum, in Lang's *Das Testament des Dr. Mabuse*, gained uppermost power over both his subordinates and the viewer by remaining invisible and having a loudspeaker transmit messages from behind a veil, in the opening of *The Lives of Others* Wiesler's authority results from nothing other than his ability entirely to command how diegetic and non-diegetic audiences perceive even passed events – absences – as fully present and embodied. Whether recorded or live, voices here have the force to enunciate corresponding images and in so doing progressively erase any remaining zones of darkness, lies and distortions, hidden truths and deliberate misrepresentations of the real. Analogous with the work of film itself, Wiesler's finger on the play and pause button of the tape recorder in this way holds sway over the viewer's entire perception and imagination, over all we can know and sense and can expect from the flickering images in front of us.

In his ground-breaking work on the role of voices in cinema, Chion once described God as the most powerful example of what he calls the figure of the acousmêtre, that is, an all-seeing figure whose voice commands the space of the visible, yet who is not part of the visual field him- or herself.[13] Wiesler's role in the opening of *The Lives of Others* is that of anti-acousmêtre. His voice completely dominates the space of the visible, both for the diegetic and the extra-diegetic audience, while his command over mechanically reproduced sounds allows him to fuse the visible and the invisible, present and past, the visual and the acoustical into airtight unity. He is all seeing and all knowing, yet not because he inhabits a place outside the visual field, but precisely because he in his role as the grand enunciator, and from within the diegesis itself, manages to elevate everything to perfect visibility. Nothing is or can ever remain hidden, Wiesler's presence suggests in the opening of the film. For him, the gift of omniscience and vocal power is a feature, not of a world of transcendental powers, disembodied deities, and metaphysical enigmas, but one of radical enlightenment and disenchanted immanence. It is the feature of a secular world in which State authorities produce utter

---

13 Michel Chion, *The Voice in Cinema*, trans. by Claudia Gorbman (New York: Columbia University Press, 1999), p. 24.

truth and transparency for the sake of the good life of the collective: Stasi eaves-dropping overthrows God's authority, his acousmêtric division of what can and what cannot be seen, only to resurrect God's former mission and power of voice within the very space of the visible.

It is now, finally, that we can grasp the full dilemma and despair that haunts Wiesler when hunched over his chair in the attic in the scene discussed earlier in this essay. The narrative, at this moment halfway through the film, carries us to the brink of Wiesler's complete disillusionment about the role of eavesdropping in 'real existing socialism': rather than to generate inner-worldly good through seamless transparency and knowledge, it simply serves the personal desires of power-hungry individuals. Disenchanted with the politics of surveillance in the GDR, Wiesler now aspires not only to enlighten the corrupt state's failed project of Enlightenment about itself, but to cancel out the very role of the anti-acousmêtre he once so masterly embodied himself. As he dreams of directly touching upon the lives of his objects of surveillance, his hope is to re-enchant a world in which relentless knowledge production and ever-suspicious secularism empower no-thing other than triumphant disasters. Yet in closing his eyes and indulging the fantasy of radical de-acousmatization, of incarnating the sounds of others in his attic, he simply rehearses what situated him as a powerful interrogation expert in the first place, namely not ever to accept any given boundaries between the vis-ible and the invisible, here and there, now and then. His desire to become and be other, to slip into Dreyman's role, secretly mimics what he no longer can and wants to believe in: the official understanding of the anti-acousmêtre as a posi-tion of the moral good.

On some level, one might want to argue that Wiesler – or the film in general – here suffers from a severe mixing of the metaphorical and the real. In closing his eyes, the audio expert metaphorically desires to relinquish surveillance's posi-tion of power, the distance of an all-seeing, pursuant consciousness; to shut down sight symbolizes his wish to collapse the border between object and sub-ject of surveillance and precisely thus undercut the Stasi's failed process of En-lightenment. Yet, we must ask, is not such a collapsing of space and distance what audio surveillance in the end is all about? Don't the eavesdroppers of film history such as Harry Caul and Gerd Wiesler, due to the perceptual immediacy even of highly mediated sounds, usually suffer not from too much but too little distance, too little rather than too much sight?

While it is tempting to belabour these questions in further detail, let me simply suggest that the mixing of metaphors in the crucial scene of *The Lives of Others* is symptomatic in nature. It expresses the extent to which Wiesler finds himself confronted with a situation to which no reasonable solution, no rational exit strategy, appears imaginable. The mixing of visual and auditory registers of symbolization in this sense allegorizes the existential antinomies that cannot but structure the life of someone who no longer believes in an ideological framework that had once aspired to replace mere belief with total knowledge and transparency. Wiesler's ultimate dilemma is one resulting not merely from his loss of faith in the Party, but from the fact that neither faith nor enchantment can simply be reinvented once you have placed all your eggs in the basket of knowledge and have proven to be an anti-acousmêtre of first rank, i.e., you have successfully demonstrated that there is nothing that can ever exceed the frames of the knowable, the sensible, and the representable. Wiesler's dilemma is that power cannot beget its own disappearance, as much as radical Enlightenment cannot produce the numinous, or a knowing subject intend non-intentionality.

We therefore might want to read Wiesler's hunched posture, eyes wide shut and ears wide open to silence, as a direct somatic expression less of a political than a post-metaphysical gridlock. His pose is reminiscent of someone situated in one of the two compartments of a church's confession booth, just that it is fundamentally unclear whether he is a priest waiting to listen to a sinner's confession, or whether he is a sinner anticipating God's words of punishment and forgiveness, as mediated through the voice of a priest. This irresolvable ambivalence about the true motivation of Wiesler's posture – Is he the object or the subject of power? Is he the one who defines or the one who breaks the frames of representation? Is he an omniscient secularized God, a fallen and faithless angel, or a subject about to confess his feelings of guilt? – defines nothing less than the film's truth. It brings to the fore the predicaments of a fully disenchanted society in which nothing about the role of the visible and the audible, and about how to frame questions of knowledge and the moral good, goes without saying anymore. Gabriel Yared's musical soundtrack, used here to sound out the constitutive silence of Wiesler's daydream, certainly knows something of this ambivalence, this confusion. As it incorporates some of the melodic elements that drive Albert Jerska's 'The Sonata of the Good Person', to be heard in full only later when played by Dreyman in response to Jerska's suicide, Yared's soundtrack here transports the viewer disorientingly between the diegetic and the non-diegetic, present and future. Nothing perhaps could be more appropriate to signify Wiesler's at once ethical and metaphysical dilemma than how Yared's music at this point fractures the integrity of narrative time and space – and in so doing presents Wiesler as a protagonist who has lost his faith in any reliable frame of reference and is torn apart by irreconcilable visions and obligations.

Beyond Heritage and Consensus

Scenes of surveillance play an eminent role in much of German art-house film-making of the new millennium. Think of the crucial role of surveillance footage in Christian Petzold's *Die innere Sicherheit* (The State I Am In, 2000), capturing a calamitous bank robbery and inviting the viewer to develop conflicting readings of what we see and hear. Think of Michael Haneke's *Caché* (Hidden, 2005) as it pictures a present observed and haunted by a past that does not want to go away. Think finally of *Dreileben* (2011), a three-part television production directed by Petzold, Dominik Graf, and Christoph Hochhäusler, in which surveillance cameras frame and pierce the entire narrative process from the very first to the very last shot. Yet more important than the diegetic presence of observation technologies in recent German filmmaking is the fact that, in particular in the films of the so-called Berlin School, the camera itself often seems to assume the role of an at once disaffected and unyielding instrument of surveillance. As it tracks the restless paths of antiheroes whose lives are struck by a profound absence of passion, direction, meaningful communication, and physical contact, the Berlin School camera typically stays deeply aloof from what it captures. It provides images that – like surveillance footage – remain distant and indifferent, curtail the viewer's processes of projection and identification, and precisely therefore seem to limit their purpose, in Siegfried Kracauer's words, to the task of solely redeeming physical reality.[14]

In recent years, the Berlin School has become the new good object of German film studies. For many scholars, particularly in North America, it has come to represent a cinema of uncomfortable and non-commercial smallness not only legitimizing German filmmaking once again internationally as part of a cinema of formal experimentation and criticality, but also challenging the way in which popular filmmaking in the postwall period has capitalized on the production of consensus and heritage values. Given the new (and in fact not so new) orthodoxies of German film studies, commercially successful productions such as *The Lives of Others* often have to fight uphill battles in order to receive the kind of attention and reading they might deserve. Good box office returns, let alone Academy Award nominations, are gauged as an automatic sign of formal deficiency and political sell out, an assault on sophisticated tastes as much as on the critic's monopoly in matters of critical meaning-making.

---

14 Siegfried Kracauer, *Theory of Film. The Redemption of Physical Reality*, with an introduction by Miriam Bratu Hansen (Princeton: Princeton University Press, 1997).

This is not the place to discuss in detail German film studies' at times almost suicidal desire to neglect or deride its objects' popular successes on the national or international stage. What I want to point out in closing, however, is the fact that the formal treatment of surveillance in *The Lives of Others* – though by no means comparable to what Petzold or Haneke have done with it during the last decade – opens a space of critical energy and ambivalence that by far exceeds the user-friendly designs of heritage and consensus cinema. While my reading in this essay has stressed what I understand to be the film's underlying Catholicism – the way in which themes of guilt, faith, disenchantment, and repentance prop up the film's overt narrative of political oppression, collaboration, and resistance – the overall point has been to point at how the choreography of sounds and sights in *The Lives of Others* destabilizes any coherent and consumable framing of meaning within the diegesis. In von Donnersmarck's view, Wiesler's dream of de-acousmatization, of collapsing image and sound into tangible presence, secretly replays and reinforces the very system he – disenchanted with the mechanics of power in 'real-existing socialism' – seeks to defy. In a world beyond faith and belief, the relation of the visual and the acoustical, of different registers of the sensible, cannot but remain a broken one. Whereas consensus comedies are eager to construct convenient frames around what is sensible in the present, and heritage films seek to package the sights and sounds of the past into marketable consumer items, *The Lives of Others* explores its theme of auditory surveillance as a narrative engine unsettling formal closure and reconciliatory acts of enframing, in both synchronic and diachronic terms.

The Lives of Others no doubt exerts considerable affective pull on its viewers, yet its formal arrangement and narrative organization should provide German film studies with good reasons to move beyond the normative opposition of (bad) commercial consensus and heritage filmmaking on the one hand, and (good) non-commercial, disaffected film art on the other. In von Donnermarck's fallen and deeply damaged world, the audible may long for being reunited with the visible, but to fulfil this dream would mean to betray one's very vision of a better and other life. Contrary to what consensus and heritage filmmaking have sought to teach us, sound in von Donnersmarck's film cannot be heard rightly. It rubs against the power of the frame and thus reveals the ways in which our modern world of omnipresent media has come to produce much less enlightenment and reciprocal communication than it had initially promised.

Sabine Hake

CHAPTER TEN
On the Lives of Objects

The historical film depends to a large degree on the filmic representation of objects of everyday life that are either associated with a particular past or, in the case of films about recent events, identified as being no longer part of the present. Production design plays a key role in conveying this sense of pastness through a heavy reliance on objects – the things that make up everyday life and the stuff with which characters surround themselves.[1] Yet by visualizing the difference between the bygone world of the narrative and the contemporary conjuncture, these objects – furniture, house wares, clothing, electronics and so forth – also resist the unique claims on physical reality that distinguish film from other visual media. Separated from the flow of life, the historical film does not partake in what Siegfried Kracauer calls 'the redemption of physical reality through film', leaning instead toward theatrical effects, illusionist tendencies and allegorical impulses.[2]

Closer attention to this object world allows us to move beyond assumptions about representation that keep the historical film under the sway of the realism-illusionism divide and to examine the enlistment of physical reality in the reconstruction of the past from a decidedly contemporary (i.e., presentist) perspective. Precisely because of film's precarious relationship to physical reality, the objects in the historical film are frequently enlisted in the imagination of times and places marked as other or introduced to establish the terms of difference. This has profound implications for our understanding both of historical narratives, as articulated through subject-object relationships, and of the meaning of history as organized through objects (or things) as the materialization of specific attitudes and ideas about the past. 'From a *theoretical* point of view human actors encode things with significance', writes Arjun Appadurai; yet 'from a *methodological* point of view, it is the things in motion that illuminate their human and social context'.[3] Accordingly, their function within the diegesis offers a useful entry

---

1 The growing interest among cultural historians and theorists in things and objects – their filmic representation obliterates the difference between both terms (e.g., in Heidegger's distinction between *Ding* and *Objekt*) – is reflected in recent anthologies such as *The Object Reader*, ed. by Fiona Candlin and Raiford Guins (London: Routledge, 2009).
2 Siegfried Kracauer, *Theory of Film. The Redemption of Physical Reality*, with an introduction by Miriam Bratu Hansen (Princeton: Princeton University Press, 1997).
3 Arjun Appadurai, 'Introduction', in *The Social Life of Things. Commodities in Cultural Perspective*, ed. by Arjun Appadurai (Cambridge: Cambridge UP, 1986), pp. 3–63 (p. 5).

point into the ideological operations that distinguish the historical film and define its precarious position between realism, illusionism and allegorization.

For that reason alone, the objects chosen to interpret – rather than merely represent – the distance between present and past should never be treated as self-evident in their function within the mise-en-scène or be regarded as secondary to the production of narrative meanings or historical insights. On the contrary, reading a historical film such as *The Lives of Others* through what I call the lives of objects allows us to better understand the unique status of objects as visualizations of both the social and cultural discourses associated with them and the forms of attachment and strategies of incorporation articulated through them. In this particular case, the objects chosen for a historical reconstruction of the GDR circa 1984 are profoundly dependent on contemporary forms of engagement: the sensory pleasures through which spectators respond to these audiovisual semblances and evaluate their cultural and aesthetic significance; the political memories and historical knowledges that guide their recognition and appreciation of period styles; and the reading strategies that integrate them into ideological formations and interpretative frameworks. It is with these larger questions in mind that I approach the culture-politics interface marked as East German through the kind of objects that visualize its historicity (i.e., its pastness) and, in the process of historicization, give rise to a decidedly West German theory of cultural production. Greater attention to the objects of everyday life is central to a better understanding of the aestheticization of history and the commodification of memory that continue to trouble postunification representations of the GDR; but it also brings into relief the pivotal role of the object in the filmic production of history, memory and nostalgia more generally. In other words, the objects in the historical film allow us to make use of the important distinction made by Philip Rosen among history, historiography and historicity, with the latter defined as 'the particular interrelations of the mode of historiography and the types of construction of history related by it'.[4]

Essential to the reality claims of film and its illusionist potential, objects occupy the centre of what Laura Marks calls haptic visuality and play a key role in the process of grasping, quite literally, the texture and textuality of the past.[5] Of course, objects in film are only visual representations of objects; yet their physical presence within the mise-en-scène can never be fully contained by the frame or

4 Philip Rosen, *Change Mummified. Cinema, Historicity, Theory* (Minneapolis: University of Minnesota Press, 2001), p. xi.
5 Laura U. Marks, *The Skin of the Film. Intercultural Cinema, Embodiment, and the Senses* (Durham: Duke University Press, 2000), p. xi.

completely integrated into the narrative. As part of production design, objects reach beyond the diegesis, evoking qualities and experiences shared with the extradiegetic practices of architecture, technology, fashion and design. Embedded in specific conditions of cultural production and consumption, objects often serve as heuristic devices in the above mentioned culture-politics interface. In this particular film, typewriters, telephones, tape recorders and television monitors, together with books and magazines, stand in for basic cultural techniques such as reading, writing, speaking and listening. They are introduced to represent the struggle between individual expression and political control or, to phrase it differently, between artist and state. Yet the fact that these tools and techniques are identified with a historically specific mode of cultural production – namely, in a socialist state that no longer exists – further complicates the filmic status of objects as objects because of their association with memory culture and historical debate, that is: with formally very different but closely related narratives about culture and politics that, not surprisingly, involve processes of objectification and *Verdinglichung* (reification).

On the one hand, the objects in the diegesis serve as markers of historical authenticity even where they are in fact anachronistic; they situate the story in a particular time and place and do so through fiction effects markedly different from, say, the spatial regimes prevalent in historical exhibitions. On the other hand, these objects construct (and hence allow us to reconstruct) a particular relationship to the past, one that is sometimes nostalgic, sometimes fetishistic, and sometimes allegorical. These two sides align the historical film in often problematic ways with claims of authenticity that have less to do with history as commonly understood than with the spectator's particular relationship to that history. The audience's familiarity with the look of an era and the filmmaker's heavy reliance on set and costume design in recreating the past are openly acknowledged in the term 'period film'. Similarly, the emotional investments in the kind of pasts mobilized in the making of national history and identity are considered crucial to the nostalgia effects of the so-called heritage film. But in ways not yet fully understood, the ideological demands on the mise-en-scène of history remain inextricably linked to the visual, narrative, affective and haptic qualities that make the objects from the past – in the diegesis and beyond – nodal points for conflicting projections, interpretations and appropriations.

Whether seen as an important contribution to coming to terms with the German division or analyzed through the lens of *Ostalgie* (i.e., nostalgia for the old East), the numerous films about the GDR made since unification rely heavily on the materiality of everyday life to evoke a political system and ideology that has been soundly defeated. What better way to consider their role in historical representation than by *not* writing about stories and characters and instead focusing on physical objects and the relationships organized through and inscribed in them? Precisely such a strategy informs my approach to the questions raised by *The Lives of Others*, a much discussed contribution to post-1989 West German representations of East Germany in films, novels, exhibition culture and historical scholarship and their shared reliance on bits and pieces from that country's vanished lifeworld in articulating decidedly contemporary views on history, politics and culture.[6]

The continuing scholarly indifference to the actual building blocks of the historical film is all the more surprising in light of the centrality of production design to German film history from Expressionist cinema to New German Cinema; the same could be said about the privileged role of objects – 'stranded objects', in Eric Santner's phrase – in staging the haunted scenes of post-Holocaust mourning and melancholia.[7] Confirming the importance of objects in imagining the politics-technology interface of the future, Fritz Lang's *Das Testament des Dr. Mabuse* (The Testament of Dr. Mabuse, 1932) with its 1962 sequel, Harry Piel's *Die Welt ohne Maske* (The World without a Mask, 1934) and Rainer Werner Fassbinder's *Welt am Draht* (World on a Wire, 1973) are telling examples of the obsessions in German cinema with technologies of surveillance; but little attention has been

---

6 The special issue of *German Studies Review*, 31.3 (2008) on *The Lives of Others* addresses many of these issues; see the articles by Thomas Lindenberger, 'Stasiploitation – Why Not? The Scriptwriter's Historical Creativity in *The Lives of Others*', 557–66; Mary Beth Stein, 'Stasi with a Human Face? Ambiguity in *Das Leben der Anderen*', 567–79; Jens Gieseke, 'Stasi Goes to Hollywood: Donnersmarck's *The Lives of Others* und die Grenzen der Authentizität', 580–88; Manfred Wilke, 'Fiktion oder erlebte Geschichte? Zur Frage der Glaubwürdigkeit des Films *Das Leben der Anderen*', 589–98; Cheryl Dueck, 'The Humanization of the Stasi in *Das Leben der Anderen*', 599–608. On the importance of marketing in this context, see Lu Seegers, '*Das Leben der Anderen* oder die "richtige" Erinnerung an die DDR', in *Film und kulturelle Erinnerung. Plurimediale Konstellationen*, ed. by Astrid Erll and Stephanie Woninka (Berlin: de Gruyter, 2008), pp. 21–52. On the West German perspective, see Anna Funder, 'Eyes without a Face', *Sight and Sound*, 17.5 (2007), 16–20 and Daniela Berghahn, 'Remembering the Stasi in a Fairytale of Redemption: Florian Henckel von Donnersmarck's *Das Leben der Anderen*', *Oxford German Studies*, 38.3 (2009), 312–33. On the centrality of gender to these revisionist projects, compare Jennifer Creech, 'A Few Good Men: Gender, Ideology, and Narrative Politics in *The Lives of Others* and *Good Bye, Lenin!*', in *Women in German Yearbook*, 25 (2009), 100–26, and Gary Schmidt, 'Between Authors and Agents: Gender and Affirmative Culture in *Das Leben der Anderen*', *German Quarterly*, 82.2 (2009), 231–49. See also Andrea Rinke's contribution to this volume. On the problem of historical authenticity, also see Wendy Westphal, '"Truer than the Real Thing": "Real" and "Hyperreal" Representations of the Past in *Das Leben der Anderen*', *German Studies Review*, 35.1 (2012), 96–111.

7 The reference is to Eric L. Santner, *Stranded Objects. Mourning, Memory, and Film in Postwar Germany* (Ithaca: Cornell University Press, 1990).

paid to the material reconstruction of the past and its enlistment in contemporary political debates, reason enough to start out with some introductory remarks on the benefits of approaching postunification films about the GDR from the perspective of production design and its objects.

There are good reasons (disciplinary as well as methodological) for pursuing such an approach: to counteract the continuous privileging in German film studies of questions of narrative in the negotiation of (national, ethnic and gendered) identities; to resist the discursive logic according to which every film about the GDR is evaluated based on criteria of historical accuracy and authenticity; and to avoid the tendency in more theoretical contributions to read films symptomatically but, in the process, bracket everything that confirms film as an aesthetic practice with a special investment in the object world. As should be apparent by now, my larger goal behind reading *The Lives of Others* through the 'totality of objects' and a thus evoked 'totality of life', to draw on two terms coined by Georg Lukács in his analysis of the historical novel, is to expand the parameters within which we evaluate the historical film and to acknowledge the uniquely filmic reconstruction of the past as an integral part of other object-based historical practices from museum exhibitions to retro consumption.[8] But whereas Lukács draws attention to objects in the name of a materialist conception of history, I use their placement in the diegesis to untangle some of the contradictions that inform all postunificiation representations of the GDR. This means to ignore much of what has preoccupied critics and scholars so far, including the film's melodramatic emplotment of German history, the problematic narrative of redemption and reconciliation, and the highly gendered figure constellations that make both possible.

Confirming my earlier comments on the blind spots of narrative analysis, the critical reception of *The Lives of Others* consists largely of symptomatic readings that quickly bypass the visual surface of history, its texture and textuality, and downplay the spectatorial pleasures afforded by the historical film as a genre with a particular investment in the look of things. Instead the Oscar-winning film has been analyzed as part of other revisionist accounts of the German division and the kind of nostalgia for East Germany known as *Ostalgie*.[9] Usually *The Lives*

---

8 Georg Lukács, *The Historical Novel* (Lincoln: University of Nebraska Press, 1983).

9 Surveys of these films can be found in Ralf Schenk, 'Die DDR im deutschen Film nach 1989', *Aus Politik und Zeitgeschichte*, 44 (2005), 31–38 and Katarina Kuperstein, *Zwischen Ostalgie and Reflexion. Die filmische Darstellung der DDR nach der Wende* (Saarbrücken: VDM Dr. Müller, 2010). On some of the broader implications, see Thomas Lindenberger, 'Zeitgeschichte am Schneidetisch. Zur Historisierung der DDR im deutschen Spielfilm', in *Visual History. Ein Studienbuch*, ed. by Paul Gerhard (Göttingen: Vandenhoeck and Ruprecht, 2006), pp. 353–72.

of Others is grouped together with more 'serious' films that approach the last decade of the GDR from a Western perspective and often focus on the Stasi as the embodiment of the East German *Überwachungsstaat* (surveillance state). Examples include two well-known films by representatives of New German Cinema, *Das Versprechen* (The Promise, Margarethe von Trotta, 1995) and *Die Stille nach dem Schuß* (The Legend of Rita, Volker Schlöndorff, 2000), as well as the successful television miniseries *Weissensee* (Friedemann Fromm, 2010). Resisting the project of national reconciliation through (failed) heterosexual romance, former DEFA directors (in a variation on the famous Marx quote) have depicted the final years of the GDR as either tragedy (e.g., *Abschied von Agnes* [Farewell to Agnes, Michael Gwisdek, 1994]) or farce (e.g., *Letztes aus der DaDaeR* [Latest from the DaDaeR, Jörg Foth, 1990]). Meanwhile mainstream productions such as *Sonnenallee* (Sun Alley, Leander Haußmann, 1999), *Helden wie wir* (Heroes Like Us, Sebastian Peterson, 1999), *Good Bye, Lenin!* (Wolfgang Becker, 2003), *NVA* (Leander Haußmann, 2005) and *Der rote Kakadu* (The Red Cockatoo, Dominik Graf, 2006) draw upon the conventions of the heritage film, including its heavy reliance on production design, in conjuring up bygone worlds, mentalities and sensibilities. The latter have played a key role in translating the problems of unification into the conciliatory registers of *Ostalgie* or, in the case of *Good Bye, Lenin!*, its humorous deconstruction.[10]

But as the latter films illustrate, *Ostalgie* is only secondarily a narrative phenomenon; like the preoccupation with heritage in postunification German cinema and culture, it is primarily based on, and articulated through, the world of objects. Most films about everyday life in the GDR use set and costume design to simultaneously serve the nostalgic pleasures of *Ostalgie* and marginalize the GDR within the visual archives of a unified Germany. At first glance, aligning *The Lives*

---

10 On *Ostalgie*, see the special volume edited by David Clarke, 'Beyond *Ostalgie*: East and West German Identity in Contemporary German Culture', *Seminar*, 40.3 (2004); Anna Saunders, '"Normalizing" the Past: East German Culture and *Ostalgie*', in *German Culture, Politics, and Literature into the Twenty-First Century*, ed. by Stuart Taberner and Paul Cooke (Rochester: Camden House, 2006), pp. 89–103; and Greg Castillo, 'East as True West: Redeeming Bourgeois Culture: From Social Realism to *Ostalgie*', *Kritika. Explorations in Russian and Eurasian History*, 9.4 (2008), 747–68. On films in the context of *Ostalgie*, also see Jennifer Kapczynski, 'Negotiating Nostalgia: The GDR Past in *Berlin Is in Germany* and *Good Bye, Lenin!*', *Germanic Review*, 82.1 (2007), 78–100; Jaimey Fisher, 'German Historical Film as Production Trend: European Heritage Cinema and Melodrama in *The Lives of Others*', in *The Collapse of the Conventional. German Film and Its Politics at the Turn of the Twenty-First Century*, ed. by Jaimey Fisher and Brad Prager (Detroit: Wayne State University Press, 2010), pp. 186–215; Nick Hodgin and Caroline Pearce, eds, *The GDR Remembered. Representations of the East German State since 1989* (Rochester: Camden House, 2011), especially Nick Hodgin, 'Screening the Stasi, The Politics of Representation in Postunification Film', pp. 69–94.

of Others with such objectifying treatments seems counterintuitive, given the implicit diagnosis of a trivialization of history. The melodramatic tone of this ambitious art film shares little with the comedic and parodistic modes prevalent in filmic and televisual simulations of the GDR as a site of retrospective projections. Similarly, its humanistic belief in the utopian power of art stands in sharp contrast to the cult of the commodity that has turned East Germany into an object of cultural consumption and performative identification. But as in earlier treatments, the film's fantasy of national reconciliation – over the body of a dead woman (as some critics have rightly noted) – is achieved through the recreation of the East as the exoticized other, a process not dissimilar to what Paul Cooke has described as colonization.[11] More relevant to my discussion, in the same way that the blanket dismissal of *Ostalgie* as sentimental kitsch is often predicated on a high-culture disregard for the materiality of history and (post)memory, the moralistic insistence on appropriate forms of engagement sometimes hides the instrumentalization of postunification representations of the GDR in the corresponding phenomenon of *Westalgie* (i.e., nostalgia for the old Federal Republic) as *Ostalgie*'s secret double. This elusive mixture of temporal detachment and emotional attachment is most apparent in the film's colour scheme, a result of von Donnersmarck's decision to shoot in analogue rather than digital technology, with all reds and blues drained from the film stock, thus creating a visual effect similar to patina. The narrow colour range, consisting largely of browns, greys and blues, has been described as key to the film's reconstruction of 1980s East Berlin 'as it really was'; it also has been criticized for contributing to the denunciation of the GDR, and of socialism, as lacking in colour and, hence, vitality.[12] Yet in less obvious ways, this historical patina can also be seen as a symptom of nostalgia for the kind of futures past associated with the two sides in the Cold War divide.

Rereading *The Lives of Others* through the lives of objects reveals the numerous ways in which production design is also informed by a postunification perspective on (the marginalization of) literature in the public sphere. In other words, the representation of the GDR as a society of writers and readers, even if the latter are Stasi agents, is inseparable from nostalgia for the divided *Leseland* (reading country) of the 1980s of which West Germany was the other half. With von Donnersmarck approaching the former East from a position of retrospection as well as extraterritoriality, his film must thus be read as displaced *Westalgie*,

11 Paul Cooke, *Representing East Germany Since Unification. From Colonization to Nostalgia* (New York: Berg, 2005).
12 'A World without Red and Blue: An Interview with Florian Henckel von Donnersmarck', *Projections 15 Seminar. European Cinema*, ed. by Peter Cowie and Pascal Edelmann (London: Faber and Faber, 2007), pp. 225–35.

that is, nostalgia for the FRG's thriving literary public sphere and its reliance on writers as the nation's moral conscience. The incessant complaints about the fundamental transformation of the public sphere in the new information age, and the attendant decline of (high) literary culture, are inseparable from legitimate concerns about the triumph of neoliberal capitalism and global consumer culture, a point made by Dominic Boyer and Anthony Enns in their analyses of *Ostalgie* as postsocialist nostalgia; yet the same concerns have inspired nostalgia for the imaginary other Germany, the old FRG, that is always present in postunification representations of the GDR.[13] In *The Lives of Others*, these two positions come together in the preoccupation with the final flourishing of literature in the East (and of critical journalism in the West) and the acute awareness of the disappearance of both worlds acknowledged in the film's melancholy tone.

Rather than reconstructing this process through the figure of Georg Dreyman, I focus on the objects that visualize his dilemmas as an East German writer and play a key role in the filmic representation of the Stasi and its observational techniques, that is, of recording, transcribing, copying, interpreting and so forth. Such a process-based approach to writing is essential for understanding the contemporary investment in the GDR as both a surveillance state and a literary culture, a structural tension captured in the terms *Stasiland* (land of the Stasi) and *Kulturnation* (cultural nation). The linkages between the two reveal the constitutive elements behind the historicization of the literary public sphere under conditions of dictatorship, the related diagnosis of a decline of literary culture today, and the melancholy attachment to the cultural life and political culture of the decades leading up to unification. Last but not least, the strategies through which von Donnersmarck distinguishes a humanistic from a totalitarian definition of literature allow us to revisit some of the criticism levelled against the film and, instead of reproducing the East-West antagonism informing many contributions, to shift attention to the aesthetic and ideological alternatives visualized through the world of objects: bourgeois humanism or socialist modernity, literary public sphere or surveillance state.

Conceptual support for rereading films about the GDR from the perspective of things – and the function of things in relation to bodies and stories – can be found in the recent turn in historical scholarship toward material culture and its recognition of the importance of product design for understanding historiography and historicity. Here Rainer Gries's definition of 'products as media' and Paul Bett's

---

13 Dominic Boyer, '*Ostalgie* and the Politics of the Future in Eastern Germany', *Public Culture*, 18.2 (2006), 361–81; Anthony Enns, 'The Politics of *Ostalgie*: Post-Socialist *Nostalgie* in Recent German Film', *Screen*, 48.4 (2007), 475–91.

notion of 'the return of history as design'[14] offer useful entry points into the parallel projects of textual analysis and historical contextualization and shed new light on the bifurcated narratives of mass culture and modernity in East and West Germany during the Cold War. In the popular films associated with *Ostalgie*, the kind of objects enlisted in a thus described return of history as design include the iconic two-cylinder car in *Go, Trabi, Go* (Peter Timm, 1990), the hilarious *Multifunktionstisch* (multifunction table, or MUFUTI) in *Sonnenallee* and the beloved Spreewald gherkins in *Good Bye, Lenin!*[15] Confirming the intricate dynamics of allegorization, fetishization and commodification, memories of GDR everyday life and material culture during the early 2000s enjoyed great popularity in television shows and are still kept alive through fan clubs, theme parties and mail order catalogues for *Ostprodukte* (products made in the GDR). Adding the perspective of musealization, the material culture of 'the first socialist state on German soil' can be found on full display in the DDR-Museum in Berlin and the Dokumentationszentrum Alltagskultur der DDR (Documentation Centre of Everyday Culture in the GDR) in Eisenhüttenstadt.[16] But what are the implications of this growing attention to GDR material culture for the analysis of a film like *The Lives of Others*? If it is true, as Daphne Berdahl and others have argued, that consumer objects open up an alternative to the privileging of the resistance narrative dominant in the East German branch of the Stiftung Haus der Geschichte der Bundesrepublik Deutschland or the Zeitgeschichtliche Forum Leipzig (ZGF), what precisely is the function of such objects in a film 'about' the paradigmatic struggle between 'Geist und Macht' (spirit and power) evoked since the 1910s as a central conflict in Ger-

---

14 See Rainer Gries, *Produkte als Medien. Kulturgeschichte der Produktkommunikation in der Bundesrepublik und der DDR* (Leipzig: Leipziger Universitätsverlag, 2003) and Paul Betts, *The Authority of Everyday Objects. A Cultural History of West Germany Industrial Design* (Berkeley: University of California Press, 2004), p. 249.

15 Daphne Berdahl, '"Go, Trabi, Go"!: Reflections on a Car and its Symbolization over Time', *Anthropology and Humanism*, 25.2 (2000), 131–41; by the same author, '(N)ostalgie for the Present: Memory, Longing, and East German Things', *Ethnos*, 64.2 (1999),192–211. A rare discussion of the filmic representation of consumer culture can be found in Michael D. Richardson, 'A World of Objects: Consumer Culture in Filmic Reconstructions of the GDR', in *The Collapse of the Conventional*, pp. 216–23.

16 See Daphne Berdahl, 'Re-presenting the Socialist Modern: Museums and Memory in the Former GDR', in *Socialist Modern. East German Everyday Culture and Politics*, ed. by Katherine Pence and Paul Betts (Ann Arbor: University of Michigan Press, 2008), pp. 345–66; Paul Betts, 'The Twilight of the Idols: East German Memory and Material Culture', *Journal of Modern History*, 72.3 (2000), 731–65; Martin Blum, 'Remaking the East German Past: *Ostalgie*, Identity, and Material Culture', *Journal of Popular Culture*, 34.3 (2000), 229–53; Jonathan Bach, '"The Taste Remains": Consumption, (N)Ostalgia, and the Production of East Germany', *Public Culture*, 14.3 (2002), 545–56.

man society and revisited, after 1989, in the controversies surrounding writers Christa Wolf and Sascha Anderson and their work as unofficial Stasi informers?

In answering these questions in the case of *The Lives of Others*, we must begin with the constitutive tension between historical representation and retrospective reconstruction as articulated through production design, including the choice of locations and the look of interiors. In early interviews von Donnersmarck repeatedly described how his production team went to great lengths to return East Berlin neighbourhoods to their original look before unification. Yet for the reasons noted above, they invariably ended up reproducing contemporary cultural topographies, with all the adjustments necessitated by urban reality and filmic fantasy. For instance, Dreyman's apartment building, a typical example of *Gründerzeit* architecture, is supposed to be in Prenzlauer Berg but the exterior scenes were in fact shot on Wedekindstrasse in Friedrichshain. Stasi colonel Wiesler lives in one of the infamous modern *Plattenbauten* (prefab high rises) found on Leninplatz and similar showcases of socialist city planning. The film team's difficulties in protecting building facades from being sprayed with graffiti overnight, recounted in the 'Making of' feature on the Sony Pictures Classics DVD, confirm the director's historicist ambitions; but these anecdotes also reveal to what degree the difference between an oppressive regime intent on controlling all forms of writing and a free society presumably powerless against such renegade acts of (re)inscription become an integral part of the promotional strategies. The choice of the famous Soviet War Memorial in Treptower Park (instead of the more neutral Teufelssee near Köpenick in the screenplay) as the setting for a conspiratorial meeting illustrates the growing emphasis during the production on East Berlin as a city with a burdensome socialist history. Meanwhile the oft-cited problems concerning the use of historical sites indirectly validate the importance of cinema as a site of collective memory. Key scenes were shot inside the old Stasi headquarter in Normannenstrasse, now the repository of the Stasi archives. However, initial plans to use the main Stasi detention centre, now the Berlin-Hohenschönhausen Memorial, were vetoed by its director, suggesting competing views on the uses of German history in the new Berlin Republic.

With the look of history in film often influenced by historical paintings or paintings from the period, it should not surprise that the production team sought inspiration from visual material produced during the GDR to recreate the disillusioned atmosphere of socialism's final decade. As a result, history returns in the form of film history, with the historical film clearly benefitting from the increasingly important role of films in history. Confirming the highly mediated nature of the genre, production designer Silke Buhr reportedly watched famous DEFA films such as *Die Legende von Paul and Paula* (The Legend of Paul and Paula, Heiner Carow, 1973) and drew on other visual sources such as photography – perhaps even Helga Paris's 1970s photo series of East Berlin neighbourhood bars or Harald Hauswald's 1987 photo book of East Berlin – to gain a better sense of the GDR lifeworld and its visual self-representations. Her exterior scenes reproduce the old-fashioned urbanity and picturesque decay that, after 1989, prompted many artists and intellectuals to move to Prenzlauer Berg and Friedrichshain and that, notwithstanding the hipster reclamation of 1970s prefab high rises as monuments to mid-century modernism, continue to be favoured over the products of GDR modern architecture and city planning. By contrast, through the postmodern alignment of modernism with totalitarianism, the SED regime in the film is reduced to the sterility of the functional public and private spaces inhabited by its representatives. Their privileges are on full display in their signature cars, the Volvo 760 state limousine reserved for the state minister or the Lada 1600 driven by rank and file Stasi officers. Beyond these few tokens of socialist luxury, the banality of life in a modern(ist) dictatorship manifests itself above all in mundane details such as the wood-panelled Stasi offices and the rubber plant in the Stasi canteen – symbols of the petty-bourgeois culture of provincialism, authoritarianism and philistinism that the Federal Republic proudly claimed to have overcome by the 1980s.

All historical films, especially those aiming at authenticity, rely on stylization to produce their ideological effects. Aware that historical authenticity is often a product of illusionism posing as realism, von Donnersmarck at one point called his approach to set design a 'making everything graphic'.[17] Corroborating his statement, the actor Sebastian Koch (in an interview included among the DVD extras) describes how the director set out to find big things in small things; he was looking for a filmic version 'truer than the true thing'. In accordance with convention, *The Lives of Others* introduces the corresponding material things primarily in the service of the narrative, to mark turning points, highlight dramatic tensions, and reveal underlying conflicts. Unlike in *Good Bye, Lenin!*, these things do not serve as means for ironic commentary or tokens of fetishistic desire. Yet it would be nearsighted to simply see them as extensions of the characters or, worst, as mere decoration. As the second part of the essay will show, the filmic transformation of objects into sites of contestation and manifestations of ambivalence can be traced from the most personal ones, especially those related to the body (clothes) and the home (furniture), to the most political ones, including those used in the acts of surveillance that *de facto* eliminate the separation between private and public sphere.

---

17 Diane Carson, 'Learning from History in *The Lives of Others*: An Interview with Writer/Director Florian Henckel von Donnersmarck', *Journal of Film and Video*, 61.1–2 (2010), 18.

To begin with the protagonists' clothes, their function as objects – or, more precisely, as membranes mediating between bodies and spaces – is two-fold: to foreground the performative nature of their identities and to locate these performances in a culturally mediated fantasy of German division. Throughout costume designer Gabriele Binder emphasizes the uniformity of menswear, suggesting that the Stasi officer and the literary author only act out predetermined roles in the performance of oppression and resistance. At the same time, she clothes the East Berlin intelligentsia in the familiar uniform of 1980s alternative culture shared by East and West: functional parkas, baggy trousers, long hair and unshaven faces or beards, further evidence of the similarities in countercultural tastes and the contemporary investment in this doubling effect. Dreyman and Wiesler´s sartorial choices identify them as professionals and, across the culture-politics divide, as inhabitants of the same world of ideologies and ideas. Dreyman's brown corduroy jacket and wool trousers, worn with an open beige dress shirt, suggests a writer or intellectual; his look is mid-career Günter Grass without the moustache and pipe. Wiesler's three-tone grey Terylene parka, with the two corduroy side flaps and three snap buttons, announces a faceless organization man, the kind found in all large state bureaucracies. His grey-in-grey ensemble, which includes a small man purse with wrist strap, resembles the standard attire of central committee members during the 1980s; comparisons to a younger and thinner Erich Mielke, the Minister of State Security, are perhaps intended.

Of course, these uniforms also point to significant differences in their meaning for the two antagonists. For the ascetic Wiesler, the uniform represents a way of denying his individuality and guarding against intimacy, whereas Dreyman moves with grace and ease, clearly comfortable in his body. The dialogic structure of the Dreyman-Wiesler relationship is sustained through the figure of Dreyman's girlfriend, Christa-Maria Sieland, whose main function is to facilitate communication between the two men and their surrogates, State Minister Bruno Hempf and Wiesler's superior Anton Grubitz. The glamorous style of the famous actress – her camel hair coat with large fur hat, her body-hugging silvery dress and her cream-coloured negligee – appears extraterritorial to both ideological projects, the denunciation of socialism as totalitarianism and the romanticization of German literary culture as oppositional culture. For that reason, the woman has to be eliminated from the narrative in a melodramatic scene that takes full advantage of the implied connection between male creativity and female sacrifice.

Similarly, the men's apartments function not only as manifestations of their different personalities; in the larger context, they also serve to illustrate the richness of bourgeois humanism and the failure of socialist modernism. Like the chamber-play film of the Weimar era, *The Lives of Others* presents the home – and the private sphere more generally – as an externalized manifestation of the main characters' internalized conflicts. The screenplay describes Dreyman's apartment as follows:

> It is a representative and generously sized Berlin prewar apartment, with few but beautiful pieces of antique furniture and large dynamic paintings in the socialist expressionist style. [...] During his inspecting of the apartment [Wiesler] stopped in front of an antique lamp: a wooden Moor with golden turban bearing the light fixture. For Wiesler, this was pure decadence.[18]

Spacious and comfortable, the actual apartment includes a low sofa and chairs in midcentury modern style, a large wooden desk and grand piano, heavy patterned drapes and curtains, numerous book shelves and side tables, simple white lamps, countless knick knacks and artworks and the obligatory potted palm found in Berlin bourgeois interiors since the *Gründerzeit*. With high ceilings and parquet floors, the rooms are decorated in a bourgeois bohemian style, evidence of the privileges accorded to the cultural elites in East German society. Some of the artwork offers pointed commentary on Dreyman's compromised position as a writer (i.e., the large marionette on the wall), Sieland's eventual betrayal (i.e., the female marble statue next to the telephone) and the complications arising from the mingling of love and politics (i.e., the drawing depicting Adam and Eve). A silver *Jugendstil* dragonfly sculpture on the armoire in the hallway captures best what for the Stasi agent epitomizes the excesses of hedonism but what for the writer signifies the rewards of a well-lived life made possible by literary productivity and political accommodation.

By contrast, the Stasi colonel lives in a small apartment in a prefab high rise described as follows in the screenplay: 'Wiesler's one-bedroom apartment is furnished with the kind of pieces most easily attainable in the GDR: thin wood furniture with steel legs. Any attempt at decoration is missing; the only embellishment is a calendar of the National People's Army'.[19] An example of the so-called P2 prototype, complete with a pass-through from kitchen to living room, the actual apartment is a showcase of modern socialist living: small rooms with low ceilings and sparsely furnished with functional furniture. Despite its textured wallpaper and brown drapes, the living room offers little comfort except for a small sofa and coffee table and a television set as the sole source of entertainment. The simple meal consumed in such a sterile environment – rice with tomato paste – only adds to the overall sense of deprivation and isolation. In the same way that the

---

18 Florian Henckel von Donnersmarck, *Das Leben der anderen. Filmbuch* (Frankfurt am Main: Suhrkamp, 2007), pp. 40–41.
19 von Donnersmarck, *Das Leben der anderen*, p. 37.

eclectic *Gründerzeit* style favoured by Dreyman comes to stand in for tradition, intimacy and a sense of belonging, the postwar interpretations of the Bauhaus legacy are now equated with alienation, coldness and social anomie. By using the presumed honesty of materials such as glass, steel and concrete in denouncing an oppressive political regime, the film effectively enlists modernism as a stand-in for the failed project of socialism, a connection established through their shared belief in social engineering and aesthetic functionalism.[20] According to this logic, the ethos of transparency symbolized by glass in the modernist aesthetic was appropriated by the project of socialist reconstruction and reinterpreted within its totalitarian regimes of order and control. The habitus of sobriety, as Theodor W. Adorno and Ernst Bloch noted in the 1950s, was to achieve the reconciliation of subject and object; but as functionalism stopped anticipating social change in aesthetic form, its direction was reversed, no longer a weapon against oppression but an expression of it.[21]

Jonathan Bach describes the contemporary attachment to this aesthetic and political project as modernist nostalgia, a longing for the longings once possible. Its manifestations in the historical imagination of the postunification years are everywhere, including in the West's continued need for the East as the historical locus of these abandoned hopes:

> The inability of unification to act as the *Aufhebung* (sublimation) of the socialist trained and capitalist-propelled desire for harmony resulted in a form of postunification nostalgia in the East that has as its object not the GDR itself, but the longing associated with the GDR. What had been a frozen aspiration for an indefinitely deferred future shifted to nostalgia for that aspiration.[22]

Not surprisingly, the close attention to the object world by film director, costume designer and set designer is most apparent in the representation of surveillance as both a technology of state control and a technique of reality construction. This connection is articulated through the actual tools and techniques of surveillance: the enormous Stasi card archives, the rows of shelves with files, the two-way mirrors, strange contraptions like the steam letter opener or the chair with removable seat (for smell sampling) and, of greatest relevance to the narrative, the moni-

---

20 See Paul Betts, 'Building Socialism at Home: The Case of East German Interiors', in *Socialist Modern*, pp. 96–132. On the role of architecture, see Greg Castillo, *Cold War on the Home Front. The Soft Power of Midcentury Design* (Minneapolis: University of Minnesota Press, 2010).

21 Theodor W. Adorno, 'Functionalism Today', trans. by John H. Smith, *Oppositions*, 3 (1988), 35–40 and Ernst Bloch, 'Formative Education, Engineering Form, Ornament', trans. by John H. Smith, *Oppositions*, 3 (1988), 45–51.

22 Bach, '"The Taste Remains"', p. 548.

tor, open-reel recorder, telephone and typewriter set up in the attic of Dreyman's apartment building. Significantly, the objects associated with surveillance – that is, with controlling the flow of information – have their counterparts in the objects involved in the circulation of information, namely the books, magazines and newspapers in Dreyman's apartment. Upsetting these clear divisions, the decision by Wiesler to take a Brecht volume from the writer's desk and read it at home marks the beginning of his momentous transformation from passive record keeper to active creator (or, rather, inventor) of a new socialist reality. That this confrontation takes place through the juxtaposition of new and old media, with literature portrayed as emancipatory and technology as oppressive, only heightens the profoundly nostalgic forms of appropriation through which *Ostalgie* and *Westalgie* converge in a postunification fantasy of the historical conflict between art and power. This mutual articulation of an East and West position on culture and politics – and their respective futures past – is inextricably linked to the technologies of observation mobilized by the Stasi colonel and the very similar techniques of visualization employed by the film director. But unlike von Donnersmarck, his uncanny double is almost entirely defined through the devices that he controls and that, in turn, control him.

Complicating the frequent description of Wiesler in terms of voyeurism (i.e., the kind explored by Hitchcock in *Rear Window*), these devices are primarily auditory in nature and include the reel-to-reel tape recorder used during his opening lecture to Stasi officers in training, his interrogation of prisoners in Hohenschönhausen and his increasingly compromised role in 'Operation Laszlo', the around-the-clock surveillance of Dreyman. There is no doubt that vision plays a key role in the film's regimes of surveillance and involves highly voyeuristic pleasures. Wiesler's use of binoculars during the theatre performance establishes his relationship to Dreyman and Sieland both as individuals and as a couple; these acts of looking, observing and ultimately 'seeing' (i.e., the truth) continue through the monitors that allow him to influence the dramatic events from afar and the windows and glass doors from behind which he maintains his position as omnipresent spectator. But it is sound and the much more intimate act of listening that facilitate his transformation from an invasive recorder of violations against socialist conformity to a clandestine defender of artistic freedom and individual free will. Headphones play a decisive role in his emotional and professional undoing: first when he listens to Jerska reciting a Brecht poem at the birthday party and, later, when he hears Dreyman play the 'Die Sonate vom guten Menschen' (The Sonata of the Good Person) after the suicide of the blacklisted theatre director. Upon receiving the news of Jerska's suicide – significantly, through a telephone call monitored by Wiesler – Dreyman sits down at the piano, reaches for the sheet music and, quite literally, turns symbols into sounds, but not before the opening theme is already heard on the soundtrack, with the slight disconnect between musical notes and finger movements continuing in the subsequent cut to the Stasi agent listening in quiet rapture on his surveillance shift. In interviews, von Donnersmarck has cited Lenin's comment on the incommensurability of listening – truly listening – to Beethoven's *Appassionata* and following through with the ruthless business of revolution as the main inspiration for the film, an inspiration acknowledged in Dreyman's use of the same quote in the diegesis. Accordingly, Wiesler begins to act like a human being and use the state apparatus in the interest of art after listening to Dreyman's soulful rendition of 'Die Sonate vom guten Menschen'. And suddenly he no longer looks like a Stasi agent but an audiophile with an expensive headset. The ideological fantasy that informs this much commented upon moment of personal redemption is central to what I have earlier described as the postunification reconstruction of East German cultural politics as the bad other of what the West German literary public sphere has been or could have been.

In fact, all forms of cultural production or consumption – and closely related, all sensory registers – in the film are depicted through their communicability or translatability: listening becomes writing, writing seeing, and reading listening. The closeup of the Stasi typescript detailing one important night in Dreyman's apartment is superimposed with scenes of passionate lovemaking, with the image of text giving rise to moving images. The closeup of Wiesler reading the stolen volume of Brecht poems motivates the first of two voiceovers, with the words of 'Erinnerung an die Marie A.' (Remembering Marie A.) merging with an elegiac musical score. The second one occurs when we see an emboldened Dreyman writing his *Spiegel* article about suicides in the GDR, with the clicking sounds of the mechanical typewriter giving rise to a musical version of the Wolfgang Borchert poem 'Versuch es' (Try It). These moments are part of a series of closeups of typewriters and typescripts that alternate with closeups of Dreyman speaking and Wiesler listening and that, taken together, are intended to show the power of aesthetic experience and the sources of artistic inspiration. Not surprisingly, the turning point in the story is announced through the relationship between two very different kinds of East German keyboards, a piano, a Roenisch made by the well-known Dresden-based piano maker, and a typewriter, a Groma Kolibri produced in Markersdorf near Görlitz.

The underlying assumptions about the transformative effects of great art and the subversive powers of the romantic artist must be evaluated against the ascendancy of digital technologies and the marginalization of literary forms by visual media during the 1980s. In other words, *The Lives of Others* can also be read as an allegory of the changing conditions of cultural production and reception before and after the fall of the Wall. The characters' preoccupation with the tools and techniques of writing, reading, listening, watching and recording is a clear indication of the growing role of technology in the changing dynamics between art and politics. Within the discursive field marked by auteurist intentions, filmic traditions and historical references, these tools and techniques serve contradictory functions: to show the workings of the East German surveillance state and its political instrumentalization of culture, to evoke the tradition of a literary public sphere still committed to the praxis of critique and, to introduce a third layer of references, to identify the emergence of a very different and more elusive culture-technology interface in contemporary media practices no longer reducible to the model of the panopticon (in the sense of Bentham and Foucault) and the state apparatus (as defined by Althusser). Considering these additional layers requires us on the remaining pages to tease out the broader implications of the allegory of cultural production and reception inscribed in the filmic representation of the scene of surveillance and its transformation into the scene of resistance.

In *The Lives of Others*, listening (and, to a lesser degree, looking) is presented as a precondition of writing, which also means: writing is confirmed as a privileged form of artistic expression. Once again, this connection becomes clear as soon as we reconstruct the process from the perspective of the object world and, more specifically, of objects as sites of multiple inscriptions. As noted earlier, headphones and recording devices function as conduits to a world of private ambitions and desires otherwise hidden from view, and listening to the voices and sounds of others gives rise to previously suppressed experiences of empathy, beauty and the sublime. These feelings cause Wiesler to intervene in the existing regimes of surveillance and, by redefining the relationship between reality and fiction, to protect autonomous art from state intervention. The turning point can be described (in accordance with Brecht's media theory) as the transformation of the medium from an instrument of reception to one of production. Unlike the writer who spends much of his days unwittingly performing for his unknown one-man audience, therein competing with his lover, the famous actress, the Stasi colonel spends much of his job actually writing: taking notes with a pencil during interrogations, typing summaries of the discussions between 'Laszlo' and his friends and, finally, inventing the fiction of Dreyman's artistic subservience to the SED regime. In that sense, Wiesler can be described as the more successful author, creating the kind of alternative reality Dreyman can only dream about with his rather conventional socialist realist plays.[23]

---

23 For further discussion of this aspect of the film see Marc Silberman's contribution to this volume.

A mechanical typewriter brings together Wiesler and Dreyman as two authors with a very different investment in the future of socialism, the power of speech and the preservation of the state. At a time when electronic typewriters had become the norm in most state bureaucracies and when computers were transforming large-scale data systems and personal writing practices in the West, both men continue to use old-fashioned writing tools: pencils for Wiesler and pens for Dreyman. The fact that Dreyman's typewriter of choice is a Wanderer Torpedo, a prewar design, suggests a direct connection between the romantic image of the writer as public intellectual and the mournful recognition of the replacement of the literary public sphere by the market place as the primary measure of relevance and success. This association is indirectly confirmed by the introduction of a second typewriter, a Groma Kolibri made in East Germany during the 1960s but in this portable version produced exclusively for the export market. The West German journalist who asks Dreyman to write about the high number of suicides in the GDR for *Der Spiegel* provides him with this untraceable model to safeguard his anonymity. The Kolibri (German for humming bird) returns to its place of origins hidden under a birthday cake – an association that, given the active role of writers in the fall of the East German regime, might be read as a veiled reference to the birth pangs of a unified Germany. Expertly identified as the model used for the *Spiegel* typescript by a Stasi graphologist, this typewriter becomes the means of transforming East German literature from what some scholars have described as an *Ersatzöffentlichkeit* (substitute public sphere) into a *Gegenöffentlichkeit* (counter public sphere), with literature no longer compensating for the lack of open political debates but becoming an instrument in its final realization. But this transformation comes at a high price: the sacrifice of individual lives and the death of political utopias.

Both losses are acknowledged in repeated appearances of the colour red as a symbol of love, death and socialism. Its symbolic powers are first acknowledged when Dreyman hides the Kolibri under a doorstep and gets red ink stains on his fingers. The corresponding passage in the screenplay, which describes him as 'Lady Macbeth extending his red hands toward his friends' (109), suggests personal guilt: over his failure to prevent Jerska's suicide, which gives rise to a newly found sense of purpose, and over his role in the death of Sieland who ends up being punished for his critical stance. Later the colour red returns as a stain on the first page of the *Der Spiegel* manuscript written by Dreyman and then on the last page of the report written by HGW XX/7, with the similarities between ink and blood clearly intended.

The Kolibri typewriter (a), correctly identified by the Stasi graphologist (b), *The Lives of Others*.

These two paradigms of writing establish the terms under which Wiesler and Dreyman end up collaborating on the same project. In the beginning, Wiesler merely records reality, with surveillance introduced as the ideal model of filmic realism. Since Dreyman is unaware of the fact that his entire apartment has been turned into a recording studio, he continues to talk openly; meanwhile, in a friend's apartment, they play loud pop music to cover up conspiratorial talk. Initially, the transfer from voice to text follows the model of writer and secretary; however, this relationship changes under the humanizing effect of autonomous

The colour red as a symbol of love, death and socialism. Dreyman with red ink on his hands (a), and a red stain on the last page of HGW XX/7's report (b).

art. At that point, Wiesler becomes the author of a very different reality that has Dreyman and colleagues working on a historical drama featuring Lenin. Years later, it is in turn the writer who, sitting in the Stasi archives, becomes a reader of his own life as invented by a man 'humanized' by an aesthetic experience and who subsequently decides to write a novel dedicated to the anonymous agent known to him only as XX/7.

To briefly summarize the broader implications of reading historical films through their objects: the contribution of objects to the visual reconstruction of the GDR is evident in the visual quality of *Ostalgie* and can be traced in everything from museum exhibitions to retro consumption. However, the role of production design in the filmic representation of the GDR and its alignment with a distinctly West German perspective on culture and politics is less obvious and has not yet received the same kind of scholarly attention. The discourses on cultural production and reception that are part and parcel of these nostalgic modes of appropriation can be examined most productively through the representation of their constitutive elements and techniques, including their strategies of transmission and transformation. In the words of Stefan Wolle, the virtual GDR has been recreated as a 'dictatorship of beautiful images' even as, or perhaps because, it was a 'dictatorship of the texts', that is: of writing, editing, transcribing and so forth.[24] The representation of the lives of objects in *The Lives of Others* reveals how this transfer from image (and sound) to writing is in fact achieved and in what ways objects are used both to articulate the opposition between socialist modernism and bourgeois humanism and to organize the profoundly nostalgic relationships among historicization, aestheticization and commodification. The objects foregrounded in von Donnersmarck's fantasy of cultural production and reception may not be part of the redemption of physical reality through film; but as I hope to have shown, they are essential to the functioning of the historical film and, by extension, its affective and ideological project.[25]

24 Stefan Wolle, 'Die Welt der verlorenen Bilder: Die GDR im visuellen Gedächtnis', in *Visual History*, pp. 332–52.
25 I am grateful to the members of the UT-Austin film studies faculty group for their insightful comments on an earlier version of this essay; thanks also to Paul Cooke for his helpful feedback. All translations from the German are mine unless noted otherwise.

Paul Cooke
Chapter Eleven
Von Donnersmarck's Dialogue with Hollywood: from *The Lives of Others* to *The Tourist* (2010)

Florian Henckel von Donnersmarck was not the only director to win his first Oscar at the 2007 Academy Awards. While the success of his debut feature was hailed by many around the world as an extraordinary achievement, perhaps the biggest story to emerge from this particular Oscar night was the award for best director. This went to Martin Scorsese, his film *The Departed* (2006) bringing the success he had famously failed to achieve on numerous previous occasions with such acknowledged classics as *Taxi Driver* (1976), *Raging Bull* (1980) and *Goodfellas* (1990). 'Can you double check the envelope?' he quips, as he receives his statuette from Francis Ford Coppola, accompanied by two other old friends from that group of filmmakers who had come to prominence during the auteur-driven Hollywood Renaissance of the 1960s and 1970s, George Lucas and Steven Spielberg.[1] As I shall discuss in this chapter, which explores the ways in which von Donnersmarck's work can be seen to engage with the films and filmmakers of Hollywood, the coincidence of these two Academy Awards seems to offer a moment of neat historical symmetry. Numerous reasons can be given for the success of *The Lives of Others* at the Oscars, from the way it engaged with German history to the very well managed promotion campaign run by the film's US distribution company Sony Pictures Classics.[2] However, for some commentators at least, an important element in the film's success was attributable to its invocation of the type of Hollywood Renaissance filmmaking for which the likes of Scorsese and Coppola were central figures, working, as Lars-Olav Beier suggests, in the tradition of 'paranoia thrillers like Coppola's *The Conversation* (1974) or Alan J. Pakula's *All the President's Men* (1976)'. Just as these films spoke to a conspiracy theory-riven post-Watergate society, *The Lives of Others* seemed to resonate with an American public living through the tired second term of an equally paranoid Bush administration, recognizing its own dystopian future in the film's portrayal of a

---

1 79th Academy Awards, first broadcast on ABC, 5pm (EST), 25 February 2007.
2 For a discussion of these and other reasons for the film's success see Paul Cooke, '25 February 2007: *Das Leben der Anderen* wins the Oscar for "Best Non-English Language Film"', in *A New History of German Cinema*, ed. by Jennifer Kapczynski and Michael D. Richardson (Rochester: Camden House, 2012), pp. 609–14.

GDR government obsessed with state security.[3] In particular, *The Conversation* was cited throughout the film's international press reception as an important reference point, most obviously in terms of its presentation of a professional wire tapper who begins to question his value system as a result of the case he is working on, but also in its mise-en-scène and broader aesthetic strategies. Thus, the 79th Academy Awards appeared to provide a forum that could not only 'right the wrongs' of the past by finally honouring Scorsese, it also showcased the work of a filmmaker who self-consciously appeared to draw on his generation's legacy.

The inclusion of Lucas and Spielberg within the party presenting Scorsese's award is also significant. While they belong to the same iconoclastic group of filmmakers that began to shake up the Hollywood industry at the end of the 1960s, they represent a very different historical trajectory. Coppola and Scorsese were inspired to make films by their exposure to the French New Wave of the 1950s and 1960s. Although they have both made very successful mainstream blockbusters, be it *Peggy Sue got Married* (Coppola, 1986) or *Hugo* (Scorsese, 2011), central to much of their work has been the attempt to imbue the cinematic mainstream with the ostensibly more challenging aesthetics of such European fare. Spielberg and Lucas have, on occasion, also drawn on this type of filmmaking, colouring their work with a darkness that one would not always expect from mainstream Hollywood productions, most obviously at the start of their careers (*THX 1138*, Lucas, 1971; *The Sugarland Express*, 1974, Spielberg). However, they are best known for films that have helped revive the sensibilities of classical Hollywood, reinvigorating its generic forms, reinventing the spectacular epics of the past and beginning the trend towards the production of large-scale blockbusting event movies that now drives the mainstream industry.[4] This is a trend, it might be noted, to which German filmmakers have made a significant contribution in recent years, most obviously in the work of Wolfgang Petersen (*The Perfect Storm*, 2000; *Troy*, 2004) and Roland Emmerich (*Independence Day*, 1996; *2012*, 2009), filmmakers that are part of a Hollywood elite which has the right of final cut and who are particularly sought after by producers due to their ability to deliver high concept spectacular movies within budget.[5]

Von Donnersmarck's work draws on elements of both these traditions, at times adopting the type of genre expectations found throughout mainstream pro-

---

3 Lars-Olav Beier, 'On the Oscar Campaign Trail', *Spiegel Online International*, 23 February 2007 (http://www.spiegel.de/international/spiegel/0,1518,466450,00.html).
4 For further discussion of the tensions between the two legacies of this group of filmmakers see Geoff King, *New Hollywood Cinema. An introduction* (London: I.B. Tauris, 2002).
5 For further discussion see Christine Haase, *Heimat Meets Hollywood. German Filmmakers and America 1985–2005* (Rochester: Camden House, 2007).

ductions, similarly seeming to look back to classical Hollywood conventions, at times drawing on aspects of the European-infused sensibility we find in Scorsese and Coppola. As I shall discuss, this is, moreover, a tendency that can be identified across a number of contemporary German filmmakers working both at home and in the United States. I begin with a discussion of the relationship between *The Lives of Others* and *The Conversation*, a comparison that has often been made but as yet not explored in any detail. In so doing, I hope to reposition von Donnersmarck's film beyond the authenticity debate it initially provoked. The relationship between Hollywood and von Donnersmarck's approach to filmmaking as identified in *The Lives of Others* is then itself compared with the way this works in his second feature film *The Tourist* (2010), a romantic crime caper starring Angelina Jolie and Johnny Depp. Here the parameters of the filmmaker's engagement with Hollywood shift, von Donnersmarck reversing the direction of his aesthetic gaze by instilling a Hollywood genre piece with some of the cultural appeal of a European auteur. This is, of course, not a new strategy for the German film industry. One thinks, for example of Eric Pommer's marketing coup in the aftermath of World War One, when the producer managed to infuse a number of productions with elements of German Expressionism in order – at least in part – to sell German movies to American audiences more effectively.[6] For many of the New German Cinema generation, mainstream Hollywood movies were a formative influence on their lives. As they came to make films themselves, Hollywood offered them not only a grammar for their own filmmaking practice but also a foil for critique, the likes of Wim Wenders and Rainer Werner Fassbinder attempting to challenge what they saw as the 'colonization' of the postwar West German social psyche by the mores of American popular culture through this same cultural language. For many contemporary German filmmakers Hollywood remains a key influence.[7] However, the nature of this relationship has changed. I examine the ways in which von Donnersmarck can be viewed as part of a trend within German filmmaking today that seeks to use a European cultural perspective to enhance rather than critique the core values of Hollywood genre cinema. In so doing, some contemporary filmmakers reveal a sensibility that is more reminiscent of Pommer's postwar project than Fassbinder and Wenders' deconstruction of

---

6 See Pommer's comments in Ursula Hardt, *From Caligari to California. Eric Pommer's Life in the International Film Wars* (Providence: Berghahn, 1996), p. 48.

7 For a discussion of some of the ways in which America and American culture impacted upon the New German Cinema see Eric Rentschler, 'How American is it: the U.S. as Image and Imaginary in German Film', *German Quarterly*, 57 (1984), 603–20; Thomas Elsaesser, 'American Friends: Hollywood in New German Cinema', *Hollywood and Europe*, ed. by Geoffrey Nowell-Smith and Steve Ricci (London: BFI Publishing, 1998), pp. 142–55.

American cultural norms. At the same time, it would, for the moment at least, appear to be an approach that continues to exclude many contemporary film-makers, like much of the New German Cinema generation, from mainstream success in the United States, the box office-pull of von Donnersmarck's *The Tourist* notwithstanding.

The Lives of Others and *The Conversation*

While reviews of *The Lives of Others* invariably suggest echoes of Coppola's film, von Donnersmarck himself tends to play down this influence, noting that he only watched the film for the first time after he had virtually completed the screen-play.[8] Nonetheless, a comparison of the two films is revealing, not only in terms of their points of correspondence but also in the ways in which they differ. Like *The Lives of Others*, *The Conversation* tells the story of a professional surveillance operative, Harry Caul (Gene Hackman), who is commissioned to eavesdrop on a conversation between a young couple as they walk through a crowded and noisy Union Square in San Francisco. Initially, like Wiesler, Caul is very matter of fact about his work, his sole interest being the production of a 'nice fat recording' of the couple talking, irrespective of its content. However, as he pieces together the conversation from the various microphones he has placed around the square, he becomes concerned for the couple, fearing that the person who has commissioned him to spy on them wants them dead. His work on an earlier case had already led to the death of his targets, and he increasingly comes to see his current case as a means of assuaging the guilt he feels for his earlier complicity in murder.

Parallels between the two films can be found throughout, particularly in the mise-en-scène, an influence that von Donnersmarck does readily acknowledge. Wiesler's attic surveillance suite is strongly reminiscent of Caul's warehouse workshop where he creates his listening devices and reconstructs the conversation. This space, part filled with large reel-to-reel tape players and other electronic devices that would have appeared state of the art in Coppola's 1974 production, resonates with von Donnersmarck's period depiction of the technology the Stasi employed. As the latter has pointed out in numerous interviews, he went to great pains to make his presentation of the Stasi operation *look* as authentic as

8 Sara Michelle Fetters, 'Other People's Lives: Conversation with Writer-Director Florian Henckel von Donnersmarck' (http://www.moviefreak.com/artman/publish/interviews_florian-henckelvondonnersmarck.shtml).

possible, suggesting that even the 'bugs' he used were real.[9] And indeed, the type of surveillance paraphernalia depicted here can be found in numerous museums throughout the GDR, often providing a type of 'chamber of horrors' exhibit to contrast the everyday *Ostalgie* artefacts that dominate such places. Nonetheless, in *The Lives of Others* this is clearly also shaped by the constellation of surveillance we find in Coppola's earlier film. As von Donnersmarck recalls:

> When I didn't like the way the assembled real Stasi equipment looked, I had Silke Buhr, my production designer, look very carefully at the way the technical equipment was set up in [*The Conversation*]. I said that I wanted the level of technical complication not greater than in this film, and I wanted the equipment to be simple enough as to still have *the man* be the most important element of it all.[10]

Even the chalkboard on the wall of Caul's workshop, where he maps out his operations, reappears in von Donnersmarck's film, here as a life-sized plan sketched out on the floor of the attic where Wiesler is based, an echo that further helps emphasize the central role of the Stasi operative – *the man* – in organizing and controlling the space. This link is then augmented by cinematographer Hagen Bogdanski's much discussed use of a colour palette of grey and brown tones and a decision to record in analogue rather than digital which seems to transport the spectator back to an earlier age. While this decision has generally been discussed as part of von Donnersmarck's authenticity strategy intent upon replicating the sound and hue of images one finds in period footage of the GDR, the filmmaker himself also sees echoes of Coppola and the Hollywood Renaissance generally in this aesthetic, if not *The Conversation* specifically.[11] Returning to Coppola's film, even David Shire's piano motif, that recurs throughout *The Conversation*, feels eerily reminiscent, albeit coincidentally, of Gabriel Yared's 'Die Sonate vom guten Menschen' (The Sonata of the Good Person), played by Dreyman in *The Lives of Others*, replicating its simple, melancholic tone.

---

9 Sebastian Handke, 'Die Wanzen sind echt: Kinodebatte über *Das Leben der Anderen*', *Tagesspiegel*, 8 April 2007.
10 Email exchange with von Donnersmarck, 15 November 2011.
11 In my email exchange with the director he suggested, 'the similarity of the films may seem so great in part because I had always been looking for that 70s film texture and colour for *Das Leben der Anderen*. A scratched, grey-beige, cool, rainy feel as found only in the 70s. It took a lot of testing to find out how to create it. [...] But this was not *The Conversation*-specific. I simply felt that the 80s colours were too garish, and the 90s and the films of the 2000s looked too clean/technical/cold [...]. The 60s were again too garish, and in the 50s they were still struggling with the technical aspects of the emulsion too much. So I defaulted to the 70s look and colours, and enhanced it through the production design'. Email exchange with von Donnersmarck, 15 November 2011.

The blackboard of Caul's workshop in *The Conversation* (a) reinvented in Wiesler's attic surveillance suite in *The Lives of Others* (b).

Again however coincidentally, Wiesler and Caul themselves would also appear to have much in common. Both are very meticulous men, as can be seen in their similarly spartan apartments that reveal almost nothing about their personal history. Both are outsiders who carefully regulate all personal relationships – Caul keeps his girlfriend at one remove, putting her up in her own flat and never bringing her to his home. Wiesler's only moment of physical intimacy is with a state-employed prostitute booked by the half hour. Both are men of faith. Caul is a Catholic who chastizes his colleague for taking the Lord's name in vain and who finds solace in a visit to confession. Wiesler is an even more devout socialist, who believes with an almost religious zeal at the start of the film in the moral superiority of the GDR as the better of the two postwar German states, and in the need for his organization to protect its socialist project from counter-revolutionary forces.[12] Most importantly, both men are changed by their current operation, beginning to identify with, and ultimately to define themselves through, the experience of their targets. As Caul becomes ever more obsessed with the details of the conversation he has recorded and his wish to warn the couple of their apparently imminent death, they invade his dreams. As he lies in bed with a woman he has taken back to his workshop, – his personal barriers already beginning to crumble due to this case – he imagines reaching out to the young woman he has recorded. His dream conversation with her soon turns into an outpouring of his most intimate memories, details that he would normally never reveal to himself let alone others, forcing him to reflect upon his clear sense of inadequacy. Similarly, as Wiesler becomes ever more entwined with his case, he comes to understand the flaws in his ideological position. As Daniela Berghahn notes, there are several moments in the film where graphic match cuts set up points of correspondence between the experience of Wiesler and his target Dreyman. One particularly striking example of this, discussed at greater length in Lutz Koepnick's contribution to this volume, is the juxtaposition of a shot of Dreyman, framed horizontally lying in bed comforting his partner, with a shot of Wiesler in silent contemplation – his eyes shut, head tilted to one side as he listens to the flat below. It would seem that Wiesler is imagining himself embracing the woman, in turn highlighting the loneliness of his life and the flaws in his value system.[13] In both films, the aural world of their protagonists, to which they gain access through their work, transports them to a plane beyond their own physical reality, forcing them to reflect critically upon their place in society and providing them with a potential model for reform.

The question of surveillance also becomes a self-referential metaphor for the act of spectatorship in both films. As Coppola himself suggests on the commentary track to the DVD release of *The Conversation*, his is a film as much about the experience of watching a movie as it is about conspiracy theories. Moreover, for all its focus on the representation of the world through sound, the film also reflects upon the limits of *visual* representation and the inevitable subjectivity of the world we experience on screen. Indeed, as many commentators note, a key inspiration for *The Conversation* was Michelangelo Antonioni's *Blow-Up* (1966), a film that depicts a fashion photographer's attempt to uncover a killer he inadvertently catches in one of his pictures, Antonioni's forensic investigation of the po-

---

12 This aspect of the film is discussed further in Manfred Wilke's contribution to this volume.
13 Daniela Berghahn, 'Remembering the Stasi in a Fairy Tale of Redemption: Florian Henckel von Donnersmarck's *Das Leben der Anderen*', *Oxford German Studies*, 38 (2009), 321–33 (p. 327).

tential of photography replaced here with Coppola's dissection of sound recording.[14] At times, Coppola consciously positions the spectator as an eavesdropping voyeur, the audience itself seeming to take up the position of a surveillance operative watching Caul coming to terms with his anxieties. Early on in the film, for example, when we first enter Caul's flat, we watch him make a phone call, the camera static as if it were a passive surveillance device being controlled remotely. When he walks out of the frame the camera remains fixed, losing him for a moment, until it is clear that he is not going to return, at which point it pans mechanically to the left, seeming to follow the sound of his voice as if part of a voice activated system through which the spectator is given access to this space.

As I have discussed in more detail elsewhere, in *The Lives of Others* there is a similarly self-conscious performance of surveillance at work that draws the audience's attention to the very act of watching a film.[15] Initially, Wiesler is constructed as a transcendent all-seeing (and hearing) spectator, a position that is established in a sequence where he first sees the man who is to be the victim of his surveillance operation. In a moment of deliberate metatheatre, we enter a 'play within the play' as Wiesler is taken to the theatre by a superior officer to watch the production of one of Dreyman's plays, starring his girlfriend Sieland. Wiesler sits in a box, at a distance from the rest of the audience, able to look beyond the performance itself, which transfixes the rest of the public. Unlike the passive voyeur of Caul's flat, Wiesler here can construct his own frame, his use of binoculars highlighting his status as the master spectator in the room, and to whom we are subsequently sutured in a series of point of view shots: of the woman's performance; of Dreyman talking to a journalist already under suspicion by the state; of Hempf whispering to his aide, a conversation that perhaps suggests to the astute agent the reason why he has been asked to come to this performance.

Most importantly, and in contrast to these other men, it would seem that Wiesler can see beyond Sieland's beauty, the woman Dreyman loves and who Hempf, we subsequently learn, is determined to have. Wiesler, at first sight, ap-

---

14 For a discussion of the various intertextual echoes of *Blow up* in *The Conversation* see Dennis Turner, 'The Subject of *The Conversation*', *Cinema Journal*, 24 (1985), 4–22; Jeffrey Chown, *Hollywood Auteur* (New York: Praeger, 1988), pp. 85–99. Brian De Palma's *Blow Out* (1981) is another striking link in this intertextual chain. De Palma's film self-consciously draws on both Coppola and Antonioni and would also appear to be recalled in *The Lives of Others*, most obviously in the shot of Jack Terry (John Travolta) embracing the murdered Sally Bedina (Nancy Allan) which seems to be reworked in the final shot of Dreyman and Sieland.

15 See Paul Cooke, 'Watching the Stasi: Authenticity, *Ostalgie* and history in Florian Henckel von Donnersmarck's *The Lives of Others* (2006)', in *New Directions in German Cinema*, ed. by Paul Cooke and Chris Homewood (London: I.B. Tauris, 2011), pp. 111–27 (pp. 123–29).

pears to maintain his distance, always standing at the edge of the main action, silently making notes and never participating actively. When he does decide to intervene it is, initially at least, in order to direct events. He decides, for example, to reveal to Dreyman the Minister's desire for Sieland, ringing the door bell to Dreyman's flat remotely from his observatory so that the writer comes down just as the woman is getting out of Hempf's car. Within the diegesis, Wiesler once again controls the frame, turning Dreyman into a spectator in his own narrative, dictating the view of the world that he is given. However, there are in fact indications from the start of the film that Wiesler's objective distance, and with it his spectatorial power, is illusory. Indeed, even during the initial theatre performance there is the suggestion that he, like Hempf and Dreyman, is in reality also transfixed by the woman's performance. For the briefest of moments Wiesler's point of view shots are interrupted by a shot/reverse-shot sequence between himself and Sieland. Just for a second the woman seems to return his gaze, leaving the man momentarily mesmerized and thereby breaking the illusion of his objective distance from events. The Stasi operative's position as a transcendent, detached observer is undermined. Wiesler is being drawn into the traditional libidinal economy of mainstream cinematic texts of desiring and objectifying the female 'other' in order to empower his own subject position. As the narrative progresses and Wiesler increasingly rejects the State's position, desiring ever more the life of the artists he observes, he becomes ever more embroiled in his case. Crucially, however, in a further echo of Caul, the more he intervenes, the less he is in control of events, his cool observation turning into a confused emotional stare. When, for example, he hears Dreyman's plea that Sieland should not go to meet Hempf, Wiesler leaves his attic for the street outside, hiding in the shadows to see if she comes out. 'What are you gawping at?', he is asked by a drunk passer-by, a question which makes it clear that Wiesler can no longer stand outside the narrative. The voyeur is caught looking. His power crumbles.

Yet while there are parallels between Coppola's and von Donnersmarck's films, there is an important epistemological difference that is also highlighted through their comparison, a difference that moves us beyond questions of filmic self-referentiality to the way the film engages with recent debates on the relationship between the Berlin Republic and its GDR pre-history. If we return to Caul's dream-state encounter with the woman in *The Conversation*, this is echoed in von Donnersmarck's film. However, here it is transformed into a *physical* encounter between Sieland and Wiesler in a café, during which he convinces her to return to Dreyman. The true nature of the world Caul creates from his recordings, as well as his further encounters with the people who have commissioned him to undertake this work, is always open to supposition, the man performing a version of the Kuleshov Effect, filling in the gaps in his knowledge with projections of empathy.

Indeed, he is ultimately proven wrong in his interpretation of the conversation. It transpires he has been set up. Rather than having discovered a couple in fear of their lives, his recording is, in fact, to be used to lure the woman's husband to a hotel room where the couple plan on murdering him. The pivotal line in the recording, which Caul hears as 'He'd *kill* us if he got the chance', should in fact be understood as 'He'd kill *us* if he got the chance'. Consequently, we learn that it is the couple themselves who are the murderers. Yet even once this 'truth' has been revealed, we are not left with a clear sense of what is happening, the extent of any corporate conspiracy or of the impact that this might have on Caul's future. We leave him playing his saxophone, sitting in his flat which he has just pulled apart in search of a bug that he believes has been placed there by the organization he fears has duped him into aiding and abetting a murder, the camera tracking in a shape that again reminds us of a video surveillance device locked in a never-ending loop. This lack of clarity is further foregrounded visually throughout the film in the repeated use of translucent material in the mise-en-scène: Caul's raincoat which he almost never takes off, even when he gets into bed with his girl-friend; the plastic screen in his workshop through which we watch him mix a drink as he is interrogated by one of his colleagues about his tricks of the trade; and most significantly, the frosted glass that obscures Caul's view of the murder he thinks he is witnessing. What we see and hear is never completely transparent, self-consciously reflecting the representational limits of the film we are watching.

In the *Lives of Others*, there is far less ambiguity in our understanding of the world we observe. *The Conversation's* final sequence, in which Caul destroys his flat, is also re-enacted in von Donnersmarck's film. However, here we always know that Dreyman has been bugged. There is never any doubt either for the spectator or for the main protagonist as to the meaning of the recordings that are made. Wiesler's imagined visualizations of what is happening in the flat below that punctuate the narrative slip straightforwardly into the actual representation of the couple's life. Any ambiguity instead comes from the written reports that Wiesler creates, which wilfully manipulate and misrepresent this reality. It is *here* that epistemological uncertainty is introduced into the representation of the world, not through its exploration of filmic reality, in turn opening up import-ant questions about the relationship of the Stasi past to contemporary debates about the nature of life in the GDR beyond the authenticity debate the film first generated.

The importance of the Stasi archive in contemporary readings of the GDR can-not be underestimated. As noted in the introduction to this volume, the opening of the files gave rise to numerous scandals, outing a whole host of public figures in the GDR as having worked with the organization. The Stasi files seemed to prove the organization's omnipresence and omnipotence. However, through Dreyman's engagement with the files as an historical archive, their status as the repository of absolute truth, as the final word on the 'reality' of life in the GDR as they have been construed either implicitly or explicitly in countless popular readings of the period, is called into question. The Stasi file is only helpful to Dreyman because it does *not* hold the truth. Like the rest of the archive, Dreyman's file is a written text constructed within a specific socio-political context by people with their own agenda, abilities and competing desires. Thus, the file's presentation of events might be shaped by Grubnitz's request to Wiesler not to put anything in his reports about the relationship between Sieland and Hempf, or by Wiesler's assistant's only partial knowledge of the 'back story' to an argument he hears between the lovers in the flat below.

Equally importantly, however, any epistemological uncertainty implied by the Stasi files is also deliberately confined to the past in the film. While *The Conversation* ends with the unsettling image of Caul being forced to live with the continuing uncertainty of his relationship to his case and whether he remains the victim of his corporate clients, in *The Lives of Others* it is clear that for Dreyman the nightmare is over. This is signalled explicitly in the final reel of the film. He has begun to move on from his tragic relationship with Sieland, suggested in the image of his new companion taking his hand on their visit to the theatre after unification. Moreover, once he learns the truth about his life in the GDR by reading between the lines of his file, he is also at last able to write again, evidence that he has finally 'arrived' in the postwall Berlin Republic. He has also now put his past behind him, signalled in the dedication of his new book to his Stasi guardian angel, an action which also, in turn, allows Wiesler to move on from his own past, giving him peace of mind that his good deed has been recognized.

This sense of resolution is further signalled in the film's straightforward adoption of mainstream genre conventions that again distance it from Coppola's film. While *The Conversation* might, as Dennis Turner suggests, 'cod[e] itself in the manner of the classic detective film, [it] refuses the closure usually associated with that genre'.[16] For its part, *The Lives of Others* works within a melodramatic mode, an aspect which, Owen Evans and others have argued, was also an important element in the film's popular appeal and which is noticeably absent from earlier surveillance dramas such as *The Conversation*. As Jaimey Fisher points out, one could not imagine Caul being moved to tears by a piece of music as Wiesler is during the pivotal moment in the film when he listens to Dreyman per-

---

16 Turner, 'The Subject of *The Conversation*', p. 7.

form 'Die Sonate vom guten Menschen'.[17] The film plays on the emotions of the audience with ever-greater force throughout the main narrative arc, reaching a crescendo in the death of Sieland. In the tradition of Michael Curtiz or Douglas Sirk – also with a nod perhaps to Brian de Palma's own reworking of *The Conversation*, *Blow Out* (1981) –, the film follows the classic melodramatic pattern of a female protagonist being punished for disloyalty to her lover, her betrayal ultimately leading to her death in the arms of the weeping Dreyman.[18] He caresses her blood-stained face, its red standing out against the muted tones of much of the mise-en-scène and contrasting starkly with the crisp white of his shirt, all accompanied by the melancholic swell of strings that might be taken straight from a Sirk weepie. And, again in similar vein to Sirk, this tragedy will ultimately lead to redemption. Dreyman will move on. Wiesler will escape the punishment his superior promises him for his obvious mishandling of his case – the fall of the Wall ensuring that he will not spend the next twenty years of his career in a windowless office steaming open the population's mail. The job we see him doing post-unification might be as mundane. Nonetheless, he will be morally redeemed, Dreyman's dedication allowing all concerned to draw a line under the past. In so doing, the film provides the sense of narrative closure typical of mainstream film-making far removed from the open-ended ambiguity of *The Conversation's* denouement. In the process, von Donnersmarck attempts to walk a line between the European sensibilities that inspired this earlier generation, directly invoking stylistic elements from Coppola's film, while also making sure that he fundamentally delivers a universally understandable melodrama of tragedy and redemption.

'You looking at me?' Returning to Europe via Hollywood in *The Tourist*

Continuing the role of the Hollywood Renaissance as a reference point for von Donnersmarck's work, in the title of a scathing review of the filmmaker's second feature Cosmo Landesman ironically recalls Scorsese's *Taxi Driver*. Rather than

---

17 Jaimey Fisher, 'German Historical Film as Production Trend: European Heritage Cinema and Melodrama in *The Lives of Others*', in *The Collapse of the Conventional. German Film and its Politics at the Turn of the Twenty-First Century*, ed. by Jaimey Fisher and Brad Prager (Detroit: Wayne State University Press, 2010), pp. 186–215 (p. 209); Owen Evans, 'Redeeming the Demon?: The Legacy of the Stasi in *Das Leben der Anderen*', *Memory Studies*, 3 (2010), 1–14 (p. 8).
18 For further discussion of the melodrama in the film see Marc Silberman and Andrea Rinke's contributions to this volume.

suggesting any aesthetic or political legacy of this tradition, however, here the reference is used as a means of underlining what Landesman sees as the failure of the film to live up to the expectations one might have had for the Oscar-winning director's first Hollywood production. The abidingly powerful depiction of Travis Bickle's (Robert De Niro) descent into violent psychosis is used to characterize what, in Landesman's view, is the vacuously 'self-regarding' performance of Angelina Jolie as Elise Clifton-Ward, the beautiful girlfriend of master criminal Alexander Pearce.[19] Pearce disappeared two years earlier after stealing $2.3 billion from his gangland boss. He has subsequently undergone plastic surgery and created a completely new and unknown identity for himself. As the film begins, he contacts Elise by messenger in Paris, asking her to meet him in Venice. Along the way, she is to pick up a stranger who she is to pass off as Pearce in order to throw both the police and his former boss off the scent. Thus, Frank Tupelo (Johnny Depp) is drawn into a dangerous story of mistaken identity, an apparently unassuming maths teacher from Wisconsin who is given the role of patsy, forced to run for his life, clambering over the rooftops of Venice and negotiating the city's canals in order to avoid the wrath of Pearce's enemies. As one might expect, in the process he appears to fall for Elise, who sashays elegantly through the city, always immaculately turned out no matter what the situation, transfixing the world around her as she moves, always in control, until she realizes that Frank Tupelo is in fact Alexander Pearce. And, after dealing neatly with both the law and the underworld, the couple finally escape into the sunset to enjoy their future together.

The Tourist can be seen as part of a growing trend amongst German filmmakers working both at home and in Hollywood towards the production of genre films. As already noted, the likes of Emmerich and Petersen have been extremely adept at working within this tradition, producing commercially very successful hi-concept blockbusters. However, for a number of others, such as Tom Tykwer or Mennan Yapo, this remains a problematic endeavour. While their European credentials offer them a way of marking their distinctiveness within the industry, at the same time they seem to prevent such filmmakers from breaking through into the mainstream. Von Donnersmarck's second feature provides an interesting case study in this regard, a film that reconfigures the discussion I have offered of *The Lives of Others*. Although a commercial success, it was almost universally dismissed by reviewers. Those few reviewers that were more positive saw its strength in an ostensibly European ability to challenge mainstream genre conventions,

---

19 Cosmo Landsmann, 'You looking at me?; Swanky locations can't make up for *The Tourist's* dull plot and smug Angelina Jolie', *The Sunday Times*, 12 December 2010.

while *looking* like a classical Hollywood film from the 1950s. This is also an aspect of the film that von Donnersmarck himself feels was ignored in much of the film's critical reception, suggesting that reviewers missed the point of 'the poise and the glamour' evoked in *The Tourist*, along with, and most importantly in terms of its 'European' credentials, its 'deceleration', that is its self-conscious rejection of any Hollywood freneticism.[20]

That *The Tourist* would draw on a European tradition is not surprising given that it is a remake of Jérôme Salle's *Anthony Zimmer* (2005), a French film which tells a largely similar story set in Cannes. Although *Anthony Zimmer* was only moderately successful commercially, it received generally positive reviews, being seen as a 'simple but stylish thriller [...] aimed at moviegoers who like both classic Hollywood and good-looking European cinema'.[21] To a degree, it seemed that *Anthony Zimmer* managed to strike the same balance achieved in *The Lives of Others* between the mainstream conventions of Hollywood and the more 'quirky' art-house tone associated with European directors. As such, some commentators expected the film to be more successful internationally than it eventually was.[22] Part of the reason for this lack of international success might, however, be attributable to its international distributors who were, almost from the start, looking at its remake potential. Both films were co-produced by Studio Canal who might well have been willing to forego international success with the French version if they saw greater profit in an English-language remake. And, as Christopher Campbell notes, it is not uncommon for the majors to put pressure on the distribution of an earlier version of a film, if they feel it might harm the business done by the remake. In this case, he suggests that Sony were worried that a wide distribution of the French film could put mainstream audiences off going to see their version, fearing that the Hollywood film would be perceived as still too 'European', and so too much like hard work to watch.[23]

The production of the remake had a number of well-publicized false starts. It was initially to be directed by the Swedish filmmaker Lasse Hallström (*My Life as a Dog* [*Mitt liv som hund*, 1985]; *The Cider House Rules*, 1999), with Charlize Theron playing opposite Tom Cruise. Hallström was then replaced by Bharat Nalluri, best known for his British television work (*Spooks*, 2002–11; *Life on Mars*, 2006–7), as was Cruise by Sam Worthington and Theron by Jolie. It was at this

20 Email exchange with von Donnersmarck, 15 November 2011.

21 Grant Rosenberg, 'Anthony Zimmer', *Screen International*, 26 April 2005.

22 Lisa Nesselson, 'Anthony Zimmer', *Variety*, 4 May 2005.

23 Christopher Campbell, 'The Originals: *Anthony Zimmer* is Lighter-Than-Light Hitchcock – Hopefully *The Tourist* is Better', *Spout. The movies you love* (http://blogs.indiewire.com/spout/archives/the_originals_anthony_zimmer_is_lighter_than_light_hitchcock_hopefully_th/).

point that von Donnersmarck joined the project, only to leave again shortly afterwards, citing creative differences with other members of the project, until finally rejoining, bringing in Johnny Depp to replace Worthington and rewriting the screenplay, in collaboration with Christopher McQuarrie (*The Usual Suspects*, Bryan Singer, 1995) and Julian Fellowes (*Gosford Park*, Robert Altman, 2001, *Downton Abbey*, 2010-).[24] This kind of development process is not uncommon in Hollywood and can go on for years. The calibre of the people ultimately brought together to work on *The Tourist* would clearly seem to have been worth the wait. There are few contemporary stars bigger than Depp and Jolie, and many in the industry were keen to see them work together.[25] They are supported by such well-known actors as Steven Berkoff and Timothy Dalton and a very well respected writing team. Cinematography was by John Seale, best known for his Oscar-winning work on *The English Patient* (Anthony Minghella, 1996) and its lavish costume design was by the multiple Oscar winner Colleen Atwood (*Chicago*, 2002, *Memoirs of a Geisha*, 2006, Rob Marshall). As one might expect given the names involved, after a slow start, the film was a commercial success, grossing a healthy $278 million worldwide on its theatrical release against a budget of $100 million.[26] It will have more than amortized its production and advertizing costs, and this before DVD and other sales are factored in which often generate far more revenue than the theatrical release. It also garnered some interest on the awards circuit, receiving three Golden Globe nominations: for best picture and for its two leads.

From the various directors connected with the project, it is clear that the film's producers were keen to draw on filmmaking traditions beyond Hollywood, while also wishing to create a thoroughly mainstream commercial movie. Most often, the film, like *Anthony Zimmer* before it, was seen to be recalling Hitchcock in its approach. While Salle appeared to capture the suspense of *North By Northwest* (1959), *The Tourist*, on the other hand, appeared intent upon revisiting the glamour of Hitchcock's romantic thriller *To Catch a Thief* (1955), Depp's Cary Grant playing to Jolie's Grace Kelly.[27] Functioning like Hitchcock's version of the French Riviera, the opulent splendour of Venice's most elite hotels, captured in all their vivid beauty through Seale's typically lavish cinematography, provides

---

24 For more detail on the production history of the film see *Sony Insider* (http://www.sonyinsider.com/2010/11/15/depp-and-jolie-cros s-paths-in-the-tourist-movie/); Kyle Buchanan, '*The Tourist*: Director Florian Henckel von Donnersmarck on How Johnny Depp Is Like a Serial Killer', *New York Magazine*, 4 January 2011.

25 Campbell, 'The Originals: *Anthony Zimmer* is Lighter-Than-Light Hitchcock'.

26 Figures taken from *Box Office Mojo* (http://boxofficemojo.com/movies/?id=tourist.htm).

27 Kathryn Shattuck, 'What's On Today', *The New York Times*, 30 July 2011.

Angelina Jolie glides through the streets of Europe, *The Tourist.*

the perfect backdrop to Jolie, upon whom the camera continually lingers, and whose costumes exude Kelly's 1950s chic, from her arm-length gloves to her silk head scarves.

The old world glamour of the film also seemed to play to the director's credentials as a member of the European aristocracy, the film's marketing making much of this connection, along with the international nature of his upbringing. This is a man, we learn, who knows the places he is presenting on screen very well, equally at home in such major European cities as he is in New York or Los Angeles.[28] That said, for several critics, despite the director's apparent insider knowledge of the locations he uses, the film ultimately simply fulfils the expectations of its title, giving the spectator a resolutely 'touristy view of Venice', never going beyond its presentation of the Grand Canal and the other well known landmarks an international audience might expect to see.[29] As such, the film can once again be seen to be working in a classical Hollywood tradition, presenting Europe as a tourist space such as was commonplace, in particular, in numerous 1950s musicals set in Paris. Indeed, von Donnersmarck at times appears to recall precisely this tradition, Jolie's hip-swinging walk echoing the stylization of a Hollywood musical and the 'to-be-looked-at-ness' of a Monroe from *Gentlemen Prefer Blondes* (Ho-

---

28 See Wolfgang Höbel's discussion of the film, 'Putzig mit Pop: Donnersmarck-Film *The Tourist*', *Der Spiegel Online*, 14 December 2010 (http://www.spiegel.de/kultur/kino/0,1518,734546,00.html).
29 Landsmann, 'You looking at me?'.

Angelina Jolie and Johnny Depp caught up in the choreography of a 1950s Hollywood musical, *The Tourist*.

ward Hawks, 1953) or a Hepburn from *Funny Face* (Stanley Donen, 1957).[30] In fact, the echoes of the 1950s musical become overt towards the end of the film when Jolie and Depp are caught up in a ball. Elise hopes finally to meet her lover, only to be manoeuvred into a dance with Frank, enveloped in the scene's choreography. It is at this point that we might finally guess the ultimate plot twist: that Frank is in fact Alexander Pearce and that the couple will ultimately live happily ever after. The couple dance. All that is missing is their song.

Interestingly, the central difficulty most critics had with *The Tourist* was precisely one of the aspects that was seen by some as so important to the success of *The Lives of Others*, namely its approach to mainstream genre conventions. *Anthony Zimmer* had been praised as a stylish thriller, the tone of which is established in an opening sequence drenched in the iconography of a classic film noir. The camera tracks a woman's legs getting out of a car on a rain-soaked night, following her as she walks slowly and deliberately into a restaurant. Cut to a courtroom where we hear the story of Anthony Zimmer, an international money launderer being hunted by the police. Cut back to the woman, shot from behind; a close up on a book of matches as she lights a cigarette, her face still hidden from the spectator, all to a soundtrack that recalls a Bernard Herrmann score from one of Hitchcock's movies. For many critics of *The Tourist*, there was a general sense

---

30 Fiona Handyside, 'Colonising the European Utopia', in *World Cinema's Dialogues with Hollywood*, ed. by Paul Cooke (London: Palgrave, 2007), pp. 138–53.

that the film did not know what it wanted to be. In its opening, we once again follow the film's female protagonist to a restaurant, this time the camera focusing on the front of Jolie's body in medium close-up, a shift which begins the process of generic confusion. Unlike Salle's sequence, here we immediately know who this woman is, not only due to the star persona Jolie brings with her to the part but also from her deliberate performance of a woman who understands the world is watching her, as if she were a model on a catwalk rather than a femme fatale in a 1940s noir, or even the female victim in a melodrama. Suspense dissolves as we watch her stylized movements, her face fixed in a wry smile, accompanied here by a soundtrack that, as Christy Lemire notes, suggests 'madcap hilarity' rather than impending danger.[31] Yet while the music seems to signal a romantic comedy, subsequent shots remain intent upon delivering a thriller. In a nod to von Donnersmarck's previous film, or even to the opening of *The Conversation*, we follow a surveillance team tracking the woman, the policemen watching Elise, enjoying their role of voyeurs in a manner reminiscent of John Cazale's performance inside the surveillance van at the start of Coppola's film as he frantically takes pictures of two girls putting on their makeup in the van's mirrored windows. Nonetheless, it is not long before suspense again gives way to comedy. Two undercover officers watching Elise as she sits in the restaurant are overheard by a waiter who thinks they want to order something, a moment that might have been taken from a 1970s *Pink Panther* film rather than Hitchcock's 1950s Europe. Yet, unlike these other films, where the audience always knows how it is supposed to react, in *The Tourist*, so its critics suggest, the spectator is never sure if the comedy that seems to erupt out of the film's hyper-stylization is intentional or rather the product of weak direction.[32]

For many, *The Tourist* was a poorly made film, for all its star cast. However, for a few, its stylization was considered so over-the-top, 'almost knowingly preposterous' as Lemire puts it, that the director actually deconstructs the genres to which he alludes. Is the European auteur unable, or unwilling, to create a straightforwardly mainstream movie? Does he, in fact, incorporate an element of the same self-referentiality one finds in *The Lives of Others*, the film's apparent pastiche of 1950s Hollywood stylization spilling over into parody?[33] The film's ostensibly knowing approach to its form is, in fact, alluded to early on, in the moment when

---

31 Christy Lemire, '*The Tourist:* a Mindlessly Enjoyable Trip', *The Associated Press*, 9 December 2010.

32 Tim Appelo, 'Globe Comedy Nom for *The Tourist*: Now, That's Funny' *The Hollywood Reporter*, 14 December 2010 (http://www.hollywoodreporter.com/blogs/race/globe-comedynom-tourist-funny-59606).

33 Lemire, '*The Tourist:* a Mindlessly Enjoyable Trip'.

Elise makes contact with Frank on the train to Venice. Noticing that he is reading a crime story, she invites the man to cast their current conversation as if it were part of a Cold War thriller.[34] The film becomes a mise-en-abyme, drawing the audience's attention to the fact that we are watching a story with this same narrative potential. This is the moment when she invites him to leave his everyday life behind and join her on an illicit journey of adventure. And, of course, Frank complies. Like every other man in the film, he cannot help but become transfixed by Elise, to the point that it becomes almost impossible to suspend disbelief, the film drawing attention to its own hyper-stylized presentation of the female lead as the spectator's object of desire. In the process, the film seems to expose the classical gender codes of a Hollywood movie. If there is any degree of parody present in the film, however, it is clear that there is no broader critique of Hollywood conventions at work. As is suggested in the director's own comments about the film, for von Donnersmarck the film is, fundamentally, an homage to an earlier age, filtered through a 'decelerated' European optic that can enhance, rather than challenge, its celebration of Hollywood glamour, encapsulated in the poise of his leading lady.

German Filmmakers, Hollywood and Genre

For Eric Rentschler, one of the key reasons why German film in the 1990s largely failed to reach international audiences was its tendency to adopt 'generic designs that are not readily exportable because they are done better and more effectively elsewhere'. Thus the cinema of the time did 'not sell abroad because it [was] perceived as both too German and yet not German enough'.[35] In the following decade, a number of filmmakers appeared to have overcome this problem, not least von Donnersmarck who, along with other makers of German historical dramas, found a way of walking this particular tightrope, making films that appeared universally accessible but with a specifically German flavour. At home, the trend towards the production of genre films that are largely unexportable, however, continues. Claudia Tronnier, head of ZDF's *Das kleine Fernsehspiel* – a longstanding showcase for new talent in Germany – for example, suggests that while 'we don't look for genre, we look for originality and encourage experimentation [...] in recent years we have seen more genre works coming from young filmmakers than in

---

34 For further discussion of this genre of filmmaking in connection with *The Lives of Others* see David Bathrick's contribution to this volume.

35 Eric Rentschler, 'From New German Cinema to the Post-Wall Cinema of Consensus', in *Cinema and Nation*, ed. by Mette Hjort and Scott Mackenzie (London: Routledge, 200), pp. 260–77 (p. 275).

the past'.[36] To be sure, at times this has led to some interesting aesthetic reworkings of classical forms, including Christian Petzold's *Jerichow* (2008) or Thomas Arslan's *Im Schatten* (In the Shadows, 2010). Both of these films have had some limited international distribution. However, while most German genre films are not exported, they can open up the possibility of working internationally for the filmmakers themselves. Although Mennan Yapo's first full length feature film, *Lautlos* (Soundless, 2004) – a thriller aesthetically reminiscent of Luc Besson's *Cinéma du look* –, did not receive a widespread international release, it nonetheless acted as a useful calling card, bringing him an invitation to direct in Hollywood. It appeared that this was a filmmaker who could weigh European style against Hollywood entertainment. His first Hollywood feature, however, the Sandra Bullock vehicle *Premonition* (2007), received very poor reviews. Although, like *The Tourist*, it was at times praised for its visual beauty, audiences found the plot too confusing. As the filmmaker himself suggests, at the premiere, 'everyone congratulated me "Mennan, your film looks great!" – "Ok, but what did you think of it?" – "Oh, I think I didn't get it. It's too … European'.[37] For Yapo, as we see in von Donnersmarck's second feature, the balance that marked their domestic production as distinctive in the minds of Hollywood executives is more difficult to achieve when they have to negotiate the machinery of the mainstream industry. As was the case with a previous generation of filmmakers who made a similar move from Germany to the US in the 1980s, mainstream critical success often remains elusive, the badge of 'Europeanness' ultimately acting as a barrier even as it provided them with their initial entry ticket. That said, the younger generation often has a far greater, and more straightforward, affection for the Hollywood dream factory than the likes of Schlöndorff or Wenders. Even if there are elements of parody in *The Tourist*, any satire is very gentle. There is none of the engagement with contemporary political issues that one finds in *The Lives of Others*. Instead, he simply wishes to rework, and potentially enhance, a classical Hollywood tradition. From the quality of cast and crew that von Donnersmarck can attract to his projects, and the commercial success this helped to guarantee for *The Tourist*, while he has some way to go before achieving the status of Emmerich or Petersen within the industry, it would nonetheless appear that this is another German director with a future in Hollywood. It remains to be seen of course, if he will have to wait for his second Oscar as long as Scorsese did for his first.

---

36 Quoted in Ed Meza, 'TV Chefs Dilute Pic Stew?', *Variety*, 7 February 2010.
37 Mennan Yapo, 'Deutsche in Hollywood: Zwei "Fuck", acht "Shit" und ein paar Dutzend Nippel', *Spiegel Online*, 4 October 2007 (http://www.spiegel.de/kultur/kino/0,1518,509359,00.html).

Eric Rentschler

CHAPTER TWELVE
The Lives of Others: The History of Heritage and the Rhetoric of Consensus

A Salvage Text

The Lives of Others. Imagine that you were hearing this title for the first time and that you knew nothing about Florian Henckel von Donnersmarck and had not seen his film. You might well think that the four words referred to an ethnographic inquiry, an account of a foreign culture, in keeping with film titles like *In the Land of the Headhunters/In the Land of the War Canoes* (Edward S. Curtis, 1914), *Trance and Dance in Bali* (Gregory Bateson and Margaret Mead, 1952) or *The Last of the Cuiva* (Brian Moser, 1987). 'The ethnographer', we read in a classical textbook about the composition of field notes, 'writes down in regular, systematic ways what she observes and learns while participating in the daily rounds of the lives of others'.[1]

Of course, if one has seen the film, such an association might well seem far less compelling. Even so, the associative richness of the terse title is striking. As in the title of Wolfgang Staudte's exemplary DEFA feature of 1946, *Die Mörder sind unter uns* (The Murderers Are among Us), the phrase intimates a tension, an implied difference between a 'we' and a 'they'. Staudte's title, however, for all its vividness, is far less ambiguous in its marked, even Manicheistic, antimony between others, who though in our midst are not like us, namely the murderers, perpetrators who must be identified and taken to task for their war crimes. The others of von Donnersmarck's film, one surmises, might be the objects of Stasi violence; they might also refer to an even larger set of others, namely a communist state and its culture of surveillance, East German society at large, a defunct republic overcome by history. 'The film is called *The Lives of Others*', said Joachim Gauck, founder of the New Forum and the first Federal Commissioner for the Stasi archives. 'For me it could just as easily be called *The Other Life*, the one that we left behind us after we finally got rid of the GDR'.[2]

---

1 Robert M. Emerson, *Writing Ethnographic Fieldnotes* (Chicago: University of Chicago Press, 1995), p. 1.
2 Joachim Gauck, '*Das Leben der Anderen*: "Ja, so war es!"', *Stern*, 25 March 2006.

In one regard, then, the initial association might not be altogether inappropriate given the title's reference to otherness, be it the lives of others or what Gauck calls the other life. Indeed, this film manifests two essential attributes of many so-called ethnographic narratives. First, it represents a foreign culture through the prism of a more dominant one and, second, it articulates that foreign culture's history from a position of power which claims for itself semantic sovereignty. James Clifford's essay 'On Ethnographic Allegory' in fact proves quite helpful in comprehending the perspectival alignment of *The Lives of Others*. Ethnography, argues Clifford, often posits its object as something that is disappearing; what is perceived to be a culture's insufficient discursive capacity and its potential dissolution supply a rhetorical justification for a representational practice which he terms 'salvage' ethnography. The other will disintegrate and be lost for all time unless it is saved (salvaged) in the form of an ethnographic record. The recorder is an interpreter as well as a 'custodian of an essence, [an] unimpeachable witness to an authenticity'.[3] *The Lives of Others* is a salvage text that enacts a redemptive Western allegory, a tale of consensus for a unified Germany.

Revisiting the Cinema of Consensus

The Lives of Others is, to state the obvious, certainly one of the most visible and successful European features of the new millennium. Let us briefly ponder its postwall place. Contemporary German cinema, speaking broadly and quite schematically, is internationally visible today above all in two configurations: (1) in a profusion of popular 'retro films' that have become increasingly plentiful since the late 1990s, and (2) in the work of the Berlin School, which gained notoriety among festival audiences and cineastes in the early 2000s and now enjoys the status of a New German Wave. And between these two possibilities there exists a dynamic and dialectical relationship. The first transforms the key German traumas of the 20th century into the equivalent of historical theme parks; the latter is a cinema of space and place which seeks, with phenomenological insistence, to remap Germany within the new European order. One revisits the past, the other reflects on and reconnoiters the topographies of the present. The conciliatory scenarios of so-called New German historical films, of which *The Lives of Others* is without question the most significant example, have boomed dramatically over

---

3 James Clifford, 'On Ethnographic Allegory', in *Writing Culture. The Poetics and Politics of Ethnography*, ed. by James Clifford and George F. Marcus (Berkeley: University of California Press, 1986), pp. 98–121 (112–13).

the last decade. These narratives spirit us back to Hitler's evil empire and the horrors of the Holocaust, and, more recently, to the Stasi state of fear and loathing. From *Aimée & Jaguar* (Max Färberböck, 1999), *Rosenstraße* (Margarethe von Trotta, 2003), *Der Untergang* (Downfall, Oliver Hirschbiegel, 2004), *Napola – Elite für den Führer* (Before the Fall, Dennis Gansel, 2004), *Der neunte Tag* (The Ninth Day, Volker Schlöndorff, 2004) and *Sophie Scholl – Die letzten Tage* (Sophie Scholl, Marc Rothemund, 2005) to *Das Drama von Dresden* (The Drama of Dresden, Sebastian Dehnhardt, 2005), *Der letzte Zug* (The Last Train, Joseph Vilsmaier/Dana Vávrová, 2006), *Anonyma – Eine Frau in Berlin* (A Woman in Berlin, Max Färberböck, 2008), *Nordwand* (North Face, Philipp Stölzl, 2008), *John Rabe* (Florian Gallenberger, 2009), *Habermann* (Juraj Herz, 2010), and *Unter Bauern* (Saviors in the Night, Ludi Boeken, 2009), recent German films have channelled the nation's historical reservoir and created a tsunami of retrospective readings (of which there have been repeated surges since 1945), an updated variation on an impetus that Anton Kaes once described as 'the return of history as film'.[4]

For New German Cinema of the 1970s and early 1980s, as is well known, that return came in the form of looks backward, looks that were both analytical and critical. Current retro films, in contrast, provide conciliatory narratives that seem above all driven by a desire to heal the wounds of the past and thereby seal them, to transform bad history into agreeable fantasies that allow for a sense of closure. 'Celluloid memory', in the words of Lutz Koepnick, 'reawakens the dead and redeems historical injustice from today's standpoint'. In this way this new series of German retro films 'present historical epochs from the perspective of post-memory'.[5] These celluloid memories, many of them driven by great ambitions and sustained by substantial budgets, consciously appeal to mass audiences and seek to create communities of consensus. Particularly when they are successful, these popular narratives assume political proportions.

Elsewhere I have sketched the impact of the genre cinema that followed the over-determined demise of New German Film in the mid-1980s. I used the term 'New German Cinema of consensus' and this notion has fostered far more discussion than I might have imagined a dozen years ago when I wrote what I thought to be an uncontroversial contribution to a collection entitled *Cinema and Nation*.[6] The appellation, I took care in saying, surely *did not* apply to all of the

---

4 See Anton Kaes, *From Hitler to Heimat. The Return of History as Film* (Cambridge: Harvard University Press, 1989).

5 Lutz Koepnick, 'Reframing the Past: Heritage Cinema and Holocaust in the 1990s', *New German Critique*, 87 (2002), 47–82 (p. 76).

6 Eric Rentschler, 'From New German Cinema to the Post-Wall Cinema of Consensus', in *Cinema and Nation*, ed. by Mette Hjort and Scott MacKenzie (London: Routledge, 2000), pp. 260–77.

films made in Germany since the death of Fassbinder in 1982 and the onset of a government-endorsed witch-hunt on critical filmmakers which was accompanied by radical changes in film subsidy policies, a fierce backlash against the *Autoren-kino*, and the advent of a new cinematic populism. Not for a moment did I forget other forces at work in this nation's film culture, indeed offbeat voices and un-reconciled visions, films with a historical ground, a postnational sensibility and a topical impetus, whose recalcitrant, if under-acknowledged, presence I empha-sized in the essay's closing passage. The problem is that these edgy films were at the time hard to see, indeed, cast to the margins or all but invisible, and for this reason remain to this day largely forgotten. The phrase 'cinema of consensus' referred to a gathering of films and filmmakers which had dominated media accounts and industry campaigns meant to bolster the film industry's public pro-file in Germany and abroad during the Kohl era, which is to say the cinema that had been most popular and therefore most conspicuous and, in that way, most symptomatic of a dominant discourse that presumed to speak as a we when it in fact mirrored the film industry's powers that be.

Likewise, I was not assailing genre cinema in general nor was I insinuating, as if I were the spawn of Horkheimer and Adorno, that films seeking to be popular can only be seen as affirmative and regressive. (After all, we no longer live in the 1970s and have ceased to worship at the altar of Screen Studies and venerate apparatus theory's deterministic orthodoxies as if they were articles of faith.) I surely was not claiming that New German filmmakers, even if many of them sought to foster an alternative culture and create an oppositional public sphere, were altogether unbeholden to genre. As a film historian who at least *tries* to get things right, how could I? Think of the significance of melodrama for Fass-binder, Schroeter, Rischert, Van Ackeren, von Trotta, and Sanders-Brahms, of road movies for Wenders, Winkelmann, and Noever, of film noir for Thome, Klick, and Lemke, of the street film for Brandner, the crime film for Geissendörfer, and the polit thriller for Schlöndorff, of anti-homeland films like *Jagdszenen aus Nie-derbayern* (Hunting Scenes from Bavaria, Peter Fleischmann, 1969), *Jaid – der ein-same Jäger* (Jaid – the Lonely Hunter, Volker Vogeler, 1971) and *Matthias Kneissl* (Reinhard Hauff, 1970), of the signature retro films from *Die BRD Trilogie* (FRG Trilogy, Rainer Werner Fassbinder, 1979–82) to *Heimat* (Edgar Reitz, 1984), of the innumerable literature adaptations, from *Nicht versöhnt* (Not Reconciled, Jean-Marie Straub and Danièle Huillet, 1965) and *Der junge Törless* (Young Törless, Volker Schlöndorff, 1965) to the abundance of adaptations during the mid-1970s, and, yes, let us not forget the movement's many comedies, from Young German Film's *Kuckucksjahre* (The Cuckoo Years, George Moorse, 1967), *Wilder Reiter GmbH* (Wild Rider Ltd, Franz-Josef Spieker, 1967), *Quartett im Bett* (Quartet in Bed, Ulrich Schamoni, 1968), *Engelchen* (Angel Baby, Marran Gosov, 1968) and

Zur Sache Schätzchen (Go for It, Baby, May Spils, 1968) to New German Cinema's *Die Reise nach Wien* (The Journey to Vienna, Edgar Reitz, 1973), *Lina Braake*, (Bernhard Sinkel, 1975) and *Der starke Ferdinand* (Strongman Ferdinand, Alexander Kluge, 1976), much less the zany misadventures of von Praunheim's and Lambert's wacky personages or the desperate screwball antics of Achternbusch's errant husbands.

What the cinema of consensus above all lacked were critical voices and incisive visions, especially in the relationship comedies (*Beziehungskisten*) from Dörrie's *Männer* (Men, 1985) to Wortmann's *Der bewegte Mann* (Maybe … Maybe Not, 1994), but also in the rude and lewd proletarian farces (*Prollkomödien*) like *Ballermann 6* (Gernot Roll and Tom Gerhardt, 1997), *Werner – Das muß kesseln!!!* (Werner – Eat My Dust!!!, Udo Beissel and Michael Schaack, 1996) or *Kleines Arschloch* (The Little Bastard, Michael Schaack and Veit Vollmer, 1997), to which my article only refers in passing. Following Georg Seeßlen, we find on the one hand 'lust, love, and social climbing somehow brought into balance, the residue of bohemian indulgences comically overcome, a retreat into the private sphere, liberality confirmed beyond a doubt by the presence of token homosexuals; on the other hand, the image of a proletarian body that refuses to grow up, for which the world consists only of eating, drinking, and teletubbery'.[7] What above all dismayed me about the cinema of consensus and its unremarkable portraits of yuppies and slobs, was the way in which this cycle of comic populism functioned in a more general turn against personal and critical filmmaking and within the wider framework of a political regime wrestling, as never before and not very well, especially after the opening of the Wall, with questions of diversity and difference. During the Kohl era there was a provincialization of German film culture as a whole; indeed in the years 1985–1995 German cinema all but disappeared from the programs of major festivals and the catalogues of foreign film distributors.

The Cinema of Consensus: The Sequel

Since my thoughts on the New German Cinema of consensus appeared in 2000, certain structures and constellations have become more apparent; indeed, it is now much easier to discern the larger picture, to recognize contours, counter-

---

7 Georg Seeßlen, 'Lacht da wer? Die deutsche Filmkomödie zwischen Otto und Männerherzen', *epd Film* 28.9 (2011), 18–25 (p. 21). Comedy, Seeßlen elaborates, can be an important vehicle for the public expression of taboos, an influential forum to display the subversive capacities of language and the body within social contexts, in ways that stimulate laughter by showing how things go wrong when things are not quite right (p. 19).

points, and fault-lines, to see how the cinema of consensus continues and has found its most prominent extension in what is commonly referred to as German heritage cinema. We surely do not have to labour unduly to make that connection; indeed, filmmakers like Joseph Vilsmaier and Florian Henckel von Donnersmarck as well as producers like Bernd Eichinger and Günter Rohrbach have repeatedly invoked and defended the consensus paradigm. They certainly know what they are doing when they appropriate the past and seek to transform it into a lucrative commodity. We should be mindful, as Randall Halle's recent book helps us to be, of the international marketing of historical films, a crucial pursuit within the German film industry's concerted efforts to optimize the exchange value of national properties as transnational commodities.[8] Buena Vista, for instance, is essential in our understanding of the success of von Donnersmarck's film as is the calculated implementation of tie-ins and extensions in Eichinger's historical features. There is something decidedly strategic (and perhaps even mercenary) about the commercial exploitation of German wartime suffering and postwar victimization in a plethora of films made during the last decade for German television. And it has of course become a truism that only German films about Nazis (and now members of the Stasi) ever get nominated for Academy Awards.

Rohrbach's essay, 'Das Schmollen der Autisten' (The Pouting of Autists) provided a trenchant apologia for a cinema of consensus; one might even call it a programmatic intervention. Let us recall the setting: several weeks before the 2007 Berlin Film Festival, Rohrbach, the well-known producer and President of the German Film Academy, published a polemic in *Der Spiegel*. In it he lashed out at Germany's movie critics, who have, he charged, little regard or respect for most filmmakers and the film-going public. Instead they champion an esoteric art cinema that appeals to their precious cinephilic sensibilities.[9] For this reason, Rohrbach, employing a medical disorder as an epithet and an insult, called these commentators autistic and went on to chide them for their hostile relation to the German film industry and their inattentiveness to the responses of their readers. Vain and self-serving, these pundits are ever ready to attack productions that harbour great ambitions and seek to please large audiences – in short, would-be consensus films. Why, wondered Rohrbach, was a film like Tom Tykwer's *Das Parfum: Die Geschichte eines Mörders* (Perfume: The Story of a Murderer, 2006) that attracted millions of viewers panned with such malice and harshness? What,

---

8 Randall Halle, *German Film After Germany. Toward a Transnational Aesthetic* (Urbana: University of Illinois Press, 2008).

9 As such, these critics might be seen as captives of what Dominik Graf calls the 'art film prison'. See Dominik Graf, Christian Petzold and Christoph Hochhäusler, 'Mailwechsel. Berliner Schule', *Revolver*, 16 (May 2007), 6–40 (pp. 33–34).

other than poor judgment and bad will, stood behind the fierce backlash against *The Lives of Others*, a box-office success blithely castigated in the press as a 'cinema of consensus'? The film's technical competence and deference to cinematic convention, after all, are hardly marks of formal incapacity and surely not just signs of commercial opportunism. Works that connect with a large and diverse spectatorship are anything but easy to make; indeed, fumed the furious producer, consensus films are daunting undertakings and surely do not deserve to be treated with automatic scorn and kneejerk dismissiveness.[10]

Shortly after Rohrbach's invective, von Donnersmarck weighed in. Speaking in a *Der Spiegel* article published on February 12, he regretted that *The Lives of Others* had not found as strong a resonance as he had hoped for or envisioned. His film, he insisted, 'doesn't have enough of a consensus yet! The consensus I strive for is a film that everyone likes, one no one can criticize'.[11] Months before he had assailed critics who had faulted the film precisely because it harboured such ambitions. How can one attack a film, he raged, that 'appeals to almost everyone, and thus to very different people! [...] Those who repeat this verdict presumably want Germany to be lumbered with the kind of mediocrity that has induced so many "consensus people", from William Weiller [sic] to Wolfgang Petersen, to flee the country! If "consensus film" is supposed to mean the same as "trivial"; or even "bad film", then I want to make a lot more bad and trivial films in my career'. 'I wish', he concluded, 'that *The Lives of Others* was much more of a consensus film'.[12]

It is striking how in the director's account 'almost everyone' and 'very different people' come together while watching his film in an act of affective *Gleichschaltung*, a mighty moment of sublation in which diversity succumbs to the higher power of consensus. And it is striking as well how he equates the quite different destinies of William Wyler, a Jewish emigrant (born in Alsace and educated in France) who came to the United States in the 1920s and established himself as a filmmaker, becoming in effect an exile after the rise of Hitler, and Wolfgang Petersen, a successful young director who happily moved to Hollywood in 1987 (and, contrary to von Donnersmarck's insinuation, did not leave West Germany because the New German Cinema refused to have him). Both individuals, insists von Donnersmarck, had 'to flee the country' because Germany was dangerous ground for popular filmmakers; his claim, in each instance, suggests that he is not unduly burdened by a knowledge of film history.

---

10 Günter Rohrbach, 'Das Schmollen der Autisten', *Der Spiegel*, 22 January 2007.
11 Lars-Olav Beier, 'Endstation Hollywood', *Der Spiegel*, 12 February 2007.
12 Annette Maria Rupprecht, 'XXL: A Portrait of Florian Henckel von Donnersmarck', *German Films Quarterly*, 3 (2006), 16–17 (p. 16).

In accordance with the director's designs, *The Lives of Others* functioned as a vehicle of consensus on various levels. Replicating *Schindler's List* patterns of reception, von Donnersmarck's film with a historical topic became a privileged object of public education and national identity formation; the wider regard that came with this exposure surely served as an effective means of generating political spin. Culture Minister Bernd Neumann arranged an exclusive showing of the film prior to its official premiere for the entire German Bundestag and, legitimating its value as a historical memory, afterwards urged that it be screened in German schools. A substantial study guide produced by the Bundeszentrale für politische Bildung (Federal Agency for Political Education) ensured that the film would serve as a seminal text in future study of the GDR and the Stasi. Prominent former dissidents like Wolf Biermann likewise, despite some misgivings, attested to the film's veracity and granted their seal of approval, claiming 'The political sound is authentic'.[13] After the film won an array of Bavarian Film Prizes early in 2007, a public podium discussion with von Donnersmarck was scheduled. The director asked that the positively disposed critic Rainer Gansera be present, but not Claus Loeser, who had panned the film. The filmmaker's participation, it became clear, had as a condition the elimination of any contrary voices. Public discourse about the film, in this way, became inextricably bound to its advertising value, which is, of course, a larger problem that faces contemporary film criticism that wishes to remain independent and indeed critical.[14]

Which Heritage? Whose Heritage?

Von Donnersmarck's production provides a paradigmatic example of what scholars describe as a distinct genre, the German heritage film. 'A genre's history', Steve Neale reminds us, 'is as much the history of the term as it is of the films to which the term has been applied; it is as much a history of the consequently shifting boundaries of a corpus of texts as it is of the texts themselves. The institutionalization of any generic term is a key aspect of [its] social existence'.[15] If we are to continue to employ the term in the context of German cinema, we would

---

13 Wolf Biermann, 'Die Gespenster treten aus dem Schatten', *Die Welt*, 22 March 2006.

14 Claudia Lenssen, 'Inszenierte Öffentlichkeit: Eine Debatte um die symbolische Macht der Filmkritik', *VDK. Verband der deutschen Filmkritik* 4 (2008), 28–30. There is, Lenssen argues, a decided lack of rules governing the interaction between public relations and film criticism in Germany. Rohrbach seems to think that the role of film critics should be to present and legitimate the film industry.

15 Steve Neale, *Genre and Hollywood* (London: Routledge, 2000), p. 43.

do well to give its conceptual and historical implications some further and more careful thought. Four critical concerns come to mind about this often used concept's pertinence within an understanding of postmillennial German film culture and suggest some ways in which we might refine our use of the term in this specific national setting.

1. *The question of appropriation which is also one of translation*: How well does the notion of heritage cinema translate, which is to ask how well does it apply in the German context? One, of course, recalls that the notion is taken from discussions initiated by British film scholars about features made in the UK and, later, France (e.g., Andrew Higson, Richard Dyer, and Ginette Vincendeau).[16] The question is one of naming, i.e., of formulating a term that accurately accounts for the distinctive terms of recent German historical features. The appeal to heritage cinema has quite often (but not always) deployed national history positively, recalling the former glory of the British Empire and putting treasured traces of the imperial past on display and employing them as cultural capital. The term 'German heritage cinema', if we follow recent scholarly exchanges (for instance the influential contributions of Lutz Koepnick), almost without exception refers to historical films that look back at 'bad' history, especially the Nazi epoch. This heritage, as the history of Academy Awards granted to postwar German films confirms, seems to be what travels best and has the greatest allure for foreign audiences. To be sure, the so-called Stasi era has come to gain equal power as a sign of a bad German past that can be transformed into successful movies. In the words of Timothy Garton Ash, 'Nazi, Stasi: Germany's festering half rhyme'.[17]

It is instructive to consider other possible appellations. In 2003 Katja Nicodemus, for instance, likened the attractions of recent history films to exhibits in a nostalgia shop (*Nostalgiebude*): 'German cinema has become a site of yearning and memory in which we search for lost times and lost paradises, in which we hallow childhood dreams and conciliatory fantasies. [...] As it fetishizes signs of the past, this new German haven of curios provides something for everyone, from tales of Nazi era resistance [*Rosenstraße*] to the Spree forest pickle dreams of the ever-present GDR [*Good Bye, Lenin!*, Wolfgang Becker, 2003] from the soccer myths of postwar Germans [*Das Wunder von Bern/*The Miracle of Bern, Sönke Wortmann, 2003] to the hedonistic grand refusals of the 1980s [*Herr Lehmann*, Leander Haußmann, 2003]'.[18] Christina Nord, writing in 2008, speaks of a 'new

---

16 See, for instance, the collection of representative essays edited by Ginette Vincendeau, *Film/ Literature/Heritage. A Sight and Sound Reader* (London: British Film Institute, 2001).
17 Timothy Garton Ash, 'The Stasi on Our Minds', *New York Review of Books*, 31 May 2007.
18 Katja Nicodemus, 'Unsere kleine Traumfabrik: Vor den Filmfestspielen in Venedig zeigt sich das deutsche Kino als Nostalgiebude', *Die Zeit*, 28 August 2003.

German naiveté'. History films like *The Lives of Others*, she argues, make a great to-do about their authenticity, without for a second acknowledging that their putative cinematic authenticity is in fact a construction and, as such, an illusion. Would-be post-ideological films produced by Bernd Eichinger and Günter Rohrbach spare the viewer reflective distance in the name of a seductive and spurious reproduction of the way things were.[19]

2. *The limited range of reference*: Nicodemus's comments about a new cinema of nostalgia make another problem strikingly transparent. To this date, with a few notable exceptions, Anglo-American discussions of heritage cinema fixate narrowly on films that deal with a small sector of the German past and diminish the larger and more diverse German sense of history (*Geschichtsgefühl*) that has surfaced in the nation's fantasy production since the mid-1990s.[20] Looking at the striking recurrence of titles and directors in recent scholarly discussions, one might very well believe that the Nazi-Stasi eras are the sole domains of contemporary German filmic retrospection. Millennial German cinema, in fact, has probed a decidedly wide range of pastness and recognized the contemporary resonance of a number of different heritages, for instance in:

- Biopics from a variety of epochs: *Der Einstein des Sex* (The Einstein of Sex: Life and Work of Dr. M. Hirschfeld, Rosa von Praunheim, 1999), *Klemperer – Ein Leben in Deutschland*, (Klemperer – A Life in Germany, Kai Wessel and Andreas Kleinert, 1999) *Marlene* (Joseph Vilsmaier, 2000), *Abschied – Brechts letzter Sommer* (The Farewell, Jan Schütte, 2000), *Der Verleger* (The Publisher, Bernd Böhlich, 2001), *Schiller* (The Young Schiller, Martin Weinhart, 2005), *Mein Leben – Marcel Reich-Ranicki* (My Life, Dror Zahavi, 2009), *Romy* (Torsten C. Fischer, 2009) and *Goethe!* (Young Goethe in Love, Philipp Stölzl, 2010).
- The postwar years and the Adenauer era, especially *Das Wunder von Bern*, but also *Marmor, Stein & Eisen* (Marble, Stone and Iron, Hansjörg Thurn, 2000), *Solino* (Fatih Akin, 2002), and *Die Entdeckung der Currywurst* (The Invention of the Curried Sausage, Ulla Wagner, 2008) as well as a plethora of recent TV movies about the destinies of German refugees after the Second World War and the ARD mini-series *Unsere fünfziger Jahre* (Our 1950s, Thomas Kufus, 2005).

---

19 Christina Nord, 'Deutsche Geschichte im Kino: Die neue Naivität', *tageszeitung*, 20 October 2008.
20 A noteworthy departure from this tendency is to be found in Mattias Frey, *Postwall German Cinema: History, Film History and Cinephilia* (Oxford: Berghahn, 2013).

- 1968 and its afterlife in the guise of the RAF: *Die 68er Story* (The Story of the 68ers, Wolfgang Ettlich, 1999), *Die innere Sicherheit* (The State I Am In, Christian Petzold, 2000), *Die Stille nach dem Schuss* (The Legend of Rita, Volker Schlöndorff, 2000), *Das Phantom* (The Phantom, Dennis Gansel, 2000), *Was tun wenn's brennt?* (What To Do in Case of Fire, Gregor Schnitzler, 2001), *Black Box BRD* (Black Box Germany, Andres Veiel, 2001), *Baader* (Christopher Roth, 2002), *Starbuch Holger Meins* (Gerd Conradt, 2002), *The Raspberry Reich* (Bruce La Bruce, 2004), *Das wilde Leben* (Eight Miles High, Achim Bornhak, 2007), *Baader-Meinhof Komplex* (The Baader Meinhof Complex, Uli Edel, 2008), *Dutschke* (Stefan Krohmer, 2009), *Die Anwälte* (The Lawyers – A German Story, Birgit Schulz, 2009), *Wer wenn nicht wir* (If Not Us, Who?, Andres Veiel, 2011);
- The 1980s and the Kohl era: *23* (Hans-Christian Schmid, 1998), *England!* (Achim von Borries, 2000), *Happiness is a Warm Gun* (Thomas Imbach, 2001), *Das Jahr der ersten Küsse* (The Year of the First Kiss, Kai Wessel, 2002), *Liegen lernen* (Learning to Lie, Hendrik Handloegten, 2003), *Die Ritterinnen* (Gallant Girls, Barbara Teufel, 2003), *Herr Lehmann* (2003), *Am Tag als Bobby Ewing starb* (On the Day Bobby Ewing Died, Lars Jessen, 2005);
- Films about the GDR, before and after unification: *Good Bye, Lenin!* and *Berlin is in Germany* (Hannes Stöhr, 2001) (both of which are Rip Van Winkle narratives with characters who sleep through history) along with the Thomas Brussig adaptations (in essence, the usual suspects rounded up in discussions of *Ostalgie*), but also *Bis zum Horizont und weiter* (To the Horizon and Beyond, Peter Kahane, 1999), *Wege in die Nacht* (Paths in the Night, Andreas Kleinert, 1999), *Deutschlandspiel* (The Germany Game, Hans-Christoph Blumenberg, 2000), *Die Unberührbare* (No Place to Go, Oskar Roehler, 2000), *Wie Feuer und Flamme* (Never Mind the Wall, Connie Walter, 2001), *Der Tunnel* (The Tunnel, Roland Suso Richter, 2001), *Führer Ex* (Winfried Bonengel, 2002), *Der Aufstand* (The Uprising, Hans-Christoph Blumenberg, 2003), *Kleinruppin Forever* (Carsten Fiebeler, 2004), *Der rote Kakadu* (The Red Cockatoo, Dominik Graf, 2006), and, of course, *The Lives of Others*.[21]

3. *The term heritage's rich (and, in current discussions among film scholars, vastly unprobed) connotations for students of German culture:* The history of this idea in the 20th century surely lends itself to other ways in which one might pursue a

---

21 In this vein, Andreas Dresen has noted that the cinematic representation of the GDR past has for the most been dominated by filmmakers from the West; this was to a degree also the case with productions made just after the opening of the Wall; it is only recently that the significant *Wende-flicks* from the GDR have resurfaced and undergone productive reconsideration. See Dresen's essay, 'Ost-West Film: Der falsche Kino-Osten', *Die Zeit*, 31 July 2009.

heritage discussion, particularly if we take into account the *Erbschaft* (heritage) debates that reach back to Georg Lukács's reflections on an appropriate and progressive classical-realist canon to exchanges in the history of the GDR regarding which elements in the bourgeois heritage might be salvageable for a socialist society. 'Every nation throughout the stormy path of its history', noted Anna Seghers, 'drags along with it, from generation to generation, what we call its heritage. Hungry for freedom it appropriates from its cultural past whatever is needed to sustain us'.[22] Particularly illuminating is Bloch's *Erbschaft dieser Zeit* (Heritage of our times, 1935) and his concept of nonsimultaneity, with its sensitivity for thoughts out of season.[23] Bloch demonstrates how nonsynchronous elements (which the Nazis appropriated and successfully exploited) represented legitimate desires and might in fact have been proved useful in the creation of an anti-capitalist heritage. In short, he talks about how one might salvage things that conventional wisdom consider to be illegitimate properties and make them viable and workable. In Anson Rabinbach's assessment, Bloch makes us mindful of 'treasures discovered in the rubble – the lost heritage of the time'.[24]

4. *The legacy of German film history as a heritage in its own right*: Within the circumscribed focus of current German heritage cinema discussion, crucial heritages, the bearers of significant experience and the objects of considerable public interest, have become obscured and overlooked, for instance, the legacy of the GDR (especially its history as represented in its film history) as well as the continuing appeal and, for many commentators, the problematic heritage of UFA (Universum Film AG), whose codes and conventions and whose notion of the well-made film, for instance, von Donnersmarck to a large degree relies on and replicates. *The Lives of Others* is, quite literally, a heritage film: it inscribes heritage in its narrative and, as a cultural artefact, enacts the construction of a humanistic heritage. In so doing, it puts on display the illusory quality of such a construction; its popular reception also attests to the seductive power of such illusions.

---

22 Anna Seghers, quoted in Anette Horn, *Kontroverses Ende und Innovation* (Frankfurt am Main: Lang, 2005), p. 36. For a more general assessment of the heritage debates in the GDR, see Wolfram Schlenker, *Das 'Kulturelle Erbe' in der DDR. Gesellschaftliche Entwicklung und Kulturpolitik 1945–1965* (Stuttgart: Metzler, 1977).

23 Translated into English as Ernst Bloch, *Heritage of Our Times*, trans. by Neville and Stephen Plaice (Berkeley: University of California Press, 1991).

24 Anson Rabinbach, 'Unclaimed Heritage: Ernst Bloch's *Heritage of Our Times* and the Theory of Fascism', *New German Critique*, 11 (1977), 5–21 (p. 5).

A Heritage for Postwall Times

In the course of time, *The Lives of Others* has, as the film's international success confirms, become for memories of the GDR what *Schindler's List* now represents for recollections of the Holocaust: a master text. Both films offer rescue narratives in which an insider (a Nazi party member, a Stasi surveillance officer) goes native and becomes a guardian angel; each depicts the transformation of a calculating collaborator into a *guter Mensch* (good person) capable of empathy. *The Lives of Others* does not want to engender discomfort nor to generate controversy. It wants to please, and, as its director has repeatedly attested, it wants to please everyone. Von Donnersmarck celebrates an art that both defies and overcomes politics and in that way harmonizes.[25] His parable fosters a heritage of the good man in which Beethoven's music can be imagined to possess anti-Communist potential: if Lenin had listened to the *Appassionata*, it is suggested, there would have been no revolution and, by implication, no GDR and no Stasi and no divided Germany. In the curriculum of words and music that constitutes Wiesler's re-education, Brecht is de-ossified; the socialist activist figures solely as a lyrical poet, not a Communist or the proponent of a critical theatre. The many references to *der gute Mensch* conspicuously recall Brecht's *Der gute Mensch von Sezuan* (The Good Person of Sezuan, 1943) all the better, it would seem, to disavow this dialectical play about the necessity of tactical behaviour for the sake of material survival. *The Lives of Others* is in fact just the opposite of Brecht's critical parable, which leaves its audience disappointed and consternated; as the curtain closes, all questions remain open.

A distinct structure of retrospection, claims Clifford, governs many ethnographic portraits; they search for fundamentally desirable human traits. In this endeavour, as stated, the recorder and interpreter of fragile custom serves as a custodian of an essence.[26] In von Donnersmarck's postwall allegory, the state servant comes to identify with a dissident; the spectator in turn comes to identify

---

25 There is a decided tension between the director's emphasis on the film's authenticity and his desire to tell a story with universal interest which could take place anywhere. In an interview on Journal DW-TV, with Stephan Bachelmeier, he stresses that both of his parents came from the East and that his family maintained an intimate familiarity with life in East Germany; an uncle of his father was in fact the Head of Protocol for Erich Honecker. The set designer, he elaborates, had been in a GDR prison for two years and knew well what the Stasi world looked like. But the film, he goes to say, is above all about 'people in an extreme situation' and not necessarily just about the Stasi and the GDR. If films are to be successful abroad, he insists, they must deal with 'large themes, large feelings'. See 'Journal Interview: Florian Henckel von Donnersmarck', accessed on 1 December 2011 (http://www.youtube.com/watch?v=QuIgJTmLov4).

26 Clifford, 'On Ethnographic Allegory', p. 110 and 113.

with the renegade agent as he turns against bad politics.[27] The narrative portrays an aesthetic education that reforms a Stasi agent and creates a larger community in which perpetrators and victims come together, in which 'alle Menschen werden Brüder' (All men become brothers), to quote Schiller's 'An die Freude' (Ode to Joy). This community is sanctified by a book whose catalyst is the oppositional director Lerska and whose patron saint is the Stasi operative; it celebrates the male bond that is made possible by Sieland's act of sacrifice (*Opfergang*), a suicide that serves as a self-punishment for the actress's collaborationist activities. The book replicates, indeed essentializes, the impetus of the film as a vehicle of redemption and as a triumph of good will in dark times which circulates in a reunited Germany. Wiesler says the book is 'für mich' (for me). As a stand-in for the film as a whole, it also speaks to us.

This salvage narrative allows us access to the presence of pastness. The camera grants the viewer an augmented perspective in the same way that the film as a whole offers a sense that what we are seeing is authentic. In that regard the spectator becomes a fellow surveiller who enjoys a more exclusive entry to the film world's sights and sounds; indeed, we see the lives of the others from a position that is far more omniscient than that of the lower-tech Stasi. Hempf's claim that observers like he and Grubitz 'see more' is of course cynical, but also doubly ironic. He utters these words while, unbeknownst to this SED minister (who himself will become an object of surveillance), he is the object of Wiesler's gaze. And, to be sure, during the operation, the Stasi's key tool will be hidden microphones – not cameras. As Wiesler listens to the others, his sonic perspective also becomes visible, which means that the viewer can see what the eavesdropper cannot. The implied audience's perspective exceeds that of the unsophisticated East German security apparatus; the contemporary spectator enjoys a privileged relation to the spectacle, a perceptual and technological sovereignty granted by the filmmaker.[28] The film is 'for us', the empowered denizens of a contemporary post-Cold War world.

---

27 Wiesler initially resembles the voyeur (*Spanner*) in Alexander Kluge's *Die Patriotin* (The Patriot, 1979), a peeping Tom with a fixed gaze. In the process of his aesthetic education he comes to ease up, to relax and enjoy other dimensions of what he sees and hears, to assume a perspective that is more open to and appreciative of possibility.

28 Note as well how the film uses a theatre setting to introduce and reintroduce discussions about surveillance, a site of spectacle where people look at people and where we, as spectators, enjoy a privileged access to specular relations. For further discussion see Marc Silberman's contribution to this volume.

In this would-be ethnographic enterprise, von Donnersmarck views himself, as statements made in innumerable interviews confirm, as an agent of authenticity and of historical memory.[29] He shot on original locations, employed contemporary phonographs and typewriters, period furniture, decor, music and colour.[30] He aimed to capture 'the inner truth of the GDR' and spare German viewers 'yet another folkloristic orgy with historical costumes'. As this last quote makes clear, von Donnersmarck explicitly sought to distance his film from the *Ostalgie* wave and did so by billing his feature as the more accurate and serious memory of life in the GDR.[31]

Many film critics praised the film for this very reason. Paul Cantor, apparently not at all modest in his reliance on the press kit, argues that until *The Lives of Others*, we had only upbeat exercises in *Ostalgie*: 'No German film had attempted to portray the brutal nature of the communist regime in East Germany'. It is as if Sibylle Schönemann's *Verriegelte Zeit* (Locked-up, Time 1990), Roland Gräf's *Der Tangospieler* (The Tango Player, 1991), and Thomas Heise's chilling *Barluschke – Psychogramm eines Spions* (Barluschke – Portrait of a Spy, 1997) had never been made – much less Alexander Zahn's low-budget production from 1992, *Die Wahrheit über die Stasi* (The Truth about the Stasi). The film, Cantor continues, was justifiably hailed 'for its willingness to confront what many Germans seemed content to let slip down the memory hole of history'. The feature 'seems destined to stand with *1984* as one of the most chilling evocations of the nightmare of twentieth-century totalitarianism'.[32] Cantor's rhetoric conspicuously recapitulates and reaffirms the director's resolve. For von Donnersmarck made a film about the GDR as if it were, as far as cinema goes, *terra incognita*, as if DEFA had (almost) never existed, as if he and his production were the privileged and primary bringers of this culture into expression, as if no one before him had really

---

29 As is also discussed in Manfred Wilke's contribution to this volume, von Donnersmarck's scenario is not altogether loyal (or authentic) in its historical reconstruction. Indeed, it takes liberties with chronology, relying for its background in great part on events and developments from the mid- to late 1970s: Wolf Biermann's expatriation in the fall of 1976, Jürgen Fuchs's *Vernehmungsprotokolle* from 1976–1977, and Robert Havemann's book *Ein deutscher Kommunist. Rückblicke und Perspektiven aus der Isolation. Der Spiegel*'s East Berlin office was closed after the publication of the so-called '*Spiegel* Manifest' in early 1978 and would not be reopened until 1985. It is essential for the film's dramatic effect, though, that the narrative take place later, closer to Gorbachev's rise to power in 1985 and the opening of the Wall.
30 Especially the ubiquitous greyness is meant to replicate visual memories of the era's dreariness and drabness.
31 Philipp Lichterbeck, 'Die innere Wahrheit der DDR', *Tagesspiegel*, 5 December 2004.
32 Paul A., Cantor, 'Long Day's Journey into Brecht: The Ambivalent Politics of *The Lives of Others*', *Perspectives on Political Science* 40.2 (2011), 68–77 (all quotes, p. 68).

tried, much less succeeded in such a historical reckoning. In this way he over-
looks or marginalizes previous endeavours, all the better to supersede them.[33]

Von Donnersmarck's film and the Schlöndorff-DEFA controversy are of a
piece, insofar as they both, in one case directly, in the other indirectly, respond
to the heritage of the GDR and the legacy of DEFA. 'I got rid of the name DEFA',
boasted Schlöndorff, the former Babelsberg studio head in an interview with the
MAZ. 'DEFA films were just terrible. They were shown in Paris, where I studied,
but only in the cinema run by the Communist Party'.[34] The off-the-cuff (and off the
wall) remark caused widespread anger and chagrin. An open letter signed by 120
prominent German directors and actors was published a few days later; the statement provided an inventory of DEFA's venerable legacy, 10,000 films in various
genres, 10 features that are considered by specialists to be among the 100
most important German films of all times, not to forget the significant body of
children's film as well as DEFA's continuing resonance, e.g., in the 2005 MOMA
retrospective of 21 features. Schlöndorff's rant was all the more curious given that
nothing specific had occasioned it.

When one contemplates the history of DEFA, there are of course many heritages that come to mind. These heritages are, in this context, pertinent and
worthy of more careful consideration and, to use Bloch's term, significant in their
non-synchronicity:

– The legacy of anti-fascist cinema, films that provide lessons in how one might
  conceptualize an anti-fascist aesthetic.
– The *Kaninchenfilme* (Rabbit Films) of 1965/66, 10 productions, noteworthy
  signs of new critical and artistic life, banned by the 11th Plenum of the SED
  Central Committee, which were rediscovered and screened after unification.
– The *Wendeflicks*, features and documentaries made in the GDR between 1988
  and 1994, the last films from East Germany with their vivid, ironic, and poignant portraits of the disintegration of a nation and the recasting of a populace.
– The essential heritage of documentarism, e.g., Thomas Plenert's patiently
  attentive camera, Heike Misselwitz's portrait of GDR women (*Winter, adé*
  [After Winter Comes Spring], 1988), Jürgen Böttcher's trainyard images (*Ran-
  gierer* [Shunters, 1984]) and postwall prospects (*Die Mauer* [The Wall, 1991]),

---

33 Cf. Clifford, p. 117. Von Donnersmarck does voice his admiration for *Die Legende von Paul und
Paula* (The Legend of Paul and Paula, Heiner Carow, 1973) on the commentary to the American
DVD edition. Andrea Rinke has also noted the resemblance between the dance scene at the start
of the inscribed theatre performance and a passage from *Alle meine Mädchen* (All My Girls, Iris
Gusner, 1980).
34 'So viele Speichen – Plausch mit Volker Schlöndorff auf seinem sonnengelben Sofa', *Märkische Allgemeine Zeitung*, 2 December 2008.

Winfried and Barbara Junge's epic *Lebensläufe* (Résumés, 1981) along with
Volker Koepp's poignant portraits of working-class destinies in Wittstock.
Despite its plethora of politically correct (*linientreu*) productions, DEFA also sus-
tained a venerable legacy of critical realism.

A Waking Dream of an Other Life

This essay began with an invocation of a film title's ethnographic connotations
and went on to consider von Donnersmarck's feature as a self-conscious consensus production that, in the name of authenticity and verisimilitude, displays tab-
leaux from the GDR as a heritage for our times. In order to create consensus, it
crafts comforting and conciliatory images from out of time, post-ideological tab-
leaux that in fact reintroduce well known Cold War panoramas which claim to be
the way things were, scenes from an imagined past marked by an emotional sua-
sion that eschews reflective distance. This is, of course, but one way of looking at
the lives of others and only one sort of heritage cinema. Let us in closing consider
another perspective which one might find in a different kind of heritage cinema.

Jürgen Böttcher's *Jahrgang 45* (Born in '45) was banned in 1965 before its completion and did not come into full view until 1990. About an hour into the film, we
see West German visitors from a tour bus gawking at young East Berliners who
sun themselves on the steps of the French Cathedral; the tourists stare with a
lurid intensity as if the strange beings before them, actors in a film about East Germany who are portraying citizens of the GDR, were creatures in a zoo or the denizens of an exotic village. But Böttcher's idlers are not just the objects of the gaze;
they also return it – as does the film as a whole. Böttcher's film both records the
importunance of Western cameras as well as demonstrating that the others on
view have lives that transcend these patronizing foreign perspectives that would
reduce them to abject others.

Jahrgang 45, like the *Kaninchenfilme* as a corpus, brought to the screen nonsynchronous energies, an everyday East German reality at odds with or even
divorced from the SED's party priorities. The film patiently measures the living
spaces of Prenzlauer Berg and the conditions of existence for young people who
reside in a state of dismay, uneasiness, and anticipation. It is a portrait of dreamers
and, as a film, both the exploration of a grand refusal to live according to official
expectations as well the expression of an alternative perspective and the hope for
a different experience. Enacting Bloch's notion of redemption, Böttcher offers a
transcendence freed from the constraints of otherworldliness. 'We need not be
afraid', argues Bloch, 'of taking note and of distinguishing the hunger for happiness and freedom, the images of freedom for human beings deprived of their

Curious onlookers from a West Berlin tour bus focus their cameras (a) on a group of young people sunning themselves on the Gendarmenmarkt (b), the regard of the visitors from the West is patronizing and haughty (c); rather than allowing themselves to be positioned as caged animals in a zoo, the youths stand up and, with cheekiness and confidence, confront the gaze and return it (d), *Jahrgang 45.*

rights, images which are contained in these dreams'.[35] Böttcher's film is extraordinary in the way it restores the essential meaning of utopia as an immanent force and provides a waking dream of the possible.

This example supplies a necessary counterpoint to von Donnersmarck's film, a different cinema with a different approach to the lives of others. *Jahrgang 45* abides today as a remnant from a cinema that might have been, insisting, with keen and unflinching nonsynchronicity, on an unpopular and untimely view of a society. Böttcher's chronicle of young rebels represents an unreconciled and unconsensual heritage within a much larger and in many regards still uncharted subterranean history of German cinema. As a film from the past, it enacts aspirations that had a real existence as possibilities despite the formidable challenges that militated against their realization. As a heritage film, *Jahrgang 45* offers a concrete historical record that commingles critique with hopefulness and affords us an altogether different ethnography, indeed a decidedly different manner in which we might envision the lives of others in the GDR and other lives that might have been.

---

35 Bloch, *Heritage of Our Times*, p. 13.

Bibliography

On *The Lives of Others*

Ansen, David, 'A Waking Nightmare. Sex, spies und audiotape in corrupt East Germany', *Newsweek*, 12 February 2007.

Beaupré, Nicolas, 'L'enfer des autres', *Vingtième Siècle. Revue d'histoire*, 91 (2006), pp. 163–64.

Beier, Lars-Olav, 'On the Oscar Campaign Trail', *Spiegel Online International*, 23 February 2007 (http://www.spiegel.de/international/spiegel/0,1518,466450,00.html).

–, 'Unter Genieverdacht', *Der Spiegel*, 49 (2010), pp. 140–45.

Berghahn, Daniela, 'Remembering the Stasi in a Fairy Tale of Redemption: Florian Henckel von Donnersmarck's *Das Leben der Anderen*', *Oxford German Studies*, 38.3 (2009), pp. 321–33.

Bernstein, Matthew H., '*The Lives of Others*: Matthew H. Bernstein on an Emotive Thriller Set in Communist East Germany', *Film Quarterly*, 61.1 (2007), pp. 30–6.

Betts, Paul, *The Authority of Everyday Objects. A Cultural History of West Germany Industrial Design* (Berkeley: University of California Press, 2004).

Biermann, Wolf, 'Die Gespenster treten aus dem Schatten', *Die Welt*, 22 March 2006.

Bradshaw, Peter, 'The Lives of Others', *The Guardian*, 13 April 2007.

Buchner, Kathrin, 'Keine Einladung zur Oscar Feier', *Stern.de*, 12 February 2007 (http://www.stern.de/kultur/film/martina-gedeck-keine-einl adung-zur-oscar-feier-582425.html).

Bulgakowa, Oksana, '*Das Leben der Anderen* – Rückschau auf einen deutschen Erfolgsfilm', *Film-Dienst*, 60.11 (2007), pp. 15–6.

Bulgakowa, Oksana, 'Das Sehen der Anderen', *Film-Dienst*, 60.11 (2007), pp. 14–6.

Cantor, Paul A., 'Long Day's Journey into Brecht: The Ambivalent Politics of *The Lives of Others*', *Perspectives on Political Science* 40.2 (2011), pp. 68–77.

Carson, Diane, 'Learning from History in *The Lives of Others*: An Interview with Writer/Director Florian Henckel Von Donnersmarck', *Journal of Film and Video*, 62.1–2 (2010), pp. 13–22.

Cook, Roger, 'Literary Discourse and Cinematic Narrative: Scripting Affect in *Das Leben der Anderen*', in *Cinema and Social Change in Germany and Austria*, ed. by Gabriele Mueller and James M. Skidmore (Waterloo, ON: Wilfrid Laurier University Press, 2012), pp. 79–95.

Cooke, Paul, 'Watching the Stasi: authenticity, *Ostalgie* and history in Florian von Donnersmarck's *The Lives of Others* (2006)', in *New Directions in German Cinema*, ed. by Paul Cooke and Chris Homewood (London: I.B. Tauris, 2011), pp. 111–27.

–, '25 February 2007: *Das Leben der Anderen* wins the Oscar for "Best Non-English Language Film"', in *A New History of German Cinema*, ed. by Jennifer Kapczynski and Michael D. Richardson (Rochester: Camden House, 2012), pp. 609–14.

Creech, Jennifer, 'A Few Good Men: Gender, Ideology, and Narrative Politics in *The Lives of Others* and *Good Bye, Lenin!*', *Women in German Yearbook. Feminist Studies in German Literature & Culture*, 25 (2009), pp. 100–26.

Der Spiegel, 'Letzter Tango', 9 (1991), p. 264.

Diamond, Diana, 'Empathy and identification in von Donnermarck's *The Lives of Others*', *Journal of the American Psychoanalytical Association*, 56.3 (2008), pp. 811–32.

Dresen, Andreas, 'Die Bilder der Anderen', *Film-Dienst*, 62.22 (2009), pp. 32–4.

Dueck, Cheryl, 'The Humanization of the Stasi in *Das Leben der Anderen*', *German Studies Review*, 31.3 (2008), pp. 599–608.

Ehrlicher, Gerhard, 'Die Realität war eine andere', *Frankfurter Allgemeine Zeitung*, 21 June 2006.

Elley, Derek, Film Reviews: Cannes: 'The Lives of Others', *Variety*, 403.5 (2006), p. 40.

Esther, John, 'Between Principle and Feeling: An Interview with Florian Henckel von Donnersmarck', *Cineaste*, 32.2 (2007), pp. 40–2.

Evans, Owen, 'Redeeming the demon? The legacy of the Stasi in *Das Leben der Anderen*', *Memory Studies*, 3 (2010), pp. 164–77.

Falck, Marianne, *Filmheft. Das Leben der Anderen* (Bonn: Bundeszentrale für politische Bildung, 2006).

Fetters, Michelle, 'Other People's Lives: Conversation with Writer-Director Florian Henckel von Donnersmarck' (http://www.moviefreak.com/artman/publish/interviews_florianhenckelvondonnersmarck.shtml).

Fisher, Jaimey, 'German historical Film as Production Trend: European Heritage cinema and Melodrama in *The Lives of Others*', in *The Collapse of the Conventional. German Film and its Politics at the Turn of the Twenty-first Century*, ed. by Jaimey Fisher and Brad Prager (Detroit: Wayne State University, 2010), pp. 186–215.

Funder, Anna, *Stasiland. Stories from Behind the Berlin Wall* (London: Granta, 2003).

–, 'The Lives of Others', *Guardian*, 5 May 2007.

–, 'Eyes without a Face', *Sight and Sound*, 17.5 (2007), 16–20.

Garton Ash, Timothy, 'The Stasi on Our Minds', *New York Review of Books*, 31 May 2007.

Gauck, Joachim, '*Das Leben der Anderen*: "Ja, so war es!"', *Stern*, 25 March 2006.

Gerle, Jörg, 'Das Leben der Anderen', *Film-Dienst*, 59.7 (2006), p. 42.

Gieseke, Jens, 'Stasi goes Hollywood: Donnersmarcks *The Lives of Others* und die Grenzen der Authentizität', *German Studies Review*, 31.3 (2008), pp. 580–88.

Handke, Sebastian, 'Die Wanzen sind echt: Kinodebatte über *Das Leben der Anderen*', *Tagesspiegel*, 8 April 2007.

Harmsen, Torsten, 'Irgendwie geht's um Stasi: 700 Schüler sehen auf Einladung Klaus Bögers *Das Leben der Anderen*', *Berliner Zeitung*, 4 April 2006.

Henckel von Donnersmarck, Florian, *Das Leben der anderen. Filmbuch* (Frankfurt am Main: Suhrkamp, 2006).

–, 'A World without Red and Blue: An Interview with Florian Henckel von Donnersmarck', *Projections 15 Seminar. European Cinema*, ed. by Peter Cowie and Pascal Edelmann (London: Faber and Faber, 2007), pp. 225–35.

–, 'My Favourite Movies: Director Florian Henckel Von Donnersmarck', *The Sunday Telegraph*, 16 September, 2007.

–, 'Thirteen Questions with Florian Henckel von Donnersmarck, Writer and Director of *The Lives of Others*', *The Lives of Others Press Booklet* (Sony Classic Films, n.d.) (http://www.sonyclassics.com/thelivesofothers/externalLoads/TheLivesofOthers.pdf).

Herrmann, Mareike, 'The Spy As Writer: Florian Henckel von Donnersmarck's *Das Leben der Anderen*', *Gegenwartsliteratur. Ein germanistisches Jahrbuch*, 7, ed. by Paul Michael Lützeler and Stephen K. Schindler (Tübingen: Stauffenburg, 2008), pp. 90–112

Hodgin, Nick, 'Screening the Stasi: The Politics of Representation in Postunification Film', in *The GDR Remembered. Representations of the East German State since 1989*, ed. by Nick Hodgin and Caroline Pearce (Rochester: Camden House, 2011), pp. 69–91.

Horn, Eva, 'Media Conspiracy: Love and Surveillance in Fritz Lang and Florian Henckel von Donnersmarck', *New German Critique*, 103 (2008), pp. 127–44.

Körte Bauer, Katja, 'Die feine Grenzlinie auf dem Weg zum Verrat', *Stuttgarter Zeitung*, 27 February 2007.

Lally, Kevin, 'Spies & Lies: Florian Henckel Von Donnersmarck Examines Recent German History in Drama About Artists and Stasi Agents', *Film Journal International*, 110.3 (2007), p. 12 and p. 28.

Lenssen, Claudia, 'Die Rezeption des Films von Florian Henckel von Donnersmarck in Deutschland', *Verband der deutschen Filmkritik* (2007) (www.vdfk.de/137-schwerpunkt-2-rohrbach-und-die-folgen).

Lewis, Alison, 'Contingent Memories: The Crisis of Memory in Florian Henckel von Donnersmarck's *The Lives of Others*', in *Limbus 1. Erinnerungskrise/Memory Crises*, ed. by Franz-Joseph Dieters, Axel Fliethmann, Birgit Lang, Alison Lewis and Christiane Weller (Freiberg: Rombach Verlag, 2008), pp. 147–63.

Lichterbeck, Philipp, 'Die innere Wahrheit der DDR. Die Stasi-Falle. Wie in Mitte gerade ein Film über die Angst im Sozialismus gedreht wird ', *Tagesspiegel,* 5 December 2004.

Lindenberger, Thomas, 'Stasiploitation – Why Not? The Scriptwriter's Historical Creativity', *German Studies Review*, 31.3 (2008), pp. 557–66.

Müller, Uwe, 'Die verlorene Ehre des Ulrich M', *Berlin Morgenpost*, 16 January 2008.

Nagel, Daniela, *Das Drehbuch. Ein Drama für die Leinwand? Drehbuchanalyse am Beispiel von Florian Henckel von Donnersmarcks 'Das Leben der anderen'* (Marburg: Tectum, 2008).

Peitz, Christiane, 'Wenn es gut geht, tanzen wir miteinander', *Tagesspiegel,* 21 March 2007.

Podhoretz, John, 'Nightmare Come True: Love and Distrust in the East German Police State', *The Weekly Standard*, 12 March 2007 (http://www.weeklystandard.com/Content/Public/Articles/000 /000/013/360jfrwt. asp).

Radow, Dieter, 'Die innere Wiedervereinigung', *Frankfurter Allgemeine Zeitung*, 12 April 2007.

Rössling, Ingo, 'Film und Diskussion: Enkel von Stasi-Opfer zeigt Flagge', *Die Welt*, 29 March 2006.

Rupprecht, Annette Maria, 'Florian Henckel von Donnersmarck: XXL', *German Film Quarterly*, 3 (2006), pp. 16–7.

Schmidt, Gary, 'Between Authors and Agents: Gender and Affirmative Culture in *Das Leben der Anderen*', *German Quarterly*, 82.2 (2009), pp. 231–49.

Scott, A.O., 'A Fugue for Good German Men', *The New York Times*, 9 February 2007.

Seegers, Lu, '*Das Leben der Anderen* oder der "richtige" Erinnerung an die DDR', in *Film und kulturelle Erinnerung. Plurimediale Konstellationen*, ed. by Astrid Erll and Stephanie Wodianka (Berlin: Walter de Gruyter, 2008), pp. 21–52.

Seeßlen, Georg, 'So gewinnt man einen Auslands-Oscar', *Die Zeit*, 22 February 2007.

Stein, Mary Beth, 'Stasi with a Human Face? Ambiguity in *The Lives of Others*', *German Studies Review*, 31.3 (2008), pp. 567–79.

Suchsland, Rüdiger, 'Mundgerecht konsumierbare Vergangenheit', *Teleopolis*, 23 March 2006.

Tilmann, Christina, 'Wer ist Florian Henckel von Donnersmarck?', *Tagespiegel*, 25 February 2007.

Vahabzadeh, Susan and Fritz Göttler, 'Dabei sein ist längst nicht alles', *Süddeutsche Zeitung*, 23 February 2007.

Westphal, Wendy, '"Truer than the Real Thing": "Real" and "Hyperreal" Representations of the Past in *Das Leben der Anderen*', *German Studies Review*, 35.1 (2012), pp. 96–111.

White, Christina, 'The Lives of Others', 32.2 *Cineaste*, (2007), p. 58.

Wilke, Manfred, 'Fiktion oder erlebte Geschichte: Zur Frage der Glaubwürdigkeit des Films *Das Leben der Anderen*', *German Studies Review*, 31.3 (2008), pp. 589–98.

Wölfel, Ute, 'Inverting the Lives of "Others": Retelling the Nazi past in *Ehe im Schatten* and *Das Leben der Anderen*', *German Life and Letters*, 64 (2011), pp. 601–18.

Wolle, Stefan, 'Stasi mit menschlichem Antlitz', *Deutschland Archiv*, 3 (2006), pp. 497–99.

Žižek, Slavoj, 'The Dreams of Others', *In these Times*, 18 May 2007 (http://www.inthesetimes. com/article/3183/).

Other Works Cited

Abteilung Bildung und Forschung der Behörde des Bundesbeauftragten für die Unterlagen des Staatssicherheitsdienstes der ehemaligen DDR, ed., *Das MfS-Lexikon*, (Berlin: Ch. Links, 2011).

Adorno, Theodor W., 'Functionalism Today', trans. by John H. Smith, *Oppositions*, 3 (1988), pp. 35–40.

Albersmeier, Franz-Josef, and Volker Roloff, eds, *Literaturverfilmungen* (Frankfurt am Main: Suhrkamp, 1989).

Althen, Michael, '*Der Tangospieler*', *Süddeutsche Zeitung*, 22 February 1991.

Altman, Rick, 'Cinema and popular song. The lost tradition', in *Soundtrack available. Essays on Film and Popular Music*, ed. by Pamela Robertson Wojcik and Arthur Knight (Durham and London: Duke University Press, 2001), pp. 19–30.

Appadurai, Arjun, ed., *The Social Life of Things. Commodities in Cultural Perspective* (Cambridge: Cambridge UP, 1986).

Appelo, Tim, 'Globe Comedy Nom for *The Tourist*: Now, That's Funny', *The Hollywood Reporter*, 14 December 2010 (http://www.hollywoodreporter.com/blogs/race/globe-comedynom-tourist-funn y-59606).

Assmann, Aleida, and Ute Frevert, *Geschichtsvergessenheit/ Geschichtsversessenheit. Vom Umgang mit deutschen Vergessenheiten nach 1945* (Stuttgart: Deutsche Verlagan-stalt,1999).

Bach, Jonathan, '"The Taste Remains": Consumption, (N)Ostalgia, and the Production of East Germany', *Public Culture*, 14.3 (2002), pp. 545–56.

Bathrick, David, *The Powers of Speech. The Politics of Culture in the GDR* (Lincoln: University of Nebraska, 1995).

Beier, Lars-Olav, 'Endstation Hollywood', *Der Spiegel*, 12 February 2007.

Berdahl, Daphne,'*(N)ostalgie* for the Present: Memory, Longing, and East German Things', *Ethnos*, 64.2 (1999), pp. 192–211.

–, '"Go, Trabi, Go"!: Reflections on a Car and its Symbolization over Time', *Anthropology and Humanism*, 25.2 (2000), pp. 131–41.

–, 'Re-presenting the Socialist Modern: Museums and Memory in the Former GDR', in *Socialist Modern. East German Everyday Culture and Politics*, ed. by Katherine Pence and Paul Betts (Ann Arbor: University of Michigan Press, 2008), pp. 345–66.

Bergfelder, Tim, Erica Carter and Deniz Göktürk, eds, *The German Cinema Book* (London: BFI, 2002).

Betts, Paul, 'Building Socialism at Home: The Case of East German Interiors', in *Socialist Modern. East German Everyday Culture and Politics*, ed. by Katherine Pence and Paul Betts (Ann Arbor: University of Michigan Press, 2008), pp. 96–132.

–, 'The Twilight of the Idols: East German Memory and Material Culture', *Journal of Modern History*, 72.3 (2000), pp. 731–65.

Biskind, Peter, *Easy Riders, Raging Bulls. How the Sex-Drugs-and-Rock'n'roll Generation Saved Hollywood* (New York: Simon & Schuster, 1998).

Black, Jeremy, *The Politics of James Bond. From Fleming's Novels to the Big Screen* (Westport: Praeger, 2001).

Bloch, Ernst, 'Formative Education, Engineering Form, Ornament', trans. by John H. Smith, *Oppositions*, 3 (1988), pp. 45–51.

–, *Heritage of Our Times*, trans. by Neville and Stephen Plaice (Berkeley: University of California Press, 1991).

Blum, Martin, 'Remaking the East German Past: *Ostalgie*, Identity, and Material Culture', *Journal of Popular Culture*, 34.3 (2000), pp. 229–53.

Bohnenkamp, Anne, ed., *Interpretationen. Literaturverfilmungen*, (Stuttgart: Reclam, 2005).

Boyer, Dominic, '*Ostalgie* and the Politics of the Future in Eastern Germany', *Public Culture*, 18.2 (2006), pp. 361–81.

Brooks, Peter, *The Melodramatic Imagination. Balzac, Henry James, Melodrama and the Mode of Excess* (New Haven: Yale University Press, 1976).

Browne, Nick, ed., *Refiguring American Film Genres: Theory and History*, ed. by (Berkeley: University of California Press, 1998).

Buchanan, Kyle, '*The Tourist*: Director Florian Henckel von Donnersmarck on How Johnny Depp Is Like a Serial Killer', *New York Magazine*, 4 January 2011.

Bulgakowa, Oksana, '*Der Tangospieler*', *tageszeitung*, 18 February 1991.

Campbell, Christopher, 'The Originals: *Anthony Zimmer* is Lighter-Than-Light Hitchcock – Hopefully *The Tourist* is Better', *Spout. The movies you love* (http://blogs.indiewire.com/spout/archives/the_originals_anthony_zimmer_is_lighter_than_light_hitchcock_hopefully_th/).

Candlin, Fiona, and Raiford Guins, eds, *The Object Reader* (London: Routledge, 2009).

Castillo, Greg, 'East as True West: Redeeming Bourgeois Culture: From Social Realism to Ostalgie', *Kritika. Explorations in Russian and Eurasian History*, 9.4 (2008), pp. 747–68.

–, *Cold War on the Home Front. The Soft Power of Midcentury Design* (Minneapolis: University of Minnesota Press, 2010).

Childs, David and Richard Popplewell, *Stasi. The East German Intelligence Service* (London: Palgrave, 1996).

Chion, Michel, *The Voice in Cinema*, trans. by Claudia Gorbman (New York: Columbia University Press, 1999).

–, *Film. A Sound Art*, trans. by Claudia Gorbman (New York: Columbia University Press, 2009).

Chown, Jeffrey, *Hollywood Auteur* (New York: Praeger, 1988).

Clarke, David, ed., 'Beyond *Ostalgie*: East and West German Identity in Contemporary German Culture', *Seminar*, 40.3 (2004).

Clifford, James, 'On Ethnographic Allegory', in *Writing Culture. The Poetics and Politics of Ethnography*, ed. by James Clifford and George F. Marcus (Berkeley: University of California Press, 1986), pp. 98–121.

Cooke, Paul, *Representing East Germany Since Unification. From Colonization to Nostalgia* (New York: Berg, 2005).

–, and Marc Silberman, eds, *Screening War. Perspectives on German Suffering* (Rochester, NY: Camden House, 2010).

–, and Chris Homewood, eds, *New Directions in German Cinema* (London: Tauris, 2011).

Dennis, Mike, *The Stasi. Myth and Reality* (London: Pearson Education, 2003).

Der Spiegel, '*Der Tangospieler*', 9 February 1991.

Dresen, Andreas, 'Ost-West Film: Der falsche Kino-Osten', *Die Zeit*, 31 July 2009.

Dyer, Richard, *Heavenly Bodies. Film Stars and Society* (London: Routledge, 2003).

–, *Stars* (1979; London: BFI, 1998).

Elsaesser, Thomas, *New German Cinema* (New Brunswick: Rutgers University Press, 1989).

–, 'Tales of Sound and Fury: Observations on the Family Melodrama', in *Imitations of Life. A Reader on Film and Television Melodrama*, ed. by Marcia Landy (Detroit: Wayne State University Press, 1991), pp. 68–91.

–, 'American Friends: Hollywood in New German Cinema', *Hollywood and Europe*, ed. by Geoffrey Nowell-Smith and Steve Ricci (London: BFI Publishing, 1998), pp. 142–55.

–, *European Cinema. Face to Face with Hollywood* (Amsterdam: Amsterdam University Press, 2005).

Emerson, Robert, M. *Writing Ethnographic Fieldnotes* (Chicago: University of Chicago Press, 1995).

Enns, Anthony, 'The Politics of *Ostalgie*: Post-Socialist Nostalgie in Recent German Film', *Screen*, 48.4 (2007), pp. 475–91.

Fietz, Lothar, 'On the Origins of the English Melodrama in the Tradition of Bourgeois Tragedy and Sentimental Drama: Lillo, Schröder, Kotzebue, Sheridan, Thompson, Jerrold', in *Melodrama. The Cultural Emergence of a Literary Genre*, ed. by Michael Hays and Anastasia Nikolopoulou (New York: St. Martin's Press, 1996), pp. 83–101.

Fisher, Jaimey, *Disciplining Germany. Youth, Reeducation and Reconstruction after the Second World War* (Detroit: Wayne State, 2007).

Foucault, Michel, 'The Eye of Power', in *Power / Knowledge. Selected Interviews and Other Writings 1972–1977*, ed. by Colin Gordon (New York: Pantheon Books, 1980), pp. 146–65

Frey, Mattias, *Postwall German Cinema: History, Film History and Cinephilia* (Oxford: Berghahn, 2013).

Freydag, Nina, 'Es braucht zehn Jahre, um über Nacht berühmt zu werden', *Brigitte,* March (2007), pp. 104–5.

Fricke, Karl Wilhelm, *Die DDR-Staatssicherheit* (Cologne: Verlag Wissenschaft und Politik, 1989).

–, *'Schild und Schwert'. Die Stasi* (Cologne: Deutschlandfunk, 1993).

Fuchs, Jürgen, *Vernehmungsprotokolle* (Reinbek: Rowohlt, 1978).

–, 'Dann kommt die Angst', in *Gefangen in Hohenschönhausen. Stasi-Häftlinge berichten*, ed. by Hubertus Knabe (Berlin: Ullstein, 2007), pp. 268–301.

Fulbrook, Mary, *The People's State. East German Society From Hitler to Honecker* (New Haven and London: Yale University Press, 2005).

Gellately, Robert, 'Denunciations in Twentieth Century Germany: Aspects of Self-Policing in the Third Reich and the German Democratic Republic', *Journal of Modern History*, 68.4 (1996), pp. 931–67.

Gieseke, Jens, *Miele-Konzern. Geschichte der Stasi 1945–1990* (Stuttgart: Deutsche Verlagsanstalt, 2001).

Gill, David, and Ulrich Schröter, *Das Ministerium für Staatssicherheit* (Berlin: Rowohlt, 1991).

Gladziejewski, Claudia, 'Script Doctors', (http://www.script-doctors.com/de/home/index.php).

Gledhill, Christine, ed., *Home is where the heart is. Studies in melodrama and the woman's film,* (London: BFI, 1987).

–, and Linda Williams, eds, *Reinventing Film Studies* (London: Arnold, 1999).

Gorky, Maxim, *Collected Works*, XVII (Moskow: Foreign Language Publishing House, 1950), pp. 39–40.

Graf, Dominik, Christian Petzold and Christoph Hochhäusler, 'Mailwechsel. Berliner Schule', *Revolver*, 16 (May 2007), pp. 6–40.

Gräf, Roland, '"Der gewöhnliche Sozialismus". Interview mit Axel Geiss', *Filmspiegel*, 5 (1991), pp. 8–9.

–, *Der Tangospieler* (http://filmmuseumpotsdam.de/de/446-1484.htm).

Grafe, Roman, ed., *Die Schuld der Mitläufer. Anpassen oder Widerstehen in der DDR* (Munich: Pantheon, 2009).

Gries, Rainer, *Produkte als Medien. Kulturgeschichte der Produktkommunikation in der Bundesrepublik und der DDR* (Leipzig: Leipziger Universitätsverlag, 2003).

Gwosc, Detlef, 'Social Criticism in the Films of Roland Gräf', in *DEFA. East German Cinema, 1946–1992*, ed. by Seán Allan and John Sandford (New York and Oxford: Berghahn Books, 1999), pp. 245–66.

Haase, Christine, *Heimat Meets Hollywood. German Filmmakers and America 1985–2005* (Rochester: Camden House, 2007).

Habermas, Jürgen, *Die postnationale Konstellation* (Frankfurt am Main: Suhrkamp, 1998).

Hahn, Annegret, ed., *4. November '89. Der Protest. Die Menschen. Die Reden* (Berlin DDR: Propyläen, 1990).

Halbwachs, Maurice, *On Collective Memory*, ed. and trans. by Lewis Coser (Chicago: Chicago University Press, 1992).

Hall, Stuart, 'Encoding/decoding' in *Culture, Media, Language,* ed. by Stuart Hall, Dorothy Hobson, Andrew Lowe and Paul Willis (London: Routledge, 1980), pp. 128–38.

Halle, Randall *German Film After Germany. Toward a Transnational Aesthetic* (Urbana: University of Illinois Press, 2008).

Handyside, Fiona, 'Colonising the European Utopia', in *World Cinema's Dialogues with Hollywood*, ed. by Paul Cooke (London: Palgrave, 2007), pp. 138–53.

Hardt, Ursula, *From Caligari to California. Eric Pommer's Life in the International Film Wars* (Providence: Berghahn, 1996).

Hepburn, Alan, *Intrigue. Espionage and Culture* (New Haven: Yale University Press, 2005).

Higson, Andrew, 'The Concept of National Cinema', *Screen*, 30.4 (1989), pp. 36–47.

–, 'The Heritage Film and British Cinema', in *Dissolving Views. Key Writings on British Cinema*, ed. by Andrew Higson (London: Cassell, 1996), pp. 232–248.

–, *English Heritage. English Cinema* (Oxford: Oxford University Press, 2003).

Höbel, Wolfgang, 'Putzig mit Pop: Donnersmarck-Film *The Tourist*', *Der Spiegel Online*, 14 December 2010 (http://www.spiegel.de/kultur/kino/0,1518,734546,00.html).

Hodgin, Nick, and Caroline Pearce, eds, *The GDR Remembered. Representations of the East German State since 1989* (Rochester: Camden House, 2011)

Holden, Stephen, '*Der Tangospieler*', *New York Times*, 3 November 1993.

Horn, Anette, *Kontroverses Ende und Innovation* (Frankfurt am Main: Lang, 2005).

Iser, Wolfgang, 'The Reading Process: A Phenomenological Approach', *New Literary History*, 3 (1972), pp. 279–99.

James, Clive, *Cultural Amnesia. Notes in the Margin of My Time* (London: Picador, 2007; corrected edition 2008).

Johannes, Günter, and Ulrich Schwarz, *DDR. Das Manifest der Opposition* (Munich: Wilhelm Goldmann Verlag, 1978).

Kaes, Anton, *From Hitler to Heimat. The Return of History as Film* (Cambridge: Harvard University Press, 1989).

Kapczynski, Jennifer, 'Negotiating Nostalgia: The GDR Past in *Berlin Is in Germany* and *Good Bye, Lenin!*', *Germanic Review*, 82.1 (2007), pp. 78–100.

King, Geoff, *New Hollywood Cinema. An introduction* (London: I.B. Tauris, 2002).

Knabe, Hubertus, *Die unterwanderte Republik* (Berlin: Propyläen Verlag, 1999).

Koepnick, Lutz, 'Reframing the Past: Heritage Cinema and Holocaust in the 1990s', *New German Critique*, 87 (2002), pp. 47–82.

–, 'Amerika gibt's überhaupt nicht: Notes on the German Heritage Film', in *German Pop Culture. How American Is it?*, ed. by Agnec C. Mueller (Ann Arbor: University of Michigan Press, 2004), pp. 191–208.

Kracauer, Siegfried, *Theory of Film. The Redemption of Physical Reality*, with an introduction by Miriam Bratu Hansen (Princeton: Princeton University Press, 1997).

Kukutz, Irena, and Katja Havermann, *Geschützte Quelle. Gespräche mit Monika H. alias Karin Lenz* (Berlin: Basisdruck, 1990).

Kuperstein, Katarina, *Zwischen Ostalgie and Reflexion. Die filmische Darstellung der DDR nach der Wende* (Saarbrücken: VDM Dr. Müller, 2010).

Landsmann, Cosmo, 'You looking at me?; Swanky locations can't make up for *The Tourist's* dull plot and smug Angelina Jolie', *The Sunday Times*, 12 December 2010.

Lane, Anthony, 'I SPY. John le Carré and the rise of George Smiley', *The New Yorker*, 12 December 2011.

Lemire, Christy, '*The Tourist:* a Mindlessly Enjoyable Trip', *The Associated Press*, 9 December 2010.

Lenssen, Claudia, 'Inszenierte Öffentlichkeit: Eine Debatte um die symbolische Macht der Filmkritik', *VDK. Verband der deutschen Filmkritik* 4 (2008), pp. 28–30.

Lessing, Gotthold Ephraim, 'Das 14. Stück' and 'Das 23. Stück', in *Hamburgische Dramaturgie*, ed. by Klaus Berghahn, rev. edn (Stuttgart: Reclam, 1999), pp. 77–81 and 121–25.

Levi, Primo, *The Drowned and the Saved* (New York: Vintage, 1989).

Lichterbeck, Philipp, 'Die innere Wahrheit der DDR', *Tagesspiegel*, 5 December 2004.

Lindenberger, Thomas, 'Zeitgeschichte am Schneidetisch. Zur Historisierung der DDR im deutschen Spielfilm', in *Visual History. Ein Studienbuch*, ed. by Paul Gerhard (Göttingen: Vanderhoeck and Ruprecht, 2006), pp. 353–72.

Lukács, Georg, *The Historical Novel* (Lincoln: University of Nebraska Press, 1983).

Märkische Allgemeine Zeitung, 'So viele Speichen – Plausch mit Volker Schlöndorff auf seinem sonnengelben Sofa', 2 December 2008.

Marks, Laura U., *The Skin of the Film. Intercultural Cinema, Embodiment, and the Senses* (Durham: Duke University Press, 2000).

Meves, Ursula, 'Die Geschichte der Atombombe: Dramatischer Stoff für einen Spielfilm', *Neues Deutschland*, 12 May 1990.

Meza, Ed, 'TV Chefs Dilute Pic Stew?', *Variety*, 7 February 2010.

Ministerium für Justiz, *Strafrecht der Deutschen Demokratischen Republik* (Berlin East: Staatsverlag der Deutschen Demokratischen Republik, 1984).

Morin, Edgar, *The Stars* (Minneapolis: University of Minnesota Press, 2005).

Mühe, Ulrich, and Christian Schröder, '"Bin ich nicht mitgeschwommen?" Ulrich Mühe und die geschlossene Gesellschaft eines U-Bootes', *Tagesspiegel*, 21 March 1993.

–, and Thomas Klug, '"Menschlichkeit bewahren": Ulrich Mühe über seine Rolle in ... *nächste Woche ist Frieden*', *Berliner Zeitung*, 25 April 1995.

–, '"Ist doch toll": Ulrich Mühe über sein Leben im Niemandsland aus Fernsehen, Film und Theater', *Tagesspiegel*, 16 April 2000.

–, 'Mann mit Botschaft. Ein Gespräch mit dem Schauspieler Ulrich Mühe', *Stuttgarter Zeitung*, 15 May 2001.

–, and Harald Heinzinger, '"Wir sind zarte Wesen". Ulrich Mühe wieder als Dr. Kolmaar im ZDF – Ein Gespräch', *Stuttgarter Zeitung*, 30 April 2002.

–, and Iris Schmid, 'Kein Alter Ego: Ulrich Mühe über seine Rolle im *Letzten Zeugen*', *Stuttgarter Zeitung*, 31 March 2005.

–, and Carla Woter, '"Grauenhaft. Das würde ich ablehnen": Schauspieler Ulrich Mühe über Homestorys, Schmerzgrenzen und 50 Folgen als TV-Pathologe', *Tagesspiegel*, 1 April 2005.

Neale, Steve, *Genre and Hollywood* (London: Routledge, 2000).

Nesselson, Lisa, '*Anthony Zimmer*', *Variety*, 4 May 2005.

Nicodemus, Katja, 'Unsere kleine Traumfabrik: Vor den Filmfestspielen in Venedig zeigt sich das deutsche Kino als Nostalgiebude', *Die Zeit*, 28 August 2003.

Nieberle, Sigrid, *Literarhistorische Filmbiographien – Autorschaft und Literaturgeschichte im Kino. Mit einer Filmographie 1909–2007* (Berlin: De Gruyter, 2008).

Nord, Christina, 'Deutsche Geschichte im Kino: Die neue Naivität', *tageszeitung*, 20 October 2008.

Outhwaite, William, and Larry Ray, *Social Theory and Post-Communism* (Oxford: Blackwell, 2005).

Peitz, Christiane, 'Wenn es gut geht, tanzen wir miteinander', *Tagesspiegel*, 21 March 2007.

Pergande, Frank, 'Die Schauspielerin, Ihr Mann und Ihr Liebhaber. Die Geschichte von Jenny Gröllmann und Ulrich Mühe klang ohnehin wie *Leben der Anderen*. Neuester Dreh. Ein postumer Rufmord', *Frankfurter Allgemeine Sonntagszeitung*, 2 March 2008.

Rabinbach, Anson, 'Unclaimed Heritage: Ernst Bloch's *Heritage of Our Times* and the Theory of Fascism', *New German Critique*, 11 (1977), pp. 5–21.

Rancière, Jacques, *The Politics of Aesthetics. The Distribution of the Sensible*, trans. by Gabriel Rockhill (London and New York: Continuum, 2004).

Rentschler, Eric, 'How American is it: the U.S. as Image and Imaginary in German Film', *German Quarterly*, 57 (1984), pp. 603–20

–, ed., *German Film and Literature. Adaptations and Transformations* (New York: Methuen, 1986).

–, 'From New German Cinema to the Post-Wall Cinema of Consensus', in *Cinema and Nation*, ed. by Mette Hjort and Scott MacKenzie (Routledge: London, 2000), pp. 260–277.

Rinke, Andrea, *Images of Women in East German Cinema 1972–1982. Socialist Models, Private Dreamers and Rebels* (Lampeter: Edwin Mellen Press, 2006).

Rohrbach, Günter, 'Das Schmollen der Autisten', *Der Spiegel*, 22 January 2007.

Rosen, Philip, *Change Mummified. Cinema, Historicity, Theory* (Minneapolis: University of Minnesota Press, 2001).

Rosenberg, Grant, '*Anthony Zimmer*', *Screen International*, 26 April 2005.

Santner, Eric L., *Stranded Objects. Mourning, Memory, and Film in Postwar Germany* (Ithaca: Cornell University Press, 1990).

Saunders, Anna, '"Normalizing" the Past: East German Culture and *Ostalgie*', in *German Culture, Politics, and Literature into the Twenty-First Century*, ed. by Stuart Taberner and Paul Cooke (Rochester: Camden House, 2006), pp. 89–10.

Schenk, Ralf, 'Zwischen Fangschuß und Unhold: Volker Schlöndorff wird am Sonntag mit dem Konrad-Wolf-Preis der Akademie der Künste geehrt', *Berliner Zeitung*, 4 December 1997.

–, 'Die DDR im deutschen Film nach 1989', *Aus Politik und Zeitgeschichte*, 44 (2005), pp. 31–38.

–, 'Go, Trabi, Go – DDR-Vergangenheit, Wende und Nachwende in Deutschen Kinofilmen zwischen 1990 und 2005', *Filmportal.de* (2005). (http://www.filmportal.de/thema/go-trabi-go-ddr-vergangenheit-wende-und-nachwende-in-deutschen-kinofilmen-zwischen-1990-und-2005).

Schindler, Stephan K., and Lutz Koepnick, 'Against the Wall? The Global Imaginary of German Cinema', in *The Cosmopolitan Screen. German Cinema and the Global Imaginary, 1945 to the Present*, ed. by Stephan K. Schindler and Lutz Koepnick (Ann Arbor: The University of Michigan Press, 2007), pp. 1–21.

Schlenker, Wolfram, *Das 'Kulturelle Erbe' in der DDR. Gesellschaftliche Entwicklung und Kulturpolitik 1945–1965* (Stuttgart: Metzler, 1977).

Schröder, Christian, 'Von Kunst mag er nur selten sprechen: Ulrich Mühe, ein Schauspieler der bei Rollenangeboten äußerst geschmäcklerisch ist', *Süddeutsche Zeitung*, 20 March 1993.

Schütte, Wolfram, '*Der Tangospieler*', *Frankfurter Runschau*, 21 February 1991.

Seeßlen, Georg, 'Lacht da wer? Die deutsche Filmkomödie zwischen Otto und Männerherzen', *epd Film*, 28.9 (2011), pp. 18–25.

Shattuck, Kathryn, 'What's On Today', *The New York Times*, 30 July 2011.

Singh, Anita, 'James Bond a Neo-Fascist Gangster', *The Telegraph*, 17 August 2010.

Smith, Murray, *Engaging Characters. Fiction, Emotion and the Cinema* (Oxford: Oxford University Press, 1995).

Snydor, Robert Lance, '"Shadow of Abandonment", Graham Greene's *The Confidential Agent*', *Texas Studies in Literature and Language*, 52.2 (2010), pp. 203–26.

Sony Insider (http://www.sonyinsider.com/2010/11/15/depp-and-jolie-cross-paths-in-the-tourist-movie/).

Stöver, Bernd, '"Das ist die Wahrheit, die volle Wahrheit". Befreiungspolitik im DDR-Spielfilm der 1950er und 1960er Jahre', in *Massenmedien im Kalten Krieg. Akteure, Bilder, Resonanzen*, ed. by Thomas Lindenberger (Cologne, Weimar, Vienna: Böhlau Verlag, 2006), pp. 49–76.

Thieringer, Thomas, 'Das Kapital: Ulrich Mühe rettet seinen Erfahrungsschatz aus der DDR. "Nicht der Schauspieler ist das Zentrum, das Zentrum ist die Figur"', *Süddeutsche Zeitung*, 10 March 1993.

Timmermann, Heiner, ed., *DDR. Recht und Justiz als politisches Instrument* (Berlin: Dunker und Humboldt, 2000).

Turner, Dennis, 'The Subject of *The Conversation*', *Cinema Journal*, 24 (1985), 4–22.

Vincendau, Ginette, *Film/Literature/Heritage. A Sight and Sound Reader* (London: British Film Institute, 2001).

Weber, Max, 'Science as Vocation', in *From Max Weber. Essays in Sociology*, ed. and trans. by H. H. Geerth and C. Wright Mills (New York: Oxford University Press, 1946) pp. 129–157.

Weibel, Peter, 'Pleasure and the Panoptic Principle', in *CTRL [SPACE]. Rhetorics of Surveillance from Bentham to Big Brother*, ed. by Thomas Y. Levin, Ursula Frohne and Peter Weibel (Cambridge, MA: MIT Press, 2002), pp. 207–23.

Wilke, Manfred, ed., *Robert Havemann. Ein deutscher Kommunist* (Reinbek: Rowohlt, 1978).

—, and Werner Theuer, '"Der Beweis eines Verrats lässt sich nicht erbringen": Robert Havemann und die Widerstandsgruppe Europäische Union', in *Der SED-Staat. Geschichte und Nachwirkungen*, ed. by Hans-Joachim Veen and Manfred Wilke (Cologne: Böhlau, 2006), pp. 91–110.

Willett, John, ed. and trans, *Brecht on Theatre* (New York: Hill and Wang, 1964).

Williams, Linda, 'The American Melodramatic Mode', in *Playing the Race Card. Melodramas of*

Black and White from Uncle Tom to O.J Simpson, ed. by Linda Williams (Princeton and Oxford: Princeton University Press, 2001), pp. 10–44.

Wolle, Stefan, 'Die Welt der verlorenen Bilder: Die GDR im visuellen Gedächtnis', in *Visual History*, ed. by Paul Gerhard (Göttingen: Vandenhoeck & Ruprecht, 2006), pp. 332–52.

Yapo, Mennan, 'Deutsche in Hollywood: Zwei "Fuck", acht "Shit" und ein paar Dutzend Nippel', *Spiegel Online*, 4 October 2007 (http://www.spiegel.de/kultur/kino/0,1518,509359,00.html).

Zander, Peter, 'Im Ausland wird man immer zuerst auf Nazis angesprochen. Das nervt', *Die Welt*, 21 March 2006.

Zbikowski, Dörte, 'The Listening Ear: Phenomena of Acoustic Surveillance', in *CTRL [SPACE]*, pp. 38–41.

Film Credits
Das Leben der Anderen (The Lives of Others, 2006, Germany), 137 Minutes

Main Cast

Christa-Maria Sieland	Martina Gedeck
Captain Gerd Wiesler	Ulrich Mühe
Georg Dreyman	Sebastian Koch
Lieutenant Colonel Anton Grubitz	Ulrich Tukur
Minister Bruno Hempf	Thomas Thieme
Paul Hauser	Hans-Uwe Bauer
Albert Jerska	Volkmar Kleinert
Karl Wallner	Matthias Brenner

Crew

Director/Screenwriter	Florian Henckel von Donnersmarck
Producers	Quirin Berg
	Max Wiedemann
Cinematography	Hagen Bogdanski
Set Design	Silke Buhr
Costumes	Gabriele Binder
Make-up	Annett Schulze
Casting	Simone Bär
Editing	Patricia Rommel
Music	Gabriel Yared
	Stéphanie Moucha

Distributors

Buena Vista International (Germany)
Lionsgate (UK)
Sony Pictures Classics (USA)

List of Illustrations

Contributors

David Bathrick is emeritus Jacob Gould Schurman Professor of Theatre, Film & Dance and Professor of German Studies at Cornell University in Ithaca, New York. His publications include *The Dialectic and the Early Brecht* (1976), *Modernity and the Text* (1989, co-edited with Andreas Huyssen), *The Powers of Speech. The Politics of Culture in the GDR* (1995), for which he was awarded the 1996 DAAD/GSA Book of the Year Prize, and numerous articles on the theory and history of 20th century European culture. He is a co-founder and co-editor of New German Critique, an interdisciplinary journal of German studies. His areas of specialization include the history and theory of modern drama, 20th century German literature, critical theory, Weimar culture, the cultural politics of East Germany, European film, Holocaust studies, and Nazi cinema.

Paul Cooke is Professor of German Cultural Studies at the University of Leeds, UK and has published widely on contemporary German culture. He is the author of *Speaking the Taboo. A Study of the Work of Wolfgang Hilbig* (2000), *The Pocket Essential to German Expressionist Film* (2002), *Representing East Germany. From Colonization to Nostalgia* (2005) and *Contemporary German Cinema* (2012). His edited books include *World Cinema's Dialogues with Hollywood* (2007), with Stuart Taberner, *German Culture, Politics and Literature into the Twenty-First Century. Beyond Normalization* (2006), with Marc Silberman, *'Screening War. Perspectives on German Suffering'* (2010) and with Chris Homewood, *New Directions in German Cinema* (2011).

Jaimey Fisher is Associate Professor of German and Cinema and Technocultural Studies as well as Director of Cinema and Technocultural Studies at the University of California, Davis. He is the author of *The Cinema of Christian Petzold. A Ghostly Archeology* (2013) as well as *Disciplining German. Youth, Reeducation, and Reconstruction after the Second World War* (2007). He co-edited *Collapse of the Conventional. German Film and its Politics at the Turn of the Twenty-first Century* with Brad Prager (2010); with Barbara Mennel, *Spatial Turns. Space, Place, and Mobility in German Literary and Visual Culture* (2010) and, with Peter Hohendahl, *Critical Theory. Current State and Future Prospects* (2001). His current book-project analyzes war films in Germany from 1914–1961. He is also editing a volume on genre in German cinema.

Ian Thomas Fleishman is a doctoral candidate in French and German Literature at Harvard University. His thesis, *An Esthetics of Injury*, treats representations of the wound as a textual model in the work of Charles Baudelaire, Franz Kafka, Georges Bataille, Jean Genet, Hélène Cixous, Ingeborg Bachmann and Elfriede Jelinek. He has also published in *Mosaic* on Marcel Beyer's *Flughunde* and in *The German Quarterly* on H.J.C. von Grimmelshausen's *Simplicissimus Teutsch*.

Sabine Hake is the Texas Chair of German Literature and Culture in the Department of Germanic Studies at the University of Texas at Austin. She is the author of six books, *Passions and Deceptions. The Early Films of Ernst Lubitsch* (1992); *The Cinema's Third Machine. German Writings on Film 1907–1933* (1993); *Popular Cinema of the Third Reich* (2001); *German National Cinema* (2008, second revised edition), *Topographies of Class. Modern Architecture and Mass Society in Weimar Berlin* (2008) and *Screen Nazis. Cinema, History, and Democracy* (2012), as well as numerous articles and edited volumes on German film and Weimar culture. Her new book project is tentatively called *Proletarians! Archaeology of a Van(qu)ished Class*.

Randall Halle is Klaus W. Jonas Professor of German Film and Cultural Studies at the University of Pittsburgh. His research interests include film theory, critical theory, queer theory, social philosophy, cultural studies, transnational studies, nineteenth and twentieth century German literature and culture. His is the co-editor with Maggie McCarthy of *Light Motives: German Popular Film in Perspective* (2002) and with Sharon Willis of the double special issue of *Camera Obscura* on Marginality and Alterity in Contemporary European Cinema (44 & 46). He is author of *Queer Social Philosophy. Critical Readings from Kant to Adorno* (2004) and *The Transnational Aesthetic. German Film after Germany* (2008).

Lutz Koepnick is Professor of German, Film and Media Studies, and Comparative Literature at Washington University in St. Louis. He has written widely on German film, visual culture, and literature, on media arts and aesthetics, and on critical theory and cultural politics. Book publications include: *Framing Attention. Windows on Modern German Culture* (2007); *The Dark Mirror. German Cinema between Hitler and Hollywood* (2002); *Walter Benjamin and the Aesthetics of Power* (1999); and *Nothungs Modernität. Wagners Ring und die Poesie der Politik im neunzehnten Jahrhundert* (1994). Co-edited or co-authored volumes include: *After the Digital Divide? German Aesthetic Theory in the Age of New Media* (2009); *Window | Interface* (2007); *The Cosmopolitan Screen. German Cinema and the Global Imaginary, 1945 to the Present* (2007); *Caught by Politics. Hitler Exiles and American Visual Culture* (2007); and *Sound Matters. Essays on the Acoustics of German Culture* (2004).

Eric Rentschler is Arthur Kingsley Porter Professor of Germanic Languages and Literatures at Harvard University. His publications concentrate on film history, theory, and criticism, with particular emphasis on German cinema during the Weimar Republic, the Third Reich, and the post-1945 and postwar eras. His articles have appeared in a variety of collections and periodicals; his books include *West German Film in the Course of Time* (1984) and *The Ministry of Illusion* (1996). He was also the editor of *German Film and Literature* (1986), *West German Filmmakers on Film* (1988), *Augenzeugen* (1988), and *The Films of G. W. Pabst* (1990). Presently he is completing a book project, *Haunted by Hitler. The Return of the Nazi Undead* and working on a manuscript titled *Courses in Time. Film in the Federal Republic of Germany, 1962–1989*.

Andrea Rinke is senior lecturer in Film Studies and Director of the MA in Film Studies at Kingston University, School of Performance and Screen Studies. She has published widely on German film and culture, including GDR cinema and post unification films, including 'Eastside Stories – Singing and Dancing for Socialism', *Film History. An International Journal. Special Issue: Cold-War German Cinema* (2003) and 'Rock 'n Roll and Passport Control – German cinema colours the past', in *Questions of Colour*, ed. by Wendy Everett (2007). Her last monograph, *Images of Women in East German Cinema 1971–82. Socialist Models, Private Dreamers, and Rebels,* was published in 2006.

Marc Silberman is Professor of German and Director of the Center for German and European Studies at the University of Wisconsin. His research and teaching focus on twentieth-century German literature, theater, and cinema. He has published the following monographs: *Literature of the Working World in East Germany* (1976); *Heiner Müller* (1980); *German Cinema. Texts in Context* (1995), and edited the *Brecht Yearbook* from 1990–1995. In addition he has edited or co-edited another 15 volumes or special journal issues, including 'The Art of Hearing', *Monatshefte* 98.2 (Summer 2006) "Cold-War German Cinema," *Film History*, 18.1 (February 2006).

Manfred Wilke is the head of the Lankwitz Division of the Research Committee SED Regime at the *Freie Universität* Berlin. Between 1992 and 1994 he was a member of the Federal Enquete-Kommission Aufarbeitung von Geschichte und Folgen der SED-Diktatur in Deutschland. He was also historical adviser for *The Lives of Others*. His recent publications include *Die Streikbrecherzentrale. Der Freie Deutsche Gewerkschaftsbund und der 17. Juni 1953* (2004) and *Der SED-Staat. Geschichte und Nachwirkungen* with Andreas Graudin (2006).

Christopher Young is Professor of Modern and Medieval German Studies and Fellow of Pembroke College. He has authored and edited numerous books on a wide range of German cultural topics, including *Narrativische Perspektiven in Wolframs Willehalm* (2000), *A History of the German Language Through Texts* (2004), *Ulrich von Liechtenstein. Das Frauenbuch* (2004) and with Sandra Linden, *Ulrich von Liechtenstein Leben, Zeit, Werk, Forschung* (2010). His *The 1972 Olympics and the Making of Modern Germany* (2010), with Kay Schiller, appeared in German translation in 2012 and won the book prizes of both the North American and the British Societies for Sports History.

Index

Note: 'n.' after a page reference indicates the number of a note on that page
Note: page numbers in *italic* refer to illustrations
Note: literary, filmic, and televisual works can be found under authors'/directors' names. A separate list of filmic and televisual titles is also provided at the end of the main index

Index of filmic and televisual titles